CROSSING
THE BORDERS
OF POWER

Michael Cooper
Best Wishes from
[signature]
19.9.07

Liberal Democrat Autumn Conference
Brighton, September 2007

CROSSING THE BORDERS OF POWER

*The Memoirs of
Colin Eglin*

JONATHAN BALL PUBLISHERS
JOHANNESBURG & CAPE TOWN

With gratitude to the progressives old and new who,
through their commitment, helped to bring about change;
and to those South Africans who,
when the time arrived, chose reconciliation and not revenge.

Published in 2007 by
JONATHAN BALL PUBLISHERS (PTY) LTD
PO Box 33977
Jeppestown
2043

ISBN-13: 978-1-86842-253-1
ISBN-10: 1-86842-253-4

Editing and index by Owen Hendry for Wordsmiths, Johannesburg
Designed by Triple M Design & Advertising, Johannesburg
Set in 10.5/13pt Minion Pro
Printed and bound by Paarl Print, Cape Town

Contents

PART I

Childhood, youth, war

Early years: Pinelands and OFS
1925-1935

I had just turned nine when my father died in July 1934. He had been ill for a long time, but had been strengthened by a deep and abiding Christian faith – and by the love and care (and equally deep faith) of his wife, Elsie.

The curtains were drawn across the bedroom windows of our thatched Pinelands home on that wintry Cape morning. And yet despite my father's long and painful illness – and the death from meningitis of Rona, their first child and daughter, aged a mere 20 months – my parents' life in the small, newly established Cape Town village had been idyllically happy. Now, the cold winds were matched by an economic depression to be faced by my mother without the companionship of the man she loved; and her primary responsibility was to look after her young son and six-year-old daughter, Lorna.

I was born on 14 April 1925; Lorna on 13 July 1927.

Carl and Elsie Eglin moved into their newly-built home in Pinelands in 1923, soon after the first few houses had been completed. The house itself was a single-storey cottage with a steeply pitched thatched roof, a tall red-brick chimney, off-white painted walls, and small pane windows tucked under low overhanging eaves. It had been designed as a wedding present by Garth Baker, a friend of my mother and an aspiring Cape Town architect. It was designated No. 10 Meadway, later named 'Caronel' after Carl, Rona and Elsie; and was our family home until my father's death.

Through the windows you looked under a canopy of pines to an open grassed park called 'The Mead'. Behind the house was a large informal garden where my father built a wooden summerhouse and a toolshed, and planted a dozen or so fruit trees. And beyond this was a part of Uitvlugt forest – a glade of tall pines that whistled in the south-east wind and provided a shady playground for schoolboys such as me and my cousins Stan, Doug and Ron Wells, who grew up next door in 'Wellesley', No. 12 Meadway.

The forest, with its soft spongy carpet of pine needles, was also an excellent place for collecting 'denneballs' (pine cones) from which we prised the pips (pine nuts). These were eaten there and then or formed a tasty and essential ingredient of 'temmeleitjie' – a tacky toffee-like sweet we used to make in my mother's biscuit pans.

Pinelands, or Pinelands Garden City, was a fresh and exciting concept in housing and community development. The driving force behind the venture was Richard Stuttaford, Minister of Housing in the cabinet of General JC Smuts, and a Cape Town businessman and director of the prestigious department store that bore his family name. Since his return to South Africa from England in 1898, Richard had taken a keen interest in housing. He was impressed by the writings and work of Ebenezer Howard, founder of the Garden City movement in England and the author of the book *Garden Cities of Tomorrow*; he followed the progress made in Welwyn and Letchworth, new garden cities in southern England.

The ravages of the great 'flu epidemic that swept through the country at the end of the Great War shocked Stuttaford and intensified his vision of devising better housing and community facilities. On 28 January 1919 he wrote to FS Malan, acting prime minister in the absence of General Smuts, then in Europe taking part in the post-war discussions that led to the Versailles peace treaty. He wished to put before him a proposal on the matter, which he was 'prepared to support with my own money, as I feel certain it will materially help towards the physical and moral improvement of our people'. He requested 15 minutes to outline his ideas, and reassured Malan that he did not propose to ask for financial help from the government.

Malan granted the interview and it went well. On 19 June 1919, the Senate of the Union of South Africa formally approved a grant of 365 morgen of the Uitvlugt Forest Reserve, on the fringes of the sandy Cape Flats, some five-and-a-half miles from Cape Town by rail, for the purpose of establishing Pinelands, the country's first garden city. Stuttaford backed the initiative with his own money, and donated £10 000 to furnish an enabling trust with its initial working capital.

By August 1921 the first houses were being built. On 5 May 1923 Smuts laid a commemoration stone at the foot of Central Avenue, and South Africa's first garden city was truly under way.

My parents were active in the life of the youthful Pinelands community. The residents in general, despite unhelpful sandy soil, were dedicated gardeners: Arbor Day was the major community festival. In the morning schoolchildren planted trees, and in the afternoon decamped with their parents to the local sports fields where young and old participated in various competitions.

While my parents shared in many civic activities, it was in the religious life of Pinelands that they became increasingly involved. At first, the new Civic Hall was the venue for inter-denominational church services – the 'children's church' on Sunday mornings and services for the adults in the evening. In 1926 the foundation stone of the Anglican St Stephen's church was laid; but my parents, both ardent Methodists, or Wesleyans as they were more commonly called, yearned to share in the spiritual intensity and lusty singing that characterised Methodist services. With a few friends they formed the Pinelands Methodist Church – with my father as the treasurer, my mother the organist, and our home the venue for regular Sunday evening services. Often, my father or one of his friends would lead the small band of worshippers.

Pinelands had no school at that time. Boys and girls cycled across to Rondebosch

Boys' and Rustenberg Girls' schools. A few boys whose parents could afford private school fees went to Diocesan College (Bishops). Nearing five, I wanted to attend school and had an aptitude for learning. Fortunately, two Pinelands women, Sheila Cassidy and Annie Nixon, opened a private school, and there I attended classes until Pinelands Primary School opened its doors in 1931.

After my father's death my mother decided it would be necessary to sell Caronel and to go out to work. She and Lorna would stay with her sister Doris and her husband Harry Hudson, who had a house high on the slopes of Signal Hill, Sea Point. I was asked whether I would mind staying with her youngest sister, Marjorie, and her husband John Berry who, with my cousins Rex and Eileen, lived on a farm near the village of Hobhouse in the Orange Free State. Although I was young to be going off, the suggestion was no shock since my parents had planned that I should spend my standard six year at a Hobhouse school, partly to learn Afrikaans, partly to experience the atmosphere of farm life.

In August 1934, at the age of nine, I arrived at 'Welgeluk', my uncle's farm, some three miles from Hobhouse alongside the gravel road from Tweespruit. The environment and community made a deep and lasting impression, stimulating two desires that in years to come became driving forces in my life. One was to become involved in politics. The other was to see more of Africa.

Hobhouse was laid out on an unimaginative square grid, marked by sand and gravel streets on a piece of land that sloped up gently from the Leeu River to a long, flat-topped, stony *koppie* less than a kilometre away. It had a police station, a post office, a garage, a farmers' co-operative, a café, a butchery, a couple of general dealers, a Dutch Reformed church, a hotel inappropriately called 'The Grand', a couple of tennis courts, and a sprinkling of single-storeyed corrugated-iron-roofed houses. My stay gave me, a young English-speaking boy from the city, an opportunity to understand something of the values, the sensitivity, the fundamentalism, the stubborn pride of the rural Afrikaner – and to experience something of the intensity of his politics.

At least once a week Uncle John and Aunty Marjorie would play tennis on the village courts. These were social occasions, not only for the tennis players who came in from the surrounding farms, but also for many of the children. On one occasion, we heard that a swarm of locusts was approaching. Tennis was abandoned and we dashed back to Welgeluk to see whether we could start some smoky veld fires to head off the swarm. Too late! By the time we arrived, the swarm cast a clinging brown-black blanket over grass, crops, trees. The next day it moved on, but left the part of the farm where it had settled stripped of leaves and greenery. The only people to whom this natural blight gave any advantage were the black farmworkers, who gathered up locusts and cooked them in four-gallon tins over open wood or dung fires.

In the early evening we would go to the rough stone-walled kraal and, amid the smell of fresh cow droppings, watch the cows being milked; the treat was to scoop up and drink a mugful of frothy milk, warm and fresh from the udder. Occasionally on a Saturday we would get up before dawn and ride on a cart drawn by two oxen which delivered the milk, in metal cans, to the cheese factory at Morgenson a few kilometres away on the gravel road to Wepener. However the trip was long, tedious and bumpy, and in winter was icy cold – a journey not undertaken too often.

When work was done, some of the workers would come across to the rondavel near the farmhouse where Uncle John kept a supply of basic household goods. Mealie meal was measured out in large tin beakers; and there were salt, sugar, matches, candles, yeast for brewing home-made beer, and, on occasion, fresh meat. Farmworkers and their families would ask for bandages or medicines to deal with ailments such as cuts, sores, colds and headaches, or explain why they needed time off to go to the *dorp*.

Farm life was very social. Tennis 'parties' were fashionable since almost every farm had its court, surfaced with the brown earth from ant heaps. There were guinea fowl shoots at the Leeu River.

The highlight of the year was harvest time. Maize and wheat were the main crops: when the mealies had turned from milky cream to rich yellow, the cobs were picked and stacked inside a wire netting enclosure to form a vertical cylinder of ripe maize. In due course a rented threshing machine would separate corn from cob. Children, black and white, armed with a variety of sticks, stood at the ready for the swarms of mice and rats that emerged from the bottom of the stack.

The harvesting of the wheat was more hectic and commercial. A team of forty to fifty black women harvesters were employed. They arrived at Welgeluk *en masse*, complete with cooking utensils, household goods and young offspring. They went through the ripened wheat field in an extended line, bent at the waist, cutting through the cluster of wheat with a swish of their razor-sharp sickles. Another team gathered the shafts of wheat and put them together in vertical bundles, while yet another team with two oxen and a cart gathered the stacks and took them to a central point on the field near the cattle kraal. The next day the hissing, steam-driven, piston-thumping threshing machine was set in motion. The shafts of wheat were fed into a dark hole in its back – and marvellous grains of golden wheat cascaded out of a funnel on the right into the waiting jute sacks.

After the harvest the workers were paid in cash and the fires were lit. Soon the smell of smoke, of boiling *mieliepap* and cooking meat, with a waft of *kaffirbier*, touched the nostrils, and the ears responded to a babble of melodious cheerful voices, mostly talking, but interspersed with African song and music. Next day the harvesters moved on. The sacks of grain were a reminder of their transient presence.

When I arrived at Welgeluk South African politics, and OFS Afrikaner politics in particular, were in a state of turmoil. The farmers – at that time the key element in South African politics, and the backbone of the Afrikaner *volk* – faced ruin. The worldwide depression, plus a stubborn attempt by the Minister of Finance, Klaasie Havenga, to keep South Africa on the gold standard, had brought them to their knees. In the OFS matters were made worse by a searing drought and a plague of locusts that travelled across the blue sky in vast black swarms, and settled on the veld in ugly clinging masses to destroy the crops and the grazing beneath them.

But for these Afrikaners, something far worse than economic or natural disasters had occurred – Afrikaner nationalism, as a consequence of which the National Party was split from stem to stern.

The two former Boer generals, Hertzog and Smuts, leaders of the Nationalist and South African parties respectively – arch political foes ever since Hertzog formed the National Party in 1914 – had joined forces in 1934 to form the United South African Party. But not all Afrikaner nationalists welcomed this act of fusion, or 'samesmelting'. The doughty leader of the Cape Nationalists, Dr DF Malan, left Hertzog and Smuts to form the Gesuiwerde (Purified) National Party.

The Afrikaners of Hobhouse, in common with so many others, were torn between their commitment to the Afrikaner *volk* and loyalty to their born hero and political leader, Hertzog. Families, congregations, communities were split between *Smelters* and *Gesuiwerdes, Hertzogite* and *Malanite.*

My uncle, John Berry, became the chairman of the local branch of the *Smelters*; his brother-in-law, Sarel Cilliers, was his counterpart in the *Gesuiwerdes.* Meanwhile, I was the only *rooinek* in the school in Hobhouse.

The *dorp* was named after Emily Hobhouse, that courageous English woman who throughout the Anglo-Boer War argued the cause of the Boers, and worked to relieve some of the misery and suffering of the women and children in the concentration camps established by the British during the latter part of the war. She was buried, not as a pacifist and liberal in her native England, but as an Afrikaner heroine at the Vrouemonument in Bloemfontein.

During my stay at Hobhouse one of its sons was leading the campaign to free the Afrikaner from the economic dominance of English-speaking South Africans. Nico Diederichs founded the Reddingsdaadbond and later became minister of finance and then the third state president of the Republic of South Africa.

A less parochial Africa seemed close. From my uncle's *stoep* one looked out across an orchard that sloped away below the house, across the neighbouring farms with their sparse peach orchards and patches of mealie lands, across the willow-lined Leeu River to Hobhouse with its roof and church steeple against the background of the brown stone *koppie*. But beyond Hobhouse one saw range upon range of majestic and intriguing mountains in Basutoland – the Malutis. For me Hobhouse was still South Africa, the Malutis were Africa.

During the first week that I was at school in Hobhouse, our class was taken to the agricultural land below the *dorp's* dam where the supervisor who was leading us, metal spade in hand, across the dam wall, was struck dead by a bolt of lightning.

I was fascinated by the Malutis and by the black men and women who came across the border from Basutoland. Red- and grey-blanketed men on small Basuto ponies. Women on foot with their upright posture, their purchases and possessions perched precariously on their heads, and their lilting voices as they greeted one another from afar. Africa lay across the Caledon River and it seemed to lie beyond my reach. Yet it wasn't.

2

High school: Villiersdorp
1936-1939

As devoted Methodists, my parents had planned for me to attend school at Kingswood College, a Methodist Church school in Grahamstown. But father's early death and our financial situation put paid to these plans. My mother, on the recommendation of a friend, suggested as an alternative that I go to the De Villiers Graaff Institute, later to become the De Villiers Graaff High School, at Villiersdorp, a country village some eighty kilometres from Cape Town. It was founded as a typical village institution in 1872 but gained considerable stature in the Western Cape thanks to a substantial endowment by David de Villiers Graaff (later to become Sir David). I was ten.

As an illiterate boy, Graaff came to Villiersdorp to work in his Uncle James Combrink's butchery. In due course, together with his brother, he took over Combrink's business and, having learned the benefits of refrigeration, built up the powerful Imperial Cold Storage Company. He went on to become a wealthy farmer and landowner; served as mayor of Cape Town; and was a member of the cabinets of both the Cape and Union governments. Sir David's son, De Villiers, and his grandson, David, were to feature prominently as adversaries in my political career.

The De Villiers Graaff School comprised substantial school buildings and well-equipped boarding hostels. It became famed for its high standard of teaching, its extended study hours, and its boarding school discipline. It also acquired a reputation as a school where 'naughty' boys from well-off homes in Cape Town were sent. On one occasion, the mother of a Jewish friend in Sea Point said to me: 'Colin, where do you live?'

'In Pinelands,' I replied.

'Then do you go to school at Bishops?'

'No, not at Bishops.'

'Then do you go to school at Rondebosch?'

'No, not at Rondebosch.'

'Well, where do you go to school?'

'At Villiersdorp,' I replied.

She held up her hands in amazement and said: 'Oi! Did you fail your standard nine at SACS?'

Although younger than the other scholars in my class, I soon adjusted to the routine, the discipline, and the camaraderie of boarding school life in a small country town. It meant: punctuality at meals, regular study hours, cold-water showers, keeping the dormitory neat and tidy. There were schoolboy pranks like 'bunking out' to raid an orchard, or go skinny-dipping in a pool of the nearby river. We would walk the girls from Spes Bona, the local schoolgirls' hostel, along a red gravel road at the edge of the town; and we would flirt when possible at the annual school hostel party. We climbed up to caves in the nearby mountain, and shot at frogs in the water furrows with homemade catapults.

There were (to us) tedious services in the Dutch Reformed church, and occasional shorter services when once a month the Anglican parson from Caledon presided in the small church at Villiersdorp. We spent our weekly pocket money at the Central Café on Saturday mornings; there were occasional cinema shows presented by Parker's Talkie Tours; and even more occasionally a play performed by André Huguenet and Linda Lindeque.

There was an intriguing mix of English and Afrikaans and rural and city pupils. Close to twenty-five per cent of the students were English-speakers, and of these a large proportion were Jewish. This meant not only that youngsters from English and Afrikaans homes were rubbing shoulders with one another on the playground, but that in many classes lessons were taught in both English and Afrikaans. Bilingualism flourished. The pupils were aware of the ebb and flow of politics in the larger South Africa.

The rapid urbanisation of Afrikaans-speaking South Africans after the Great Depression combined with the nationwide celebration in 1938 of the 100th anniversary of the Great Trek to give tremendous impetus to the strengthening of Afrikaner identity and the rise of Afrikaner nationalism. The ruling United Party was deeply divided since its leader, General Hertzog, decided to push through the so-called 1936 'settlement'. In terms of this, 'native' voters of the Cape Province were removed from the common voters' roll and given a so-called *quid pro quo* in the form of three white representatives in parliament elected on a separate voters' roll, plus the promise of 15 million morgen of land for occupation in the native reserves – a forerunner of the Bantustans that were to emerge under the National Party in the 1960s.

Almost simultaneously, events in the outside world had an impact. Italian forces under Mussolini, in disregard of the League of Nations, invaded and conquered Abyssinia. German forces under Adolf Hitler marched into the demilitarised Saargebiet, took over Austria in a bloodless Anschluss, seized the Sudetenland from Czechoslovakia, and were now threatening Poland. A war between Great Britain and Hitler's Third Reich seemed inevitable.

Hitler's campaign of vilification and discrimination against Jews in general, and against the Jewish citizens of his country in particular, was increasing in momentum and brutality. Hundreds of thousands of Jews were emigrating from Europe, mostly to America, but some thousands came to South Africa, where anti-Semitism also reared its ugly head. It became part of the political debate and manifested itself in new pro-Nazi organisations such as the Greyshirts, and stormtrooper-style movements such as the Ossewabrandwag.

The political showdown in South Africa came early in September 1939. War had broken out between England and Germany. General Smuts, then the deputy leader of the United Party, moved a motion in parliament supporting Britain in the war. Hertzog, prime minister and leader of the United Party, moved for neutrality. Smuts's motion was carried by 13 votes; Hertzog resigned as prime minister, and rejoined the National Party; Smuts became prime minister. On 6 September 1939, South Africa was at war.

These traumatic political events, inside and outside South Africa, were often the subject of intense discussion and heated debate on the school playground and in the dormitories. They made a profound impact on the scholars at De Villiers Graaff High School – and certainly sharpened my political awareness and stimulated my interest in politics.

Two months after war had been declared I completed my schooling and left Villiersdorp at the age of 14. A month later I was relieved and pleased to hear that I had passed my matriculation examination with what was known as 'first-class honours'.

3

Cape Town University, 1940-1943

In February 1940, having qualified for a bursary sufficient to pay for my basic tuition fees, I went up to the UCT campus to register as a student for a Bachelor of Science degree in quantity surveying. This decision arose partly out of my mother's days as a secretary in Parker and Forsyth, a prominent firm of Cape Town architects, and partly from the recommendation of a family friend who was a partner in a firm of quantity surveyors with the charming rural name of Shepherd, Quail and Wood.

The course for which I enrolled fell under the Faculty of Architecture, introduced at UCT for the first time in 1940. After a few months of the academic year, two of the students pulled out of the course and I found myself the only student taking it. That first year was extremely demanding, mentally and emotionally, especially for a 14-year-old straight from boarding school. There was the transition from the imposed discipline and regulation of the school to the freedom and the need for self-discipline of the university campus. There was the change from a style of education based on memorising to one based on thinking, understanding and applying.

Morning classes and tutorials were held at the main campus on the slopes of Devil's Peak, and the afternoon ones at the School of Architecture at the Hiddingh campus at the top of Government Avenue in Cape Town. As I lived at home in Pinelands, I spent hours each day on foot and by train getting from one venue to the other. Fortunately I was well built and physically strong. My years away at school in Hobhouse and Villiersdorp had given me experience in handling personal problems on my own and helped me to develop a comparatively mature sense of self-confidence.

The head of the School of Architecture was Professor Thornton-White, commonly referred to as TW. A man of moderate build, receding hairline, thick-rimmed spectacles, a goatee beard that partly hid the wound he received during World War 1, and with a colourful bow tie and a cigar, TW cut a fascinating figure. He was passionate about architecture, and expert in his knowledge of wines. Indeed, he enjoyed nothing better than having students and staff around to his home for a convivial evening of wine-tasting.

His great interest in the planning and development of the extension of Cape Town's foreshore and his frequent absence from the school while engaged on this project prompted one of the students to chalk this rhyme on the blackboard:

There's Professor TW
Who'll seldom trouble you.
He is gaining renown
By planning the town
But should he stray
Down your studio way
Don't forget to mention
The 'Foreshore Extension'.

As the only student taking the course, I was introduced to and kept in close touch with Bernard James, my lecturer in quantity surveying. This relationship became an enduring and rewarding one. Bernard became my mentor in quantity surveying; but more than this he took a fatherly interest in me, and helped me to shape my judgement of people and issues.

In 1948, when, after the war, I had qualified as a quantity surveyor and done a year of practical work in the office of a building contractor, I joined Bernard as a junior quantity surveyor. In 1952 I became a partner in Bernard James and Partners, and remained one for more than fifty years.

Bernard James and Partners is a remarkable professional institution. Not only has it remained intact since Bernard James founded it in 1936, but it has done so without any formal partnership agreement. I could not have wished for a more congenial, rewarding, and (considering my intense involvement as a politician) a more accommodating relationship than I enjoyed with my partners.

A few names: Bernard James, the team leader; Ralph Aitchison and Dick Baragwanath; Frank Moore, who shared an office with me during our first years at the firm; Harold Phinn, who was persuaded to come back from Australia to head up our team working on the vast Tygerberg Hospital project; Wally Brink, Roy Bailey and Billy Steele in Windhoek; Graham Thomas in Johannesburg; and in the nineties and the two-thousands, Donald Steward and Adrian Buckland who led the team in Cape Town.

They were all more than professional partners: they were friends and confidants. While not necessarily agreeing with me on every issue, they all understood and supported the thrust of my activities in public life. They made it possible for me to take up public office as a town councillor, a provincial councillor, and an MP – yet remain a quantity surveying partner. They were prepared to endure the inconvenience and face up to the risk of having a professional partner who was at the same time an active and outspoken politician.

No student at UCT from 1940 to 1943 could escape the impact of the war. There were traumatic setbacks such as the fall of France, the surrender of the South African Second Brigade at Tobruk, the forced occupation of country after country in Europe. There were the emotion-wracked battles of Britain, El Alamein, and Stalingrad; the entry of the USA into the war; General Rommel's retreat from Africa; and the invasion of Europe, when on 6 June 1944 Allied troops landed on the beaches of Normandy.

In line with the rest of the country, the students at UCT were divided on the war. A majority of white citizens supported the effort. But a sizeable minority led by Hertzog and Dr Malan's Reunited National Party opted for neutrality. A small but militant minority that identified with the Ossewabrandwag opposed the war effort altogether and favoured a Nazi victory.

This division precipitated the withdrawal by the anti-war faction from UCT's traditional sporting, social and cultural organisations and led to the formation of a number of new bodies that reflected the anti-war sentiment. Student life was divided; student emotions were polarised.

In 1941 the university authorities established the University of Cape Town Training Corps. This enabled students and staff to join a part-time military unit through which they could receive some basic military training in preparation for the day when they would leave to join the military forces. Although barely sixteen years old, I joined this corps and received my first mild introduction into military life.

In the initial stages, activities were divided into lectures and parade ground drill at the upper campus on Saturday mornings. In the July mid-year vacation we were packed off in a troop train to Zonderwater, a vast tented training camp near Cullinan, north of Pretoria, for three weeks of intensive 'field training'. This was tough going for pampered students from Cape Town in the freezing winter of the red-dusted Transvaal highveld. During the end-of-the-year vacation a number of us went on to selected courses such as musketry, camouflage and field intelligence at Voortrekkerhoogte Infantry Training School outside Pretoria.

By 1942 the training had become more intensive. The anti-aircraft unit assembled on Saturdays at the base camp of the Tenth Light Anti-Aircraft Artillery Regiment at Ottery for intensive training on the maintenance and use of the Bofors 40mm anti-aircraft gun. By the time our proficiency in the use of this weapon had been tested by live 'shoots' at a drogue towed behind a slow-flying aircraft off the beach at Strandfontein, we were considered ready to perform some effective service by manning operational Bofors gun sites.

During the university term we each took one day off in ten to man the anti-aircraft gun that had been installed on top of the Colosseum building at the corner of St George's and Riebeeck streets. Our sleeping, eating and ablution quarters were in a prefabricated building that had been erected on top of the adjacent Garlick's building. Immediately below us was Garlick's bakery. In the early morning when the delicious aroma of bread being baked wafted up to us, one of us on guard duty would tap on the window of the bakery and ask the friendly baker for a couple of loaves of his excellent freshly baked bread. He always obliged.

In parliament the issue was kept alive by debates on the neutrality motions introduced by the National Party opposition. Communities and at times families were divided. There were speeches, meetings, rallies – and assaults by bearded members of the Ossewabrandwag on soldiers, and vice versa. There were even occasional acts of sabotage on troop trains and military installations. No-one was neutral.

My family life was greatly disrupted. My mother, 'following the flag', signed on for military service. For some months she worked as a secretary at SAAF Area Head-quarters at Youngsfield near Cape Town and was later transferred to serve as secre-tarial assistant to the chief of the SADF at headquarters in Pretoria. My sister Lorna was at boarding school in Wellington in the Cape, and during the school holidays stayed with my mother's sister Doris Hudson and her family in Sea Point. I was liv-ing in lodgings close to the university in Alma Road, Rondebosch.

On 14 April 1943 I turned 18 and began to think about volunteering to do mili-tary service on a full-time basis. After discussions with Prof. Thornton-White it was agreed that, provided I completed the first six months of my fourth year, I would be credited with having completed the full four years of my surveying course.

For the next few years my life was going to be very different.

4

You're in the army now

In June 1943 I reported for military service to the Castle in Cape Town. My university education, and my parents' long association with Captain RJ du Toit MP, the chief recruiting officer for the Cape Command, earmarked me for an officer-training course. However, at this stage in the war, the military were not looking for officers. I was assigned to the Tenth Light Anti-Aircraft Artillery Regiment, stationed at a camp at Ottery on the outskirts of Cape Town. I was given the rank of bombardier and the role of instructor on the Bofors gun.

My duties were not onerous. I had time to take part in athletics meetings – I was a reasonably competent thrower of the javelin – as well as in inter-unit cricket and rugby matches. Except when on guard duty, I could obtain a 'weekend pass' which enabled me to enjoy the comfort of our home in the newer part of Pinelands and the conviviality of the wartime social life in the Cape Peninsula.

During this period I first came to know Joyce Cortes, an 18-year-old curly-haired blonde, who, with her parents Leslie and Rose, had emigrated from London in 1938. Les, a printer by trade, had come to join his brother-in-law, who had a printing business in Parow, an overwhelmingly Afrikaans-speaking northern suburb. Joyce was enrolled first at Parow Primary and then at Parow High School, and matriculated in December 1943 as a very competent English-Afrikaans bilingual shorthand typist. She and I spent many hours together as part of the Pinelands clan: dances in the local civic hall, evenings at the cinema, and weekends at the beach, often entertaining troops from the UK, Australia and New Zealand when their convoys stopped over in Cape Town *en route* to England or the Middle East.

Joyce enrolled in the local Voluntary Aid Detachment of the Red Cross and was frequently called out on duty whenever crowds were expected to assemble. She also started doing regular spells of duty at the short-staffed Mowbray Maternity Home. She and I were close, but never reached the stage at which either of us felt exclusively beholden to the other. This did not mean that I didn't feel pangs of jealousy when I heard that she was to go to one or other social function with someone else.

During my days at Ottery I met a wider and rougher range of South Africans than in the somewhat closed environment of Pinelands and the university. Apart from the troops who came to Ottery for retraining prior to being 'sent up North', the main body of the Tenth Light Anti-Aircraft Regiment consisted of enlisted men with no intention of doing their service farther afield than Cape Town.

They fell roughly into two groups. One comprised 'old boys' who had seen service with the First South African Division up North and who had been sent back to South Africa for various medical, personal or compassionate reasons. The other I can only describe as 'roughies'. One sensed they had joined up not out of any sense of duty but because the army would provide them with food, clothing, housing, pay and some focus to their otherwise unfocused lives. They were constantly at loggerheads with the disciplinarians, and often described themselves, justly, as '*daggarokers*', '*bandiete*' or 'gangsters'.

After a few months at Ottery I became restless. I hadn't joined up to spend my army career at base camp. I sought and obtained a meeting with the officer commanding my unit and explained my wish to 'go North'. I was assigned for active service in the Middle East.

A round of farewells from my friends, and an especially tender farewell from Joyce; words of advice and loving prayer from my mother; and I boarded a troop train on the first leg 'up North'. Then followed a few days of preparation at a transit camp at Voortrekkerhoogte outside Pretoria, and it was on to Zwartkops military airbase to board a 'Dak' DC3 for our journey northward. The flight to Cairo took four not-too-comfortable days strapped into the canvas seats in a plane that had no insulation, air-conditioning or cabin pressurisation, and that bumped and lurched as it made its way doggedly over the mountains, plains and deserts of Africa.

On the fourth day, after a long haul following the course of the Nile, we eventually touched down at Cairo West airport. An hour in a troop carrier, and finally we were shown to our bungalow in the sprawling South African base camp at Helwan. After a few days we were issued with fresh desert-style clothing and equipment, learned some words of basic soldier's Egyptian, and saw films at 'Shaftos' – Egyptian-owned open-air cinemas, which had an appalling record of breaking down midway through the film. After a weekend savouring the mysteries and excitement of wartime Cairo, we boarded a troop train to the local army headquarters, located in the desert not far from Ismailia. While we were waiting to be called in, I saw, to my astonishment, over the brow of the nearby sand dune, a ship's funnel and two masts gliding past. On the other side of the sand dune was a cargo ship making its way through the Suez Canal.

Once we had been signed in at the HQ of our new unit, the Forty-third Light Anti-Aircraft Regiment, we were taken southwards to a point where the Canal joins the Great Bitter Lakes at Deversoir. Here a small skiff rowed by Achmat, a wiry Egyptian, came to take us across to our Bofors gun site on the western edge of the Sinai Desert.

For the next few weeks the Bofors gun site was to be my 'home', which I shared with Sergeant Meltcalfe, eight other South Africans and Achmat. Life followed a regular daily pattern – spells of guard duty spread over 24 hours, turns at kitchen fatigue, daily gun maintenance and gun drill, rifle and Bren gun target shooting, get-fit jogs along the edge of the canal – we were warned against wandering into the desert for fear of mines – and spearing delicious large crabs. A variety of ships passed by, and we occasionally asked the crews to throw empty crates overboard to supplement our fuel supply.

We followed the news, and especially the progress on the various war fronts, as closely as we could on our mobile radio set. But of course, what we wanted to hear most of all was news from home. This made the arrival of the mail truck, which stopped on the other side of the Canal once or twice a week and brought letters, magazines, and occasional food parcels from home, a very special event.

Occasionally the gun site routine was broken by an air raid alarm. We would take up our positions and scan the skies for an enemy intruder. As it turned out, the only intruding enemy was a high-altitude reconnaissance plane, way out of the range of a Bofors shell.

Two soldier colleagues who remained in my mind for many years were Jan, a tough, tanned young farmer from South West Africa; and Peter, a pale, shy-natured bank clerk from Cape Town. Jan was a first-class marksman, and an outdoors man who revelled in the work and the routine of army life. Peter was essentially an indoor man. He pulled his weight as a member of the gun site team, but one felt that this was out of a sense of duty rather than being done with relish. One felt that Jan was the kind of man one would like to have alongside one in any tough encounter with the enemy. Peter would do his best, but one wondered how he would shape up in a battle.

A few months later, during the battle for Monte Solé in the Apennines in Italy, I saw how the strain of battle, with the danger of death, impacted on individuals in unexpected ways. I was just short of the crest when Jan, with no greeting, scurried down the mountain to the safety of the dead ground below. On reaching the crest I enquired about him and was told that under fire his toughness had gone, his nerves had snapped, and he had been ordered to quit the battle zone.

Late that afternoon, after a couple of German counterattacks had been repelled and it appeared that the enemy was withdrawing, I came across Peter in a slit trench in an area that had come under intense enemy mortar fire. His eyes were bloodshot; his face was pale and smudged. But he was alert, his rifle was still at the ready. He grinned broadly and shouted triumphantly: 'Corporal, we made it!'

To Italy and Monte Solé

Towards the end of July we were instructed to prepare to leave our gun site; a couple of trucks took us back to Ismailia to join other gun crews of our regiment. From there we were taken on to Port Said where our regiment's CO, Lieutenant Colonel Frank Mellish, announced that we were going to Italy to join the Sixth South African Armoured Division and be converted from an anti-aircraft regiment into a number of infantry companies. One battery would become a company in the Witwatersrand Rifles / De la Rey Regiment; another in the Royal Natal Carbineers; another in the Royal Durban Light Infantry Regiment; and my battery would become D Company in the First City / Cape Town Highlanders.

My arrival in Italy was an emotional experience: to be in Europe, to be in Italy, steeped in ancient culture and architecture, to be in Taranto, the scene of a great air and sea battle earlier in the war. Above all, to be ready to play my part in the defeat of the Nazis.

My first impression was how old and stately the buildings were. There were no shacks and no corrugated-iron roofs; instead, stone, brick and plastered walls and brown-red tiled roofs. In the countryside there were no barbed-wire fences. Hedges and stone walls separated the farm fields.

I did a stint of guard duty at a nearby prisoner-of-war camp. One night I was detailed to do picket duty with some British military police. Their main function seemed to be to visit the brothels in the area to ensure that all was in order. As a sexually innocent 19-year-old from South Africa, this was a fascinating and eye-opening experience. What struck me were the remarkably good relations between the military police and the madams, which I have no doubt they put to good use when off duty.

A few weeks later we boarded a convoy of trucks and headed north, past the Allied air base at Foggia, and then west through the mountain town of Benevento. At Caserta, just short of Naples, we turned north again, past the old town of Capua and on to the Sixth South African Armoured Division's training camp near the village of Piedmonte de Alife. Here we were issued with small two-person tents, which became our temporary homes on the farm fields sloping down to the Volturno River.

By this time the battle line was moving away from us. The battle for Cassino had been won. Rome had fallen. The Arno River had been crossed, and the vanguard of General Mark W Clark's US Fifth Army, of which our South African Division was a part, was heading for the Apennines that stood between the Allied forces and the industrial heartland of northern Italy.

Having realised we were likely to be engaged in combat at much closer quarters than we would have as anti-aircraft gunners, we got stuck into the battle training with a will. We were toughened up physically and emotionally, and taught the practical skills of infantry warfare. Route marches, map reading, camouflage, mock battles, liaison with mortar and artillery support, handling of Sten and Bren guns and rifles and hand grenades – there was not much time for relaxation. However, in the late afternoon there was sometimes the opportunity to cool off in the river. In the evening, when we were not too exhausted, we played bridge or poker by candlelight in our tents.

Once we were taken to Cassino, a few kilometres north of our camp. There we saw the mountain barrier that blocked the way north, the mountain-top monastery that had been bombed to rubble, the devastation of the town, and the fields pock-marked with shellholes. It was awesome. Our instinctive reaction was: 'Thank God *we* didn't have to capture it.'

As I had not only matriculated but completed four years of university studies, I was sent on a course in battlefield intelligence with a view to becoming D Company's intelligence corporal. At the Military Intelligence Training School outside Naples I was immersed in an intensive three-week course. The curriculum included recognising the sound of shells, bullets and mortars flying overhead; observing signs of enemy movement and gunfire; briefing patrols; map reading; taking down and relaying the daily news bulletins to the troops; and reporting back to Regimental Intelligence.

One of the benefits of my training stint was that it afforded me the opportunity of visiting Pompeii and Herculaneum, and of enjoying my first experience of Italian opera, Puccini's *La Bohème* and Verdi's *Il Trovatore*.

I returned to Piedmonte de Alife as the 'intelligence corporal' of my company. On 14 November, under orders, I boarded a truck that took me past Cassino and up to Rome where I spent two days – loving every minute. Then I went north, sleeping over in Perugia before going on to Florence and the town of Prato where the headquarters of the Sixth Division was located. The next leg was up, up and over the Apennines on a winding muddy road, packed with vehicles of all types. Beyond the crest of the Apennines we stopped at the mountain village of Castiglione dei Pepoli – 'Castig' as it was called by the South Africans. Near its picturesque tower at the fork of two roads in the centre of the village was the base for the Twelfth South African Motorised Brigade.

Today Castig is the site of a magnificent South African war cemetery, with white gravestones, green lawns and red and white roses all cared for by the Commonwealth War Graves Commission and townsfolk of Castiglione. From there the road went downhill to the narrow valley of the Setta River as it flowed northwards, eventually to reach the Po valley. The further north, the more intense the signs of men and machines of war. Trucks, tanks, field guns, Bailey bridges, brigade and regimental insignia festooned the tortuous route through the small, partially destroyed villages and farmsteads. At the busy little river town of Pian di Setta, we turned left out of the valley and zigzagged our way up the adjoining mountainside.

For the first time I heard the sounds of war: the occasional blast from some heavy artillery sending a shell into German-held artillery; a screech and crunch as the German gunners responded.

Ahead, some eight kilometres to the north, was the mountain massif of Monte Solé and Monte Caprara, still firmly in German hands. Signs on the bends of the roads said: 'Do not stop on this road, you are in sight of the enemy!'

Eventually our truck reached Grizzana, a small village on the ridge of the range of mountains separating the valleys of the Setta and Reno rivers. Looming over Grizzana from the south was Monte Stanco, captured at great cost only a month before. From there I was taken to First City / Cape Town Highlanders regimental headquarters and introduced to Lieutenant Basil Crisp, the regimental intelligence officer, who briefed me on procedures relating to an intelligence corporal's duties. I was equipped with a Sten gun, binoculars, compass, maps and writing material, and taken by jeep around the mountain to 'Pink House', a farm building that was the operational head-quarters of C Company, commanded by Major Lionel Murray.

Major Murray, who had already been awarded the MC and was to be awarded a bar for his leadership during the battle of Monte Solé in April 1945, took me under his wing with his intelligence team to teach me as much about the terrain, the enemy disposition, and my duties as he could in the two weeks before the rest of D Com-pany joined the winter line. Strange how the wheel of fortune turns – 13 years later, when I became a member of parliament for Pinelands, Lionel became my provincial councillor – and a year later my political adversary.

On the first night in Pink House I thought every shell was heading for me, until some battle-hardened colleague told me: 'If you can hear the shells they are not go-ing to hit you. The one that hits you is the one that you don't hear.'

I soon became adept at map reading and at recognising the sounds and sights of warfare, the puffs of smoke from enemy artillery, and the different sounds that enemy projectiles made as they passed overhead. I learned how to brief patrols as they went out and how to debrief them on return. After three weeks at Pink House, D Company arrived, and I rejoined them to take up my intelligence responsibilities.

D Company, commanded by Major Gerry Boland, had its headquarters in a cluster of farmhouses, nicknamed Foxhole, on the slope of the mountain overlooking Griz-zana. Each of the three platoons was allocated a farmhouse on the forward slopes of the mountain, from where they carried out night patrols in the direction of enemy lines. Occasionally they came into contact with the enemy and suffered casualties. On one occasion a patrol walked into an ambush and were taken prisoners-of-war.

Our farmhouse bases also experienced sporadic shell and mortar fire. To avoid at-tracting attention troops in the forward-position houses had to keep the windows facing the enemy line shuttered. They had to avoid using the front of the houses, and could not light fires, which emitted smoke during daylight. One forward observation post that eight of us took turns to man during the night, was a quaint little cemetery at Campiaro. It was in a commanding position, perched on the side of the mountain with one wall bordering on no-man's-land and the adjacent wall facing down the road to Vergato, a town in the Reno River valley occupied by the enemy.

The cemetery was rectangular, approximately twenty metres by thirty metres. Among the neat rows of graves were three new ones, each of which had a simple wooden cross and a German steel helmet placed on the ground in front of it.

At either end of the cemetery the walls were constructed to form four rows of horizontal 'boxes' – each wide, high and deep enough to accommodate a coffin. The coffin was slid into the box, which was then sealed with a slab of marble giving the name and particulars of the dead person entombed in it. Not all the boxes were oc-cupied, and these we used as sleeping quarters when not on guard duty. A tight fit, but warm and dry.

Autumn was turning to winter, mud was turning to ice, and rain first to sleet and then to snow. We were supplied with warm clothing including duffel coats and white-hooded overalls for when we were in forward positions. Patrolling became more difficult, but observation easier. Tracks made in the snow during the night betrayed troop movements the next day. Melted snow on the roofs of barns and houses was a sign that people were living in them. On the other hand, walking on the frozen surface of ploughed fields and rutted roads was hazardous. Trying to keep warm, especially when the wind was blowing, was a priority. One way was to stand behind a Sherman tank parked behind a farmhouse and soak up the warmth of its exhaust, which was kept running while the tank's batteries were recharged.

At Christmas there was a church service for those of us who were billeted at, or close to, Foxhole. There were extra rations, including some fresh mutton 'acquired' by our enterprising quartermaster, some impromptu singing, and much nostalgia and deep thoughts of home. Then winter dragged on, with the monotony broken by occasional visits to Castig for showers, fresh clothes and relaxation away from the front line.

The arrival of mail from South Africa did not always boost morale. There were those who were hoping to receive letters but did not get them; it was worse still for those who did get them, only to find that their relationship with their girlfriend, fiancée or wife was no more. Prolonged separation under wartime conditions played havoc with many people's personal relationships.

Occasionally the mail included a food parcel from home or from the Gifts and Comforts organisation headed by 'Ouma Issie', the wife of the prime minister, General Smuts. These parcels included such luxuries as tins of butterscotch and other sweets, biscuits, a comb, shaving equipment, playing cards, a magazine and sometimes socks – which were renowned among the troops for not fitting properly.

In February I was fortunate enough to have my name drawn out of the hat to go to Rome on a week's leave. It was a long and uncomfortable journey on the back of an army truck, starting in a snowstorm as we went up the winding road towards Castig. We stopped to pick up a gunner who was going down to Prato. There was a dusting of snow on the top of his army cap and on his shoulders; his army-issue glasses were frosted over; icicles hung from his moustache; his ears were blue lumps of flesh. After a while he warmed up and relaxed, and, to our amazement, he was Boy Louw, one of the heroes of the Springbok rugby team that toured New Zealand in 1937, the last tour before the war.

I had a magical few days – hot showers, regular meals, clean clothes, plus the grandeur of Rome. There was the Pantheon, the Trevi Fountain, the Colosseum, the Castello St Angelo, St Peter's, the Victor Emmanuel II memorial; nearby the memorial was the small balcony from which Benito Mussolini, only a year before, had harangued his cheering fascist admirers. *The Barber of Seville* resounded in the open-air arena at the Baths of Caracalla, and on top of all this there was an audience with

Pope Pius in the Vatican, shared with some three hundred other Allied troops. I sent my mother a card from the Vatican post office in which I suggested she should break the news quietly to my grandfather, an old-fashioned member of the 'anti-papist' school. My card crossed in the post with a letter from my mother telling me that granddad, Frank Wells, had passed away on the very day that his grandson had an audience with the Pope!

When I arrived back at Prato on the way to the front line, I found that our regiment had been pulled out for a spell of rest and recreation. Instead of going to the Apennines, we proceeded westwards along the Arno River valley to the village of Quiesa, midway between the historical town of Lucca and the seaside resort of Viareggio.

The break from front-line duties was good for morale. Apart from a daily parade, occasional guard duties and route marches, we were allowed to relax. There was plenty of rugby, soccer and hockey, as well as visits to Lucca and to Pisa to see its Leaning Tower. We arranged dances in the community hall of Viareggio, attended by local Italian *signorine*, chaperoned by their mothers, more intent on reaping a harvest of sweets, chocolates and cigarettes than protecting the chastity of their daughters!

However, all good things have to come to an end. I was told to join a party that would go ahead of the regiment to our new positions 'somewhere in the Apennines'. At short notice on 3 April we were packed into army trucks and taken back to Prato and on to Gardaletta, where we forded the Setta River and marched back to the small village of La Quercia. Towering ominously above La Quercia as it nestled in the valley under the arches of a railway overpass was the massif of Monte Solé.

Colonel Angus Duncan took us into a *casa* for a briefing, crisp and to the point. In a few weeks' time the Allied spring offensive would commence. The Sixth South African Armoured Division had been given the task of opening the road to Bologna. To do this, the Twelfth Brigade would have to capture the mountain massif formed by Monte Solé, Caprara and Abelle. The Highlanders had been assigned to capture Monte Solé. Suddenly, that mountain we had gazed at all winter from a safe distance was in front of us, forbidding, frightening, challenging.

Casualties were likely to be heavy. Yet there was a sense of pride that *our* regiment had been chosen for this pivotal battle task, and quiet determination to show we could do it.

The task of the forward party was to prepare for the regiment to take over from the Ninety-first US Cavalry Reconnaissance Squadron that had been holding the line while we were relaxing at the Quiesa. Unfortunately for us, the Americans, knowing they were not going to be asked to capture Solé, did little patrolling to locate the German forward positions. A debriefing of any American intelligence counterpart provided me with scarcely any information of value. Added to this, the Americans had laid mines in a defensive pattern in the terrain in front of them, but had kept no accurate record of their location!

What did impress us about the American soldiers was the quantity and quality of their equipment and supplies. Canned and packaged food, field cookers, eating utensils, sleeping bags, torches, 'candies', compasses – all were available in quality and abundant quantity. We had a good 'haul' when the Yanks pulled out and the rest of the Highlanders moved in.

The sappers were called in to clear paths and tracks leading to Monte Solé, and our men on forward patrol were instructed not to stray from them. The days that followed were totally directed to preparing for the 'big one' – the actual attack on Monte Solé. Our assembly area was on the reverse slope of the hillside, out of sight and just out of enemy mortar range. My function, together with my colleagues in the regiment's intelligence team, was to get all the information we could about enemy positions and the terrain that we would have to traverse to the summit. During the day we had forward observation posts monitoring the area between Monte Solé and us; at night we sent reconnaissance patrols forward for information and to probe the enemy's front positions. Once I accompanied a team of signallers to take a telephone cable as far along a track leading to Solé as possible; and on the night of 15 April, I was to be one of the squad who used the same track and telephone cable on our way to Solé.

Piece by piece the picture of the route we would have to take, and of what we could expect from the enemy, was put together. The plan of attack unfolded. Bombers and fighter-bombers of the US Air Force were to bomb and strafe the Solé/Caprara/Abelle massif for a full day. Lionel Murray's C Company and Gerry Boland's D Company, who were to undertake the initial assault, would move forward along two farm tracks – one on the left and one on the right of Hill 501 leading to Solé. Where the tracks joined at Casa Casetta, and with their mountain objective in full view, the two companies would lie up while a combined barrage of big guns and mortars pounded the terrain.

On 13 April we were told we would attack Monte Solé on the evening of the 14th – which happened to be my 20th birthday! I thought of my family and friends back in Pinelands. In turn they would be thinking of the birthday boy. In the evening while they were in church, unbeknown to them, I would be engaged in battle.

Then, on the 14th, low clouds prevented the US Air Force from bombing the massif: our attack had to be postponed.

On the 15th the skies were clear. Wave after wave of medium bombers flew over us to attack targets in the enemy's rear. Then fighter-bombers bombed, strafed and rained rockets and incendiaries on the enemy. Watching Solé being pounded from the air was good for our morale; not so good was when, in the course of a strafing raid, a USAF fighter bomber mistook its target and sent a string of machine gun shells ripping through the area where we were assembling. A group of Italian muleteers and their animals took the brunt of this wayward attack. Our supply train was badly disrupted; one South African and four Italians were killed, and others wounded. This single burst of aircraft fire gave us some inkling of what the German troops must have been feeling.

At 8.30 that evening our moment arrived. The assault on Monte Solé and Monte Caprara commenced.

The Battle of Monte Solé, 15-17 April 1945

From the time we started moving forward the adrenaline was pumping. It was all very real, and yet unreal: there was nothing artificial about the noises and dangers and death of battle, yet one had to pinch oneself to persuade oneself that it really was happening.

My first numbing shock was when stout-hearted 'Constable' van der Merwe, the runner at Company HQ, walking just behind me along a narrow track just short of Casa Casetta, trod on an enemy anti-personnel Schuh mine. My first reaction was bewilderment: 'What the hell has happened?' My second was to attend to Van der Merwe. Part of his foot had been blown off, and his ankle badly injured. A field dressing to close up the wound; a tourniquet to stem the flow of blood; a shot of morphine to ease his pain; and a call for a stretcher-bearer on the very field telephone line I had helped install two nights earlier.

Then: 'Where do we move from here? Forward? Backward?' Forward it had to be. So we scrambled up the bank at the side of the track and went ahead along the edge of an adjoining field. Boland, two signallers and I followed No. 1 and 2 platoons as they moved up the spine to the summit of Monte Solé. The going was tough as we were heavily laden with equipment, and the mountain had been pulverised into sand and jagged stone by guns, mortars and aircraft. At times the sound was deafening; when mortar bombs whistled over, we threw ourselves flat.

While we were making our way up Solé we got word that our forward platoons had driven the enemy from their fortified positions along the crest of the mountain. A short while later stretcher-bearers and walking wounded who came struggling down the steep mountainside made it clear that success had not been without its price.

Boland decided to establish his Company HQ in a vacated German dugout some metres short of the summit. As I was carrying the field radio, I went on to the summit to establish communication between the forward troops and Company HQ. The Solé ridge was exposed to enemy mortar and machine gun fire, so I used an entrenching tool that was part of my equipment to deepen a shallow slit trench the Germans had left behind. Just as well, too, for no sooner had I snuggled down in my hand-hewn haven than a piece of shrapnel from a mortar bomb snapped off the aerial from the field radio I had lugged all the way to the top.

With my radio out of action, I could not provide a link between the forward platoons and HQ. I scrambled down to the headquarters dugout to hear, on the set tuned into Regimental HQ, the message: 'Sunray is dead, Sunray is dead. Sholto Douglas has taken over as Sunray.' Lieutenant Colonel Angus Duncan, the officer commanding the Highlanders, had been killed by a mine when he stepped from a jeep near Casa Pudella onto the verge of the rough track going towards Monte Solé.

I spent the next few hours helping the signallers establish a field telephone communication between Company HQ and No. 1 and 2 platoons who were securing our night's gains, using trenches which the Germans had dug along the crest. I went back to the top of Solé and was talking on my field telephone to my friend Ray Paul of No. 2 Platoon, when I heard the whine of approaching mortar bombs. I dived into the nearest trench as the first bombs exploded. 'Ray, can you hear me?' I shouted into the mouthpiece. A voice came back: 'Yes, I can. But there's no need to shout. You're sitting on my back.'

The next morning we endured more enemy mortar fire, as well as Spandau machine gun fire. The men in the forward positions to the front and on the right side of the crest repulsed two enemy counterattacks. By late afternoon the Germans pulled back and Monte Solé was firmly in South African hands.

Major Thomas's A Company and Major Swabey's B Company passed through northwards and, after a fierce battle, captured Monte Abelle, the last of the trio of mountains blocking the route to Bologna. It was the task of a company of the Royal Durban Light Infantry under command of the FC / CTH to drive the enemy from ridges that ran eastwards from Monte Solé. They did this, but suffered heavy casualties in fierce hand-to-hand fighting.

On the morning of the 17th we began counting the cost: friends killed, others wounded and evacuated by stretcher to casualty clearing stations and then to field hospitals. It was time to move off Solé. Collecting what equipment we still had, we moved forward down the quiet northern slope, turned left as Monte Abelle rose before us, and emerged at the 'nek' between Solé and Caprara, which was still guarded by three Sherman tanks. From that vantage, Caprara looked particularly forbidding. No wonder it needed all the toughness and resolve of the men of the WR/DLR to wrest it from the Germans.

Weary, grateful that we were still alive, and frankly somewhat proud of ourselves, we went down and back past the cemetery of Casaglia, past Casa Casetta where we had formed up two nights before, and down the farm track to La Quercia in the Setta River valley, away from the bomb-blasted and battle-scarred face of Monte Solé.

At La Quercia there were showers and clean clothes and warm rations. We unwound, we relaxed, we revelled in a few hours without strain or tension. But as the regiment regrouped, the gaps in our ranks became starkly apparent. Although Solé was out of sight, our previous 48 hours were not out of mind.

The reward was victory for our regiment. The recognition was a DSO, four MCs, a bar to an MC, a DCM, eight MMs, two bars to MMs, one US Silver and one US Bronze Star, and three Mentioned in Dispatches. The cost was 30 men killed and 76 wounded. It had been a watershed in our lives.

From Monte Solé to war's end

On Saturday 21 April, having rested and regrouped, we were on the move again – this time as part of the Eleventh Motorised Brigade. Once again we crossed the Setta River, climbed into a convoy of army trucks and jeeps, and set off northwards along Route 6620 towards Bologna. After about ten kilometres we reached the confluence of the Setta and Reno rivers and the junction of main roads up from Florence and Pistoia in the south and then heading northwards to Bologna.

We passed through the outskirts of Bologna which, on the same day, was being liberated by a brigade of the Polish army. By this time the Germans were in full retreat, save for delaying actions at river crossings, and attempts by pockets of enemy troops to resist being trapped in a ring of Allied forces. Near the town of Finale a fierce battle ensued between South African tanks, supported by the FC/CTH, and German anti-tank guns and hand-propelled anti-tank rockets and a lone Tiger tank. At times we went ahead on foot.

Most of the roads on top of the embankment were two to three metres above the surrounding farmlands, and to use them exposed us to enemy fire. Splitting up and using field tracks meant an absence of visual contact, and we kept in touch through our cumbersome backpack field radios. After a couple of kilometres we decided to meet in order to take stock. To our consternation, when we clambered back onto the road, we found that the road had split into two slight forks, and there were a thousand or so well-armed enemy troops in the fields between the two arms of the fork, and between us and our regimental comrades. We scurried back down to the farm tracks, called the tanks, and in a very short time the enemy troops had surrendered.

We pressed on, expecting to meet further resistance when we came to the River Po. To our relief the enemy had already retreated northwards and we were able to cross at Ostiglia on a combined Bailey and pontoon bridge that our South African engineers had constructed. From then on it was helter-skelter, mopping up pockets of enemy troops and making for the key cities further north.

The Sixth South African Armoured Division was told to head north-east of the town of Treviso. We made good progress interrupted only by a clash with the Germans at our crossing over the Brenta River. However, when we reached Camposampiero, a few kilometres inland from Venice, we were told to turn about and head west to Milan.

The next morning we had the unique experience of seeing military vehicles carrying senior German officers passing us in the other direction *en route* to surrender. On 2 May we arrived at the outskirts of Milan where the regiment moved into the small village of Carugate in the neighbourhood of the town of Gorgonzola. A regimental parade was called, at which we were told that the enemy high command in Italy had surrendered. The war in Italy was over.

Exaltation, yes; relief, most certainly. However, as the impact of the news sank in I was filled with a strange sense of emptiness – and of irrelevance. Suddenly I realised that all my knowledge, skill and training in warfare were now redundant. So were the tanks, guns, shells and military ordnance. The generals, the officers, the NCOs and the privates were all equal in their irrelevance. The war, which for so long had filled my life and my emotions, was over.

A few days later, on 8 May, in a BBC broadcast, Winston Churchill announced that the German high command had surrendered, and that the war in Europe was over.

Return to Egypt and home

VE Day started a new chapter in the lives of the millions in Europe, and in those of many who, like me, had come to rid the world of the threat of Nazi and fascist domination. As the guns fell silent and the bombs stopped raining down, the gates of the concentration camps swung open, and those who were still there were released. Prisoners of war began to return, and the Europeans, their lives shattered and dislocated, assessed the cost and the horror of war and began their lives again. Uppermost in the minds of people like me, who were now 10 000 km away from South Africa, was the question: 'When are we going to return home?'

This question was never satisfactorily answered. We were kept in the dark or were fed vague statements like 'soon' or 'in the near future'. We never knew definitely until we received orders to embark on a troopship or aircraft for the return journey.

Added to this the repatriation was done in two stages. Soldiers were told that their category for repatriation had arrived and that they would be taken by air or sea on the first leg of their journey back to South Africa. They said their farewells to their comrades, and in many cases to their Italian girlfriends; excitement was high as they left. However, disillusionment set in when they were taken only as far as the army camp at Helwan outside Cairo, where the process of waiting and the uncertainty as to when they would finally go home started all over again.

Vague statements led to widespread rebelliousness, and the troops waiting in Helwan went on the rampage. Buildings were set alight, equipment and installations were damaged. Fortunately, no lives were lost.

For myself, having joined up only in June 1943, nearly four years after the outbreak of the war, I was 'J' category for demobilisation. With nine categories from A to I ahead of me, the only certainty I had about my repatriation was that it was not going to happen soon. And so, in spite of all the restrictions imposed by military service, I set about making the most of my days in Italy.

During the two weeks that we spent on the outskirts of Milan the mood among the troops was a mixture of buoyancy and serious thought. The trauma of war was over, but for the first time we began to learn from uncensored sources of the death and destruction and human misery the war had brought to Europe. Added to this were first-hand accounts of the bestiality of the Gestapo, of the horror of the Nazi concentration camps, and of the callous killing of millions of men, women and children in Hitler's gas chambers.

Where we were, Italian society was far from at peace with itself: the air was thick with tension – tension between old-time fascists and new communists; between collaborators and the resistance fighters; between the many who had suffered and the few who had prospered. Bands of partisans roamed around conducting revenge killings, often on the flimsiest of grounds. Young women accused of collaborating with Germans had their heads shaved as a mark of shame and disgrace. Others, identified as traitors, were killed and their bodies thrown into the nearest river.

In the light of all this, and the virtual collapse of the Italian security forces, we South Africans conducted regular motorised patrols through Milan as a show of force. On one patrol we stopped outside the service station where only a few days before the mutilated bodies of Benito Mussolini and his mistress Clara Petacci – cornered by partisans and killed while trying to escape to Switzerland – had been hung by their feet from a metal beam as a crude expression of revenge and contempt.

A few days after the end of the war a special parade of the regiment was held at which decorations and medals were awarded to a number of officers and men of the FC/CTH for gallantry during the battle for Monte Solé and Monte Abelle, and the fighting that followed on the way to the River Po. On 14 May the whole of the South African Armoured Division assembled for a victory parade on the motor racing circuit at Monza – an impressive and moving occasion at which General Mark Clark, who had commanded the Fifth US Army when the Sixth South African Armoured Division was part of it, awarded American medals to a number of our men. Among these was the Legion of Merit (Commander) to the commander of our division, General Everard Poole.

We saw something of the towns of Lecca and Como, and enjoyed the beauty of Bellagio and the clear, sparking water of Lake Como. On one outing I set off with a backpack full of cigarettes which I had saved from my rations and wanted to sell on the black market to buy a camera. In those days, when printed Italian lira notes were of no value, cigarettes were 'standard currency', and the various brands enjoyed fixed rates: US brands such as Camel and Lexington were 10 liras a cigarette; UK Players, 9 liras a cigarette; Springbok and C-to-C, 8 liras a cigarette. Less popular brands were down to 6 liras a cigarette.

As I got off the truck at Como, the inevitable man with the 'borsa nera' (black bag), the symbol of the black market business, met me. I followed him through the back streets until we arrived at a circus tent, and behind it the caravan office. I clambered up some steps and went inside to be introduced to an incongruous couple: a large, fat lady in a plain cotton dress with cutaway armholes from which protruded massive arms under each of which was a bush of dark hair; and a circus dwarf whose chin was just level with the tabletop. After some haggling the deal was done, and with my backpack stuffed full of lira notes I was ready to leave. But, 'No,' said the fat lady, 'we must drink to the success of the deal.' Four small glasses were produced into which a colourless liquid was decanted. With a 'Saluté!' the liquor was gulped down. I coughed and spluttered: I had drunk my first 'grappa'.

29

The 'borsa nera' man accompanied me back to the main street and directed me to a camera shop, and a short while later I emerged with my backpack empty, but in my hand a handsome second-hand German Voigtländer camera. I often wondered who had owned it before me, and how it had found its way into the camera shop.

After three weeks on the outskirts of Milan, our regiment was sent to Genoa and then on to liberate the seaside resorts of Rapallo, Santa Margherita and Portofino. There were no tourists; the only signs of war were rows of concrete blocks built into the beaches to repel a sea invasion.

Being billeted at the splendid Hotel Santa Margherita, a serviceman could not have had a more congenial life. There was swimming, cycling, yachting, walking across the headland to San Frutuoso, and dancing in the evenings. All too good to last, though. A couple of weeks later we were sent inland to Poirino, a nondescript village south of Turin. From there it was on to garrison duty in the Val da Aosta on the border between France and Italy. French claims to Italian territory were causing great tension. Regimental headquarters was in the alpine village of Courmayeur, while our company was sent to Val Ferret, a beautiful valley blocked by a glacier at one end and flanked along the northern border with France by the Mont Blanc massif. I was billeted with others from Company HQ staff in the Albergo Golf, a small upmarket hotel that had opened just before the war started. The air in the Val Ferret was exhilarating, and the alpine scenery magnificent. We went for long hikes during the day, and played bridge in the evenings.

Frequently we held discussions about the world around us, about what South Africa was, and what we'd like it to be. Our officers did nothing to discourage us; on the contrary, some of the talks took place on the initiative of the Army Information Officer attached to our brigade. One issue was whether a war memorial should be built in South Africa, and if so, what form it should take. The dominant view was that there should be a memorial, but that it should be a living one that served the community, not merely a monumental structure. After various proposals, the decision was that it should take the form of a top-quality children's hospital. The servicemen, in overwhelming numbers, volunteered to donate two days' pay towards what was to become the Red Cross War Memorial Children's Hospital at Rondebosch in Cape Town.

During the post-war weeks, personal relationships between Gerry Boland and me became strained. Boland was a salesman/clerk in a skins and hide business in Port Elizabeth. I was a university student aspiring to be a quantity surveyor. Eventually I was transferred from Company headquarters to No. 3 Platoon, meaning shifts of guard duty, and occasional border patrols. Nevertheless there were compensations. Firstly, the men of No. 3 Platoon, as a result of battlefield experiences, had developed a great sense of camaraderie and mutual supportiveness. Secondly, one of its outposts was at a cable station halfway up Mont Blanc, and spells of duty in the snow halfway up Europe's highest mountain were in themselves an experience. The remoteness of the outpost did not prevent us from occasionally using the cable car to ferry some of the young ladies from the valley for partying and dancing.

While I was with No. 3 Platoon, Lieutenant Moyle, the regimental 'I' Officer, discussed the possibility of me entering the diplomatic service. This would have meant release from duties, and immediate secondment to become a 'diplomat in training'. Attractive though the proposal was, I decided I should finish my studies at UCT. Then, when I returned to Val Ferret, I found that I had been successful in my application to go on an architectural study tour of northern Italy.

I was taken down to a village on the shore of Lake Maggiore where the group that was to take part in the course assembled. Our first stay was in Turin where the vast Fiat organisation hosted us. We went on through Alba and Savonna to Genoa. After a day there it was on to La Spezia, Viareggio, Pisa and Florence, where we spent a fascinating two days with professors Bartol and Thialdi from Florence University. Particularly moving was our visit to the church of St Croce, where the two professors were overcome when they saw, now that the protective sandbags were being removed, that the precious statues that had been entrusted to their care were still intact.

Over the Apennines we passed by Castiglione and Monte Solé, and on to the historic town of Bologna, and then Venice – where we spent three days, partly as students of architecture and partly as wide-eyed tourists. Our course took us on through Padua, Vicenza, Verona and Lake Garda to Milan. Here the course ended with a visit to Milan cathedral, the modern Montecatini building, said then to be Europe's first aluminium-clad high-rise building. We rounded off the course by attending a performance of *Lucia di Lammermoor* at La Scala opera house.

Our stay at Val Ferret ended with a move to Turin where we stayed for the best part of August and September, billeted in an Italian army barracks quite close to the centre of the city. Duties were not onerous, but our brigade had been sent there as a 'show of strength' as political tensions were running high, and the settling of old scores from the fascist and wartime eras resulted in frequent assaults and killings. An occasional corpse floating down the river was indicative of what was going on behind the scenes.

Meanwhile, as a result of repatriation, the number of the personnel of each of the regiments was reducing. Back in Turin all the regiments comprising the Eleventh Brigade were consolidated into a single brigade unit. I was despatched to this unit's headquarters where, for a reason that was never divulged to me, I was asked to set up a brigade office filing system. I did this with alacrity, for once I was on the office staff in charge of filing I would be freed from doing guard duties and route marches, and from the formal discipline of an infantry battalion.

Apart from my office duties, life in Turin was dominated by sport and socialising. There was no shortage of young ladies to take part; and I struck up a friendship with Mariella, an attractive and thoughtful lass who was doing a part-time course in the humanities at the University of Turin. Mariella and I traded English and Italian lessons, usually English in the late afternoon in offices she shared with some of her student colleagues, and Italian in the evenings when we went to restaurants and nightspots on the banks of the River Po.

Mariella and her friends helped me to learn something about Italian politics and about the emotions of the people emerging from fascism, a war, surrender and a German occupation. I watched the political battle lines being drawn in Turin, as in the rest of the industrial heartland of Italy, between the Communists led by Pietro Nenni, and the conservative Christian Democrats led by Palmiro Togliatti.

Japan surrendered. My friendship with Mariella faded, and was replaced by a succession of dates, first with Daisy, then Lily and then Rosie – an interesting sequence of acquaintances for someone who had no pretensions of being a horticulturist.

The pattern of evening outings was interrupted on one occasion when the celebrated South African pianist, 80-year-old Dr Elsie Hall, came to entertain the troops. The rumour doing the rounds was that Dr Hall had come to Italy on the personal suggestion of her friend General Smuts. In the circumstances the officers took no chance of there being a small audience for her. A regimental parade was called and a roll call taken – then trucks took the men to the Conservatory of Music, for most of them to listen for the first time to a recital of classical music.

By the end of September the brigade unit, by then considerably reduced in numbers, was sent down to Alassio, a resort town on the Italian Riviera, where a small group of us stayed in the Albergo Internationale. Life was pleasant, but of no consequence. We were not getting on with our careers. We felt that we were wasting precious time.

At long last, in mid-December, I was among those told to pack up and be ready to be repatriated. There was a flurry of goodbye parties, and plenty of fond farewells. After my return home I kept up a correspondence with three of my lady friends from Alassio. Whether Joyce, who was to become my fiancée and then my wife, altogether approved of this, I was never sure.

On Tuesday 18 December I started on the first leg of my long journey home. The first night was spent at Sportona; the next day we boarded a troop train at Novara, a functioning railway junction in northern Italy. At four o'clock the next morning we had to pack our kitbags and detrain as a bridge over a river was down. We walked across a makeshift road bridge to a train waiting for us on the other side. Then we set off on the long haul down the Adriatic coast of Italy, stopping first at Bologna, and then at Ancona and Pescara, before arriving at Foggia two days later.

The ten-day wait in the bleak soulless transit camp in mid-winter was the longest two weeks of my stay in Italy. Christmas with a church parade and an army ration dinner came and went, and so did New Year's Eve with scarcely a cheer. On New Year's Day 1946 I was put on standby to leave. My last 'action' before leaving was to get rid of a Luger pistol that I had taken off a dead enemy soldier near the Cento de Finale and had looked after with great care, with a view to taking it back to South Africa as a trophy of war. However, in our final transit camp there were repeated warnings of dire action being taken against anyone taking weapons back home. I went to the camp latrine and dropped my precious trophy into the pit. I had finally said goodbye to the war.

On Wednesday 3 January we arrived in Taranto where we boarded a troopship named *Felix Roussel*, and departed from Italy. My experience and observations had taught me that, while there could be something noble in the cause for which a war was fought, there was nothing noble in war itself. War dehumanises and brutalises, not as a grisly consequence, but as a deliberate strategy for success.

On 7 January 1946 the *Felix Roussel* docked in Port Said. A train took us on an overnight journey through the desert and across the Nile Delta, back to the camp at Helwan.

One evening while at the camp at Helwan, when I was feeling in an especially nostalgic mood, I settled down at a small table outside my bungalow and, helped by the beauty of the night sky over the desert, I wrote down my reflections on my experiences under the title, *So deep is the night*:

'Do certain tunes and melodies bring memories back to you? Vivid memories of past experiences? If they do, listen to the haunting tones of one of Chopin's pieces, known to most of us as 'So deep is the night', and relive with me a few moments of the past.

'I was sitting in one of our little Pinelands churches. My embarkation leave was drawing to a close. As the organ filled the church with the rich notes of its throbbing music I was thinking; thinking of my days at home, my friends, my family, the daily rounds to which I had become accustomed. During those few moments a thousand scenes flashed across my mind. I would be leaving soon. Perhaps that was what made me realise how dear my home, my friends, and the life I had always taken for granted were to me ...

'I had just left Port Said and we were on our zigzag course across the Mediterranean to Italy. I found myself on a four-hour watch at the stern gun. Night was drawing on and, as I leaned on the rail watching the silhouettes of the other ships of the convoy merge with the surrounding darkness, I heard from below the notes of that tune coming clear and sharp from the brass reeds of a mouth organ. The ship forged its way through the inky ocean carrying its human cargo to feed the machine of war. What did the future hold for each of us? How many of us would stay on the battlefields of Europe? What was war really like? The music stopped. My watch was over. I joined the sleeping hordes on the deck below ...

'Eight o'clock Sunday evening. Silence except for the scraping of boots on stony ground and the occasional clank of metal. Suddenly, hell is let loose. Searchlights pierce the gloom, tracers weave their fiery pattern, the big guns roar and belch flame, machine guns crackle, mortar bombs hiss and burst, the air is filled with a shriek and the crash of shells, mines explode, men are being killed – So this is war! Throughout this cannonade of death I hear the music of my tune. I see myself in that quiet little church at home. I wonder. Could they be playing it again this night?

'The war was over. In Italy conflict was giving way to revelry, war to peace, and fascism to freedom. I was standing with a friend on a wooden bridge overlooking the crowd swaying to the rhythm of the music. The music stopped; some applause; and then from the orchestra playing on an island in the artificial pond came the notes of my tune. My thoughts started wandering again. A sob from beside me made me look around. My partner was crying. "What is wrong?" I asked. "I was just thinking," she said, "thinking of the terrible war, the misery and suffering, and wondering what is going to become of the world and all its people after all they have been through."

'I wondered too, but found no answer to my thoughts.'

Reaching judgement on wartime atrocities

I returned to Monte Solé with Joyce in the spring of 1965. We approached along the new autostrada that wound its way through the Apennines from Florence *en route* to Bologna. We crossed over the Setta River at the village of Gardaletta then doubled back on a gravel road that ran along the west bank of the river in order to get to La Quercia where we would start our ascent to Monte Solé.

We struck trouble just outside La Quercia when we came across an injured motorcyclist lying in the road. Joyce, remembering what she had learned in her wartime first aid lessons, tried to staunch the flow of blood from the side of the poor man's head. It was obvious that he had been drinking and, noting the shotgun that he carried on the side of his cycle, we presumed that he had been celebrating the opening of the local hunting season.

In no time we were surrounded by a group of peasant women, who amidst cries of anguish and displays of emotion when they saw their stricken cyclist/hunter friend, screamed abuse at us for having knocked him down, and threatened to call the police. We did our best to explain that far from having knocked their friend down, we were trying to save his life. In due course, in a chorus of protests and cries of grief, we moved on. We parked our car on a farm track, a short distance above La Quercia, from where we started our ascent of the mountain.

We had to cross a number of sloping ploughed fields before we reached the ruins of the cemetery at Casaglia from where we would tackle the final slopes of the mountain itself. Going up the ridge was tough. The path was overgrown with bramble, and the ground was a mix of loose stone and sand. Eventually we reached the summit. Joyce was excited to see the spot that had been the focal point of so many of my wartime reminiscences. We found the network of trenches that the Germans had dug and nearby, to my surprise and delight, found the shallow trench that I had scooped out of the earth early on that morning of 16 April 1945. In front us was a white marble obelisk standing on a stone base. I wondered what the inscription on the obelisk would be. 'In Memory of the First City / Cape Town Highlanders'? Or perhaps of the 'Sixth South African Armoured Division'? But as we came closer we saw that the obelisk was topped by a red star and inscribed 'In memory of the gallant partisans of the Brigada Stella Rossa'.

This unexpected memorial perplexed us. What was the Brigada Stella Rossa, and why was it being commemorated on Monte Solé?

We scrambled down the mountain with our questions unanswered, wondering what was in store for us when we got back to La Quercia and those villagers. However, to our surprise we were greeted with open arms. The Italian cyclist had come round and explained how the wheels of his cycle had slipped from under him as he was taking a sharp bend in the road. The Italians realised that we were not villains. We were given a basket of fruit, and before we moved on we sat down for a round of drinks with our new Italian friends.

Joyce and I continued to make enquiries about the mystery of the obelisk dedicated to the partisans of the Brigada Stella Rossa. But it was only some years later that we learned of one of the most chilling stories emanating from wartime Italy. Ruined farmsteads, flattened churches and the silence of the grave tell part of a harrowing chapter in the saga of Monte Solé. In 1943, before the Allied forces reached the area, peasant farmers and townsfolk from the surrounding villages of Marzabotto, Grizzana and Monzumo formed a partisan resistance unit known as the Brigada Stella Rossa ('The Red Star Brigade'). Under the leadership of 26-year-old Mario 'Lupo' ('The Wolf') Musolési, the Brigade grew to some twelve hundred strong. At night it wreaked havoc with the German communication and supply lines and repeatedly inflicted casualties on the personnel of their rear echelons. During the day the men of the Brigada Stella Rossa melted into the tree-covered slopes of Monte Solé. Try as they could, the German troops were unable to capture them. They started taking hostages and executing civilians in reprisal. This did not subdue the partisan fighters.

Eventually Field Marshal Kesselring called in SS Major Walter Reder and instructed him to neutralise the Monte Solé area 'even if this meant going beyond the normal limits of warfare'. Shortly before dawn on 29 September 1943, Reder and his SS stormtroopers moved in with Spandau machine guns. Systematically and ruthlessly, they shot and killed the men, women and children who lived in the area. Some were massacred in the churches at Casaglia and San Martino. More than a hundred were lined up and machine-gunned in the cemetery on the road on the ridge. In two short weeks 1 830 civilians were annihilated. Livestock was slaughtered. Farmhouses and churches were laid waste.

In 1951, Major Reder was convicted of war crimes and sentenced to life imprisonment. Sixteen years later, in April 1967, he petitioned the Italian president for clemency. The president referred the petition to the mayor of Marzabotto, the town under whose authority the Monte Solé area fell. The mayor deferred to his town council, and in turn the council referred the issue to a referendum of the victims' next-of-kin. The next-of-kin voted unanimously that Reder should stay in jail, and the town council of Marzabotto issued this statement:

'What we want is that it never be forgotten that it was not an act of war that was committed here, but a horrendous massacre, an inhuman reprisal against unarmed people, an act of cowardice and of hatred and of nothing else. For this reason pardon is unthinkable.

35

'The verdict is final. But it does not apply only to Reder: it would be absurd to claim that it did. It applies to Nazism, fascism, war, violence, intolerance, racism, hatred for any nation, all that hinders the path towards peace, the peaceful co-existence among all nations. It applies to Reder and all the Reders that now exist, all who may emerge in the world; all those who hate people and their most simple and noble feelings.

'It applies to Reder, Nazism, and fascism, and not to the German people or Austria.

'There is no hatred in Marzabotto! Hands extend and arms open towards all men that are men, towards all those who have and will perform, even in the most dramatic moments, a human gesture.

'Reder has no nationality. Nazism has created him, has deprived him of all human feeling, and has turned him into a perfect synthesis of Nazism, of fascism, of war.

'They may as well not bother to wait for him in the Alte Adige: Reder will not come to start new massacres; he will remain where he is. To the President of the Republic we will bring the vote of Marzabotto, the vote not only of the Italian people, but also of all peoples who want peace, and fight for it.'

Another 20 years on Reder was released to die at home. Today there is silence on Monte Solé – the silence of a community that was obliterated.

PART II

Towards a political future

5

Back home in Pinelands
1946-1948

On 17 January I started my journey home, reversing the route of my journey 'up north' in 1944 – by army truck from Helwan camp to Cairo West airport; then by DC3 to Khartoum, Kisumu and Ndola; arriving in South Africa at the Waterkloof air station in Pretoria and then on to a troop train bound for Cape Town. On the first evening home there was a passionate reunion with Joyce, a gathering of friends and family, and a quiet meal at our home in Pinelands. We shared it with Uncle John and Aunt Marjorie Berry, who had sold their farm in Hobhouse and moved to Cape Town.

The next day my mother and I went to Gordon's Bay. Motor cars were not readily available in those days, so we went by train from Pinelands to Cape Town, then by train to the Strand, and on by bus to Gordon's Bay. We sat on the grass under the milkwood trees that flanked the small beach and talked about past experiences and future plans, earnestly but slightly uncomfortably; we were coming together again after having been separated by differing worlds of experience.

My first task was to complete the demobilisation process; the next was to get back to university where I had to complete the final year of my BSc course in quantity surveying. This was more easily said than done, since the mood and cadence of army life was very different from that of a university. I disciplined myself; I made a conscious effort. I was helped by the fact that many fellow students were also returning soldiers.

During the immediate post-war years of '46 and '47 ex-servicemen dominated the student body at UCT; not because they were more numerous than the other students, but because on average they were a few years older, more mature, and determined to make up for the academic years they had forfeited.

In December 1946 I graduated with a BSc as UCT's first graduate in quantity surveying. My association with Bernard James resumed, and he invited me to join his firm, soon to become Bernard James and Partners. However, Bernard, based on the experience of his own career path, suggested I first work for a year with a firm of building contractors to experience the construction industry 'from the other side'. Accordingly, I went to work for William Harper, one of the major building contractors operating in the Cape; in those days, £35 a month, not a princely salary, was the going rate for a 'quantity surveyor in training'. In 1948 I joined Bernard James.

Since the start of the war, Pinelands had grown at least twice in size from a close-knit community in thatched-roofed houses to a more diverse one living in modern suburban houses spread away from the core of 'old Pinelands'. Its 'coming of age' in 1947 was marked by a change in its civic status – from being governed by a village management board dominated by the Garden Cities Trust, the founding and development institution, to a fully fledged municipality governed by a six-member municipal council.

The suburb was – and is – infused with a strong sense of community, for which there were a number of reasons. Among these were its status as a separate municipality surrounded by the larger Cape Town municipality; its character as a Garden City; and the fact that its residents reflected a social, economic and cultural homogeneity. As a consequence of its founding philosophy, a key issue in the late 1940s and 1950s was whether commercial enterprises such as service stations, shops and offices should be permitted; and if so, where should they be located and what form should they take? How would the profits that would accrue to the Garden Cities Trust be used to benefit Pinelands as a garden city?

I was actively involved in matters both as an individual and through community organisations such as the Pinelands Young People's Club, of which I was the founder chairman; the Pinelands Civic Association, of which I became chairman; and the Pinelands Municipal Council to which I was elected, and on which I served from 1951 to 1954. The Young People's Club combined social, cultural, sporting and civic elements, and played a significant role in many young residents' lives. It had its origins in the discussions of a number of young people who met regularly over a milkshake or orange juice at The Wattle House – a café housed in a cottage built in the 1920s as the estate office of the new village, and still then Pinelands's sole commercial establishment. Yet, in the rapidly expanding post-war years, the village's earlier cohesiveness was depleted and replaced by division and exclusion based on whether one lived in the old or the new Pinelands; and on the life experiences of servicemen and those too young to have served. It was decided to form a club to bridge these new divides and at the same time to serve the needs and stimulate the community interests of the young.

The club forged a relationship with the Pinelands municipal council, which agreed that it could have the use of the civic hall on Friday evenings. This relationship did not prevent us from interacting critically with the council.

I also became involved in ex-service related activities, becoming a member of the Memorable Order of Tin Hats (MOTHS), a social and welfare organisation of ex-servicemen; and in due course became the Commander of the Southern Floe Shell-hole based in Pinelands. Then there was the Institute of Citizenship, an organisation established to promote civic awareness and responsibility among the citizens – especially the young – of Cape Town. So I laboured at my profession on weekdays and Saturday mornings; played rugby, tennis and badminton depending on the season;

engaged in community and committee work; and seriously courted Joyce. My life was busy and fulfilling. The restrictions, anxieties and disruptions of wartime were things of the past.

We also became more mobile. While some occasionally had the use of their parents' cars, in 1946 I used the money I had saved on military service to buy a second-hand dark-green-and-black two-door sports model Morris 8. Although not always mechanically reliable, it was inexpensive to run and easy to maintain. It was light enough to be pushed down the road to start the engine when, as frequently happened, the battery failed.

For many years after the war I, in common with other Pinelanders, travelled to my office in Cape Town by train, then came home for lunch on a special express train that ran between Cape Town and Pinelands. We got around: twenty or thirty of us spent occasional long weekends at Prospect Holiday Farm at Ceres, while Die Mond at Hermanus was the site of a regular camp over the Easter weekend. Added to these benefits my Morris 8 was a cosy nook for frequent kiss and cuddle goodnights with Joyce outside her home.

South Africa's first post-war election was due to be held on 26 May 1948. I took a keen interest, but with my activities focused on community affairs I had not yet become directly involved in party politics. Nonetheless, I returned from the war with a deep revulsion for Nazism and fascism, and with a realisation that systems based on racial discrimination and exclusion were no longer acceptable. I understood very clearly that through the United Nations Declaration of Fundamental Human Rights the rest of the world had set out a new moral code as the basis for interpersonal and intra-national relations.

This fundamental break with the past was driven home when India, within a year of attaining its independence in 1947, used the UN as a platform to condemn South Africa's racist policies. The developed countries of the West slowly, and at times begrudgingly, started to move away from colonial-style politics based on discrimination. I sensed a new international order developing – yet in South Africa, as the world was busy transforming itself, white South Africans carried on much as before.

Prime Minister Smuts proclaimed that 'separation was dead and segregation had fallen on evil days'. However, his United Party continued much as before under the banner of 'White Leadership with Justice'. The National Party opposition under Dr Malan reflected the resistance of the white community to change, and appointed a small committee under NP stalwart Paul Sauer to devise a slogan suitable for fighting the coming election. The committee came up with one word: 'Apartheid'.

Apartheid, beginning as a slogan and a concept, became a policy, a philosophy, a political driving force for the division of those who supported it from those who opposed it. It mushroomed in the vocabulary of languages around the world as a word that, without elaboration, defined the evil of the system of race discrimination in South Africa, and would become the code word for racial discrimination in any part of the world.

As the general election drew closer it was clear that Smuts was under pressure. There were disgruntled ex-servicemen; there were post-war shortages ranging from housing and jobs to white bread and 'skaapvleis'. However, Smuts and his UP colleagues, confident that they would win, took no serious steps to ensure they would not lose.

On the 27th early results, mainly from the urban areas, were comforting for the UP. But as the results from peri-urban areas and the platteland started coming in, the picture began to change. A key outcome was that of the constituency of Standerton, where Smuts was being challenged by a political newcomer, Hennie du Plessis. The following morning, as I walked through the concourse of the Cape Town railway station, I saw the newsbill of Die Burger, one of the National Party's most supportive newspapers: 'Smuts Uit! Nekslag vir die Regering!' Smuts was out; the government had been ousted.

The National Party, in alliance with Klaasie Havenga's Afrikaner Party, had won the election by a single seat in parliament. Remarkably, it had done so in spite of only having received 41,1 % of the vote. Like many others in South Africa I was shattered. These people had refused to fight the Nazis; had opposed and at times undermined the war effort; had declared they would tighten the screws of discrimination; and were now going to determine my country's future.

A few days later I called on my Captain, RJ du Toit, member of parliament for Pinelands, and told him that I wanted to start working to get rid of the Nats. I joined the United Party; I was put on the committee in Pinelands. I had started on a lifetime in politics – 56 years.

6

Early days in politics
1948-1953

The years that followed the NP's accession to power were extremely busy. I remained heavily involved in the community affairs of Pinelands, and became chairman of the Pinelands Civic Association, an office made more demanding by the establishment of the new Pinelands Ratepayers Association as a rival to the older body. To a large extent the formation of the Ratepayers Association reflected the growing divide between the old and the new Pinelands, a divide both demographic and emotional. The new Ratepayers Association wanted a complete break with the past, with the previous village management status, and with the domination by the Pinelands Garden Cities Trust.

Just before Christmas 1948, Joyce and I announced our engagement. We married on 10 September 1949 in the little Methodist church founded by my parents. At the time, Joyce had risen to Commandant of Voluntary Aid Detachment 50 of the Red Cross. Her colleagues, resplendent in their Red Cross uniforms, provided the guard of honour.

For the first few months of our married life Joyce and I lived in a part of my mother's house that had been converted into a small flat. However, with a baby on the way we decided we needed a house of our own. I purchased a plot in Camp Road on the northern perimeter of Pinelands, and asked Hugh Floyd, my friend from university and army days, who had graduated as an architect, to design a house for us. Number 15 Camp Road was a single-storey building with a shingle roof and wide projecting eaves. It was small but comfortable, and very well designed. With alterations from time to time it provided a wonderful home for us and our three daughters until 12 years later when, with a tinge of sadness, we moved to a more spacious home on the other side of Pinelands overlooking Mowbray golf course.

During these years I was hard at work as a quantity surveying assistant at Bernard James; not only was the firm in an expanding phase but, with a partnership in the offing, I was determined to prove my competence and commitment. In 1952, together with a colleague, Frank Moore, who like me had served in the Sixth South African Armoured Division in Italy, I became a partner in BJ&P. Over a cup of tea, Frank and I were recounting some of our wartime experiences. I told him how, on the morning after we had captured Monte Solé, I was sitting watching some engineers trying to widen a farm track below the ridge with the help of a bulldozer. A soldier was standing on a small platform at the rear of the bulldozer. As it was trying to push away a large boulder, it overturned and tumbled down the hillside. The driver was killed, but the man on the rear platform managed to jump off in time. 'Quite a coincidence,' said Frank. 'I was the man who jumped off!'

In politics, my responsibilities started growing significantly. Within a month of the National Party's victory I was made a member of the Pinelands branch committee of the United Party. A couple of months later I found myself a member of the committee of the Pinelands constituency, with four local branches. A few months later I was appointed as a delegate to the Cape Peninsula Council of the United Party.

I found the UP in the Peninsula in disarray. It was in a state of shock and disbelief at its defeat at the polls. This was intensified by the fact that the coalition between the NP and the Afrikaner Party (AP) had won the election with just over 41% of the vote against the UP's 48,1% (constituency-based elections could lead to such a result). Morale was low; organisation was pathetic; policy and ideology were confused and ambivalent. In this situation, the old-guard leadership looked for someone other than themselves to blame.

Against this depressing political background I started to reorganise the branch structures in the constituency and to bring some sense of direction and of purpose into their activities. Fortunately, I was not alone. An unstructured team, largely of younger people who understood the benefit of good organisation and the necessity of clarity on policy and political objectives, came into being within a short time. It started to exert some influence on the local UP hierarchy.

In 1950 General Smuts, leader of the UP, died. I never got to know him personally, but listened to him addressing party congresses and interacting with concerned members of the Cape Peninsula Council of the UP. He was impressive, yet strangely detached from the changes taking place in the political attitudes of ordinary citizens. With his intellect, his personality, his role as a wartime leader and his status as a world statesman, Smuts was a critical factor in the fortunes, cohesion and evolution of the UP. Many UP members, Sappe as they called themselves, were motivated by a deep personal loyalty to Smuts and what they perceived he stood for. His death left a leadership vacuum – and for all his intellect, he left the UP with a legacy of ideological and policy ambiguity that was starting to erode its relevance.

In the 1930s, when relationships between the English and the Afrikaans sections of the electorate were the dominant issue, the UP was significantly relevant. It was certainly so in the war; but as wartime emotions faded and the issue of English and Afrikaans relationships began to give way to the predominance of black-white relationships against the background of a changing world order, the UP under Smuts had been unable to redefine its policy in a manner that ensured its continued relevance. Added to this, the UP had been unable to put forward a substantive alternative to the concept of apartheid.

It was against this background that JGN Strauss, an advocate who had served in the Smuts cabinet as Minister of Agriculture, was elected the new UP leader. He was intelligent, articulate and dedicated; however, what was not known was whether he had the qualities of leadership that would enable him to inspire his party to renewed relevance and to forge emerging disparate elements into a united and effective team.

The elevation of the NP to power evoked emotional and hostile reactions among many ex-servicemen – despite the fact that the vote of disgruntled ex-servicemen played a part in helping to get the NP elected. Based on the activities of the party, and in particular the views of its extremists, the Nats were perceived to be Nazis or at best Nazi sympathisers. The NP's commitment to making South Africa a republic threatened the country's status as a member of the Commonwealth. Laws were enacted such as the Repeal of the Indian Franchise Act, the Population Registration Act, the Suppression of Communism Act, the Separate Representation of Voters Act, and the High Court of Parliament Act – the architecture of apartheid. All this proved that the NP could not be trusted with democracy and good governance. Standing out above all other issues was the government's determination to remove the Coloured voters in the Cape Province and Natal from the common voters' roll. This was seen as a dishonourable breach of the solemn undertaking given to the Coloured people by Prime Minister Hertzog's white government when the 'natives' were removed from the common voters' roll in 1936. It was seen to be a breach of entrenched clauses in the South African constitution, and as such a violation of the constitution itself.

In 1951 the Nats introduced the Separate Representation of Voters Bill into parliament, where it was passed by a bare majority of the Assembly and the Senate sitting separately. It was challenged in court – and on 29 March 1952, in a unanimous judgement, the Court of the Appellate Division declared that the Act 'was invalid, null and void, and of no force and effect'. Then on 22 April the government responded to this judgement by introducing the High Court of Parliament Bill, a measure designed to give parliament, sitting as a court, power to override parliament sitting as a legislature!

Against a background of frustration about the ineffectiveness of the UP and mounting anger at the government's actions, groups of anti-nationalists started to emerge outside political party structures. Thus, the War Veterans' Action Group grew in the space of a few months to become a significant political movement called the War Veterans' Torch Commando – and was formally constituted at a national conference on 26 June 1951. The office-bearers were: president 'Sailor' Malan; vice-president Dolf de la Rey; chairman Louis Kane-Berman; and vice-chairman Ralph Parrott.

Membership was open to anyone who had served in the South African or Allied services in any war, and its founding principles were limited: to uphold the spirit and the solemn compacts entered into at the time of Union as moral obligations of trust and honour binding upon parliament and the people; to secure the repeal of any measures enacted in violation of such obligations; to protect the freedom of individuals in worship, language and speech, and to ensure the right of free access to the courts; to eliminate all forms of totalitarianism, whether fascist or communist; and to promote racial harmony in the Union.

The Torch Commando did not envisage becoming a political party. It believed that in order to implement its principles 'the Nationalist government must first be unseated'. It resolved to co-operate with the UP and the Labour Party as instruments for achieving this objective; there would be no mergers of parties, but a common anti-government front to remove the Nationalists from office at the next election. Only after the Torch Commando had achieved this would it consider its role in the future. As a consequence of this decision it entered into an agreement with the UP and the LP to form joint election committees.

The relationship between the Torch Commando and the UP was not an easy one. The Commando was shocked at the state of disarray they found in many UP formations, and frustrated by the old-fashioned approach that many of the old-guard office-bearers had to effective organisation. They sensed that while their assistance was wanted, their intrusion into the political terrain was resented. Many of the old guard feared that their vested interests would be threatened.

These background issues notwithstanding, the joint election committees worked well, and the effectiveness of organising for the elections improved significantly. The Torch Commando held a nationwide campaign in which parades through the streets of towns and villages were held by supporters carrying flaming torches made of a jam tin nailed to a wooden staff about a metre long, and filled with oil-soaked cloth which was set alight.

When the campaign arrived in Cape Town, my uncle Major Frank Wells and his two sons, Douglas and Ronald, and I went from Pinelands to the Grand Parade in Cape Town to join in the protest march. When we arrived there at about 7.30 pm the Parade was a milling mass of people. Some were already bearing their flaming torches aloft while others were queuing at lorries at the Castle end of the Parade, where they were to receive their torches. In due course, led by Malan and De la Rey, the procession, marching four abreast, moved from the Parade along Darling Street, up Adderley Street, right into Wale Street and right again down St George's Street, at the bottom turning right at the War Memorial and up Adderley Street again and back to the Grand Parade.

The procession over, we listened to speeches by Malan and De la Rey and other senior members, at the conclusion of which they called on us to disperse in an orderly fashion. Most of the protestors did, but some decided to march up Parliament Street towards parliament. Just short of their destination they encountered a cordon of troops and police. A scuffle between the police and protestors took place, and some of the metal railings around the DR Church Groote Kerk were damaged.

The march made a tremendous impact on the citizenry of Cape Town. However, not surprisingly, the Nationalists were quick to respond by referring to the 'disgraceful behaviour of the protestors who had tried to march on parliament and in the process had done damage to the Groote Kerk premises'.

I was elected chairman of the Pinelands branch of the Torch Commando and made the branch representative of the organisation's Cape executive committee. I accepted the added workload with gusto. I was caught up in the spirit that pervaded the Commando, and enjoyed working with other members on the committees.

The office of the Torch Commando in Cape Town, where Eric Oettle was the secretary, was a hive of creative activity. The meetings of the executive committee were refreshing for the frankness of the opinions expressed and the high standard of discussion and debate that took place. There were no secret agendas to promote or vested interests to protect.

Given the constitutional issue that was at the core of the Torch Commando movement, and which remained at the forefront of its activities, it was not surprising that lawyers and advocates were often at the helm of most discussions and decisions. Among them was Leslie Rubin, soon to become a senator representing the 'Native people'. He was quick-thinking and nimble as he dealt with issues; and there was Gerald Gordon, always careful to examine all sides of the issue. Michael Corbett was always thoughtful, thorough and committed – and it was not surprising that 50 years later, as Chief Justice Michael Corbett, he administered the oath of office to Nelson Mandela when he was inaugurated as first president of the new democratic South Africa.

The Pinelands branch of the Torch Commando expanded rapidly. Our function, in parallel with other branches in the Peninsula, was to give support to the UP and its candidates in Nationalist-held or marginal constituencies. This included attendance at public meetings and ensuring that they were not disrupted; registering voters; and setting up the election organisation in the allocated constituency. We attended meetings in nearby Nationalist-held constituencies such as Vasco, Bellville and Tiervlei and others further afield such as Bredasdorp, Malmesbury and Piketberg. This last was specifically targeted as it was represented in parliament by Dr Malan, the prime minister and the leader of the National Party.

It was at meetings at such places as Epping Gardens Village, Tiervlei and Bellville that I first encountered PW Botha. As the senior NP organiser in the region he would arrive with a posse of fellow organisers and at times ask questions – but generally disrupt meetings by raising spurious points of order, by disputing the chairman's rulings, by heckling, and by getting his supporters to drown the speakers by shouting or singing. As a consequence many of the meetings ended in disorder.

In the Torch Commando we set up a system of communication and mobilisation based on a chain of telephone calls. In Pinelands we could get a convoy of up to thirty fully laden motor cars to assemble at a pre-determined rendezvous once a few words of the coded password had been sent. Morale was high, and the esprit de corps good. Ex-servicemen relived the spirit of camaraderie and unity of purpose of the war.

Membership of the Torch Commando grew to more than two hundred thousand, and it became a factor with which the UP had to reckon. In spite of the Commando's declared policy of no mergers, there were behind-the-scene talks between representatives about a possible coalition or merger. On 18 August 1952 a small delegation from the Torch Commando, headed by Louis Kane-Berman, met Sir de Villiers Graaff to discuss the issue. They concluded that 'the principle of a merger is desirable, if possible', and considered a set of policy proposals submitted by Graaff followed by a draft statement outlining the basis for such a merger.

However, the matter was not taken further and the draft statement was never issued as a public document. It was outdated in parts: when it referred to cardinal principles such as 'No mixing of blood' and 'Total residential segregation' it was racist. In retrospect, had it been issued, it would have split the Torch Commando and caused significant rumblings within the UP.

What the draft statement revealed was that the tactics of the UP leadership represented by Graaff were made up of three elements. The first was to ensure that, with the assistance of the Commando, the electoral organisation of the opposition was as effective as possible. The second was to attack the NP directly on the constitutional crisis it had created over the Coloured vote issue. The third was to try to outflank and even to outbid the NP on the conservative right on the 'native non-European issue'.

In 1952 Sir de Villiers Graaff was elected the Cape provincial leader of the UP. This gave fresh hope to the embattled members of the party in the Cape – for Graaff appeared to have all the credentials of the leader they were looking for. He was a member of a well-connected Cape family; his father had been elected mayor of Cape Town in 1891, and had served in both the Cape and Union cabinets; General Louis Botha, the Union's first prime minister, was his godfather. He was a graduate of UCT and of Oxford; a good sportsman; wealthy; a lawyer and a farmer. He had a good war record. He spoke fluent English and Afrikaans. He was popular, and had the ability to evoke strong personal loyalties.

What was not known about Graaff was whether he had a vision for the future of South Africa, and whether he would have the will and the skill to lead his party to redefine itself in respect of the new challenges that were emerging in the field of black-white relationships.

Maitland election campaign, 1953

In February 1953 I called on Colonel Jack Bowring, the organising secretary of the UP in the Cape Peninsula. I told him I had six weeks leave due and would like to use them to help in the forthcoming election. 'Good – you've come at just the right time,' he said. 'Last night Zach de Beer was elected as the UP candidate for Maitland [a newly delimited constituency]. He's looking for an election agent to manage his campaign. I'll give you his telephone number.'

I knew Zach from the Villagers Football Club where he and I had played rugby in the same team. While at UCT Zach had been president of the SRC; he had graduated as a medical doctor, and in recent times been invited to speak at anti-government protest meetings. Personable, intelligent and fluently bilingual – as well as being recently married to Maureen Strauss, daughter of JGN Strauss, leader of the opposition

– Zach was an up-and-coming politician. I phoned him and he was delighted by my offer. After a discussion with the constituency committee, chaired by Guy Titterton, I was appointed Zach's election agent for the Maitland contest.

Maitland comprised four polling districts, each drawn from the former constituencies of Malmesbury, Vasco, Salt River and Mowbray. Its predominantly white voters were a mix of English and Afrikaans speakers belonging to the middle and lower income groups and spanning the spectrum of entrepreneurs, professionals, private-sector employees, public servants, railway workers and pensioners; 782 Coloured voters were registered in the satellite village of Maitland Garden Village.

The constituency had never been contested as a single entity, so it was difficult to predict the election result. Both the UP and NP considered it marginal. Both believed it could be won only through tremendous organisational effort, and gave it priority rating.

Zach, a first-time candidate at the age of 24, and I, a first-time campaign manager at 27, knew we faced a substantial challenge. Zach set about the task of contacting his voters and introducing himself to community leaders. My immediate tasks were first to structure the organisational system to be used in the election, and then to recruit key personnel who would ensure that the system functioned effectively.

In 1953 there was no television or radio advertising, no phone-ins or chat shows. There were no cellphones. The majority of voters did not have telephones – nor did they own motor cars. The Electoral Act restricted the amount of money that could be spent in each of the constituencies, and limited the numbers the parties could employ in the campaign. These factors meant that communication with the voters would be primarily through door-to-door canvassing by voluntary workers.

In addition, on election day, in each of the polling districts, sufficient volunteers would be needed to provide cars and drivers to ensure that every voter who had indicated they would vote for Zach were ferried to the polls, and returned home afterward.

There was no shortage of volunteers. Zach was seen as a most attractive candidate, and political feelings were running high. The NP appointed Louis Weichardt, the leader of the Greyshirts, a pro-Nazi and anti-Semitic movement, as its candidate for Maitland. Inevitably, the members of the Cape Jewish community were determined to demonstrate their feelings by helping Zach in whatever way they could to keep Weichardt out.

I evolved a comprehensive electoral system based on two 'canvass cards' for each voter. This provided essential back-up to door-to-door canvassing, to the re-canvassing of doubtfuls, to the tracing of missing voters, to the arrangement of postal votes, and to preparing transport arrangements for polling day. This 'Maitland system', which with minor modifications was taken over by the Progressives, was still being used in the Cape Peninsula 30 years later until the abolition of constituencies and the use of computers made it redundant.

The Nats hammered away on the theme of apartheid, and to an extent on the dangers of communism; Weichardt kept a low profile. Meanwhile, Zach's campaign theme centred on the breach of the pledge and the violation of the constitution, as well as what would today be called a 'failure to deliver'. Our man's public meetings were well-attended but rowdy thanks to NP hecklers and the presence of a couple of NP organisers who came to launch questions at the candidate.

Zach's final election meeting was held in the Martin Adams Hall in the predominantly Nat area of Ysterplaat. The hall was overflowing with the Nats, and the atmosphere was tense. We posted some well-built men from the Torch Commando in strategic positions in the hall to deal with any scuffles. The speakers were Zach and Captain Jack Basson, the UP candidate for Sea Point.

Zach spoke in measured terms – driving home the message of the time with forceful logic. Basson, who had a reputation for enjoying the rough and tumble of election meetings in Cape Town's northern suburbs, was more robust and aggressive in dealing with hecklers who soon revealed the thrust of the Nats' campaign. Sitting in the middle of this group was a woman with a celluloid doll in each hand. One was black, the other white; one was a boy, the other a girl. At intervals – to loud cheering and jeering from the Nats – the woman would raise the dolls aloft and start banging them together, shouting: '*Dis wat julle wil hé!*'

As a reaction to the Nats trying to remove the Coloureds from the voters' roll, the UP had produced the slogan: 'Vote for the Right to Vote Again. Vote UP'. Every now and then the Nats chorus would chant: '*Stem vir die reg om weer te stem. Stem vir Solly en Sam.*' The Solly referred to was Solly Sachs, a prominent communist trade union leader, and the Sam was Sam Kahn, a leading communist, whom the Nats had removed as a member of parliament in terms of the Suppression of Communism Act.

Despite all this, the meeting ended with a huge vote of confidence in De Beer. Alas, there was a different kind of drama later in the evening when his father, with whom Zach was a partner in his medical practice, died of a heart attack while driving home.

When the results of the election were announced, Zach had won with a majority of 2 105 votes to become the youngest person to be elected as a member of the Union parliament. But in the election as a whole, the NP had increased its seats from 70 to 89, while the UP had its seats reduced from 65 to 57. The UP was bound to enter into a difficult phase of its existence; the Torch Commando had failed to remove the NP from office. Apart from my exhilaration at having managed the successful election campaign, for me the redeeming feature was that, in addition to Zach de Beer, a number of progressive-thinking individuals had been elected to the UP's team in parliament.

Formation of the Liberal Party, 1953

The result of the 1953 election was a blow for the UP, and a shattering blow for the old guard in its hierarchy. Its leaders had convinced themselves that had it not been for poor organisation the party would have won in 1948; they had believed that with good organisation and a cautious non-committal approach to the 'non-European is-sue' the UP could win in 1953. Thanks largely to the Torch Commando, the UP's elec-toral machine had become remarkably good. What the leadership had not taken into account was the appeal that apartheid had for the voters, and the organic growth of Afrikaner nationalism.

A widespread, and rather uncomfortable, realisation arose within the UP that there would have to be a serious rethink of its 'non-European' policy – and in partic-ular on where it stood in relation to apartheid. While Zach de Beer kept me in touch with the tensions that were building up, and the discussions in the newly elected par-liamentary caucus, I went back to being a quantity surveyor.

For its part, the Torch Commando found itself facing a crisis of purpose and iden-tity. Having failed in its important objective of getting rid of the Nationalist govern-ment at the polls, it was left without a strategic or tactical objective. Added to this, having lost the battle over the constitutional representation of the Coloureds, it was bereft of the one issue around which its members could remain united. The Com-mando faced three choices. It could continue as a limited-objective pressure group. However, since the next election was five years off, it was unlikely that it could main-tain its initiative and enthusiasm over this extended period.

It could, secondly, consider transforming itself into a political party. This would be well-nigh impossible; the Commando had no comprehensive political policy, and its members would have widely diverging views on what such a policy should be. It had compromised itself by not being decisive enough on the admission of Coloured ex-servicemen to its ranks. In addition, should it become a political party, it would find itself competing not only with the UP but with the Liberal Party and the Federal Party, both in the process of being formed.

The third choice was to disband. Much to the relief of the UP, and indeed with some encouragement from the party's leadership, this is precisely what the Torch Commando did.

After 1948, various attempts were made to rally liberal elements within the po-litical mainstream. Non-Afrikaner churches, universities and newspapers in gen-eral espoused liberal opinions – some with more, some less, vigour. Inside the UP itself, hopes had been pinned on the brilliant Jan Hofmeyr, who was groomed to be the successor to the ageing General Smuts. When Hofmeyr died suddenly in 1948, a number of us formed the Hofmeyr Society as a 'think tank' and pressure group within the party.

In 1952 I was one of a small group who met twice in Cape Town to form the South African Liberal Group 'with the object of trying to provide a political home for those of us in South Africa with definite liberal feelings'. At that stage the group had no fixed idea about the shape it should adopt – except that 'the Group should not, for the time being, become politically active, and that the time was not opportune for a public appeal for membership'.

An interim committee, under the chairmanship of Dr Oscar Wollheim, was set up to develop membership by invitation and to call meetings in Cape Town from time to time; and, possibly, to set in motion 'preliminary steps for the calling of a closed conference of members of other parts of the Union in December or January'. Further meetings were held in Cape Town in August and November at which a draft constitution and a revised Programme of Principles was adopted 'in the interests of all the people of South Africa'. It affirmed and committed itself to:

- The essential dignity of all men and women irrespective of race, colour or creed.
- Freedom of worship, assembly and expression.
- The development of South Africa's human and material resources for the benefit of all, and the need to control state or other monopolies.
- The elimination of all bars to the acquisition and utilisation of skill.
- The freedom of every individual to own property.
- The active propagation of a spirit of tolerance and mutual understanding among the various sections of our people.
- Such free and compulsory education as would ensure opportunities for all to develop to the limit of their intellectual capacities.
- The inherent right of all civilised men and women to vote and to have a direct voice in the government of the country.
- The achievement of the Group's objects by constitutional and democratic methods.
- The charter of the United Nations as the basis for the regulation of international affairs.

The first annual meeting of the group, which evolved into the South African Liberal Association (SALA), and which included members from outside Cape Town, was in January 1953.

During that year membership of SALA increased around the country, as did interest in the concept of forming a Liberal Party. However, activities in the liberal field were overshadowed by the general election held on 16 April.

Following the electoral defeat of the UP and the Labour Party, the move to convert SALA into a fully fledged political party gained further momentum. Support for this was most pronounced in the Transvaal, where members appeared to adopt a more radical approach to policy and action than the traditional liberals of the Cape. A meeting of the SALA council was convened, to be held in the boardroom of the *Cape Times* on Saturday and Sunday 9-10 May, to consider the issue. In the week prior to the meeting the *Times* carried articles speculating that a Liberal Party was about to be formed – a speculation made more credible by featured photographs of Margaret Ballinger, Leo Marquard, Oscar Wollheim and Donald Molteno, all leading members of SALA.

I stated my case against forming a Liberal Party at that time. It rested essentially on the fact that, at the election only a month before, a number of liberal-minded individuals had been elected to parliament as members of the UP. These included Jan Steytler, Helen Suzman, Zach de Beer, John Cope, Ray Swart, Ronald Butcher and Townley Williams. I argued that there was an opportunity of liberalising the UP from within. My arguments were promptly knocked on the head by Walter Stanford and Donald Molteno, who, to my complete surprise, reported that they had been to see Sir de Villiers Graaff, the newly elected Cape leader of the UP, at his holiday home in Hermanus. In contrast to my views, Graaff had encouraged them to proceed with the formation of a Liberal Party, as 'he would prefer that his UP was not perceived to be on the left of the South African political spectrum'!

Perhaps I should have realised from this that any attempt to liberalise the UP from within would be resisted by Graaff. In fact, liberals such as Helen Suzman, Jan Steytler, John Cope, Ray Swart, Zach de Beer and I continued to try to shift the UP to a non-racial and progressive position. It was only six years later, with Graaff as national leader of the UP, that the showdown between 'conservatives and progressives' took place – splitting the UP and triggering the formation of the Progressive Party in November 1959.

At the Cape Town meeting, however, when the issue was finally put to the vote, a two-thirds majority saw the formation of the Liberal Party. Ballinger was elected president, Alan Paton and Leo Marquard its vice-presidents, Oscar Wollheim chairman, and Leslie Rubin vice-chairman. Although I announced that I would not join the Liberal Party, the council invited me to stay on for the rest of the day's proceedings. Then I dashed back home to Pinelands, hoping to be in time to hear the eight o'clock evening radio news.

In those days the SABC relied on the external service of the BBC for its 8 pm news review. The news reader started as follows: 'This is London calling. Before we give you details of today's news stories, here are the headlines from around the world ... [In] South Africa, the news of the formation this weekend of two new political parties.' There followed the announcement that in addition to the Liberal Party formed in Cape Town, a Federal Party had been formed in Natal!

I should not have been surprised. Ever since May 1948, the English-speaking voters of Natal had become increasingly frustrated, and at times had threatened to take political action on the basis of what they called the 'Natal Stand'. In politics, provincial nuances had come fully into play.

The inaugural meeting of the Liberal Party was held in the Cape Town city hall a month later under the chairmanship of Leo Marquard. The party adopted a non-racial common roll franchise subject to certain educational or economic qualifications; a year later it voted for the principle of a universal adult franchise subject to certain transitional arrangements.

Province to parliament, 1954-1958

The formation of the Liberal Party caused considerable anguish for me. Together with a number of 'progressives', I was starting to play a leading role in the UP in the Cape Peninsula, and had recently been elected unopposed as the UP member of the Cape Provincial Council for Pinelands. In the 1950s, the councils played an important role at the delivery end of schooling and hospital services. They also had a supervisory role in relation to local government, though they had no original powers, and were to a large extent agents of the central government. Nevertheless, the experience afforded me some valuable training and interesting political opportunities.

I served on the Teaching Hospitals Board, which had responsibility for Groote Schuur Hospital, Somerset Hospital, Peninsula Maternity Home, and other medical institutions connected to UCT's medical faculty. I maintained regular contact with the schools and school committees as well as community organisations in the constituency, and soon learned the responsibilities and functions of a public representative and the critical importance of being responsive to the voters.

However, my political activities extended far beyond my responsibilities as a provincial councillor. I belonged to a group of younger supporters of the UP, most of whom had been active in the Torch Commando, who acted as a pressure group in an attempt to make the party organisation more effective and to persuade the Cape Peninsula wing to take a liberal view on local issues. A modest yet signal achievement was to get the UP to abandon its traditional view that black citizens from outside the Peninsula were not permitted to come and work there. The cartoonist of *Die Burger* had great pleasure in depicting the chairman of the UP in the Peninsula opening a sluice gate at the top of the Hottentot's Holland mountains near Sir Lowry's Pass – over which work-seekers flooded, then as now.

I was put in charge of formulating and presenting the UP's proposals for the re-delimitation of the Cape Peninsula to the Delimitation Commission presided over by Judge Rumpf. I roused the ire of the old guard who were accustomed to overwhelmingly safe seats by coming forward with a plan to dilute these seats by incorporating a certain number of NP voters from adjoining Nationalist seats. Had my proposals been accepted by the commission, the UP in the Peninsula would have gained a seat or two. The commission decided otherwise – much to my regret and the relief of the UP old guard!

As a 'public representative' I had access to the various councils and congresses of the party; and in due course was elected first vice-chairman then chairman of the UP in the Cape Peninsula. So I got to know the leading party personalities in the Cape, and attained insight into the infighting and intrigue endemic in the UP at that time.

In the Provincial Council itself, members of the UP caucus were experiencing their own trauma of adjustment: it lost control to the Nationalists in 1954. Moving into opposition did not come easily to the senior UP members. It can be said that the problems facing the Cape Council were part of those facing the UP as a whole – and being played out in particular in the parliamentary caucus. The UP was in a state of tension; its leader JGN Strauss was under great pressure. His detractors within the party asserted that he had under-performed in 1953. Others argued that he lacked leadership qualities. Arthur Barlow, a member of the caucus and a long-standing critic of Strauss, continued to snipe at him.

For its part, the English-language press in general was critical of his performance, and Strauss was also placed under great pressure by the Nationalists in parliament. The Nats now asked him to state whether, if they succeeded in removing the Coloureds from the common voters' roll, the UP would restore them should it return to power. Strauss avoided responding for as long as he could until finally, under mounting pressure, he made a statement so equivocal that it merely added to the UP's, and his, problems. Seven liberal UP backbenchers declared that they disassociated themselves from his statement. Although I was not a member of the parliamentary caucus I wrote to Strauss expressing my disapproval: an action for which I had the support of my constituency committee.

After some days of negotiation the seven members accepted a compromise statement, but exercised their right to reaffirm in parliament their commitment to restoring the Coloured voters to the common roll. Dr Bernard Friedman, a senior member and outspoken liberal, resigned his seat over the issue and was replaced at the ensuing by-election by former senator and old-fashioned conservative Louis Steenkamp. The question being asked was: if the UP could not come to grips with a relatively easy issue, how could it possibly get to grips with the dominant black issue?

Strauss never really recovered from this debacle. He carried on, until in his absence from a congress of the UP held in Bloemfontein in 1956 – in circumstances which do no credit to the party hierarchy – Sir de Villiers Graaff replaced him as leader. Realising that the news that Strauss was to be removed would come as a great shock to his wife, Joy, who was at home in Johannesburg, Zach de Beer, whose wife Maureen was Strauss's daughter, and I travelled through the night to tell Joy what was happening before she read about it in the morning newspaper. In a station wagon belonging to Harry Oppenheimer we raced through the night to arrive at the Strauss home in Linksfield a few minutes before the *Rand Daily Mail* was delivered. Joy was stunned, but reacted with great composure.

In November 1954 Dr Malan resigned as prime minister, and at 80 retired from politics. He was succeeded by JG Strijdom, leader of the National Party in the Transvaal. Strijdom was a hard-line, uncompromising Afrikaner nationalist. He declared that he believed in *baasskap*, which he defined as mastery, domination and compulsion. He also made it clear that he was determined to settle the Coloured vote issue, and with that the constitutional dispute over the entrenched clauses. It was his scheme to enlarge the Senate with additional senators nominated by the Nationalists to achieve the requisite two-thirds majority necessary to alter the Union's founding document. To do so he also increased the number of judges of the Appeal Court from five to 11, to dilute the voice of the incumbent judges, who had declared the government's three attempts to remove the Coloureds to be invalid. In 1956 the Separate Representation of Voters Bill was reintroduced, and was passed with the aid of the enlarged Senate. When it was taken to the enlarged Appeal Court it was approved with only one judge, OD Schreiner, dissenting.

As the screws of apartheid were tightened the mood of the Coloured people of the Cape was one of disillusionment and anger. I was learning at first hand what the Group Areas Act, the Population Registration Act, the Immorality Act, the Mixed Marriages Act, the Separate Amenities Act, and job reservation were doing to Coloured communities, families and individuals. I was learning of what the pass laws and the basic lack of human rights were doing to black people. Apartheid was evil.

The visit of Chief Albert Luthuli to Cape Town in 1956 broadened my perspective on the extent of the denial and deprivation that had been imposed on black South Africans ever since the time of Union. In a public letter to Strijdom in May 1957, Luthuli emphasised this ugly reality, yet also conveyed a message of hope and pointed the way to a peaceful future: 'My people crave for an opportunity to work for a great united South Africa in which they can develop their personalities and capabilities to the fullest with the rest of the country's population in the interest of the country as a whole.

'I would, for emphasis, reiterate that it is our ardent desire ... to see human conduct and relations motivated by an overriding passion for peace and friendship in South Africa and the world in general, and so we would strongly be opposed to black domination, or any other kind of domination from whatever source, as we are uncompromisingly opposed to white domination. We regard domination, exploitation and racialism as arch enemies of mankind.'

At times as I sat in the back row of the little Methodist church in Pinelands on a Sunday evening I pondered these realities. Good people surrounded me; yet their goodness was defined in their relationship with God. It had little or no relevance to people outside their white community. Religious compartmentalisation was given effect by carrying out religious activities on the basis of separate churches and separate synods for Coloured and black, and white Methodists. I asked myself why these good white Methodists in Pinelands were not angry, or apparently not even concerned at what was happening to the other South Africans living around them.

I decided to call on Rev. CK Storey, the Methodist minister in the neighbouring suburb of Rosebank, who was also the head of the Methodist Church of South Africa, to discuss the matter and to put a proposal to him. My proposal was that the Methodist Church in the Cape Peninsula undertake a project to put each white family in touch with a black family, and vice versa. They would get to know one another, and to understand one another's problems, needs and aspirations. Where necessary each could help the other – especially in the case of a black family that was a relative newcomer to Cape Town. I added that I wanted my daughters, as they grew up, to have some black friends.

Rev. Storey said that he understood both the objective and the proposal, and would like to have time to think about it. A few weeks later he thanked me for my proposal and said it had merits, but that taking relevant factors into consideration he would not be able to implement it. He agreed that the Methodists in Pinelands had a faith that existed within the context of the white community of which they were a part; and that if he attempted to extend their experience and faith to include persons from the non-European community, it was likely there would be resistance from members of the congregation. It could even result in some members leaving the Church.

I left frustrated and disillusioned. I was saddened by the realisation that the Church, which meant so much to my parents, and of which I was a member, was going to put racial exclusiveness ahead of Christian inclusiveness. I had misgivings about the role the Church was playing in the evolving South Africa.

In August 1957 I received news that my mother had died of a heart attack in the village of Limbeeck near Brussels while on a touring holiday in Europe with her sister Marjorie, Marjorie's husband John Berry, and my sister Lorna. It had been decided that Elsie should be buried in the local village cemetery. Arrangements were accordingly made, but a problem arose when a Protestant clergyman could not be found to conduct the funeral service. Mindful of my mother's strong Protestant commitment, the family decided to conduct a graveside service themselves. Marjorie read some verses from the Bible; Lorna, at the time serving as a missionary in Kenya, said a prayer; and Elsie May Eglin was laid to rest in a foreign country far from home.

By now, the 1958 election was only a few months away. The political parties were in the grip of nomination fever, and I decided I would like to become a member of parliament to continue my political work, especially that of attempting to reform the UP. There was considerable support for my candidature in the councils of the UP in the Cape Peninsula. The majority of the members of the party committees in the Pinelands constituency indicated they would like me as their candidate. I sensed that, while Captain RJ du Toit, the sitting MP for Pinelands, was widely liked as a person, he was becoming ineffective as a public representative.

Du Toit, whom I presumed was aware of this, approached me with the proposal that I stand as a candidate in a Nationalist-held or marginal constituency and that he again contest Pinelands. In the event that I lost the election, he would resign his seat and I could then stand in Pinelands at the subsequent by-election. I was loth to enter nomination deals, especially this one, since I was sure that it would not find favour with the constituency committee in Pinelands. I wrote to the chairman, and stated I was not prepared to follow the course Du Toit proposed unless I was advised to do so by the leader of the party.

Graaff, far from advising me to accept the proposal, advised me against it. He was opposed to individual candidates doing private deals, and in addition, in the case of the Pinelands constituency, it was most likely that if I did not stand someone else would – and in every likelihood would defeat Du Toit in the nomination contest. The upshot was that Du Toit did not stand for nomination, and I was elected unopposed as the UP candidate for Pinelands.

When, on nomination day for the 1958 election, no other parties put forward a candidate for Pinelands, I was declared a member of parliament three weeks before the general election itself. I did, however, have election responsibilities, in particular, as a bilingual politician, to address campaign meetings in predominantly Afrikaans and Nationalist constituencies. Bellville was considered particularly important. Jan Haak, the sitting MP, was the Nat candidate, and Zach and I were on the lookout for a suitable opponent. We hit on Pieter de Kock who, like Haak, had been prominent in student politics at Stellenbosch University. Pieter was still in Johannesburg working for Anglo-American – and both he and Harry Oppenheimer were taken with the idea of Pieter standing against Haak. The UP, under our prodding, put a special effort into the Bellville campaign; with no election in Pinelands my constituency workers were assigned to Pieter; in addition, a group of progressive-minded supporters, some of whom had been introduced into politics through the Torch Commando, and who had been working behind the scenes with me, went out to Bellville.

The upshot? I was safe in Pinelands; Zach retained Maitland with an increased majority; but Pieter, in spite of his hard work and the support he received from an enthusiastic election team, was roundly defeated by Haak. Further, as the results from the rural areas started coming in, the prospects for the UP looked bleak. Pieter, Zach and I decided to travel to Caledon where the result in the Hottentot's Holland constituency, which Graaff was contesting, was expected in the late afternoon. From four o'clock on, crowds started gathering outside the local town hall where in due course the presiding officer emerged to announce the result. To the cheers and jeers of the Nationalists, and amidst tears from many exhausted UP supporters, he announced that Japie de Villiers, the Nationalist candidate, had defeated Graaff.

The final tally was National Party 103, UP 53. To rub salt into the opposition wounds, this was the first time the Nationalists had managed to obtain an overall majority of the votes cast nationwide.

Lasting friendships, 1954-1958

During my provincial council years I developed friendships that, over the years, played an important part in my life. My relationship with Zach de Beer was fashioned by our shared political philosophy and concern at the lack of direction and thrust of the UP. It developed into one of mutual trust, understanding, support, common purpose, and the shared enjoyment of each other's companionship and sense of fun. We shared confidences. We engaged in joint analyses of political situations. Together we fashioned our vision of the future. Fortunately, the companionship embraced our wives as well. Later, after Zach and Maureen separated and Zach married Mona, the friendship between the Eglin and De Beer families continued.

Not that Zach and I always agreed. He often approached a course of action from the vantage point of 'the great persuader', whereas my approach was that of a strategic manager. Zach tended to judge individuals largely in terms of their intellect; I looked

Top: Great-grandparents Morris with their four daughters, *c*1870. Florence Elizabeth, on the left with black neckband, married James Francis Wells and had two sons and six daughters, one of whom was my mother, Elsie May Wells.

Left: A sturdy 18-month-old in a kiddies' push-chair of the 1920s at *Caronel,* our family home, in Pinelands, 1926. No rival to Henry Ford!

Above: With my sister Lorna in the garden of our home in Pinelands.

Right: Getting set for a Sunday afternoon drive, with my father at the wheel and me standing in the dickie seat.

Below: My father Carl and mother Elsie with her sister Doris at Camps Bay.

Bottom: Back home from boarding school with my mother and sister.

Above: Wartime (1944-1945) photographs exchanged between Joyce Cortes, later to become my wife, and me.

Left: Joyce in her Red Cross uniform (Voluntary Aid Detachment) outside her Pinelands home.

Left: Joyce and me after our marriage service in the Pinelands Methodist church, 10 September 1949.

Bottom: D Company HQ, First City/Cape Town Highlanders, at Melzo, Italy, a week after the war ended in May 1945. I am fourth from the right in the back row.

Opposite page
Top: First Progressive Party parliamentary caucus in its caucus-cum-storeroom at parliament, January 1960. Harry Lawrence, chairman (centre), with Dr Jan Steytler, leader, seated on his left.

Bottom: With Ray Swart and Oscar Wollheim, Durban 1965. (*The Daily News*)

Top: 1966 election, Sea Point – my publicity machine assembling.

Bottom: 1970 election, Sea Point – Harry Oppenheimer with Arnold Galombik and Jack Rumbelow after addressing businessmen at a Progressive Party house meeting.

Top: Being introduced to President Kenneth Kaunda by Zach de Beer at State House, Lusaka 1971.

Bottom: With President Leopold Sedar Senghor, Dakar 1971. (Presidency of the Republic of Senegal, Photos Section)

Above: With Minister of Constitutional Affairs
and Attorney General Charles Njonjo and Helen,
Nairobi 1971.

Opposite page: With Joyce at an
interdenominational service on Signal Hill in
support of Reverend Bernard Wrankmore who
had been fasting for 67 days, demanding a judicial
inquiry into the death in detention of Imam
Haroun, October 1971. (*The Argus*, Cape Town)

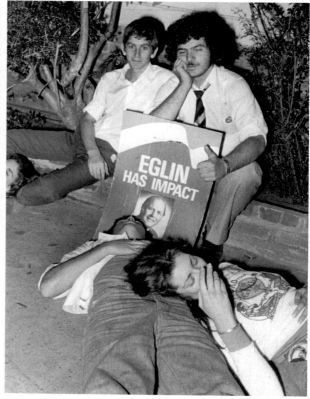

Prog breakthrough – 24 April 1974

Above: 1974 election, Sea Point – Barry Streek, the campaign organiser, looking to the youth vote. (*The Argus,* Cape Town)

Right: The long wait for the result. (*The Argus,* Cape Town)

Bottom: The joy of winning.

Outside the polling station after it had been announced that I had won Sea Point by 839 votes. In front of me, advocate Gerald Gordon and Frederik van Zyl Slabbert who had won in Rondebosch; behind me David Graaff, the defeated United Party opponent, and his wife Sally. (*The Argus*, Cape Town)

In conversation with AD (Jim) Blankson who accompanied Van Zyl Slabbert and me on our visit to Nigeria in 1974. (Keystone Press Agency, New York)

Top: Celebrating my 50th birthday with Linda, Susan, Caryl and Joyce at a bierfest in the Drill Hall, Cape Town, April 1975. (*The Argus*, Cape Town)

Bottom: With my colleagues in the Progressive Federal Party parliamentary caucus after the 1977 election, when the party became the official opposition. (*Cape Times*, Cape Town)

Right: A photograph by Harry Tyler that was used on posters, election pamphlets, and publicity material from 1977 through to 1989. (Harry Tyler Photography)

Bottom: Enjoying a lighthearted discussion with United States ambassadors Andrew Young and Donald McHenry at the United Nations headquarters in New York. (Keystone Press Agency, New York)

Opposite page
Top: 1981 election, Sea Point – driving home a point. (*The Argus*, Cape Town)

Bottom: 1981 election, Sea Point – queuing up to vote for Eglin and Hirsch. (*The Argus*, Cape Town)

Above: My PFP parliamentary colleagues and me being
sworn in as members of the House of Assembly after
the inauguration of the Tricameral constitution: State
President PW Botha and cabinet ministers Piet Koornhof,
Magnus Malan and Adriaan Vlok looking on sternly.
(*The Argus,* Cape Town)

to their sense of judgement. Zach was subtle; I was direct.

While Zach spent a number of years in the boardroom at Anglo-American, I stayed on in Cape Town. He went to live in Johannesburg, and for a while in Zambia. Yet when we met there was no need to explain where and why we stood on current issues: we carried on where we left off 'yesterday'.

In June 1954 the new parliamentary caucus of the UP, elected 15 months earlier, instead of having settled down as a team, was being debilitated by bitter political infighting. Already the fault lines between the conservatives and the progressives were manifest. Tony Delius, poet, author, journalist and parliamentary correspondent of the *Cape Times*, acting, I suspect, with an eye to the future, told me I should meet Helen Suzman: 'She is bright, and one way or another she is going to make an important impact on the political scene.'

A few days later Helen, Tony and I lunched together in the Oak Room of the old Manchester Hotel at the corner of Strand and Burg streets. That was the start of a personal and political friendship that gathered strength under the strains and challenges of opposition politics during the apartheid years. It held together during arduous journeys around Africa and China; and remarkably survived the strain of two strong-willed characters for 50 years.

Having at times witnessed Helen's belligerence in defence of what she believed to be right, and having heard her whiplash tongue when roused to anger by injustice or bullying, I have often said to myself, 'Thank God I have been on Helen's side!'

From the time that Zach came to parliament in 1953, Harry Oppenheimer, then the UP MP for Kimberley, took a liking to him. He appreciated Zach's intellect; he enjoyed his company; he liked his style, as a person and a politician; he shared his liberal yet pragmatic approach to broad national issues.

It was initially through my friendship with Zach that Harry and I got to know each other. As the turmoil in the UP during the 1950s wore on, Harry, Zach and I found ourselves engaged in discussions. We met on occasions at his townhouse in the Buitensingel area of Cape Town, or at Little Brenthurst in Parktown, Johannesburg – home for Harry and his wife Bridget. We met at UP congresses.

Oppenheimer combined a keen intellect, a sound judgement and a depth of knowledge with an interest in and a concern for individuals. He had a diffidence of style that often concealed his toughness of mind and strength of will. Until Harry died at the age of 91, I enjoyed his friendship and his company, his wise counsel and steadfast support. While he did not identify himself with the 'progressive group' in the UP caucus, he was foremost among its liberal thinkers, and in the van of those trying to impart some vision, relevance and clarity to the UP's 'non-European policy'.

He once fairly described himself as 'a liberal, with my feet firmly on the ground'. In 1956 Harry asked Zach to accompany him to a Commonwealth Conference on Constitutional Reform in the United Kingdom, after which he conceived the idea of using the Senate as a mechanism for resolving the dilemma over non-European political rights in the UP, which had been aggravated by the Nationalist government stripping the entrenched provisions from the constitution.

Two concepts were central to Harry's thinking:
- that non-Europeans should have direct representation in parliament; and
- that this representation would have to be extended in the future.

Harry's assessment was that these concepts could be achieved only with the approval of a simple majority of the whites. In addition, he held the opinion that a mechanism should be created to protect these rights from being diminished unless the proposal had the support of a two-thirds majority of the white electorate.

With the assistance of constitutional experts he developed these ideas further into a proposal for the reform of the Senate, which he then presented to Graaff. Graaff in turn took Harry's proposals to the committee of the UP considering revisions to the party's constitutional policy; and in due course the UP's Senate Plan, dubbed 'die Graaff Senaat' by the Nationalists, emerged and was adopted by the party congress in 1957 as an integral part of the UP's new constitutional policy.

Certain important features of the Oppenheimer plan were omitted from the UP Senate Plan, notable among them the omission of direct representation of non-Europeans. Under the UP Plan parliament was to remain all-white. Harry was disappointed, but recognised there were widely divergent views within the party. However, his disappointment turned to disillusionment as he saw the Plan presented differently by different UP speakers to different audiences. Increasingly, the Plan was presented as a device for maintaining white political domination.

Inevitably, the concept was misunderstood by the voters, and instead of resolving the party's dilemma exacerbated still further differences within its ranks. Harry intended to stay on in parliament and continue with his efforts to persuade his party to reform. He decided to improve his Afrikaans; and as a first decided he would like to take two young Afrikaans-speakers on an extended visit to the Mountains of the Moon on the border of Congo and Ruanda on the understanding that the three of them would converse only in Afrikaans while on the expedition. He asked Zach and me for suggestions, and we put forward the names of Hannes Fagan and Pieter de Kock, two young lawyers from Cape Town from families with impeccable Afrikaner credentials.

Harry, Hannes and Pieter set off on their linguistic mission. However, they had scarcely arrived at their Central African destination when Harry was called back to Johannesburg. Burglars had broken into Little Brenthurst and stolen valuable jewellery. Hannes and Pieter stayed on in the Mountains of the Moon.

Undeterred, Harry invited Pieter to become his political personal assistant. This was certainly a gain for Harry, but a loss for Zach and me, since Pieter – with whom we had developed a close bond of personal and political friendship – would have to move to Johannesburg to take up the job.

Pieter had grown up as a youngster in the Western Province town of Caledon, where his father had been a prominent member of the National Party.

One Sunday evening shortly after Pieter had been appointed, Harry invited Pieter and me to join his father Sir Ernest and himself to dine at Brenthurst. We were reminded that on Sunday evening, dress was black tie and dinner jacket. De Kock and I arrived in our black dress suits, white shirts and black dress ties to find a very relaxed-looking father and son wearing coloured dinner jackets instead of black-jacketed dress suits. Harry's jacket was of burgundy-coloured velvet with darker shaded collar, lapels and buttons. Sir Ernest's was a toned-down version of Joseph's multicoloured dreamcoat –made of silk with a pattern of gold, red, purple and blue squares, and dark purple collar lapels, collar and buttons.

I was fascinated by the two Oppenheimers: Harry was extremely polite and always referred to Sir Ernest as Papa. The relationship between the two was obviously very close, the son scholarly in manner and diffident in style, the father's eyes reflecting a razor-sharp mind and a direct and appropriate choice of words.

At one stage during the evening either Pieter or I ventured a comment about shares. Harry responded by saying that 'of course we don't really dabble in shares on the market, we are long-term investors'. Sir Ernest's response was that he believed there were only two ways of making money from shares: the one was by using your head, the other by using your bottom. We said we could understand how you could use your head, but how you could use your bottom? With a smile he said: 'You just sit on it.'

Harry's intention of staying on as an MP was cut short when in 1957 Sir Ernest died. The new circumstances demanded he leave parliament to take over from Sir Ernest as head of the Anglo-American Corporation and De Beer's Consolidated Mines. Yet he did not actually leave politics, continuing to take a close interest in the unfolding situation. But more than this, he believed that the advantages he had been privileged to enjoy, and the important position he held in the economic sphere, increased – rather than diminished – the scope of his political responsibility.

He was to play an important role in the formation of the Progressive Party and its development over the years. Within a couple of weeks of the PP having been formed in 1959, Harry came down to Cape Town to address a group of businessmen. I can recall his words: 'We businessmen here tonight have been fortunate people. We have been privileged. Most, if not all of us, grew up in secure homes. We had caring parents. We enjoyed the advantage of a good education. What is more, we had the advantage, which many others in South Africa did not have, and still do not have today, of being able to turn to good effect the opportunities that are available in our country. Indeed, we are fortunate. We are privileged. And that imposes on us a duty to try to put right the things in our country that we all know are wrong, and that cry out to be put right.'

Oppenheimer played a vitally important role in keeping the PP alive during the 1960s, when Helen Suzman was on her own in parliament, and the party was badly beaten in one election after another. He provided the funds that enabled the party to keep its head office functioning, and for campaigns that the party undertook from time to time. He addressed meetings of businessmen at which he urged them to support the PP. At the Grand Hotel in Cape Town, in September 1963, he said: 'I believe that it is our duty to run this risk, because the Progressive Party is more than just a political party in the ordinary sense, aiming at one law being passed or another law being withdrawn. This is a party which, as small as it is, is the bearer of a very great tradition – a tradition of seeing that justice is done to the individual man. I believe that we should work for that, and that we should run risks for that, even if we don't see the immediate chances of success.

'There is something in crying out in anger and fighting, when you see injustice done, not because you see a way of ending the injustice, but simply because it is right to protest against what is evil in this world.

'And if we have the courage, we will succeed, because we are a party which, I think, is facing up to facts and therefore we are not full of easy optimism, because we can't be when you look at the very grave facts which are before us. But we have a logical policy, we have a humane policy and we have a policy which, if it can be shown to be growing in South Africa, will reconcile us to our friends in the Western world and by doing so will give us the time to see that the changes – the great radical changes – which have got to be made in South Africa will be made, but will be made in peace and without bloodshed.'

In the circles in which he moved he always spoke up for the party and its objectives. He spoke in support of Helen in her election campaigns in Houghton, and during the 1970 election spoke at informal house meetings in support of my candidature in Sea Point.

I know that at times he was disheartened at the lack of progress that the party was making among the white voters. However, his commitment never wavered.

Turmoil in the UP, July 1958-1959

With my first parliamentary session imminent, the issue of dovetailing my political with my quantity surveying activities needed to be resolved. I would devote approximately 50% of my time to each, and financial arrangements would reflect this. As things turned out, over the following three years and four months I devoted approximately 90% of my time to the most traumatic years of my political career.

Apart from the excitement of my first session as an MP, there was the sudden death of prime minister Strijdom, the election of Dr Hendrik Verwoerd as the new prime minister, the 'wind of change' speech by UK prime minister Harold Macmillan, followed by Dr Verwoerd's 'new vision' speech and turmoil in the UP caucus. The UP was to split at a congress in Bloemfontein, followed by the formation of the Progressive Party (PP). More fundamental apartheid laws were enacted, such as the Extension of University Education Act, the Unlawful Organisations Act, the Promotion of Bantu Self-Government Act, and various amending acts that tightened the screws of apartheid.

Then there was the attempt on the life of Dr Verwoerd at the Witwatersrand Agricultural Show, the referendum on a republic, South Africa's exit from the Commonwealth, the passing of the new republican constitution, and the snap election called by Verwoerd – in which I and nine other PP MPs lost our seats. Only Helen Suzman retained hers.

Violence and confrontation rose.

The ANC split to form the Pan-Africanist Congress (PAC) under the leadership of Robert Sobukwe. As a consequence of a nationwide anti-pass law campaign there were clashes between black citizens and the police at Langa, Nyanga, and elsewhere around the country, leading to the fatal banning of the ANC and PAC. The ANC went underground and there followed the establishment of Umkhonto we Sizwe, the massacre at Sharpeville, the declaration of the state of emergency, and the historic march of thirty thousand blacks on Cape Town.

During this period I was awarded a Foreign Leader grant by the United States government. I spent 90 days in America, observing the Kennedy/Nixon presidential election and studying the relationship between the states' governments and the federal government in the deep south of America. How fortunate I was to have tolerant and understanding professional partners and a loving and supportive wife and daughters.

In July 1958 I was sworn in as a member of what was going to be the last parliament of the Union of South Africa. The Chamber had been the focal venue of debate and decision-making in national politics since 1910. I recalled the roles of the three Boer generals, Botha, Hertzog and Smuts, in leading the Union of South Africa from 1910 to 1948. I recalled the momentous decision on 6 September 1939 to go to war against Hitler's Germany. I recalled sitting in the gallery during my student days, listening to leaders like Hertzog and Malan, Smuts and Hofmeyr, arguing for and against neutrality against the background of a world at war. I recalled listening from the gallery to Nationalist members sniping with increasing intensity at a United Party government drifting along, enveloped in an aura of self-satisfied complacency.

The challenges entailed not only dealing with an apartheid government, but dealing with my own UP, which in a fast-changing national and international environment appeared to be sliding into a state of confused irrelevance.

The first few weeks of the session were characterised by a triumphant National Party, led by blunt-speaking JG Strijdom, and a surprisingly resilient UP, led by a courteous, cautious De Villiers Graaff. Graaff, who had lost his Hottentot's Holland seat in the recent election, returned to the new parliament as the member for Rondebosch after Colonel Pilkington Jordan, the sitting member, resigned to take up a seat in the Senate.

The session had only just got into its stride when on 21 August Strijdom, who had been ailing during the recess, died suddenly of a heart attack. The new leader of the NP, who would become the prime minister of South Africa, was Dr Hendrik Frensch Verwoerd, the Minister of Native Affairs. Verwoerd was born in the Netherlands, attended a primary school in Rhodesia before coming to South Africa while still a child, and received a doctorate in applied psychology from Stellenbosch University. He had a reputation for being a hardliner Afrikaner nationalist, and for holding views on the race issue with fundamentalist fervour.

In the late 1930s he went to Cape Town harbour to protest against the arrival of Jews from Europe. In 1947, as the editor of *Die Transvaler*, he refused to publish any reference to the three-month long visit to South Africa of King George VI and *Queen Elizabeth* and their two princess daughters.

As the Minister of Native Affairs he had initiated the Tomlinson Commission, which was to investigate and recommend on the development and the future role of the Bantu homelands. He was the driving force behind both the concept and the enforcement of Bantu Education, and while everyone realised he would be a force to reckon with, no-one foresaw the impact that he was going to make on politics and history in South Africa.

Within the UP caucus there was a strange, almost eerie silence – a general expectation that at some stage the caucus would review the recent election in the light of the disastrous result for the party, and discuss the way forward. Yet no such review or discussion was encouraged, or asked for, by the leadership. In the last week of the session Andrew Brown, a new member who was a prominent businessman and financier from Johannesburg, asked whether there was to be an opportunity to review the situation. Graaff responded, saying he intended to appoint a recess committee to examine ways and means of propagating UP policy. He felt there was nothing basically wrong, but that we had been unsuccessful in presenting it to the public.

In due course Graaff appointed this committee, comprising Gray Hughes, Hamilton Russell, Zach de Beer, Vause Raw, John Cope and Boris Wilson. Its work proved fruitless: the majority of its members argued that before it could decide on how to present UP policy, it had to know what the policy was. By this they meant, not only where the party stood, but also where it was heading and what the implications would be when applied in the dynamic situation of a multiracial South Africa. In the end the members, with the exception of Raw, reached agreement that in broad terms the UP would have to face up to the implications of South Africa being a multiracial country, and that this would require a forward-looking interpretation being placed on its policy.

Raw's dissent did not surprise me. In discussions I had had with him, he had made it clear that while he had a less restricted view on Coloured political representation, 'over his dead body' would he agree to the UP advocating any extension of the franchise to natives. In January 1959 Graaff said that in view of the fact that the committee could not reach agreement, he would not respond on its findings, or take the matter further.

Meanwhile, Dr Verwoerd's political hypothesis was straightforward. It would not be possible through discrimination, in the form either of *baasskap* or the UP's policy of white leadership with justice, to maintain political domination of a minority over a majority in South Africa. On the other hand, he asserted, extending political rights to the majority in a multiracial parliament would inevitably lead to the swamping of whites.

Separate development – what some would call 'grand apartheid' – would create 'independent homelands' where blacks who were to be deprived of their South African citizenship could exercise their political rights separately.

He created separate universities for blacks, Coloureds and Indians. Existing universities would become white by closing their doors to blacks, Coloureds and Indians. Then he abolished the three native representatives, and in so doing deprived blacks, who formed the majority of the population, of all representation in parliament.

Japie Basson, a member of the NP, voiced his objection to the removal of the native representatives before the establishment of independent black states. He was expelled from the NP and subsequently formed the National Union. The fact that blacks were stripped of all representation in parliament was based on Verwoerd's concept that in due course they would also be stripped of their South African citizenship. This caused deep resentment among black South Africans, and strengthened their resolve to struggle for full and equal citizenship.

I was given the opportunity to express my strong feelings on the matter in parliament, and at the same time hone my debating skills. By the time the debates were over, I felt that I was no longer a parliamentary novice. A different kind of debate was taking place in the ranks of the UP and especially within its parliamentary caucus. Verwoerd's 'New Vision' for South Africa, as set out in a speech on 27 January, gave focus to progressive members of our caucus, not so much on immediate franchise arrangements, but on the direction for their alternative vision for South Africa. It posed questions to the UP: if you reject the concept of political representation evolving towards separation, do you accept the alternative, that representation must take place within multiracial structures? Do you believe that within those structures you can maintain black participation on the basis of discrimination?

In the caucus there was general agreement that Graaff should reply to Verwoerd. He would do so towards the end of the session. He said that in the mean time it would be helpful to him and the party if each member of caucus would say what he or she thought of UP policy and how it should be presented. To avoid giving the impression that the caucus was having a series of special meetings, the Native Affairs Group, which met each Tuesday morning, should be expanded to include all members of the caucus so that discussion on policy could be continued.

The impact of the discussions at these meetings over the next three-and-a-half months was disastrous for the UP. There was a fundamental cleavage in the caucus on the basic approach to the race issue. Thus, for instance, Douglas Mitchell said: 'Let's stop beating about the bush, I'm in the party because it stands for *baasskap*.' When challenged, he replied: 'The white man will stay the political boss in South Africa.' On the other hand Douglas Smit, a former secretary of native affairs, said: 'I'm not going to press the issue, but I'm one of those old Cape members who believes in equal rights for all civilised people. You should have some kind of standard economically, socially and politically. People who pass that standard should be fully accepted.' Other views were heard as well.

On 5 May when the debate on the prime minister's vote took place, it was anticipated that Graaff would spell out the UP alternative to Verwoerd's vision. He did not do this. Instead he challenged Verwoerd on the immorality of his policy in relation to the political rights of Coloured citizens. During the course of the interaction on this issue, UP policy on the Coloured vote emerged as follows:

- The UP would restore to the common roll those Coloured persons in the Cape Province and Natal who had been removed from it.
- Registration of further Coloured voters onto the common roll would be on the basis of higher qualifications to be negotiated with Coloured leaders.
- The vote on the common roll in the House of Assembly would not be extended to the Transvaal or the Orange Free State. Coloured people in those provinces would have representation in the Senate on a separate voters' roll.
- There would be no extension of voting rights to Coloured women.
- In both the Senate and House of Assembly Coloured representatives would be white.

Graaff's failure to respond to Verwoerd on the key issue of separate development or multiracialism, and his conservative presentation of UP policy for Coloureds, did nothing to resolve UP tensions in the caucus. There were two specific and highly divisive issues.

One was that of land for the native reserves; and the other was the common roll as a form of representation in parliament. It was not the policy of the UP to have a common roll as a basis of representation for all citizens of all races in parliament. However, the UP's policy did permit persons who believed in the common roll to be members of the party and within the party to propagate the common roll as a policy.

The land issue went back to 1936 when the 'natives' were removed from the common roll in the Cape Province and Natal. At that time a commitment was made by the UP government to purchase some fifteen million morgen of land for the South African Native Trust for use by natives in the South African Native Trust, later to become the Bantu Trust, and still later the South African Development Trust. The fact was that by 1959, 23 years later, much of that land had not been purchased. The UP, in government, had been under regular attack from the NP for 'giving white land' to the 'natives'.

Before the session adjourned in June, Graaff presented the caucus with his policy formulation. This was essentially that the UP would agree to increase the number of native representatives in the House of Assembly from three to six, but they would continue to be white. Divisions deepened and tempers were frayed. In this tense atmosphere caucus adjourned for the parliamentary recess, and the party started preparing for the national congress which was due to take place in Bloemfontein on 14 August.

The Bloemfontein Congress, July 1959

After the session Zach and I spent a lot of time analysing the events of the past few months, and planning ahead for the congress scheduled for August. Our assessment was that the situation in the UP was grave. Not only were there serious policy and personality clashes, but under Graaff's leadership the party seemed unwilling to come to terms, or incapable of coming to terms, with the changed environment caused by its drubbing at the last election, the election of Verwoerd, and increasing restiveness and resistance of the non-white communities. Pressures for change, internal and external, were building up in Africa, the Commonwealth and the United Nations, and among South Africa's own black citizens. While Coloured, Indian and black people were still calling for negotiations, it was clear that the time for finding a peaceful solution was starting to run out.

Our assessment of what was likely to happen at the UP congress was threefold. Firstly, it was unlikely that those progressive members who were not part of a structured group would try and get the UP to change the details of its policy in a liberal direction.

Secondly, if the policy resolutions put to congress were in line with the recommendations that Graaff had discussed with caucus, they would be adopted. There would be some criticism in the debate, and some opposition to aspects of these resolutions, but in themselves they would not cause any members to break away from the party.

Thirdly, should the conservatives, led by Mitchell and Steenkamp, force the issues of the common roll or the purchase of land to the vote, and succeed in having them accepted as UP policy, we would resign; and we had good reason to believe that a number of our other progressive colleagues would do likewise.

The mobilisation of the conservatives, under Vause Raw's direction, led us to the opinion that the last option was precisely what Mitchell and Steenkamp planned. Not that they wanted to drive all the progressives out of the party: they wanted to put the progressives in their place, so that the fractious debate over policy would come to an end, and the party could project itself as truly conservative. For them, a limited purge of progressive members would suffice. Word had it that they had John Cope, Helen Suzman and Boris Wilson in their sights, with Ronald Butcher from Natal to satisfy Mitchell's extreme dislike of him.

Graaff was fully aware of the tactics that the conservatives were putting into place and of the consequences should the UP turn backward.

Harry Oppenheimer, who remained a good friend of Graaff throughout these troubled times, became aware of the moves to close the party to those who believed in a common roll. At one stage Oppenheimer came to Cape Town to discuss this with Graaff and subsequently wrote a letter to him in which he said he hoped that the UP would overcome these difficulties. However, he made it quite clear to Graaff that if at any time the UP did slam the door on the common roll, he, Harry Oppenheimer, would be forced to stand outside the UP.

Graaff was concerned that Zach and I were not being as amenable as he would have liked. He tried to persuade Oppenheimer to get us to toe the line – and Oppenheimer said he would do no such thing. Indeed, he made it clear that he was as upset as were Zach and I, and shared our points of view. One associated event was that Graaff asked Zach to write a memorandum giving the reasons why the party leader should oppose Mitchell's land resolution. Zach did so, and added 'that I hold extremely strong views on this and that should the land resolution be passed as proposed by Mitchell, I will consider it a backward step which will cause me to leave the party.'

Zach and I kept in close touch with Jan Steytler, Cape provincial leader of the UP. He was a medical doctor and farmed in the Queenstown area of the Eastern Cape. A down-to-earth, straight-speaking politician, he took a fundamentalist approach to the great racial issue facing South Africans: his guiding premise was: 'Racism is wrong', and discrimination on the basis of race must come to an end.' As one of the four provincial chairmen who, with Graaff, formed the UP leader's guiding commit- tee, Steytler had frequent meetings with Graaff – and as the congress approached, Graaff was under no illusions where Steytler stood on the common roll and land is- sues.

During my first years as an MP, I sensed that Graaff saw Zach and me as young men who should be groomed for leading roles in politics. I felt able to express my concern at the direction the UP was taking, pointing out that the group of young people who had played an active part in the 1958 election had decided they could not work for the UP in the 1959 provincial election. I mentioned that I had letters of resignation from members who were disillusioned with the increasingly conserva- tive tenor of Graaff's speeches. I also told Graaff of the progressive mood among a student's study group at Stellenbosch which I addressed on 'a United Party view of the future', at the conclusion of which the students said they had enjoyed my pres- entation, but that it was very different from the conservative projections Graaff was making.

To cap this, the next morning I received a letter of resignation from Len Read, my excellent constituency chairman, who some years later became a most respected reg- istrar of the University of Cape Town. Read's reason was the same – the conservative direction in which Graaff was taking the UP. I put it to Graaff that if he was indeed trying to move the UP in a conservative direction, he must accept responsibility for the resignation of Read and others. In a quiet matter-of-fact response Graaff said he was quite prepared to accept that responsibility.

A week before the congress, Zach, who had been working with Marais Steyn on Graaff's speech, told me that the leader had decided the congress should not proceed with the land resolution, and further that neither he nor the head committee should introduce a resolution on the common roll. We firmly believed Graaff had decided the risk of a split was too great, and he would squash any resolution on either matter.

Indeed, a couple of days before the congress, we met Victor Norton, editor of the *Cape Times*, at the Civil Service Club. Norton asked us whether we foresaw any serious problems. In the light of Graaff's decision to prevent the common roll and land issues coming to a head, we did not anticipate there would be – so as a result of these comments, there was no *Cape Times* reporter at the congress!

At Steytler's suggestion we travelled to Bloemfontein via Queenstown, where we met him at his farm. He brought us up to date with developments in the committees on which he served as leader of the UP in the Cape Province. It also gave us the opportunity of assessing the situation developing inside the party, and the impact this could have on proceedings at the congress.

The day before the congress, we attended a meeting of the head committee, a large body comprising MPs, senators and a representative from each constituency. This committee's function was to run through the agenda and any resolutions that had been received, and decide whether there were any items on which it should intervene. It also considered matters on which it should introduce resolutions or amendments. Graaff made it clear he was opposed to the land resolution to be proposed by Mitchell, and asked Mitchell not to proceed; but Mitchell was adamant, and Graaff stated he would oppose it. Mitchell and his conservatives seemed determined to have their way. A showdown loomed.

Session in crisis

There were no resolutions on the common roll from either the central executive or the head committee. However, there was one from a small party branch in the rural constituency of Heilbron in the Orange Free State, to the effect that 'this congress does not believe that the common roll is the correct policy for the representation of the Native people'. It was decided that the branch could move the resolution if it so wished, but that the head committee would not be associated with it.

In introducing the debate on the policy motions, Graaff repeated much of what he had said in parliament in response to Verwoerd. In essence, his five points of UP policy were:

- The rejection of Bantustans.
- The need for all groups to be represented in the central legislature.
- An increase in the number of native representatives in the House of Assembly from three to eight.
- The implementation of the 1936 Act that made provision for six native representatives in the Senate.

· That all these representatives be white.

Without giving advance notice, Louis Steenkamp drew attention to the motion on the common roll that Heilbron had placed on the agenda. He proposed it be considered at the same time as the discussion on Graaff's five policy points. Then, after Graaff had responded by saying that he thought such a procedure would be fair, Steenkamp proceeded to propose a formal resolution to the effect that 'this congress welcomes the statement by the leader of the party, that political representation for native people in the future must be on the basis of a separate roll and not on the basis of a common roll.'

In fact, Graaff had not made any reference to a common roll and had not ventured into the issue of how political representation should evolve in the future. Furthermore, Steenkamp's move to link the common roll to Graaff's speech was contrary to the attitude adopted by the head committee – a clear indication of the strategy he was going to adopt at the congress.

As the first speaker after Steenkamp, I called for a rejection of his resolution. I was not pressing for congress as a whole to embrace the common roll, but pointed out that there were a number of members, of whom I was one, who believed in this form of representation, and that it was our constitutional right to do so. Steenkamp's resolution would deny us this right and close the door to the common roll in the future.

My speech turned out to be the signal for an all-out onslaught on the 'liberals' in the party. Conservative speaker after speaker said that people who believed in the common roll should not be members of the party. Members such as Suzman, Cope and Boris Wilson were singled out. At a late stage, Graaff intervened and appealed to delegates to calm down and to accept one another's *bona fides*, whereupon Mitchell waded in again.

Late the following morning Graaff, in winding up the debate, asked for support for his five-point resolution. He went on to ask for support for Steenkamp's resolution on the basis that his interpretation of the words 'in the future' meant that the resolution bound the UP not to advocate a common roll – unless and until a future congress decided otherwise. It was obvious that this interpretation was specious, since every resolution of congress was binding unless and until a future congress decided otherwise.

Each of Graaff's points was approved by an overwhelming majority. Steenkamp's resolution was put separately and approved by about 80% of the votes.

Had the congress concluded its business and closed at that stage it was probable that some individual members would have resigned during the next few days but that there would not have been immediate mass resignations from the party. However, what had happened was not enough for Mitchell. He moved his 'land resolution' in an impassioned speech, conjured up the picture of native 'impis' marching, of women being raped, and urged that we 'look [at] what is happening in other parts of Africa'. He added that in terms of policy, 'as long as the Nationalist government is in power … the UP is opposed to spending any more on the purchase of land for the natives'. Zach commented to me that Mitchell and Steenkamp had been making similar speeches long before Verwoerd came forward with his Bantustan policy.

At the conclusion of the debate, Graaff asked delegates not to support Mitchell's motion. He said that while they might gain some political advantage, there were people who believed a moral issue was involved. The delegates voted two to one for Mitchell and against Graaff. Zach and I, sitting near the back, realised that we had come to our personal political Rubicons. We were due to fly back to Cape Town that evening but decided to cancel and stay in Bloemfontein to work out our next step. Zach left the hall to cancel our flights and, while I was sitting on my own, an extremely agitated Sydney Waterson came up to me and said: 'Look, Colin, I don't care what you fellows are going to do, but I'm getting out of the party over this.'

Waterson was one of the most senior UP MPs, having been elected to parliament as the same time as Harry Lawrence in 1929, and having served in the cabinet of General Smuts. I told him what Zach and I had decided. Waterson said he was going to quit the congress, but before doing so he would tell Graaff that he was leaving the party. He walked up to Graaff, who was on the platform, and after a brief discussion rejoined me and Zach, who had returned. Then he left the hall – but first agreed to meet Zach and me at the Bloemfontein Club once the congress had adjourned.

We sent a note to Steytler telling him that we had arranged to meet Waterson, and got a note back asking us to meet him in the Maitland Hotel at 6.30 pm. In the foyer we came across Townley Williams, Ray Swart and Clive van Ryneveld – all as upset as we were. We told them of the 6.30 pm meeting in the Maitland Hotel. Douglas Smit was equally agitated, but muttered: 'I'm angry. But I'm not going to let Douglas Mitchell drive me out of the party!' An angry Helen Suzman said: 'I'll be there.'

At the Bloemfontein Club, where Waterson was waiting for us, Hamilton Russell joined us. Waterson said to Russell: 'Hammo, I was party to the 1936 settlement. It was a bad thing we did. We took the votes from those people; now I'm told that I'm not going to give them the land we promised them. It may be easy for these other younger fellows, but I'm determined on this issue. I am out.'

Russell said he was out in any case. He sat to one side and wrote a note which he handed to Zach, and asked him to give it to Graaff. Then he departed for Cape Town.

When we joined Steytler at the Maitland Hotel we were not clear what our next step would be; however, we agreed that we would have to issue a public statement that we could not accept the land resolution, and decided to tell Graaff what we intended doing. Zach, who had given Russell's letter to Graaff when they bumped into each other on the steps of the club, pointed out that Graaff was on his way to the airport to catch his flight back to Cape Town. We decided Steytler and Waterson would dash to the airport to see Graaff before he flew out. Upon their return an hour or so later, Steytler and Waterson reported that they had told Graaff that they had come on behalf of a number of members who were extremely upset at the tenor of the congress and the resolutions that were passed. They put it to Graaff that he should not leave for Cape Town but stay in Bloemfontein in order to discuss the situation with these members. Graaff asked them to use their influence to persuade the objectors not to do anything until they could see him in Cape Town the following week. Steytler and Waterson said they could not guarantee this.

Graaff decided to fly on while Steytler and Waterson returned to the Maitland. The die was cast.

The breakaway from the United Party commences

When Steytler, Waterson, Helen, Zach, Williams, Swart, Van Ryneveld, Jackie Beck (a Cape MPC) and Steytler's brother Willie and I met that evening in room 309 at the Maitland Hotel, it was the first time we had done so as a group. We did not have a collective view on any steps we would take; yet it soon became clear that none of us would accept the land resolution, and that all believed we should make a public statement to this effect. Waterson was most insistent on rejecting the land resolution, and agreed that the statement would be issued in his name, after which we would each endorse it.

We tried to contact Percy Plewman, our MP colleague from Johannesburg North, whom we knew would also refuse to accept the land resolution. He was not available to meet us. We did contact Leo Boyd, a member of Natal provincial executive committee, and a rival to Douglas Mitchell for leadership of the UP in Natal. He joined us within a few minutes – but was both cautious and meticulous by nature, and we had to revisit the decision and go through the draft statement word by word before Boyd felt he could join us.

Helen Suzman, who was anxious – once it had been agreed to issue a statement – to leave for Johannesburg, signed at the bottom of the page on which the statement would be written, and departed saying: 'I know what it is going to be. I'm on my way.'

Well after midnight the statement, written in Zach de Beer's well-rounded handwriting, was agreed to, signed by those present, and issued to the press: we issued it to Bunny Neame, the *Rand Daily Mail*'s political correspondent. It read: 'The United Party congress today took the decision to oppose further purchases of land for native settlement by the present government. This is a clear breach of the promise given by the [UP] in 1936 and as such a backward step from the 1954 statement of … policy. We cannot accept this decision; we shall take the earliest opportunity of seeing Sir de Villiers Graaff and discussing with him our future position within the party.

'We are deeply disturbed by the whole undertone of congress, which in our opinion failed to face up to the increasingly imperative problems of our multiracial country. We have had no opportunity of consulting with other party members who may share our views.'

The following morning, most newspapers around the country carried front-page reports on the statement and the preceding rumpus at the congress. Within a few hours of the news breaking, four more UP members of parliament, John Cope, Ronald Butcher, Prof. 'Sakkies' Fourie and Boris Wilson, and some members of provincial councils and office-bearers of the UP, endorsed our rejection of the land resolution.

Zach and I decided the next morning to go to Johannesburg before returning to Cape Town. We wanted to have discussions with the press as well as with key UP supporters who were not at the congress. In particular we wanted to meet Harry Oppenheimer, who was due back in Johannesburg after a visit to Rhodesia. Zach went by air. I followed by car with Percy Plewman, who was distressed that he had not been available to sign the statement. Had he not been at a cinema he would have signed.

During our journey, Plewman expressed thoughtful views on the need to have a liberal approach to national problems. He felt he had an obligation to inform certain key supporters of his views before announcing them to the press. We dropped him at his home and he said he would contact us in the morning. But then he said he 'needed more time'. It became clear that Plewman was not going to associate with us: he remained in the UP and three years later was sent to Port Elizabeth to oppose Jan Steytler, who became the leader of the Progressive Party and eventually stood in Port Elizabeth South in the next election. Ironically, Plewman, who would have been on Steytler's side had he not been at the cinema in Bloemfontein, defeated Steytler.

Zach and I spent the morning at Suzman's home where we had discussions with key members of the press, including Laurence Gandar, editor of the *Rand Daily Mail*, and Joel Mervis, editor of the *Sunday Times*.

I flew back to Cape Town where to my surprise I was met by about a hundred cheering supporters. From the airport Joyce and I went back to our Pinelands home, which, with Steytler's arrival later that afternoon, became the communications centre for the dissenting group. It soon became clear that Graaff and his loyalist colleagues were fighting back vigorously. Mitchell, upon reading our statement in the press, demanded that every UP MP and MPC in Natal send a telegram of support to Graaff. Then Waterson, who had agreed to see key people on our behalf, did not do so. His appearance was dejected; and he told us he did not want to see Graaff as part of a three-man delegation but would see him on his own. There was no fight left in him.

On Monday morning Waterson saw Graaff, after which it was apparent that he was not going to stand by his rejection of the congress resolution. Steytler saw Graaff and a couple of hours later announced his resignation from the party. This triggered off similar announcements by Zach, Ray Swart, and Townley Williams who was in Durban. They came in for some criticism for not having first stated their case to Graaff. Cope, Wilson and Suzman, who had flown to Cape Town, also resigned after seeing Graaff.

When I saw Graaff I did not resign immediately; I was due to meet my Pinelands constituency committee that evening, and had I resigned before then would not have had the opportunity to put my reasons for opposing the congress resolution. Graaff, who had his arm in a sling following a riding accident, looked far from his cheerful self. He opened the discussion: 'Colin, what have you done? Why did you issue that statement?'

I responded: 'Why did you leave Bloemfontein? You should have realised the seriousness of the situation.'

Graaff replied that after speaking to Waterson and Steytler at the airport, he realised there were a number of disgruntled members – but he did not think they would take this kind of action, which must inevitably lead to their expulsion. I could not help feeling that Graaff had either misjudged the seriousness of the situation or else, in spite of the seriousness, believed that loyalty to him would prevent us from acting.

I pointed out that I had been serious when I attacked Steenkamp's resolution. Graaff's reply was that was why he had given congress his personal interpretation of the Steenkamp resolution. I then said that I understood that Zach, in a memorandum to him, had said that if congress passed the Mitchell land resolution, he, De Beer, would consider this a backward step that would force him out of the party. Graaff responded that he had asked Zach to prepare a memorandum presenting the strongest case against the resolution, although 'I thought he was pitching his case a little high'. I pointed out to Graaff that while he was sitting next to Steytler on the platform, Steytler had asked him to stop the resolution since it would split the party and he would have to leave.

Graaff said: 'Steytler did say something to that effect but I thought that he was terribly agitated.'

As for Waterson, he had told me that when the resolution was passed he was going to resign: 'He left me and went up to the platform where I saw him speaking to you and I presumed he told you what he was going to do.'

Graaff said: 'Yes, Sydney Waterson did speak to me – but frankly he was so flushed and agitated that I thought that he might have been drinking.'

I summed up: 'There were four people who each in his own way had emphasised to you the seriousness of the situation, yet your reaction was to tell them that they could see you in Cape Town in a few days' time.'

I did not tell Graaff that I knew Oppenheimer had written to him before the congress informing him that he, Harry, would have to leave the UP should the congress close the door on the common roll.

At the meeting of the combined Pinelands committees of the UP that evening I stated my case. Lionel Murray, who had not been present at the congress, stated the case presented by Graaff. Questions were asked and answers given. On instructions from Graaff the chairman announced that no resolutions would be put. The meeting concluded with me confirming that whatever the consequences might be, I would adhere to the statement we had made in Bloemfontein.

7

The Progressive Party is formed

The following day I confirmed to Graaff that I remained committed to rejecting the congress resolution, and resigned from the UP. That same day, while still in Cape Town, Steytler telephoned Prof. ZK Matthews of Fort Hare to get an informed opinion on the land issue from a respected black South African. Among the points they touched on were the following:

· Earlier, the UP had passed a motion that further purchases of land for 'native' occupation under the 1936 Act should be suspended while the National Party was in power and wished to use this land to add to its Bantustans. Matthews responded to the effect that 'the economy of South Africa is indivisible, and … territorial apartheid is impossible from an economic point of view'.
· Asked whether the African people attached special importance to the 1936 undertaking to purchase 7,5 million morgen of land for occupation, Matthews answered in the affirmative, adding that 'My people feel that they have insufficient land. They have been promised more land by the white people and they would regard any departure from this promise as a breach of the white man's word.' The need, he emphasised, was 'for more land, not Bantustans'.

By Tuesday, all the so-called 'progressives' in the UP's parliamentary caucus, barring Clive van Ryneveld, had resigned. A Rhodes Scholar, outstanding sportsman, and a younger member of the Cape Town establishment with a good personal relationship with Graaff, Clive was under tremendous pressure from the leader. That morning, Tony Delius, the parliamentary correspondent of the *Cape Times*, showed Steytler a statement Van Ryneveld was about to issue to the press: it took the form of a humiliating apology. Steytler was so furious with Graaff for pressuring Van Ryneveld into issuing this statement that even though he no longer had any status within the UP, he phoned Graaff and told him that common decency demanded the statement be amended.

Two mornings later, I had a call from Zach to say that Van Ryneveld, having agonised over the matter, had decided to resign from the UP and to join the yet-to-be-formed Progressive Party. He had to endure some immediate embarrassment, but overcame this and went on to do thorough and insightful work as an MP in the PP, concentrating on the disaster of Verwoerd's Bantustans.

Waterson, who might have teamed up with the Progressives, withdrew his objection to the 'land resolution' and stayed on in the UP. Hamilton Russell framed his letter of resignation to Graaff in the form of an 'offer to resign' – and in the circumstances Graaff chose not to accept it. Russell stayed on in the UP until 1963 when he resigned from the party and from parliament over its support for the draconian 90-day detention bill. He subsequently joined the Progressives, and although he never returned to parliament, he played a prominent PP role in the Cape Peninsula.

That left Harry Lawrence, in Italy with his wife Jean and their two sons. He had missed the UP congress. Some of his colleagues had heard him speaking out for more realism and vision; some, including Graaff, had sensed Lawrence's growing frustration with the UP's apparent unwillingness to face up to the realities of South Africa as a multiracial country. Most people saw him as a spirited fighter, a great parliamentarian, and a loyal party man. After all, he had served in the UP and its predecessor, the South African Party, since 1929 when he was elected MP for Salt River. He had been a cabinet minister in successive UP governments under Hertzog and Smuts from 1938 to 1948. In 1938, when first appointed to the cabinet at the age of 36, he was the youngest person ever in such a post and was described as 'the youngest minister in the Empire'. So the speculation was: 'What is Harry going to do? On whose side is he going to be?'

Zach and I were confident he would be with us in rejecting the congress resolution; as the result of a confidential conversation we had had with Lawrence at his home shortly before he departed for overseas, however, we realised it would be wrong to say anything in public before he himself had done so.

The first word from Harry came on Sunday morning, 30 August, when he phoned Brenthurst, Harry and Bridget Oppenheimer's home in Johannesburg, where Zach and I happened to be lunching. Lawrence asked Oppenheimer to tell Zach and me that we should not worry about him. However, we should leave it to him to handle the matter in his own way. Public speculation on his position continued until 16 September, when he issued a statement from London in which he indicated his intention to resign, but stated that he would not take the final step until he had returned to South Africa. Some six weeks later, he and Jean arrived back at Cape Town harbour to be met by a large and excited contingent of 'progressives'. The following evening, at what turned out to be a very hostile meeting of his UP constituency committee, Lawrence announced his resignation.

It was wonderful for Zach and me to have this respected parliamentarian, together with his wife, working with us in Cape Town. For us younger people, the decision to resign had primarily political consequences; for the Lawrences it would mean losing friends and severing loyalties built up over years of distinguished public service. It would mean starting afresh on a hard new road in a hostile environment, at a stage and an age when they would be entitled to enjoy a leisurely retirement.

As was generally anticipated, Harry Oppenheimer, on his return from Southern Rhodesia, contacted Graaff to inform him that in view of the decision of congress to close the door on the common roll he would have to resign from the UP. On 20 August, following a public statement by Graaff on the dispute, Steytler issued a statement on behalf of the ten who had resigned from the UP. He repeated our total rejection of the land resolution:

'We cannot go back on the solemn undertaking in the 1936 Settlement to buy further land for the Bantu people in South Africa because of some hypothetical change, which may come about in the status of the native areas in the far distant future. The buying of land is not only necessary to fulfil the pledge of 1936, but it is essential for the task of rehabilitating the Bantu reserves. We believe the time has come when white people should stop making important decisions affecting non-white people without regard to how the latter think or feel ... [W]e have come to the conclusion that the temper of the Bloemfontein Congress showed a complete unwillingness on the part of most delegates to face up to the challenge of contemporary events here and in the rest of Africa.'

Ten days after the UP congress, a number of us who had resigned met in Johannesburg at Helen Suzman's home. Among us were 11 MPs, five MPCs, four candidates nominated to contest the provincial elections, plus a few individuals who had been senior office-bearers in the UP. While some of us knew one another from caucus or party activities, many were making acquaintance for the first time. While all had been frustrated with the UP, none of us had anticipated that we would soon be out of the UP and meeting to decide on the new road ahead.

We reviewed the situation and developed plans. An interim steering committee, under the chairmanship of Jan Steytler, was appointed – charged with the responsibility of making arrangements to establish a new political party. Three sub-committees were established to develop policies on constitutional and franchise matters, financial matters and race relations. The sub-committees were to operate in Johannesburg, Cape Town and Durban, and report back to the interim steering committee.

At the conclusion of our weekend meeting, we stated that the UP had breached a solemn undertaking, and added: 'We believe it to be our duty to continue our service to South Africa, outside the ranks of the UP, convinced as we are that South Africa must face up more squarely than it has in the past to the problems flowing from the multiracial composition of the nation.' Accordingly, we would proceed to form a new political party based on 'our duty to maintain Western civilisation and to extend it progressively to all the peoples of South Africa'. There had to be increasing participation by all races in the economic and political life of the country, and the removal of restrictions that prevented participation. This development would take place through co-operation based on consultation, and recognition of individual aspirations as well as group sentiments; and the right of groups to maintain their own character.

I had decided I should hold a meeting to report back to my Pinelands constituents on recent events and the decisions I had taken. Some of my constituents, who liked me as a 'son of Pinelands', were bemused and confused by events, and I wanted to explain the rationale for, and the morality of, my decisions: to get them on my side.

As I walked down the central aisle of the St Stephens church hall to take my place on the platform there were some cheers and some jeers and hisses, yet considering all the circumstances the audience was relatively subdued. I explained that this was not a formal meeting organised by a party, but a gathering, based on an invitation from me to my constituents. There would be no chairman, and no motions would be put at the conclusion of proceedings. I told them that the land resolution was a breach of a solemn pledge given by a white South African government to black South Africans, taken without any consultation with them. I understood the consequences of the stand I had taken, and had a responsibility to my country that was greater than my loyalty to a party.

A long question-and-answer session followed. There was some heckling and some interjection – in the main serious, and reflecting the desire of many of those present to get more information on an issue with which they were still grappling. Had a vote been put I might well have got a vote of confidence, albeit by a small margin, but I was sure that I gained more by keeping the meeting informal and personal and by not pressing people to come to a conclusion before having had time to dwell on the issue.

I had two immediate organisational priorities. The one was to secure a base for myself and the newly formed Progressive Group in Pinelands. This I did with the help of a number of individuals who had been key members of the UP branch committees, plus a number of recruits interested in political developments. Joyce, who was not by nature a political creature, but had an intuitive sense of assessing what was right and what wrong, blossomed into one of the most ardent and effective supporters of our cause. Joyce had a superb way with people; her gentle yet firm and persuasive manner offset some of the gruffness and intolerance I tended to display at times.

The second organisational priority, which I shared with Zach, was to expand the very small foothold that the Progressive Group had in the Cape Peninsula. This was more difficult. The UP public representatives of MPs, MPCs and city councillors outnumbered us, even more so for the six months of the year when parliament sat. The Graaff family had for generations been a prominent component of the Cape Town establishment, whose members had for decades been admirers of General Smuts and ardent supporters of his United Party. So it was important to get the sympathy, and possibly the support, of the two English-language daily newspapers, the *Cape Times* and the *Cape Argus*.

Zach and I were on good terms with the editor of the *Times*, Victor Norton. He shared our philosophy and supported the morality of the action we had taken. However, he was a close friend of Graaff, and over the years his newspaper had become embedded in the ethos of the Cape Town establishment and the UP. This ambivalence was reflected in the qualified support he gave to the new progressive initiative.

Morris Broughton of the *Argus* was a different kind of person, less an integral part of the Cape Town establishment and not as close to Graaff as Norton. He was overseas at the time of the breakaway, and the acting editor trod water until he returned. Zach and I were able to ensure that a detailed memorandum was on top of the documents on Broughton's desk when he returned. The *Cape Argus* came out strongly in our support, and was scathing in its criticism of the behaviour of the UP at Bloemfontein.

By November, when the inaugural congress was held, the Progressive Group was functioning on a firm basis in the Western Cape. It had an office in Cape Town, branches in the Peninsula, and contacts in a number of rural towns. While the UP's hold on the Cape Town establishment had not been broken, it had been significantly eroded. The PP's voluntary workforce comprised not only people who had resigned from the UP, but many from outside the ranks of the UP who saw the progressive movement as constructive and worth working for. The congress was attended by 200 delegates and 150 observers, and took place in the Cranbrooke Hotel in Johannesburg on 13 and 14 November 1959. In an atmosphere laden with enthusiasm and emotion the delegates resolved unanimously to form the Progressive Party of South Africa based on the following principles:

· The maintenance and extension of the values of Western civilisation; the protection of fundamental human rights; and the safeguarding of the dignity and worth of the human person, irrespective of race, colour or creed.
· The assurance that no citizen of the Union of South Africa would be debarred on the grounds of race, religion, language or sex, from making the contribution to our national life of which he or she might be capable.
· The recognition that in the Union of South Africa there was one nation which embraced various groups differing in race, religion, language and traditions; that each group was entitled to the protection of these things and to participation in the government of the nation; and that understanding, tolerance and goodwill between the different groups must be fostered.
· The maintenance of the rule of law.
· The promotion of social progress and improvement of living standards through the energetic development of a modern economy based on free enterprise, whereby the national resources of men and materials could be fully utilised.
· The promotion of friendly relations with other nations, more particularly those who shared the heritage of Western civilisation.

Jan Steytler was elected leader, and Harry Lawrence chairman of the party. All the public representatives who had resigned from the UP, with the exception of 'Sakkies'

Fourie, were elected to the national executive. Fourie, a committed pro-republican, decided that, in view of the congress's decision to oppose the proposed republic, he would not be able to join the PP; but he co-operated with Progressive MPs in the ensuing sessions of parliament, and, as soon as the republican issue was resolved in 1961, joined the PP and stood as its candidate in Sea Point.

Other members on the national executive were Max Borkum, Pieter de Kock, Dr Bernard Friedman, Murray Hofmeyr, Dr Ellen Helman, Harold Marcus, Morris Mayers and Ralph Parrott from the Transvaal; Basil Muir from Border; Prof. Hansi Pollak from Natal; and Jack Bleiman, Ian Gordon-Forbes and Donald Molteno from the Western Cape.

There could be no going back – but we knew that to develop the PP into a viable entity before the next general election in 1963 would be difficult and demanding.

8

Another year of trauma
1960

After the political traumas of 1959, 1960 commenced quietly. In the Western Cape, the Progressive Party was in buoyant mood: the formation of the party had been reasonably well received by the press. Lawrence was back in Cape Town. Walter Stanford, one of the three native representatives in parliament as a member of the Liberal Party, who was well known and well liked in the Cape, had resigned from the LP and joined the PP.

Other prominent Cape liberals who joined us were Gerald Gordon, Leonard Thompson and Jack Causton. Jan Botha was appointed regional director. Zach and I had got to know Botha when he was the editor of the Afrikaans UP-supporting weekly, *Die Weekblad*. He had attended the Bloemfontein congress as an observer, and was shocked by what he had seen and heard. At the Maitland Hotel after the congress, he bumped into Steytler, Zach and me; Steytler asked him whether, if we decided to break away from the UP, he would work for us. Botha replied: 'I'm not sure about that, but after what happened … I will certainly not be able to stay in the UP.'

There was a practical problem: we could not assure Botha of an adequate regular income. However, Botha had an agreement with David Marais, a friend and cartoonist who worked for the *Cape Times*, to publish his cartoons annually; and since Botha was keen to go into publishing, this was the basis on which we agreed he could proceed while also working for the PP. He and Marais were later priced out of the market when the *Cape Times* asserted its right to publish the cartoons.

The parliamentary session opened sedately, with 12 PP members, plus 'Sakkies' Fourie as an independent, taking up their seats on the rearranged opposition benches. During the no-confidence debate, Verwoerd surprised everyone by announcing a referendum of white voters on the issue of South Africa becoming a republic. On 5 February, Jan Steytler moved the following motion encapsulating the essence of the PP's constitutional thinking. It was that the PP:
- accepted the permanent multiracial character of the South African nation and society, and accordingly rejected any policy designed to partition the Union; and that
- to establish our multiracial state on a stable and durable basis, a new constitution was needed that contained adequate safeguards for each of our racial communities against domination by any other; accorded each community its due share in

government; guaranteed the fundamental rights and liberties of the individual, irrespective of race or colour; ensured for every South African citizen the political rights to which his qualifications entitled him; and proposed to decentralise legislative and executive power in the interests of a reasonable degree of provincial and local self-government.

In his forceful manner, Steytler slammed Verwoerd's newly-announced 'Bantu' policy as 'totally and absolutely impracticable' and 'a dangerous deception of the white man in South Africa'. He added: 'Every party or person who accepts that the permanent population in South Africa will consist of whites, natives, Coloureds and Indians, will inevitably be forced to grant human rights on the basis of merit, and not on the basis of skin pigmentation … Do we want to live in peace or do we want to live as enemies in South Africa? We have accepted unambiguously the common voters' roll as the basis on which the non-whites in South Africa are to be given political expression. I have said, and I say again, that the yardstick will be the qualifications and the capabilities of the individual and not his colour.'

He concluded his speech by announcing the names of those who had agreed to serve on a commission to be chaired by Donald Molteno, whose mandate was to consider and make recommendations to a future PP congress on constitutional and franchise matters.

There then occurred an event that had fundamental implications in both domestic and international fields. It was the British prime minister Harold Macmillan's 'wind of change' speech. Addressing parliament in Cape Town, Macmillan drew a line in the sand defining the fundamental approach of Britain and the Commonwealth, and indeed the international community, to the race issue. Verwoerd's impromptu and forceful response reciprocally drew the South African government's line in the sand.

Apartheid had become an international issue.

There were signs of increasing black resistance to the segregationist measures being imposed on them – in particular, new regulations that made it compulsory for black women to carry reference books. In various parts of the country there were demonstrations, stay-at-home actions by workers, and clashes with police. The Pan-Africanist Congress, led by Robert Sobukwe, and the ANC launched campaigns of defiance against the pass laws. Blacks in increasing numbers were refusing to carry passes; others courted arrest by handing their passes in at police stations; others burned their documents in public. The mood reached crisis.

On 21 March, at Sharpeville, 69 blacks were killed and scores wounded when police opened fire on a crowd outside the police station. An estimated thirty thousand blacks marched from Langa to Cape Town to demand that their leaders be released from prison. On the day after the march, which was peaceful, its leaders – asked by the police officer in command in Cape Town to return to discuss the matter – were summarily arrested.

Subsequently, in Langa and Nyanga, there were clashes between the police and protestors, resulting in some deaths and the burning of property. Sensing that white statutory authority was being challenged, the government responded with an iron fist. Langa and Nyanga were sealed off. Citizen Force units were mobilised. A state of emergency was declared in various parts of the country.

The government added another weapon to its arsenal of oppression: the Unlawful Organisations Act. This enabled it to ban organisations such as the ANC and the PAC and to seize their assets. Any person continuing to promote such an organisation, or any of its objects, would be silenced by banning or imprisonment.

The debate on the bill on 29 March was the first real test of the will and the relevance of the newly formed PP. The House of Assembly was packed when FC Erasmus, the Minister of Justice, rose to move and motivate its adoption. He and other government members painted a picture of mounting black resistance on the one hand, and on the other the government's determination to crush it. To do this it needed the power to ban the ANC and the PAC.

Graaff, on behalf of the UP, responded. In his own studied style, he agreed that the situation in the country was serious; he blamed the National Party government and its policies for 'the deterioration of relations between European and non-European'. Then he went on to argue that 'if we are to maintain standards of civilisation which we know and have brought to South Africa, then it is vital that there should be a strengthening of the European population'. He called for change of attitude 'so that we can have a more humane and reasonable administration of the laws applying to the non-European peoples, so that we can obviate racial friction, resentment and frustration in our community', and went on: 'I support this Bill because as a result of the policies of this government you have a situation of emergency in South Africa. I want to go further and say that in such a state I am prepared to assist the government to the maximum of my ability, especially when I am entitled to review their actions each year here in parliament ... I believe it is the duty of any responsible opposition to assist in the maintenance of law and order, but once law and order has been restored, then I am in a position to tell this government what I think of it, and to criticise the manner in which it has exercised [its] powers ...'

There was a hush in the house when Jan Steytler rose to speak. To the anger of both the Nationalists and the UP, he announced that the PP would oppose the bill outright.

I was to second Steytler. It was my baptism of fire; I stated: '[T]he bill ... can only promote extremism. A bill such as this makes moderation in the racial field impossible. It drives these organisations underground, and causes them to employ methods which make it even more difficult for the state to deal with the troubles, and which make it more difficult for law-abiding citizens ... It remedies nothing ... We believe that the situation calls for consultation, not for banning. We ask the government to desist from this legislation before it turns the situation into one in which it will be too late for all of us.'

The Unlawful Organisations Bill was passed by parliament, with only the members of the PP and the native representatives voting against it. The ANC and PAC were outlawed; their assets were confiscated; as anticipated, their structures went underground.

This was an historical turning point. By deciding to turn its back on negotiation, and instead to impose its will on the majority by force, the National Party was signing the death warrant of apartheid; it was really an admission of defeat.

The turmoil continued. More than eighteen thousand people were arrested in terms of the emergency regulations. There were protest marches and further stay-at-home campaigns. The economy was hit by a marked outflow of capital.

The situation was exacerbated when, on 4 April, Verwoerd was shot in the head and wounded while attending the Witwatersrand Agricultural Show. The would-be assassin was a white man who was subsequently declared to be of unsound mind. While Verwoerd was recuperating, Paul Sauer, the senior cabinet minister and acting prime minister, made statements that indicated a willingness to rethink aspects of policy such as the pass laws. A couple of us in the PP looked for a mechanism to help to move the political process forward. We developed the idea of asking Harry Oppenheimer and Anton Rupert, respected citizens and leading businessmen, one English, one Afrikaans, to make a joint appeal to the NP to review its race policies and consult black leaders.

I put the proposed plan to Oppenheimer, who expressed his willingness to play his part. Steytler and I, accompanied by Gerhard Krone, a keen Progressive with good Stellenbosch connections, met at Rupert's Stellenbosch home, and we put the plan to him. He was in substantial agreement with its objectives, which he thought had some merit. However, he stopped short of agreeing to participate in it, responding that 'the small farmers along the banks of the Berg River, who [gave] me a start with my business, and who have supported me ever since, would not understand how I, as a pro-republican Afrikaner, could join forces with an anti-republican English-speaker in challenging the National Party government.'

I was left with the impression that the views attributed to 'the small farmers along the banks of the Berg River' were, in reality, his own. The issue of the republic was at the top of the white political agenda – so it was hardly an appropriate time for the pro-republican Rupert to appear to be teaming up with the anti-republican Oppenheimer.

Japie Basson's National Union entered into an election pact with the UP. In October it polled 46 448 votes and Basson was re-elected to parliament. The Union, however, was to prove short-lived, and Zach and I held discussions with Basson with a view to him throwing in his lot with the Progressives. Basson said he had a responsibility towards his two organisers, Hennie Serfontein and Hans Strijdom. But after further negotiation, Serfontein and Strijdom left the National Union and became staff members of the PP. Basson, having secured employment for his two organisers, disbanded the National Union – and joined the UP! It was only in 1977 when the UP itself disbanded that Basson joined us in what became the Progressive Federal Party.

Verwoerd's republican referendum was scheduled for 6 October. The PP decided to mobilise the voters against the NP proposal under the slogan of 'Reject this Republic'. Our rationale was that the principle of the republic as a constitutional form was not the issue – the referendum had been designed by Verwoerd to bring about a republic designed by Verwoerd. Coloureds, Indians and blacks would have no say; and, save for four Coloured seats, they would have no representation in the republican parliament. These racial provisos – apart from being offensive – would jeopardise South Africa's continued membership of the Commonwealth.

The Nationalists won the referendum with a narrow majority: 52,29% for the republic and 47,71% against. Verwoerd announced his intention to have the Republic proclaimed on 31 May 1961.

During this period I saw a lot of Anthony (Tony) Delius, a leading political journalist, author, poet and political philosopher. Tony and his wife, Tina, were constituents of mine whose house in the suburb of Rondebosch was kept under constant surveillance and occasionally searched by the Special Branch of the Security Police. Tony was fairly phlegmatic about these intrusions on his domestic privacy, but not Tina. A very outspoken woman, she usually gave the police a piece of her mind, but often ended up giving them a cup of coffee before they left in the early hours of the morning. Occasionally when Tony wanted to discuss political developments away from prying eyes or ears or hidden recorders, he would phone and suggest that we go for a walk and a chat on the slopes of Devil's Peak. I usually returned home physically tired from the exertion, but mentally refreshed from listening to Tony's skilful analysis and creative thinking.

He was a thorn in the flesh of the Nationalists. His critical observations appeared in the *Cape Times* each morning in a column titled 'Adderley' – and made some Nats squirm and others angry. He was brought before the Speaker on a couple of occasions, and eventually his accreditation as a parliamentary gallery correspondent was withdrawn.

PART III

Ascent to leadership

9

Learning freedom in the USA

Within five days of the referendum I was winging my way to London *en route* to Washington. I had been awarded a Foreign Leader grant by the United States government. This would enable me to travel in the US for 90 days, to follow the Nixon-Kennedy presidential election, and to visit some of the southern states to observe and study the relationship between the state and federal governments.

On 11 October, Zach de Beer's birthday, I landed in New York. Zach was visiting New York with Harry Oppenheimer and we had arranged to meet at the Pierre Hotel, where he was staying, and from there to go out for his birthday dinner. There were delays. By the time I managed to get through to the Pierre Hotel I was told that De Beer had waited until 10 pm, but as I had not arrived he assumed I had been delayed in London – and went out to dinner. All I could say was, 'Damn!'

Later, walking, I could not believe my eyes when I saw walking towards me Zach de Beer accompanied by Derick de Villiers and Frikkie Botha, two senior members of the South African foreign service. Having had their dinner, like most out-of-towners coming to New York, they decided to see the bright lights of Times Square. A celebration followed.

The following morning I went down to a discount store in West 57th Street to purchase a camera and a tape recorder. I decided, to enable Joyce and my daughters to enjoy my experiences in America as best they could, that each week I would air-mail them a tape on which I would have recorded the sounds and the story of that week's experiences. When I returned home we could rerun the visit by means of a colour slide show. It worked like a charm – Joyce, Linda, Susan and Caryl came with me on a tape-recorded journey from New York to Washington, to Boston, Niagara Falls, Chicago, the Rocky Mountains, San Francisco, Los Angeles, Disneyland, the Grand Canyon, New Orleans, St Petersburg, Louisville – and back to Washington and New York. With me, they watched the reflection of the setting sun on the glass walls of the skyscrapers of New York gradually fading away and being replaced by myriads of bright lights. And 80 kilometres out to sea, looking back they saw the glow in the sky from the lights of New York.

The main reason for staying in New York for a couple of days before I went to Washington was to listen to the speeches at the opening session of the United Nations General Assembly. 1960 was a vintage year as far as heads of government attending the United Nations were concerned. The Cold War was entering a very tense phase. I did not see Nikita Khrushchev banging his desk with his shoe, but I did listen to both him and the young Fidel Castro. Khrushchev was unexpectedly humorous at times; Castro was predictably fiery.

Once I had settled in, I went down to the Washington office of the Institute for International Education in Massachusetts Avenue, where I met the two people who were going to guide and assist me for the next three months. They were Sue McCall, who was to look after my travel, accommodation and financial arrangements; and Ernst Linde, a quiet and scholarly 30-year-old who was to work out the details of my programme and to adjust it where necessary.

Linde introduced me to the US Congress, and in particular to the functioning of the committee system. Together we visited the campaign headquarters of both the Republican and Democratic parties. Thereafter my first stop was Boston, where I enrolled at the Harvard University Graduate School of Education and attended a weeklong series of discussions and lectures in the Longfellow Hall. For sightseeing, *en route* to Chicago, I stopped over at Buffalo to visit the Niagara Falls. They were impressive, but too hemmed in by man-made structures. For me, the Victoria Falls with its natural setting and awesome scale remained number one.

In Chicago, my guide and mentor was Brooks Johnson, a tall good-looking black man who worked for the Institute of International Education. He also had an interest in the launch of two new journals, *Ebony* and *Jet*, designed to reach the growing market of black readers. With the assistance of the mayor, we visited urban renewal schemes in the South Side, and had discussions in the campaign offices of the two parties. I met Professor Gwendolyn Carter, a leading Africanist academic, with whom I later developed a warm friendship.

On the evening before the presidential election I was part of a crowd that gathered outside the radio and television studios in Ohio Street, where Vice-President Richard Nixon was broadcasting his last appeal to the nation. He emerged to the cheers of the crowd. Close to me was a group of young girls who were chanting, 'We're all for Nixon – mighty, mighty Nixon!'

A weary-looking Nixon, hands waving aloft, thanked the crowd and encouraged them to vote, and to vote Republican. That done, he was off to catch a plane for the finale of his campaign, a midnight parade down Wiltshire Boulevard in Los Angeles. I met Brooks's attractive young wife and a number of his friends, and at his home in the South Side we watched the election results coming through. Everyone was rooting for Kennedy, and soon after midnight it was clear that Kennedy was going to be the next president of the United States of America.

After a two-day train journey I found myself in San Francisco. There, not surprisingly, most of the discussions, newspaper articles and television shows centred on an analysis of the election results. However, I did find time to go and listen to Nat King Cole singing at a local nightspot.

A daylight train journey through the seemingly endless cultivated farmlands of central California brought me to Los Angeles, where I stayed at the Biltmore Hotel on Pershing Square in the heart of the city. I went to the University of California in Los Angeles and to the California Institute of Technology for discussions on the American political scene, and my analysis of the situation in South Africa. While in LA I met up with Bill Arthur, a young Australian MP, who, like me, was visiting America on a Foreign Leader grant.

In New Orleans I quickly realised I was in the deep south – the southern vegetation, the traditional southern architecture, the slow drawl in the accent of most people, the number of black people on the sidewalks, the pace that was so much slower than I had experienced in the cities of the north. I found it all rather attractive until I met a representative of the White Citizens' Council. His opening comments to me on hearing that I was a South African were: 'Yeah, you know how to deal with them niggers.' This was followed by a lecture on the merits of 'state rights' and a tirade against federal government interference in the south.

Over the weekend in the grandstand at the New Orleans racetrack I found segregated restaurants, drinking fountains and rest rooms. But more was to come. On the Monday morning, acting on the advice of Linde, my programme organiser, I took a taxi to Desire Street where the school named the William MacDonagh No. 42 was likely to be the scene of a showdown over school integration.

The federal government had announced it would send federal marshals to protect any black children who wished to attend the school. When three black children were admitted a few days later, the white parents decided on a boycott. Rumours were rife in the area that a young white Methodist parson was going to break the boycott by taking his two young daughters to school. As a result crowds, led by rough-looking, coarse-sounding female jeerleaders, waited outside the parson's small painted timber house. After a while he emerged holding the hands of his daughters.

A howl went up. The crowd, whose numbers had increased by now, surrounded the parson and his daughters as they continued on the sidewalk to the school. Local police, who were on the side of the 'jeerleaders', prevented the crowd from molesting the parson and his daughters physically; but there was no attempt to stop the pushing and shoving and jeering and swearing. The display of emotional hatred of blacks that I witnessed outside the school was something that I had not seen even in apartheid South Africa.

My last stopover before returning to Washington was in Louisville, Kentucky. While 'state rights' were also an issue in this Middle American state, the tensions and emotions were far less evident than in the deep south. After a couple of days of debriefing with Linde in Washington, and confirming contacts I had made during my visit, I went back to New York to complete a remarkable three months in the US.

My odyssey came to an end at four o'clock on the afternoon of 16 December when the *Queen Elizabeth* pulled away from the pier at New York harbour and sailed down the Hudson River and out into the Atlantic. In the main, I left exhilarated by what I had seen and heard of the country and its people, and its considerable achievements. But I also left with some question marks: what I witnessed of the conditions of the inner cities of Chicago and Los Angeles, and the racial bigotry of New Orleans.

I found the United States constitution with its decentralisation of power, its checks and balances, and its powerful bill of rights to be a fascinating model from which I believed the Progressive Party could gain when fashioning its own constitutional model for a future democratic and non-racial South Africa.

The presidential election also held a deep meaning for me. It demonstrated the magical role the ballot box plays in the democratic process. For when all the razzma-tazz was over, there was a peaceful transfer of tremendous power that, in the end, was determined by millions of ordinary citizens exercising their rights. I was reminded of the simple analogy expressed by my parliamentary colleague 'Sakkies' Fourie, who said: 'There are only two ways of transferring power. The one is by marking crosses on the ballot paper, the other is by putting crosses on the graves.'

I was invigorated by the spirit of enterprise, of self-reliance, and the belief in their ability to succeed which permeated US society, and which comprised the driving force behind the country's remarkable achievements. I knew I would return to the US, which I did frequently over the next four decades. I wanted to maintain the per-sonal contacts that I made, and to learn more from the nation's achievements and mistakes.

But more than this, I needed at intervals to escape from the cloying and insidious atmosphere of apartheid to recharge my commitment to liberal democratic values.

On my way back to Johannesburg I stopped over in Nairobi for a couple of days to see my sister Lorna, who in 1953 had gone to Kenya as a missionary and school-teacher. Kenya was in a transition phase – moving towards independence, which it attained in 1963. It was still being ruled from Great Britain, but there was a legislative council, and Kenyan citizens ran a number of administrative departments.

I had an interesting discussion with Tom Mboya, a young trade unionist, member of the legislative council, and a rising star on the political scene.

I met Daniel Arap Moi, at that time a member of Ronald Ngala's Kenya African Democratic Union (KADU) and a member of the legislative council, and deputy sec-retary for education. We exchanged questions about each other's country, and at one stage he said to me: 'As a member of the Commonwealth Parliamentary Association I get a lot of documents about South Africa. I know in statistical terms about South Africa's achievements in the fields of education, health services, housing, and so on. I acknowledge these achievements.'

He paused, and looked seriously at me: 'But, to me, there is something that is more important than these material achievements, and so, I put the question, "Can I, as an African, go to South Africa and live with dignity?"'

Before I could react Moi said, 'There is no need for you to answer.'

10

The Progressive Party develops
1961-1970

The 1961 session of parliament was dominated by the republican issue, and produced no more surprises from Verwoerd in the field of race policies. The government introduced the new Republic of South Africa Constitution Bill. It differed significantly from the original NP model, and did little more to the constitution than replace the governor-general appointed by the Queen with a president to be elected by parliament.

The bill confirmed that, save for the four white persons representing the Coloured people, the new South African Republic was going to have a whites-only constitution. Verwoerd, on behalf of his government, stated he would prefer that the Republic be a member of the Commonwealth; however, he made it quite clear that he would proceed with a republic even if it was not a member. He submitted a request for South Africa, upon becoming a republic, to be admitted to the Commonwealth.

Then at the subsequent conference of Commonwealth prime ministers, held in London in March, Verwoerd, following pressures which he interpreted as including a threat by some members to withdraw from the Commonwealth should South Africa be admitted, withdrew his request. This move cut short the debate, and South Africa, as a republic, would no longer be a member of the Commonwealth.

While Verwoerd's action pleased a few hard-line Afrikaner nationalists, it caused deep concern among many sections of the white voters who felt uncomfortable at the thought of being isolated. They were unhappy at the prospect of breaking long-standing links in the sporting, cultural, educational, and even the defence fields. Businessmen were unhappy at the thought of severing Commonwealth economic links. Export farmers were concerned at the loss of Commonwealth preferences.

Two very different discussions took place at that time: one in parliament, the other at a meeting of students at Stellenbosch University.

Upon Verwoerd's return from London the National Party was very much on the defensive, while the United Party, with Douglas Mitchell leading the charge, was in a really aggressive mood. The debate in the House of Assembly on our loss of Commonwealth membership, which probably reflected the mood of many South Africans, swung steadily in favour of the opposition. The 'hoor-hoors' from the Nationalist benches became less frequent and more muted. The NP's customary self-assured posture sagged: their attendance and support were not as enthusiastic as usual.

An intervention from deputy minister BJ Vorster, on the second afternoon of the debate, turned matters around for the National Party. Vorster's ten-minute speech was reasoned, somber, defiant; it played on the deep emotions of Afrikaner nationalists:

'I do not know what awaits South Africa. I do not know whether we shall continue to exist as a nation. I believe that we shall do so, because I believe that we were placed here in South Africa for that purpose. I still believe, and my people still believe, and the supporters of the honourable members opposite still believe, that we shall continue to exist, no matter what difficulties may be facing us at the moment, and no matter how the future may look ...

'But should it happen that this nation must go under, let us then go under because it is our fate, not because it is our fault!

'I feel in my heart that under this prime minister there is a possibility that the Afrikaans-speaking and English-speaking peoples will come to find one another on the basis of common love for South Africa, and on the basis of common allegiance to the Republic of South Africa.'

The initiative had swung away from the opposition.

The other related event in which I was involved at that time was an annual debate at the University of Stellenbosch at which, at the invitation of the students, the parties in parliament were invited to state their views to a lively student audience. Etienne Malan of the United Party, I from the Progressive Party, and deputy minister Blaar Coetzee of the National Party were invited – and after drawing lots, were scheduled to speak in that order.

Malan, who gave too much attention to detail, and attempted to score points off secondary issues, stated the UP case to a largely subdued and unreceptive audience. Amid considerable banter I rose to speak, and judging from the response of the audience, managed to put the Progressive Party's case in a lively, provocative, yet thought-provoking way. Blaar Coetzee, an excellent rough-and-tumble debater, was next: the students were just waiting for Blaar to 'sock it to them'.

When he was midway through his opening comments one of the university's professors opened the door at the side of the tiered lecture theatre and gave a note to a student in the front row, asking him to pass it on when he had read it. As the students, one after another, read the note in an apparent state of concerned disbelief, they stopped following what Blaar was saying, and started their own debate.

In due course the chairman announced that a report from London stated that South Africa was out of the Commonwealth. With that, he adjourned the meeting.

The 1961 election

When parliament went into recess towards the end of June, I was admitted to hospital for some surgery to my back. On the eve of my discharge, Verwoerd announced an October election; the next poll had been scheduled for 1963, but Verwoerd said that, having adopted a new constitution and proclaimed South Africa a republic, he wanted the republican era to start fresh with a new parliament. A secondary motive, unstated, was to destroy the fledgling PP before it had a chance to get off the ground.

Not that he feared the PP in numerical or electoral terms: but he was concerned at the possible growth of support for a political philosophy he totally opposed. It was clear from the political events of the past two years that he would be much more comfortable with a large UP opposition than with a small PP one.

For the UP the election was a godsend. The republican referendum had polarised the voters; now the UP could focus its efforts on the destruction of the PP, knowing it would have the support of the Nationalists.

As the PP did not have the resources to contest the election on a 150-wide constituency front, it decided to contest 26. These included seats held by PP MPs, except for Queenstown and Edenvale, marginal seats that would be hotly contested by the UP and the NP. Strategically, Steytler was moved to Port Elizabeth South and Sakkies Fourie to Sea Point. At a later stage when an NP candidate was nominated, turning Zululand into a marginal seat where the splitting of the opposition vote and the prospects of a Nationalist winning a traditionally opposition seat would have damaged PP prospects elsewhere in Natal, Ray Swart withdrew from Zululand.

In the Western Cape, in addition to contesting five seats in the Cape Peninsula – which included Salt River, Maitland and Pinelands, held respectively by Lawrence, Zach and me – we decided to contest the two NP heartland seats of Stellenbosch and George. Stellenbosch was important because of its large student vote, as well as a strong anti-Verwoerd current among the townsfolk. George was a lost cause – but it was the seat held by PW Botha, leader of the NP in the Cape Province. WJM ('Oogies') van Heerden was prepared to beard the lion in his den.

The PP faced a policy problem. After its inaugural congress, Steytler referred the constitution and franchise to the Molteno Commission, and in November 1960 the commission reported back on the franchise, the bill of rights, and the Senate; but had not yet completed work on the balance of its assignment – federalism, the judiciary, amendments to the constitution, and the national convention at which we proposed to draw up and agree the constitution. In consequence, at the 1961 election the PP could present some of its constitutional proposals, but not a comprehensive package. This made it relatively easy for the UP to distort PP policy and to exploit prevailing fears and prejudices. The Progressives fought the campaign around the concept that it was time for a non-racial alternative to apartheid; its slogan was, 'Look Ahead – Think Ahead'.

This was asking a lot of the white voters: racial discrimination, in one form or another, had existed in South Africa throughout the colonial, union and apartheid eras.

I had a wonderful team of workers in Pinelands. Some had come with me when I left the UP and formed the PP. Others had joined the PP since then. Yet others were

young people becoming involved in politics for the first time – among them a scholar from Rondebosch Boys' High, Ken Andrew, who 20 years later had a great win
against the Nat cabinet minister Dawie de Villiers, and became MP for Gardens. For
more than twenty years Ken was a friend, colleague and benchmate, until we both
retired from parliament at midnight on 13 April 2004.

With a team of volunteers Joyce ran the campaign office with great skill and determination. Night after night she was there, sorting out canvass cards that had been
returned, updating the records, and preparing for the volunteer workers who would
arrive the next day at the office. At Joyce's side was a woman I had not seen before
in Pinelands. Her name was Joan Fowle. She and her husband Les, a staff member
at UCT, lived in Pinelands with their daughter and two sons. After the election she
continued to work with Joyce in Pinelands and in 1971, when I became the leader of
the party, she became my secretary.

During the stressful years of 1971-79 she was more than a competent and loyal secretary – she was a confidante, a sounding board, a gatekeeper, and especially when it
came to matters of human relationships, an unobtrusive advisor. She came back for
a second round as my secretary and advisor when I again became the leader from
1986 to 1988.

Lawrence, Zach and I, together with other PP candidates in the Western Cape,
were comprehensively beaten. In George, poor Oogies van Heerden took a real drubbing. Elsewhere in the country, where loyalty to Graaff was not so prominent, PP
candidates fared marginally better. In the Transvaal and Natal they lost a few seats
by fewer than a thousand votes, with John Cope losing in Parktown by a mere 85
votes. The PP star was Helen Suzman, who won Houghton by 540 votes. In total the
PP polled 72 479 votes, to the UP's 357 210.

At this election Max Borkum, Helen's election campaign manager, came to the
fore. At the time of the breakaway from the UP and the formation of the PP, and
during the traumatic three years that followed, I had come to appreciate his political
acumen. However, the manner in which he managed Helen's campaign in Houghton
was masterly. Borkum, not satisfied with this victory, went on to repeat the process in
1966 and again in 1970. He was a leading stockbroker with a vast range of friends and
contacts in the business community; and was invaluable during my years as leader;
he kept me in touch with the Johannesburg business community and made me aware
of political trends within it.

During the lonely '60s and into the '70s and beyond I saw much of Borkum socially, politically, in business and at rugby test matches. He was a good friend and
generous host. As someone who did not seek high office, he preferred to operate behind the scenes. He had a nose for politics and an understanding of where the power
lay. At times when I was not quite sure what Borkum was up to I could always relax:
he was a committed Progressive, and in the cut and thrust of politics it was good to
have him on my side.

The Progressives were disappointed but not despondent. They had a foothold in parliament. They had a hard core of dedicated supporters. They had established an organisation on which they could build for the future. But more than this, the PP had succeeded in projecting the concept of 'merit not race' as an alternative to apartheid.

At one function the chairman – calling on Zach and me to say a few words – introduced us as 'these brilliant young men who have great futures ... behind them'. His words, spoken to an emotional audience, reflected their disappointment at our defeat. Time alone was going to tell whether the implicit prophecy would come true.

The start of the long haul

In October 1961 the former MPs went home, in most cases to their businesses and professions. Steytler, who remained as leader, went to his farm in Queenstown. Zach, who carried on as chairman of the national executive, joined an advertising and public relations agency in Cape Town. He had given up his medical practice a year or so before, when he decided that he could not do justice to being a medical practitioner and an MP at the same time. Ray Swart, who continued to play a leading role in Natal, went back to his law firm in Durban. I, who carried on as Cape provincial chairman, went back to Bernard James and Partners.

Around the country, defeated candidates, election workers, members of the committees and regional formations, went on with life – but resolved to continue to promote the Progressives' non-racial philosophy. For them, being a Progressive meant more than belonging to a political party. It meant embracing a philosophy of non-racialism; of applying that philosophy in their personal relationships; and promoting it within the community and the society. The issue was one of persuading voters to adopt a new attitude towards their fellow South Africans, to judge individuals on their worth as human beings and not on the colour of their skin: on merit and not on race.

So in spite of the electoral setback the party grew. New branches, some large, some small, were established. Party volunteers raised money, canvassed for support, held meetings in their homes, organised public meetings, issued statements, wrote articles, campaigned on issues. They contested by-elections and took the PP's message of merit and not race to the voters.

And Helen Suzman? She braced herself for what was going to be a tough and probably protracted assignment. Few would have predicted that Helen would play the extraordinary and inspiring role she did during the next 13 years. She showed courage, tenacity, skill, consistency, combined with a commitment to principles and a concern for people. She made a profound impact on the people and the politics of South Africa. She gave young people hope. She gave older people courage. She made people realise that simple justice was something worth fighting for.

Helen and I developed a close political relationship and a good understanding of each other. Although I was a partner in my firm of quantity surveyors, and played my part in helping to build up the firm, I remained a political activist, analyst and strategist. Added to this, I lived in Cape Town, and was at hand if Helen needed me during the parliamentary session. I combined the roles of consultant, advisor, friend-in-need, and broad shoulder-to-lean-upon when Helen felt she needed my opinion, advice or assistance. Of course, she could have managed quite well on her own.

Early on, she developed an extended network of informal advisors whom she would call upon for assistance and advice when necessary. These people were generally experts in their own fields, such as economics, labour, law, education, health services, pass laws, and so on. In addition, Helen had a superb political researcher in Jackie Beck, a law graduate from UCT. She had been a political analyst and researcher for a number of years, and had been a member of the Cape Provincial Council, fluent in English and Afrikaans and with fine, attuned political judgement.

I could write at length about Helen and her achievements, inside and outside parliament, but perhaps I should simply recall the comments I made about her 40 years later when, in November 2001 in Copenhagen, I addressed the executive committee of Liberal International in recommending Helen as a recipient of the Liberal International Prize for Freedom for 2002:

'The curriculum vitae of Helen Suzman is an impressive record of service, achievement and public recognition. Yet, it says nothing of Helen Suzman the person, or Helen Suzman the courageous champion of human rights, nor of Helen Suzman who in the dark days of apartheid did more than any other person to keep liberal values alive in South Africa.

'Helen Suzman is no political demagogue, no armchair crusader. During her 36 years in parliament she was a "hands-on" politician and tenacious fighter for the causes in which she believed. She had a straightforward political creed: "I hate bullies. I stand for simple justice, equal opportunity and human rights. These are the indispensable elements in a democratic society, and are well worth fighting for."

'It was during the 13 years from 1961 to 1974, when Helen Suzman was the lone representative of the liberal Progressive Party, that she faced the apartheid bullies head-on. Alone she stood up against detention without trial, alone in parliament she spoke up against oppression, alone she defended human rights and the rule of law. When not busy with parliamentary duties she visited political prisoners and detainees, attended political trials, went to find out what was happening in the squatter camps and to the people being harassed under the pass laws or being dispossessed of their homes or their land.

'Armed with first-hand information she returned to the fray, exposing harassment, badgering the apartheid ministers and bureaucrats, and succeeding in making a difference to the lives of many thousands of people. Using parliament as a platform, she demanded the attention of the apartheid rulers; she got the ear of the media; she endured the vilification of the racial bigots; and she earned the respect of the oppressed. She was a role model for those who believed in liberal values as the basis for a just society.'

After she retired from parliament in 1989, she continued both in her public service and in her personal campaign in the defence of liberal values. She served as president of the South African Institute of Race Relations. She was a member of the Independent Electoral Commission that supervised South Africa's first democratic election in 1994. She served as a member of the South African Human Rights Commission from 1995 to 1998. As an individual she continued to speak out against injustice.

I can recall one day in 1997 when a number of us gathered at the presidential residence in Pretoria to witness President Nelson Mandela award the Order of Merit (Gold) – the highest South African civil decoration – to Helen Suzman and three male South Africans. Mandela, in his warm, genial way, said: 'I am honoured to bestow this significant award on four distinguished citizens of our country. In deciding on three of them I followed my head. In the case of the other, I am afraid I followed my heart. I shan't tell you who that other person is – but she gives me a lot of trouble!'

As many countries in Africa move towards political systems based on democracy, human rights and the rule of law, the pioneering work that Helen Suzman did in the southern tip of Africa must not be underestimated. She has proved that 'one person can make a difference'.

The Molteno Commission

During 1962 the Molteno Commission, which Jan Steytler had appointed early in 1960 to make recommendations on aspects of Progressive Party policy and franchise policy, completed its work and reported back.

It was the first attempt by any political party or organisation in South Africa to formulate a comprehensive constitutional model for a non-racial and democratic South Africa. The Freedom Charter adopted by the Congress of the People – representing the African National Congress, the South African Indian Congress, the South African Coloured People's Organisation, the Congress of Democrats and the South African Congress of Trade Unions – at Kliptown in June 1955 set out the kind of country it envisaged for the future, but stopped short of presenting a detailed constitutional model.

The recommendations of the commission were viewed with scepticism by most black leaders, and rejected by those who fought under the simplistic banner of black majority rule. Inevitably, they were also rejected by the NP – and derided by the UP, which said that constitutions were not worth the paper they were written on, and bills of rights were meaningless. Yet for 30 years the commission's recommendations formed the only coherent basis for constitutional evolution and co-existence.

Molteno recommended a common voters' roll; a bill of rights; formalising the powers of provinces; sharing national revenue between national and provincial governments; a financial and fiscal commission on which the provinces were represented; an independent judiciary in which judges would be appointed on the recommendations of a judicial commission; the entrenchment of the constitution by means of a special majority; and a national convention to draw up the constitution.

These became of the essential features of the democratic Constitution adopted in 1996. It was only in February 1990 that President FW de Klerk removed the obstacles to the establishment of the Convention for a Democratic South Africa (Codesa); and only then could the process of negotiation, recommended by the Molteno Commission, commence.

The body was drawn from a wide and deep spectrum of non-racial talent. The chairman of the commission was Donald B Molteno, QC. Its members were: Leslie Blackwell, a former MP and judge of the Transvaal Provincial Division of the Supreme Court; Prof. Edgar H Brookes, professor of History and Political Science, Natal University; Dr S Cooppan, Department of Economics, Natal University; A van der Sandt Centlivres, ex-chief justice of the Union of South Africa; Zach de Beer, MP and chairman of the PP's national executive; Kenneth Heard, senior lecturer in Political Science, Natal University; Prof. JS Marais, professor of History, Wits University; Selby Ngcobo, lecturer in Economics, University of Rhodesia and Nyasaland; Harry Oppenheimer, former MP, and director of companies; Arthur Suzman, QC; Prof. LM Thompson, professor of History, UCT; and Dr RE van der Ross, principal of Battswood Training College. The honorary secretary was Yvonne M de Villiers.

The commission was asked to report on proposals for a reformed constitution 'which will contain adequate safeguards for each of our racial communities against domination by any other, will accord to each a share in government, will guarantee the fundamental human rights and liberties of the individual, irrespective of race and colour, and will decentralise legislative and executive power in the interests of a reasonable degree of provincial and local self-government'.

It was also asked to make provision for:

- suitably qualified citizens of a defined degree of civilisation belonging to any population group to be able to participate in the government of the country, according to their ability;
- constitutional safeguards through a reform of the Senate and otherwise to prevent the exercise of unchecked power by any one group over any other;
- the decentralisation of legislative and executive power by devolving on the provinces such powers or functions as need not be exercised by the central parliament and government in the interests of peace, safety and welfare;
- a guarantee, by inclusion in the constitution of an entrenched bill of rights, of the fundamental human rights and liberties of the individual, such as freedom of religion, speech, movement and association, equal protection under law, and the equal status of the official languages;
- the maintenance in South Africa of an independent and learned judiciary, impartial justice and rule of law;
- recommendations for a future government to summon a national convention,

representative of all racial communities, to recommend to parliament a reformed constitution.

After considerable discussion, the party adopted a non-racial common-roll franchise subject to minimum educational, income-related or property qualifications; and provided for a supplementary voters' roll for persons who did not qualify. It linked this system to a bill of rights that outlawed discrimination and committed the government to providing basic education for all.

The PP's rejection of race as a qualification for the franchise, together with its rejection of separate racial voters' rolls, presented white voters with the challenge of abandoning race as a basis for full citizenship and of facing up to the reality of a shared future for all citizens of South Africa. The party's decision to link educational and economic qualifications with a bill of rights that outlawed racial discrimination – and contained a commitment to achieve basic educational standards for all – pointed to a universal franchise in the future.

The PP was mindful of the fact that it was dealing with a constitutional model that it would propose and support, but that the final constitution would have to be the product of negotiation at a representative national convention.

The PP and its successor, the Progressive Federal Party, at times adjusted the Molteno Commission's constitutional model. The most important of these changes occurred in 1978 when it replaced the educational and property qualifications for the franchise by a universal adult franchise.

The commission concluded with a stern warning: 'For our recommendations to be efficacious their implementation depends on a vital time factor. If white coercion and domination continue until the non-white nationalist forces are in a position decisively to challenge it, it will, in our view, be too late to attempt inter-racial conciliation on the basis of a reformed constitution …'

In the 1960s when Jan Steytler, who was no constitutional lawyer but was blessed with a down-to-earth approach on political issues, was asked whether he believed that a constitution based on the PP model would ever succeed, he would answer: 'One day South Africa will be governed in this way because there is no other way in which South Africa can be governed.'

Many years passed before Codesa started its work. However, the conditions that materalised in 1990 were in fact those that the Molteno Commission had stated were essential for negotiating a non-racial democratic constitution. In Tuynhuys, the citadel of white power in 1991, was a white Nationalist leader who decided to negotiate before he had lost. At the same time, in prison, there was a black ANC leader who decided to negotiate before he had won. The synergy between them created a unique window of opportunity. Using that window we were able to negotiate a constitution respected by all instead of having to live under a political system imposed by one section on another.

Ending civil liberties

In the early 1960s the press, the churches, the universities and other organs of civil society came under increasing pressure from the government to conform to Verwoerd's master plan. It was a period of protest, confrontation and alienation; it was the period when with BJ Vorster, the new Minister of Justice, at the helm, the security laws were toughened up, and the security apparatus of the state strengthened.

Civil liberties were eroded. The police were given increased power to interrogate suspects. The definition of sabotage and terrorism was widened. Concepts like house arrest and detention without trial were introduced.

In 1963 the '90-Day Detention Bill' was passed by parliament, and in 1965 a bill was passed that extended the period of detention to 180 days. During this period Helen Suzman, the lone representative of the PP in parliament, displayed remarkable courage, skill and commitment to principle in opposing the slide towards authoritarianism. The stand she took was in sharp contrast to the behaviour of the UP. Time and time again the UP vacillated before eventually coming down on the side of the Nationalists.

The hurtful impact of apartheid laws such as job reservation, separate amenities, race, class and group areas, was increasingly being felt by the Coloured people – most of whom lived in the Cape Province. Rejected by the NP, disillusioned by the ambivalence of the UP, and in contrast aware of Helen Suzman's stand in parliament, many moved towards the PP. New branches were established, both in the Cape Peninsula and in the towns and villages of the Western Cape.

An election for two Coloured representatives in the Cape Provincial Council was due to be held in 1965. After much discussion, and at the insistence of its Coloured members, the PP decided to contest the election. It realised that the campaign was going to be tough, and that the party's resources were limited. In both seats, the sitting MPCs were from the UP.

One constituency included the Cape Peninsula and surrounding Western Cape as far as the towns of Paarl and Wellington. The other, which included the rest of the Cape Province, was so vast as to make an election campaign well-nigh unmanageable. Although the campaigns themselves were going to be orchestrated by the party's regional organisations in Cape Town, Port Elizabeth, East London and Kimberley, I, as Cape provincial chairman, was responsible for the overall direction of the campaign. For this purpose a large upstairs room in our new family home in Pinelands was converted into the campaign headquarters.

In due course Dr Oscar Wollheim and Oogies van Heerden were nominated as candidates: Wollheim for the Western Cape seat and Oogies for the Northern Cape seat, covering the rest of the province. Both were deeply committed to non-racialism and basic liberal values. Oscar had a doctorate in education, and for some years was the principal of the WT Welsh Native High School in East London. He was an activist, with a remarkable ability to mobilise people. He was one of the founders of the Liberal Party and of the Civil Rights League.

Oogies had stood against PW Botha in George in 1961. In World War 2 he had been a fighter pilot, flying Spitfires, an aircraft which he continued to adore. He too had been a member of the Liberal Party, and had a human touch and warm personality. He was deeply upset by the injustices in South Africa and the hurt they did to ordinary people.

Our first task was to register Coloured men who wished to vote. Because Coloured voters had been taken off the common roll – and because of their consequent widespread disillusionment with parliamentary politics – the number of registered Coloured voters had dropped sharply. By the time the voters' roll was closed for the election their numbers had doubled.

While Oscar was campaigning in his constituency, Oogies set off to do what he could in his campaign to win the rest of the Cape Province. We equipped him with what seemed to be a reliable second-hand Peugeot, paid some money into his bank account, wished him well, and told him we did not want to see him back in Cape Town again until he had been returned as the elected MPC for the Northern Cape.

Oogies did a remarkable job. He first made his way to Kimberley, stopping *en route* at Beaufort West and other towns and villages in the Karoo, making contacts, rallying support, and establishing networks. He then went down through Graaff-Reinet and other towns and villages to Port Elizabeth; from there up to Grahamstown and East London; and then back down the coastal route through Knysna, George and Mossel Bay to towns on the fringes of the Western Cape.

When the polls closed it seemed to us that Oscar had won, but we had no idea how Oogies was doing. The next morning the *Cape Times* billboards read: 'PROGS WIN'. Oscar had indeed won, by 3 629 votes. We had to wait 24 hours for the second *Cape Times* billboard: 'PROGS WIN AGAIN'. Oogies had won by the narrow margin of 284 votes, but on a remarkably high percentage poll, 70,3% for such a vast constituency.

However, our victory led to a chain of events with far-reaching consequences. An election for four MPs to represent the Coloured community was due to be held in 1966. This led to a debate within the party as to whether it should nominate candidates for this election, in terms of its first strategic objective: not to persuade black South Africans to become liberals, but white South Africans to become non-racists.

The party decided it could promote this objective by using parliament as a platform for confronting the custodians of apartheid head-on in their citadel of power by probing, questioning, exposing and attacking, while at the same time putting forward a liberal democratic alternative to a system of white domination and black exclusion. After extensive consultation with PP formations and community leaders around the Cape Province, four candidates were selected: Steytler for Boland, Wollheim for Peninsula, Hamilton Russell for Outeniqua, and Oogies van Heerden for Karoo.

Amid this period of turmoil over the issue of Coloured representation, Verwoerd was assassinated on 6 September 1966. Dimitri Tsafendas, a parliamentary messenger, handing Verwoerd some papers at his desk in the House of Assembly, stabbed the prime minister in the chest. There was pandemonium. Verwoerd was taken to hospital but was dead on arrival.

The NP caucus had to elect a new leader. Balthazar John Vorster, the Minister of Justice, emerged victorious and was sworn in as prime minister. An ideologue had been replaced by a securocrat.

Vorster immediately made it clear that he was not going to allow the four PP members to come to parliament as Coloured representatives. His government introduced the Prohibition of Improper Interference Bill, which was designed to prevent any persons of one race becoming involved in the political affairs of another race group. The bill – now called the Prohibition of Political Interference – was passed in 1968. The last vestiges of Coloured representation in parliament and the Cape Provincial Council were abolished.

A Coloured Representative Council, functioning outside parliament, was established. The Prohibition of Political Interference Act, in effect, made it illegal for parties such as the Liberals and the PP to be involved in Coloured political activities. The Liberal Party, which appeared to be concentrating on extra-parliamentary activities, decided to disband. The PP, after extensive discussions with its Coloured, Indian and black members, decided to continue 'even if we are compelled to fight on as a uni-racial political organisation'.

It did so subject to a very clear commitment: to work for the day when the Prohibition of Political Interference Act was no more and it would be possible to restore its former members to full membership.

The 1966 election

In 1966 I started my long political association with the Sea Point constituency. I represented the voters of Sea Point in parliament for 30 years, from 1974 to 2004.

Sea Point constituency stretches along the Atlantic coast between the mountains and the sea, and includes the towns of Sea Point, Clifton, Camps Bay, Llandudno and Hout Bay. Taking into account the majestic backdrop, at times covered with a blanket of white cloud, the verdant Hout Bay valley, the coves and bays that snuggle into the shoreline, the snow-white beaches, and the blue Atlantic beyond, I have often said that I represented the most beautiful constituency in the world; but one not without problems.

I made a bad strategic error in designing the election campaign. My image of Sea Point had been that of a place where young people lived or came to enjoy themselves. They sunbathed on the beaches, went surfing, gathered in large numbers on the promenade, and frequented the many coffee bars, restaurants, cinemas and discos. I aimed to draw them in.

But the profile of Sea Point was not that of young people: the suburb had an extraordinarily high percentage of the elderly. So while most of the young people did vote for me, the majority of voters supported the UP. In future my activities in Sea Point – whether services such as an advice office, clinics on pensions or rent control, or attending to the problems of individuals – would give high priority to the needs and concerns of the LOLs, the 'little old ladies'.

Captain Jack Basson, my UP opponent, defeated me by a majority of 4 055 votes. On matters of race he was extremely conservative, and had no qualms about seeking the support of white voters by pandering to their prejudices; clearly, in the political climate of that time, they were not receptive to the PP's non-racial policy.

One positive by-product of the campaign was that I was brought into touch with members of the Jewish community of Sea Point. The suburb had the largest Jewish population in the Cape Peninsula, and the Green and Sea Point Hebrew congregation was the largest in South Africa. These people were warm-hearted, creative, hard-working and generous. While individualistic by nature, their religious commitment and their strong sense of community acted as overarching factors. As voters in 1966 they were complex. In general, the younger members were more outward-looking and liberal. Older members, especially those who had lived for decades in towns and villages in rural areas and who had only recently retired, were conservative on political issues.

A number of the older Jews had come to South Africa from eastern Europe in the early part of the century, and in the 1930s, to escape the tyranny of the Nazis. They remained grateful to South Africa for allowing them to make their new homes here. In consequence, they felt it was not appropriate to criticise the government too harshly or too publicly.

Little did I realise at that stage what an important role members of the Sea Point Jewish community were going to play both in my future electoral successes and in helping the PP in its efforts to infuse the broader community with liberal democratic values.

Robert Kennedy comes to town, June 1966

In July 1965 I returned to Washington, to be met by Waldo Campbell, a US foreign service officer, whom I got to know when he was stationed in South Africa. Campbell told me that Senator Robert Kennedy had telephoned the State Department to ask whether they knew anyone in Washington who could give him advice on whether or not to accept an invitation from the Academic Freedom Committee of UCT to deliver the annual Academic Freedom lecture in 1966.

I told Campbell I had been asked by the students to try to contact Kennedy – since they were concerned that he had not responded to their invitation. So I met Kennedy.

His anteroom in the old senate office building buzzed with activity and the clatter of typewriters. After a quick handshake, even before we sat down, Kennedy had rapped out questions and I made my responses.

'Should I accept it and go to Cape Town?'

'From a South African point of view, I've no doubt that you should go.'

I gave him two reasons. First, the students at UCT – as at other universities around the country – were showing tremendous spirit in the face of apartheid. They would be hugely encouraged by someone of his standing taking the trouble to speak to them on home ground. Second, the universities were under great pressure from the government, and would be strengthened in their resolve to resist if someone like him identified with them in their struggle.

Kennedy paused for a moment, then responded: 'I'll accept the invitation. I will deliver the lecture. However, there are two conditions.' This was said with a smile. 'The first is that you and your wife will host Ethel and me to supper at your home after the lecture. Secondly, will you keep in touch with Adam Wilinsky, my speech-writer, as the text of my speech is developed?'

'Sure,' I replied.

Wilinsky, a bright young lawyer from New York, came into the office and we had a brief introduction. Later contact with the senator was maintained in Cape Town, where on three occasions I met emissaries from Kennedy to discuss aspects of his visit. The discussions took place in the home of Pete and Alicia Watrous, the US consul general. Then Zach de Beer joined me at the next discussion, with John Nolan, a partner in a Washington law firm who subsequently became the US ambassador to Ireland. We focused on the tone rather than the content of Kennedy's lecture. We suggested that the students wanted to know about America's achievements, but also about its problems and failures. It was important that he should let them know that they did not stand alone and that they were part of a world community of young people striving for a better world.

On 6 June 1966 I met Kennedy in Johannesburg, and then flew with him to Cape Town. Wilinsky, in discussion with Kennedy, had been putting the finishing touches to a speech that Kennedy was to make to students at Stellenbosch the next day. That evening the lecture would take place in Jameson Hall at UCT. Kennedy would then go to the Hiddingh Campus in Cape Town for refreshments with a group of students, then to my Pinelands home for a light supper and an opportunity to meet some of our friends.

Jameson Hall was filled to capacity, and thousands of people crowded onto the steps and the forecourt and along University Avenue. Kennedy's address was a masterpiece. It made a tremendous impression not only on those who were present but also on those who read it in the press and listened to it subsequently on recordings.

He began: 'I come here because of my deep affection for a land settled by the Dutch in the mid-seventeenth century, then taken over by the British, and at last independent; a land in which the native inhabitants were at first subdued, but relations with whom remain a problem to this day; a land which defined itself on a hostile frontier; a land which tamed the rich natural resources through the energetic application of modern technology; a land which once imported slaves, and now must struggle to wipe out the last traces of that former bondage.'

Kennedy paused, smiled, and said: 'I refer, of course, to the United States of America.'

The audience roared their applause. They were at ease with Kennedy, who reached through them to a much wider audience. Youth, he said, is 'not a time of life but a state of mind, a temper of will, a quality of imagination, a predominance of courage over timidity, of the appetite for adventure over the love of ease.' At that moment he gestured to 83-year-old Chief Justice Albert Centlivres, the chancellor of UCT and the leader of the university in its fight for academic freedom. Everyone present immediately understood what he meant by 'youth'.

For the specifically young he had this message: 'Few will have the greatness to bend history itself, but each of us can work to change a small portion of events – and in the total of those acts will be written the history of this generation. Each time a man stands for an ideal, or acts to improve the lot of others, or strikes out against injustice, he sends forth a tiny ripple of hope.'

His conclusion: 'All of us will ultimately be judged and as the years pass, we will surely judge ourselves, on the effort we have contributed to building a new world society and the extent to which our ideals and goals have shaped that event.

'Our future may lie beyond our visions, but it is not completely beyond our control. It is the shaping impulse of America that neither faith nor nature nor the irresistible tides of history but the work of our own hands, matched to reason and principle, will determine our destiny.'

I had invited to my home a number of my political friends. They included Edward King, the Anglican Dean of Cape Town, Donald Molteno, Frank Bradlow, a prominent businessman and historical researcher, Donald Woods and a couple of his journalist colleagues, and local Progressive Party office-bearers and campaign workers.

When the Kennedys left there was a crowd, mainly of young people, waiting outside hoping to see Kennedy and if possible shake his hand. The next day Joyce went to the local school to work in the tuck shop. She noticed that one of the girls had her hand bandaged, and asked: 'Have you hurt your hand?' 'No, Mrs Eglin,' the girl replied. 'Senator Kennedy shook my hand last night and I don't want it to rub off too soon.'

When Kennedy drove to Stellenbosch, Woods was with him. Indeed, Woods often told of travelling with Kennedy that day and how it irked Allister Sparks of the *Rand Daily Mail* to have been scooped by Woods of East London's *Daily Dispatch*. Kennedy went on to Groutville to talk to Chief Albert Luthuli, banned president of the African National Congress, and to Johannesburg to address a meeting of the Bar Association.

His visit to Soweto turned out to be the real *tour de force*. Thousands of residents flocked to see him and Ethel, and along the route he stopped to address the crowds, standing on the roof of his car. Kennedy had a remarkable ability to relate to people and make them feel that they mattered, and that he cared. He was modest in style, yet confident in his commitment to the future. He was inspiring. As the editor-in-chief of the *Rand Daily Mail* wrote: 'Senator Kennedy's visit is the best thing that has happened to South Africa for years. It is as if a window has been flung open and a gust of fresh air has swept into a room in which the atmosphere had become stale and foetid.'

Of course, as we know, in 1968 Kennedy decided to seek nomination as the Democratic Party's candidate in the presidential election in November. Shortly after midnight on the evening of 4 June, after addressing a campaign function at the Ambassador Hotel in Los Angeles, he went to the kitchen to meet and thank the staff; and there he was shot and killed by an assassin.

A year later, on 6 June 1969, Joyce and I, who were in Washington, were invited by Ethel Kennedy and her family to attend a solemn ceremony at Arlington National Cemetery where Robert Kennedy's remains were re-interred next to the grave of his brother, President John Kennedy.

A community under pressure

By the mid-1960s the government had decided to give full throttle to the implementation of the Group Areas Act. Whole areas in and around the cities and towns were declared white, and that meant physical removals. Communities were utterly disrupted: in Simon's Town, Coloured people who had served the navy and the shipyard for generations would have to go; the 40 000 Coloured people in District Six, who had lived there and brought vibrancy to the southern side of Cape Town for generations, would have to go; and so would the Coloureds of Idas Valley, part of Stellenbosch, as well as those on the west side of Paarl and in the whole of South End in Port Elizabeth.

This process of dispossession and eviction was applied time and time again throughout the Cape Province. The PP held public meetings to stir the white conscience. I can still hear the distress in the soul of a Coloured woman who stood up at a crowded protest meeting in South End and said: 'They are destroying my home. They say they are going to give us houses. Don't these people know the difference between a house and a home?' I heard the bitterness in Cuthbert Lauriston, a school principal and veteran of World War 2, outside his house in tree-lined Grave Street in Paarl: 'When I think that we are all going to be pushed out of our homes in Grave Street I ask myself, Why did I go and fight in a dirty white man's war?'

To no avail: prayers, protests and people were brushed aside as Verwoerd's racist juggernaut rolled on.

During this period I came to know Norman Daniels, who had lived with his wife Linda in Lavender Hill in the heart of District Six. Norman was a quiet and thoughtful man, a trade unionist in the clothing industry; he served on the Cape Town city council as an elected ward councillor, joined the Progressives, and was elected as one of the Western Cape's representatives on the party's national executive committee. In 1972, after years of loyal service to the people of Cape Town, he ceased to be a councillor when the Nationalist-controlled Cape Provincial Council stripped the Coloured people of their municipal franchise and created a series of separate Coloured management committees.

When the bulldozers moved in on Lavender Hill, Norman and his family moved to a house in Kensington, a mixed-race suburb quite close to Cape Town. I knew his younger brother Eddie – though not as well as Norman. This was partly because Eddie was an active member of the Liberal Party, and partly because he served a 15-year prison sentence on Robben Island.

Unbeknown to Norman, Eddie, together with some students from UCT, had become involved in the African Resistance Movement (ARM), an organisation responsible for a number of acts of sabotage including blowing up electric pylons. Inevitably, a number of members were arrested and detained under the security laws. Under the tremendous pressures to which they were subjected in detention, some turned state witnesses. Three were charged with 'furthering the aims of communism' and sentenced to five years imprisonment, partly suspended. Eddie – who had only primary school education – was charged with David 'Spike' de Keller, a white law student from UCT. They were both found guilty of sabotage in November 1974; the white law student got 10 years' imprisonment; the Coloured youngster, 15 years.

Within two years De Keller, following an approach to Prime Minister John Vorster by his father, was released from prison. Eddie was in jail from 1974 to 1989. If there could be any redeeming feature about serving a prison sentence on Robben Island, it was that Nelson Mandela, Prisoner 46664, befriended Eddie, the lone Liberal among the hundreds of members of the ANC, the PAC and other liberation movements on the island.

The tide of political protests that characterised the Cape scene during the 1960s reached a climax when in 1968 the Nationalist government enacted legislation that finally stripped the Coloured people of any say in parliament. Three repressive laws did the deed: the Prohibition of Political Interference, the Separate Representation of Voters, and the Coloured Representative Council acts.

When one considered these acts, together with all the other repressive legislation and government action, it was not surprising that the UN, on 13 December 1967, at its 21st session, condemned South Africa's apartheid policies as a 'crime against humanity'.

Black in the USA

During the 1960s and 1970s I made a number of visits to the United States. Joyce accompanied me in 1969, and again in 1972 when Linda, my eldest daughter, joined us. My wife enjoyed these visits, but when I asked her to accompany me again in 1974 she said she would prefer it if I went on my own. I was taken aback, but clearly two extended holidays in America listening to me over and over again talking to my US friends about politics was enough for her.

Washington DC was usually the focal point of my visit. It was the centre of politics and its associated media activity, and as a result of my long association with members of the US foreign service in South Africa, many of my friends and contacts lived there.

My political access gave me an informed introduction to the places I visited, and since I generally gave lectures or took part in symposiums, my board and lodging was paid for. As a keen observer and a regular visitor I was able to gain insight into the issues and trends prevailing in US politics. It struck me strongly that black Americans displayed the same prejudice towards Mexican-Americans as white Americans in the deep south displayed toward African-Americans. They seemed to resent the intrusion of Mexicans into 'their' areas, and feared for their jobs.

My South African background gave me a basis for comparison of certain developments. In 1964 I was at the University of Wisconsin-Madison as a guest of the Africanist Association and where John Shingler, a former president of NUSAS, was the acting head of the university's Africa Studies Department. I participated in a debate. A group of about forty modern history postgraduate students were asked to respond to the topic: 'Whether or not the president of the US should base his policy towards South Africa on the basis that there would be a revolutionary change of government'.

A forest of hands went up, and for the next three-quarters of an hour student after student made the case that there was indeed going to be such a revolution. At the conclusion, Shingler introduced me, a white South African, a former MP in the white parliament, and a member of the liberal Progressive Party.

I differed with the students and explained why I would not give the president such advice. In essence, the Nationalists had strong electoral support; the country had an effective military and security force; and the economy was in good shape. Black resistance forces had been seriously dislocated by bannings, and placed under great pressure by repressive security legislation. It would be a long time before they could regroup and mobilise to seriously challenge the South African government.

The students reacted with hostility. There were comments such as: 'You are a fellow traveller.' 'You are part of the apartheid system.' 'You are on the side of the police.' After a while, a middle-aged black man standing at the door raised his hand to speak: 'This young man from South Africa is correct!' he said. 'There is not going to be a revolutionary change in South Africa in the short term. That is why I got out.'

He turned out to be AC Jordan, a former lecturer at UCT, who on one occasion was slapped in the face by a white policeman while walking on the sidewalk in Rondebosch. His son Pallo returned to South Africa in 1991 and served as a cabinet minister in both Nelson Mandela's and Thabo Mbeki's administrations. I don't know whether Pallo is pleased to be reminded of the occasion when his father came to my rescue.

In 1969 I found America frustrated and divided. The Vietnam war was starting to expose the nerve ends of society. Universities were already in protest mood, and seethed with anger when state troopers shot and killed four student protestors at

Kent State University. Black power was challenging the conformism of US politics. Black power leaders were speaking out openly, and black power salutes were given at the Olympic Games in Mexico – making the issue clear to the rest of the world.

I tried to learn what I could about this new phenomenon in the brief time I had at my disposal. I wanted to understand its origins and objectives: I read what I could; I tried to follow what was happening; I had discussions that included two extremely helpful ones with George Farmer, a black American who was the former leader of CORE (Congress for Racial Equality) and at that time Assistant Secretary of Health, Education and Welfare in the Nixon administration.

On my return to South Africa I included my talks with Farmer when I wrote: 'Black Power. Black studies. Black dormitories. Black Panthers. Black Americans. Black is beautiful ... It is not a party, it is a phenomenon ... But to what extent is Black Power the counterpart of white apartheid in South Africa? Is it as ideological as white exclusiveness in South Africa is ideological?'

Farmer had told me: 'You could be wrong if you were to think of black Americans as a monolithic group.' I commented: 'Certainly if political leaders and forms of political expression are a guide, Farmer is correct. Black Americans do not form a monolithic group. Black Panthers talk of revolution, Black Muslims of separation ... On the other hand, black citizens join the Democratic and Republican parties, others become councillors, mayors, congressmen and senators through the ordinary processes of ballot-box democracy. A black judge sits on the bench in the Supreme Court. Farmer himself holds a key post in the federal administration. Those who believe in violence and revolution are relatively few in number. Many more would not be shocked by violence, for in one way or another, they have lived with or close to it for much of their lives.

'But most black Americans want to become full citizens, full in the meaningful sense of the word. They believe they have to marshal their forces, their talents, their votes, their energies in order to assert themselves. But why not as ordinary Americans – why as black Americans? Why Black Power? Why "Black is beautiful"?

'Again and again Farmer and others explained. Firstly, in spite of the progress, especially over the past two decades, in spite of laws and court judgements which declare them equal in law, black Americans are not full, equal citizens in the real sense of these words. Years, often generations, of living in underprivileged conditions have left many of them in a position where they cannot use the opportunities which equality in law might appear to have given them. And even when legal barriers have been removed, racial barriers have remained.

'They have become convinced that the remaining obstacles can only be removed if they assert themselves at all levels in the society and government. Black Power represents the harnessing of this collective effort. But there is a second reason for this urge for black assertiveness. Black Americans don't feel that they are full Americans. They sense that they are "out" while others are "in". America is emotionally a white society to which they do not fully belong ...

'Other immigrant communities brought with them a culture, a history, a tradition, often a language and a religion. They tended to congregate in areas that gave them a sense of security and a measure of political power. In due course they were absorbed into the mainstream of American society – a process made easier by the fact that they were white, and so was the society. But the black American was different. He had been prised loose from his African heritage, his communal links were broken, in slavery he was not able to set down new roots; he was without any political power ...

'Today black studies, black art, black history, are a search for a heritage in Africa from which their forebears were forcibly removed. These things are to provide the cultural base, with black power to provide the political base. Then, like other immigrant communities, black Americans will feel secure and strong enough to move out as equals into a wider society. Then, they will be in a position to assert themselves, to change the exclusive character of the American society. When that society has blackness as one of its facets, "Black Americans" will be able to be just "Americans".'

Was this racist? No, said the people with whom I discussed these matters. 'Of course there is an extremist element that would like to subvert black power for their own revolutionary purposes. The black American is not anti-white, but he wants an America of which he can be part ... [Most] black Americans want to become full citizens, full in the meaningful sense of the word; they believe they have to marshal their forces, their talents, their votes, their energies in order to assert themselves.'

On 16 December 1969 the Black People's Convention held its first national congress in South Africa.

Synthesis, October 1970

In October 1970 a few of us met in Cape Town at the invitation of Dr Louis van Oudenhove, a prominent Cape Nationalist, to consider forming an inter-race and inter-party discussion and study group. The purpose of the group would be twofold. First, to stimulate dialogue between people from different backgrounds with different political points of view. Second, to explore to what extent it was possible to reach consensus around a selected topic.

The original exploratory group comprised Van Oudenhove, Colin Eglin (PP leader), Japie Basson (UP frontbencher), Dr Richard van der Ross (a prominent Coloured leader), Chief Mangosuthu Buthelezi (the Zulu leader), Ebraihim Albertus (of the Cape Malay community), and Monassa Moerane, editor of *The World*.

In due course, Synthesis – as the discussion and study group was called – added to its numbers Dr Frederik van Zyl Slabbert (a prominent Stellenbosch University sociologist), Curnick Ndamse (a member of the Transkei cabinet), Prof. Nic Olivier (of Stellenbosch University), Pat Poovalingam (a prominent member of Durban's Indian community), and Prof. Nic Rhoodie of Pretoria University.

Synthesis met on a monthly basis, usually on a Saturday and, whenever practical, at the home of one of its members. The consensus-seeking discussions were stimulating, but perhaps more important was that the frank and open-ended discussions that took place broke down the personal barriers that race and politics had set up between the members.

While discussions at Synthesis were indeed 'off the record' and participation was by invitation only, there was nothing secretive, let alone sinister, about the group. But against the background of the rigid apartheid of that time, the fact that individuals from different races and political persuasions were meeting regularly aroused the curiosity of journalists. It must have been a source of great excitement to PM Vorster who at public meetings and in parliament 'exposed' the existence of what he described as a 'sinister organisation'.

At a meeting in January 1974, it was decided that Synthesis should continue as an inter-racial and inter-political study group but that its membership should be expanded. However, in a subsequent letter to members, Van Oudenhove expressed his reservations and stated that in his view Synthesis should adhere to its founding objectives. He formally proposed that Synthesis should:

- continue to explore ways and means of promoting a regrouping of political forces that could entail meaningful participation in political power by all races;
- formulate systematically and eventually publicise its findings for a potentially stable solution of the South African co-existence problem; and
- seek to maintain relations with countries in and outside of Africa, with a genuine interest in the realistic solution of the South African racial problem, and to maintain peace, order and co-operation south of the Sahara.

Synthesis continued to function for a number of years. It expanded its membership to include businessmen, political scientists, politicians from various parties, and media editors. It invited experts, often with opposing views, to lead the discussion. In this it provided a forum for imparting information and exchanging opinions on topical issues. However, in spite of its founding objectives and Van Oudenhove's proposals, it developed into a broad-based discussion group instead of a focused study group that wanted 'synthesis' on problems of co-existence in a multiracial South Africa.

Nevertheless, it was no coincidence that four of the original members – Basson, Slabbert, Olivier and Eglin, who began with very different political commitments – found themselves in 1978 playing leading roles in the regrouped Progressive Federal Party. And it was partly through Synthesis – and partly because Chief Buthelezi and his wife Irene had on occasion stayed at my home in Pinelands – that I got to know Buthelezi on a personal basis. In spite of the differences in our status and in our roles in politics, as well as differences, at times, on specific issues and strategies, our friendship matured and increased over the next 35 years.

The crucial election, 1970

During the latter part of the 1960s, strain developed in the relationship between Jan Steytler and me as leader and chairman of the national executive of the PP respectively. There was no dispute over matters of policy or party objectives; but there was a distinct cooling-off in our personal relationship.

I was extraordinarily busy, with professional commitments to my quantity surveying partners; I travelled abroad a great deal; I assisted Helen as best I could; as chairman I projected the party and its organisation to the best of my ability, impatient for results. Steytler, on the other hand, since the 1966 election had withdrawn increasingly to his farm 'Mountain Range' in the Queenstown area. He was available to address party meetings when asked to do so, but was not taking initiatives or driving the party as leader. When I referred requests to him, he increasingly asked me to draw up a statement, or issue a statement or follow-up statement on behalf of the party. I knew full well that the press wanted statements from the leader of the party.

An additional problem was that Steytler's political duties combined with his farming activities had at times placed him under financial pressure. I formed the opinion that he was not fulfilling the role of leader with the enthusiasm and energy that had characterised his leadership in earlier years.

Other than the political dimension, I led a happy family life. In December 1969 Joyce and I decided to take our three daughters, then aged 19, 17 and 12, to Europe on their first overseas holiday. This six-week excursion included Athens, Rome for Christmas, Paris, London – and then three weeks in the New Year at the skiing resort of Wengen in Switzerland. There we joined up with E Buller Pagden, his wife Lindy and their two sons. Linda had a holiday romance with Manfred, her ski instructor, who as a stunt skier doubled for George Lazenby in one of his 007 films shot in the Alps.

Zach had introduced Buller and Lindy to Joyce and me in the early 1940s, and our family spent many happy holidays with the Pagdens on their farm near Addo in the Sundays River valley. Buller was a prominent lawyer, a director of companies and a leading personality in Port Elizabeth.

With the five-year electoral cycle drawing to a close, the PP once again was gearing up for a general election in 1970. Although there was nothing encouraging for the PP in the mood prevailing among white voters, Helen Suzman's performance in parliament was an inspiration for all and we decided to fight 19 seats around the country, concentrating on a few we thought we had a chance of winning. I was nominated to stand in Sea Point. Together with my team of Progressive supporters, I was determined to try to turn the tables on Jack Basson – a tall order since at the 1966 election he had defeated me by 6 794 votes to 2 739.

Oogies van Heerden was appointed my election agent, and Rob Petersen, an up-and-coming student leader, was put in charge of youth mobilisation. Marlene Silbert, assisted by Joyce, took charge of the Sea Point campaign office. Additional election offices were opened in Camps Bay and Hout Bay.

Shortly before the start of the election was officially proclaimed, I paid a short visit to London. On arrival back at Cape Town airport I was met by bad news. Basson had again been nominated as the UP candidate, and had announced he would fight his campaign under the slogan 'Keep Sea Point White'. Oogies was worried that, given the mood of the voters, this slogan would prove a winner.

Basson did manage to scrape home in the election – but ironically his racist slogan proved a turning point in my political fortunes, and to an extent in those of the PP.

In the process of deciding how best to counter Basson's tactics, I had asked a group of political science students from UCT to help me in a market research project among voters in Sea Point. The PP's preliminary canvassing had shown that one-third of the voters were UP, one-third Progressive, and the remainder doubtful or undecided. Our survey concentrated on this remaining third. Each of these voters was asked three questions:

- Would you prefer Sea Point to be kept white?
- Do you think it is practical to keep Sea Point white?
- Would you vote for a candidate who fought under the racist banner 'Keep Sea Point White'?

In round figures the answer to the first question was 90% 'Yes'; to the second 50% 'Yes' and 50% 'No'; to the third it was 90% 'No'.

While there were many subsidiary issues, the PP campaign thereafter centred on rejecting the racism epitomised in Basson's slogan. What was rewarding and stimulating was that instead of pandering to their prejudices, we appealed to the best in people; and the voters, faced with a moral choice, responded with their best. I did not make the mistake of 1966 by ignoring the 'little old ladies'. Indeed, during the five years between elections we had paid special attention to their problems and needs. In this I was helped immeasurably by a number of doctors with medical practices in the constituency who were able to sensitise me to the problems of older voters.

During the campaign I came to know Bennie Rabinowitz and his wife Shirley, both of whom became lifelong friends. Bennie, a Rhodes Scholar and lawyer turned property developer, was gregarious by nature, generous, outspoken and motivated. He played a key role in mobilising a team of young professionals; and apart from supporting the PP with their votes, and often with their money, these people played a significant role in persuading their traditionally conservative parents and friends of an older generation to look ahead and vote PP. Sea Point in 1970 saw youth power at its best.

The English-languages newspapers did not like Basson because of his slogan. The *Cape Times*, under Anthony Heard, gave me extensive coverage; and a number of prominent citizens and community leaders endorsed my candidature. On our side we had Ann Washkansky and Beryl Blaiberg – the widows of the world's first two heart transplant patients – photographed with me next to a banner stating 'Get with

Eglin'. We commissioned Dave Marais to produce a series of cartoons around the personality of 'Fearless Frank' who gave reasons why he would be voting for Eglin.

I was also helped by a number of prominent PP speakers. Harry Oppenheimer flew down from Johannesburg to address a couple of 'house meetings' attended by businessmen. Zach de Beer spoke at Hout Bay. Maurice Zimmerman, a trade unionist and prominent Springbok rugby player, drew a crowd of 600 at the Camps Bay civic centre; and 2 000 people listened to Helen at a final meeting in Sea Point's Weizmann Hall.

At the end of her talk a PP sympathiser asked her whether the party would unban the Communist Party. In her usual forthright manner she said 'Yes'. She added, naturally, that should the CP break the law or behave unconstitutionally, it would feel the full weight of the law.

The matter was not allowed to rest there. Basson skilfully exploited newspaper reports of the meeting, and of a meeting he had addressed that same evening at a home in Durbanville. Then over the weekend before the election he plastered the constituency with posters stating that the PP was going to unban the Communist Party, without citing the qualifications Helen had set out at the meeting.

He managed to shift the emphasis of the campaign away from the discredited slogan of 'Keep Sea Point White' to the dangers many perceived to be posed by the Communists. I remain convinced that had it not been for Helen's magnificent record in parliament and for the converts she made at the Weizmann Hall meeting, I would have lost by more than 231 votes. However, when the presiding officer announced that Basson had won by those 231 votes, the UP supporters in the crowd gathered around the polling station hailed the result with jubilation. The result, so close yet decisive, was greeted with shock and dismay by the Progressives.

In an editorial in the *Cape Times*, Gerald Shaw wrote: 'The Sea Point result was in some ways the most encouraging development in the whole election. It demonstrated, in the clearest possible terms, that there are growing numbers of young South Africans who cannot be politically stampeded by tub-thumping appeals to their worst instincts, by McCarthyism posturing and "swart gevaar" tactics generally … The tide is indeed turning. The young voters have set the examples.'

But around the country, except in Houghton where Helen retained her seat with an increased majority, and to a lesser extent in Sea Point where I came close to victory, the PP continued to fare badly. We polled a total of 51 760 votes. The brutal message was that the PP had lost ground since its first election in 1961 when it polled 68 045 votes.

Within a few days we met in the party's Sea Point office to launch the '232 Club' – the basis of a sustained effort by PP supporters to make sure that the party wiped out the 231-vote deficit and won the next election in Sea Point. Helen continued to be an inspiration for the party, and the 1970 election enhanced my reputation within the PP.

PART IV

Wider circles of understanding

11

Leader and strategy

In late 1970 Jan Steytler informed the PP national executive that he would not be standing for re-election as leader at the next national congress. Harry Lawrence was charged with the task of sounding out key party members on the issue of a successor. In the course of this process he asked me whether I would be available. I told him that I would consider the matter, but would first discuss it with my quantity surveying partners; and also with Zach de Beer, whom I thought would be most suitable for the position.

A few days later I met Harry Oppenheimer and Zach in the study of Brenthurst. We made a frank assessment of the merits and the availability of Zach and me. The upshot was that I would make myself available as leader, while Zach would do what he could to assist me on the managerial side of the party. Oppenheimer offered to make an arrangement with Bernard James and Partners to enable me to take on the leadership – at least until the next election, when hopefully I would be elected to parliament.

In due course Lawrence told me I was the preferred person for leader and should prepare myself for the congress and the task ahead.

I knew that if I was to have any chance of succeeding, the change of leadership had to be (and had to be seen to be) more than a ritual exchange of personalities. Ideally, it should be a new era for the party – invigorated by fresh initiatives, characterised by renewed enthusiasm, and strengthened by the belief that the PP could make a difference.

I gave much thought to the long-term strategic objectives of the party and the short-term tactical steps needed to achieve them. I was convinced that despite the power of the government, its apartheid laws and the strength of its security apparatus, one day moral, demographic, economic and international factors would combine to end apartheid. The task of a liberal democratic party was to help bring that about as soon as possible, and to ensure that when it took place there was enough goodwill for South Africans to negotiate a new democratic society that would be respected by all sections of our people.

To achieve this, the Progressives would have to work in harmony with the many factors that, in spite of apartheid, were starting to shape our country's destiny. My task would be to persuade whites that their future lay not with apartheid, but with multiracialism. Equally, I would have to show blacks that there were a growing number of white South Africans who wanted to live in harmony as a united democratic nation.

To advance these strategic objectives the party would have to take immediate practical steps to promote awareness of our aims and to demonstrate the PP's relevance. Relevance would not be achieved merely by mobilising existing white opponents of apartheid. It would need to involve cultivating supporters of the NP as well. It would require reaching out to the disenfranchised.

The key national congress was held at the civic centre in Camps Bay. Branch and regional representatives were there in full force, and a number of invited guests were present. The theme of the congress, 'Priorities for the Seventies', dominated the décor.

After opening formalities Steytler made a farewell speech, and left the congress to carry on. Everyone present was mindful of what he had meant for the party. All were aware of his courage and forthrightness during the founding years. Now he was gone.

I was elected unopposed as leader of the party. I knew that from that moment my life would be changed: there could be no turning back. Accordingly, I had structured my acceptance speech around three tasks for the party.

The first was fundamental. It was to keep alive a set of values based on the belief that the individual human being was the touchstone of value in any society. It was the individual citizen's rights, freedom, welfare, prosperity and happiness that society should cherish and the state should serve. This task involved a commitment to the concept of human dignity, to the rule of law, to parliamentary democracy and to simple justice.

I said: 'No matter how long or how hard the road might be, we in the Progressive Party must continue to stand committed to work for a just society. We must fight injustice wherever we see it. Justice is at the root of any worthwhile society. Justice is at the root of good race relations. It is justice which is at the root of human happiness.'

Within the broad interpretation of liberalism, it was important that the PP adopted an approach to policy that was people- and not doctrine-dominated, humanistic and not mechanistic. Important though ideology was as a guiding factor, ideology should not be followed for its own sake, and policies flowing from ideological concepts should be judged, not in terms of their political correctness, but in terms of their impact on the citizens who made up our nation.

Task two was to deal effectively with the here and now: 'It is all very well to have noble ideals, and well-thought-out policies for the future, but what is equally important is to have practical plans to deal with the problems of today. Indeed, ideals and future policies become much more meaningful ... related to the realities of the present scene.' I identified five urgent issues: manpower, education, the family, the cities, and political co-operation. New structures would help make the party effective:

- Each regional council would set up a small action group, in which young members would play a significant role, to identify on an ongoing basis any situations in which the party should take immediate action.
- Five committees would advise the party on current issues and assist it in examining aspects of policies in greater detail. The chairmen would be: Economics and Manpower – Harry Oppenheimer; Education – Dr WG McConkey; The Family – Prof Hansi Pollak; The Cities – Prof. Wilfred Mallows; Political Planning – Zach de Beer.
- The party had to be more than a pressure and protest movement. It had to make an impact on political thinking, on political behaviour – and on the ballot box.

I said: 'We must give these changing attitudes political meaning and political impetus. We must prove to be a political vehicle for South Africans who are sick and tired of old-time party politics; for the growing number of people of all political parties who share *verligte* views and want to join their fellow South Africans in an exciting process of constructive change.' I identified 'the modern city Afrikaner' as most likely to breach the barrier of traditional politics in the following few years.

I argued that the party must provide real political motivation for young people – the wonderful, invigorating section of our nation. Rob Petersen, I added, had been appointed as a full-time national director of youth affairs.

The party should be prepared to commend the government when, or if, it took steps in the right direction; to co-operate with others in opposition when a national issue was at stake; to review the details of its policies from time to time to ensure that it met changing conditions; and to discuss the future of South Africa with *verligte* citizens no matter what party they might be supporting at that time.

However, I stressed that the party should do none of these things at the expense of its principles: 'Never, never, never, must we step back from our goal of a fuller, freer, happier life for all South Africans – of the right of each and every South African to make his contribution to society and to the nation, not on the basis of his race, colour or creed, but on the basis of his ability and his worth.'

My immediate task was to get my message of a rejuvenated, motivated and goal-orientated party across to PP workers, members and supporters as well as to the broader voting public. But how? In 1970 there was no television in South Africa. The only local radio available was the SABC, which behaved like an agent for the ruling party. The Afrikaans-language press was either controlled by the NP or committed to supporting it. This meant that the English-language press was the prime medium for communicating the PP's new message.

I spent a considerable amount of time briefing journalists and editors, and the English-language press recognised my election as the start of a new era in opposition politics. They were quick to understand both the message and the strategy. They gave the start of the new era extensive coverage by way of in-depth interviews, news reports and editorial comment. My task was to keep the momentum going. Fortunately, I sensed a new groundswell of interest in the party, as well as a fresh spirit of enthusiasm among its members.

With Suzman in Africa

When I succeeded to the leadership, events elsewhere in Africa over the past 15 years had had a tremendous impact on political attitudes inside South Africa. I realised it was important for the PP, with its vision of a multiracial South Africa playing a leading role in Africa, to have channels of communication with leaders around the continent. Building such channels would enable us to present our vision and objectives; more importantly, they would enable us to learn first-hand of the challenges facing Africa and of the attitudes of its leaders towards this country.

I conceived the idea that Helen Suzman and I should undertake to visit a number of African states. The logistics of arranging this from South Africa would be difficult – getting visas, gaining entrée to and making appointments with political leaders, dealing with the media, organising transport, accommodation and communications. There were political risks involved as well. If we returned home without having opened doors of communication, the party would have suffered a serious setback. On the other hand, should we succeed, and return with a constructive message for the fearful voters, the relevance of the PP would be enhanced, and its vision of an apartheid-free South Africa would have taken a big step forward.

Since Helen would be overseas at the time we were due to start our tour, we decided that my wife Joyce and I would go to Botswana to meet Seretse Khama and his wife Ruth again. I would then travel to Paris to obtain visas for Senegal and the Ivory Coast. Our plans also included trips to Ghana, Kenya, Tanzania, Malawi and Zambia.

In Dakar we visited Goree Island from where several million slaves had been dispatched to the Americas. We met businessmen, academics, politicians, journalists, and people involved in development projects.

We had an hour-long meeting with President Leopold Senghor; he could not have been more charming or hospitable. The presidential building, although modest in scale, appeared to have been inspired by the architecture of the Palace of Versailles. The furniture and the interior décor had a Louis XIV feel about them. The brightly dressed guards outside, and ushers in formal dress with large ornamental buttons on their backs at waist level, completed the scene of 'a piece of France in Africa'.

President Senghor was one of the leading African politicians who had pressed for self-determination for the African territories. He was an intellectual, a philosopher and a writer, and developed the concept of negritude. He promoted African art and literature; he had served as a deputy in the French national assembly, and as minister-councillor for cultural affairs, education and justice in the French government. He also represented France at UNESCO.

When we asked him what message we could take back with us, his answer was one that was repeated over and over again during our African visit: 'Tell South Africa that we Senegalese are not anti-white. We are anti-apartheid.'

While Helen and I were in Dakar arrangements were made through the Gambian high commissioner for us to travel by car to Bathurst (now Banjul), the capital of the river state of Gambia, for a meeting with President Sir Dawda Jawara. We left the arid semi-desert outskirts of Dakar, and passed through a few small towns and villages before arriving in the tall grass country in the vicinity of the Gambia River. We passed from what had formerly been French to British territory.

The relaxed dress, the haphazard positioning of houses and huts that marked Francophone Africa gave way to orderly lines of houses and huts, schoolchildren in regulation uniforms, and police in dark-blue serge uniforms and low peaked caps. On the north bank of the Gambia River we found that the ferryboat had already left for the south bank where Bathurst was situated. Afraid of being late for our appointment with President Jawara, we were persuaded to climb aboard a goods ferry that was about to leave.

Helen and I, dressed in our best to see the president, crossed the river on a crowded barge amid building materials, drums of petrol, vehicle spares, with a couple of hundred goats in a wired-off space nearby.

Jawara greeted us warmly. He had led Gambia to independence in February 1965; was his country's first prime minister; and became its first president when Gambia became a republic within the British Commonwealth. By training he was a veterinary surgeon, having passed his intermediate BSc examination at Acclimata College in Ghana and gone on to qualify after six years at the University of Glasgow in Scotland.

Our discussions ranged over the situation in South Africa and the problems facing the people of Gambia. He looked forward to the end of apartheid and wished us well in our efforts to try to achieve this. After lunch, Helen and I were ready to start our journey back to Dakar. As there was no ferry about to leave for the northern shore, arrangements were made for us to be taken back on a police launch. Halfway across the river we passed the ferry heading south for Bathurst, and waving to us from the deck was our driver!

We would have a long and irritating wait in a hot reed-covered shelter waiting for him. While there we watched some boatmen in dugout canoes landing a large fish on the muddy riverbank. Helen, herself a keen fisherman, wanted to find out what kind of fish it was. She trod carefully to the edge of the river bank and asked one of the fishermen, 'What is that?'

The fisherman looked at her and in equally basic English replied: 'It is a fish!'

Helen laughed with us: she had shown that if you ask a simple question you are likely to get a simple answer.

A greater frustration than our muddy wait awaited us in the Ivory Coast where we were looking forward to meeting President Felix Houphouet-Boigny. To our amazement, at the immigration counter at Abidjan airport, we were told our visas had been cancelled. There was no explanation, simply an instruction to remain in the transit lounge until we had to leave on the next plane to Ghana.

It was only years later that a French source recounted the events and the issues that led to our visas being cancelled. Apparently, at the time we arrived in Abidjan, behind-the-scenes communication was taking place between the South African and Ivory Coast governments, which could lead to reciprocal visits at ministerial level. The South Africans were angry at the generous reception Helen and I had received from President Senghor, and did not want anything similar in the Ivory Coast. In consequence, the South African government asked the French government to intervene and persuade Houphouet-Boigny not to go ahead with our planned meeting. The upshot was the cancellation.

Our reception in Accra was very different. It was exciting to be in Ghana, the 'Black Star' State, the first modern African nation to get independence (in 1957). We learned that almost the entire population of Ghana comprised Sudanese negroes, and the name Ghana itself was that of the Sudanic empire stretching across to West Africa between the fourth and tenth centuries.

There was scarcely a mention of Kwame Nkrumah, who had led Ghana to independence and played a major role in African liberation prior to his overthrow in 1964. When his name was mentioned, it was in relation to his lust for power and the great assets he was alleged to have accumulated. Yet when I returned to Accra some thirty years later, I was made aware by the impressive monument and mausoleum that had been built to honour him that Nkrumah had been reinstated as 'The Redeemer' and a leading figure in Africa's struggle.

The day after we arrived we were ushered into President Kofi Busia's office in the Christianborg Castle, once a slave stronghold and now the seat of presidential power. After an external degree in history at London University, Busia won a scholarship to Oxford. He lectured in African Studies at the University of the Gold Coast, and during his voluntary exile from 1960 to 1966 he became a senior member of St Anthony's College, Oxford. He became a member of parliament in the 1950s to oppose what he saw as Nkrumah's growing dictatorial tendencies.

Our meeting was most cordial. He was well informed about the situation in South Africa, and held the view that dialogue should not be excluded as a weapon in the armoury of the strategy for the elimination of apartheid. As with Senghor, his message was: 'We are not against whites. We are against apartheid. We look forward to the day when South Africa can once again be part of the community of African nations.'

From Ghana we took a varied path to Nairobi in Kenya. Our official host was Charles Njonjo, whom I had got to know from my visits to see my sister Lorna in Kenya. He was attorney general and Minister of Constitutional Affairs in President Jomo Kenyatta's cabinet. We never got to see Kenyatta, but held discussions with Vice-President Daniel Arap Moi as well as with Njonjo and other senior politicians. Many senior people in government had been educated at South African universities.

The Kenyans found race discrimination distasteful, yet they were pragmatic in the way they dealt with South Africa. While their sympathy lay with the liberation movements, they did not follow the hard line of isolation and boycotts when it came to matters like trade, transport and investment. We were invited to attend parliament as 'distinguished visitors'. To our surprise the Speaker interrupted proceedings to laud Helen for her brave stand against apartheid, and me and the PP for the efforts we were making to bring apartheid to an end. Members are not allowed to applaud in the debating chamber, but this did not prevent them stamping their feet and banging their desks with approval. At one stage it sounded as if a herd of buffalo was rushing through the chamber.

We did not know what to expect in Tanzania. However, we received a kind reception from government officials at the airport, and that afternoon, instead of going to State House, we were taken to President Julius Nyerere's beach house a few kilometres out of town. Nyerere immediately showed why he had the reputation of being intelligent, charming and creative by nature.

He was born near Lake Victoria, the son of Chief Nyerere Berito and his 18th wife. His education in Catholic schools laid the foundation for his profound Roman Catholic faith. After obtaining a diploma in education at Makerere College in Uganda, he went to Edinburgh where he completed an MA, majoring in English literature; he enjoyed translating the works of Shakespeare into Swahili.

His political record was impressive. He led what was called Tanganyika to independence in 1962 – then achieved the unification of Zanzibar and Tanganyika to create Tanzania in 1964. Beyond the borders he played a leadership role in the founding and the evolution of the OAU. Our discussion ranged over events in South Africa, the implementation of the '*ujamaa*' policy – his vision of African socialism for Tanzania – and the Lusaka Manifesto of 1969. This document, which in my opinion gave one of the best analyses of the situation in the South African region, and was one of the most hopeful documents to emerge from Africa, was adopted by the heads of state of the countries of the southern region. The author was Julius Nyerere.

While Helen and I did not always agree with what the president said, nor he with us, we came away from the beach cottage with a warm feeling that we had made a friend. In 1975 I resumed discussions with Nyerere on the Lusaka Manifesto. I put it to him that in the light of the statement southern African leaders would prefer negotiation to war, yet the leaders were not willing to seek a negotiated settlement on the Rhodesian issue.

He replied simply: 'You cannot negotiate between totally unequal parties. At present Ian Smith's regime, with the support of the South African government, is in an overwhelmingly powerful position. This power will have to be weakened and that of the liberation forces strengthened before there can be any talk of negotiation.'

Our African trip took Helen and me to Blantyre in Malawi. Helen had been warned that women were not permitted to wear slacks, miniskirts, or any figure-revealing dress, and men were not allowed long hair. The Chief of Chiefs, Life President Dr Hastings Kamuzu Banda, had so decreed.

Banda left Malawi as a child of 13, to walk south to South Africa. He stopped at Hartley in Southern Rhodesia for a while before arriving in Johannesburg, where he worked for eight years as a clerk and interpreter on the Witwatersrand Deep mine. His ambition was to become a doctor. With financial assistance from an American Methodist bishop, he managed to get to the States where he was the only black student at the University of Chicago. He received a BSc degree before his medical degree at McHaray Medical College, Nashville. He studied further at the universities of Glasgow and Edinburgh.

He stayed on to practise as a medical doctor in Liverpool and London, and returned to Malawi in July 1958 after an absence of more than forty years. When, after a turbulent few years, Malawi attained independence in July 1964, Banda became president.

Once Helen and I had been ushered into his presence, Banda directed the staff to leave so that we could speak frankly. He was wearing dark glasses, which prevented us from making eye contact. Soon the discussion developed into a monologue, and unfortunately Banda had very definite views on most of the issues facing the southern African region and its political leaders. He was pragmatic about South Africa and was more concerned about the situation developing in Malawi's neighbour, Rhodesia.

He struck us as a man with a keen intellect, a strong will and a highly individualistic approach to issues: a leader to be reckoned with. Nonetheless, while pleased to have met him, we were at the same time relieved that the meeting was over.

Our last stop was to be in Lusaka for a meeting with President Kenneth Kaunda. Fortunately Zach de Beer, who had been appointed as head of Anglo-American's mining activities, was on hand to meet us. He and Mona helped us to relax in their comfortable home.

Kaunda's father, David Kaunda, was a Church of Scotland missionary and teacher. Kenneth followed in his footsteps, becoming a schoolteacher before entering politics, and remaining a devout Christian. His political creed – faith in the common man, and non-violence – was based on a study of Gandhi and a visit to India. During Zambia's pre-election period he was banned and imprisoned yet did not abandon his commitment to non-violence. When a white housewife was stoned to death in the Copperbelt, Kaunda was reported as saying: 'The battle is not anti-white, it is anti-wrong. We can never fight racialism by being racialists ourselves.'

At lunch, Kaunda, a teetotaler, asked that we first enjoy some 'presidential wine' – orange juice. Later the waiter offered the guests normal wine, which he poured from a bottle covered with a white napkin. A peep under this revealed that it was South African wine. Some sanctions!

Kaunda had his finger on the pulse of what was going on in South Africa. Apart from his own government information gatherers, he was helped by the presence of the ANC's African headquarters in Lusaka, and a regular air service between Lusaka and Johannesburg bringing in a steady stream of South African businessmen, academics and journalists. Indeed, Lusaka was the political crossroads of the southern African region.

Kaunda was interested to hear Helen's and my perspective on events in South Africa and to find out what progress the PP was making among the white voters. It was clear that he was no rigid ideologue, but that he was driven by a deep compassion for people suffering under injustice.

The South African press, with the exception of the newspapers supporting the government, was positive about our mission and achievements. John Worrall, a journalist who covered our visit extensively, summed it up in the following words: 'The Suzman-Eglin team was a perfect partnership. Hers was the celebrity name everybody knew, and it is amazing how much is known about the South African political scene, even in countries as remote as Senegal. Colin Eglin, large, amiable, tolerant, outspoken, sincere, gave the operation an air of political solidity. He made a great impression with his masterly analysis of the South African scene. Never was there, outside South Africa, a better spokesman for the Progressive viewpoint.'

Nationalist supporters preferred to call the journey a waste of time, or to lampoon us in cartoons showing me playing Tarzan to Helen as Jane in the jungle, or Helen and me as pith-helmeted explorers on a futile journey to nowhere. We brought back a simple but powerful and positive message for white South Africans: 'The black leaders of Africa are not anti-white. They are anti-apartheid. They want to welcome South Africa into the community of African nations. They want South Africa to play a full role in the development of Africa. But these things can only happen when apartheid is abolished.'

I felt my gamble had paid off.

Seeking common ground

With the help of a few friends in Cape Town I was able to maintain my contacts with *verligtes* in Stellenbosch. In the north, Piet Vermeulen, the stalwart Transvaal chairman of the PP, was busy extending his contacts with *verligtes* in Pretoria. Around the country PP members interacted with reform-minded Afrikaners in their own communities; indeed, PP members played a significant part in the formation of the group known as '*Verligte* Aksie' (approximately, 'Enlightened Action').

It was not enough. The commitment I had made on behalf of the PP – to reach out to the modern *verligte* Afrikaner – required concrete and visible action. I arranged for the PP to invite a number of prominent Afrikaner academics to a symposium, a no-holds-barred interaction between them and a few of my senior colleagues, on the issue of the PP's message and its strategic objectives. The venue was Silverton, outside Pretoria.

Participants were well-supplied with party documents, and while many were sceptical as far as the attainment of our objectives was concerned, there was remarkably little hostility towards the concepts we presented to them. There was even a degree of fascination with the Progressive alternative.

Another idea that I hit on was for the PP to establish an Afrikaans-language journal as an instrument for publishing *verligte* opinion. The objective was to enhance the PP's relevance among Afrikaners in general, and *verligte* Afrikaners in particular. I had no immediate bright ideas for a possible name for the journal. During the discussion I had with Jan van Eck about his appointment as editor, his wife, who had been silent throughout, asked whether she could make a suggestion: 'How about *Deurbraak* (Breakthrough)?' *Deurbraak* it became, and *Deurbraak* it remained for the ten years of its existence.

The publication was sophisticated and informative – well-received by those in its target markets. It carried articles and statements by – and stimulated debate among – people such as Jakes Gerwel, Adam Small, Allan Boesak, Allan Hendrickse, Dick van der Ross, Mangosuthu Buthelezi, Nthato Motlana, André Brink, WA de Klerk, Breyten Breytenbach, Jan Sadie, Monassa Moerane, Danie Craven, Hassan Howa, Marinus Wiechers, JS Petersen, AJ Venter, AM van Schoor, CJ Maritz, Theo Gerdener, Blaar Coetzee and Percy Qoboza.

Student leaders such as Michiel le Roux (Stellenbosch), Lieb Loots (Rand Afrikaans University), Karel Zaayman (Pretoria) and Steven Jooste (UCT) also had their say; and the letters column reflected the strongly held views of its correspondents. Subjects tackled included the ongoing *verligte/verkrampte* tussle, the Coloureds, Africans, urban blacks, sport, student politics, the press, police, censorship, Africa, South West Africa and labour matters.

An interview that had a major impact took place in the 1970s between Van Eck (who edited *Deurbraak*) and Schalk Pienaar, the respected doyen of the Afrikaans journalistic fraternity. Asked what his attitude was towards the Angola affair – and South Africa's military engagement in that country – Pienaar responded: '*Dit was 'n ligte mistakie aan ons kant.*' Colloquially, this 'little mistake' admission reverberated in media and political circles for months. Indeed, many years after Pienaar's death in 1977, he was remembered for his superbly crafted response, and '*'n ligte mistakie*' became part of the Afrikaans lexicon.

By presenting the PP's policies and objectives in a style that was informative rather than slick propaganda, *Deurbraak* helped the party to get our message across to an important number of academics, businessmen and opinion-formers. *Deurbraak* was one of the instruments that contributed to the process of change in the mindset of white people.

For example: Van Eck arranged a speaking engagement for me at the University of the Orange Free State. As I had attended primary school in the small OFS village of Hobhouse (after Emily), I decided to make the famous Boer champion my focal point. I recounted to the students her anger at the fact that thousands of women and children had been driven from their homes and herded into concentration camps. I reminded them of her compassion for those who were suffering. I recalled her courage in confronting her own government over the injustice of the Anglo-Boer War. Then I put a few question to my student audience:

· If Emily Hobhouse was in South Africa today, on whose side would she be?

- With whom would she be angry?
- For whom would she have compassion?
- Who would she be confronting over the injustices being done?

The students listened in thoughtful silence.

While these and similar Progressive initiatives in interacting with 'modern city Afrikaners' were an important part of seeking to influence the white electorate to move away from apartheid, given the multiracial composition of our nation, it was not enough. If we wanted to counter the polarisation along racial lines, we had to increase our communication and interaction with leaders of disenfranchised black South Africans.

This was no easy task. Many of those leaders were in prison. Others were banned or in exile. Yet others were not interested in dialogue with white politicians. Nevertheless, the task of establishing channels of communication was essential. Helen, through her work as a member of parliament, her campaigning against the pass laws, and in particular her visits to Robben Island, had extensive contacts. Other members of the PP had contacts in the parts of the country where they lived and worked. These had to be extended.

As part of this project we decided to establish contact with the black leaders coming to the fore in the 'homelands' that had recently been established as part of what was termed Grand Apartheid. This was the geographical division of the land of South Africa on race lines. There were eight new homelands, and the task of establishing contact with their leaders was shared between Helen, Ray Swart, Piet Vermeulen and me. Progressive delegations visited all the homelands and succeeded in holding discussions with the political leaders. These dealt with the PP's objectives and its policies; with developments in the homelands; and with the vision the leaders held out for the future.

The government was not pleased. It tried to make it as difficult as it could for us, though in time its opposition wilted in the face of Suzman's determination to succeed. By the end of the exercise I was satisfied that communications had been established, and that the PP had a better understanding of the problems and the aspirations of the homeland leaders.

It subsequently emerged that at least some of these leaders were sympathetic to the party's policies, and shared much of its vision for the future of South Africa.

The PP had adopted the recommendation of the Molteno Commission that South Africa should have a federal system of government. The Nationalists envisaged the homelands developing into independent states. The UP's response was to declare that it rejected independent states and stood for white leadership over all of South Africa. While the PP also rejected the notion of homeland independence, it argued that regional decentralisation should be accommodated within a federal system of government. The party's view was that the form the constitution should take had to be negotiated and agreed by the representatives of all sections of the South African people.

I asked Donald Woods, editor of the *Daily Dispatch*, which was free of ties with any party or group, to convene a broad-based multiracial conference of leaders to discuss federation as a formula for the future. Woods agreed, and tackled the task with energy and enthusiasm; he had the backing of his newspaper and the support of serious businessmen who sponsored the conference, which was held at Bulugha, a coastal resort north of East London, on 9-11 November 1973.

The participants represented a significant proportion of the people of South Africa. The editors of all leading South African newspapers, or their representatives, attended as observers.

The conference took the form of an informal interaction workshop chaired by Knowledge Guzana and Alex Boraine. The speeches were relatively brief, and the interventions spontaneous. In order to broaden the impact of the conference Woods arranged for the proceedings to be published verbatim in the *Daily Dispatch*.

At the conclusion of the conference, the delegates unanimously adopted the following Declaration of Consensus, stating that:

- they affirmed the need for urgent change in South Africa;
- they declared a belief in the fundamental right of each citizen – irrespective of race, creed or colour – to live a full life with dignity, opportunity and justice under the rule of law;
- they agreed, against the background of the realities of South Africa, that a federal form of government embodying autonomous states free of racial exclusiveness was most likely to create the conditions under which these rights would be achieved; and that
- in view of fears of group domination and discrimination, the rights of each individual would be protected by a bill of rights entrenched in the federal constitution.

A committee to plan further steps in promoting the 'Bulugha Declaration' was elected. It was significant that there was no support for breaking up South Africa into a number of independent states. Nor was there support for the granting of rights on the basis of race. The conference had been part of the process of building bridges across the racial divisions of the National Party.

Mayhem at the cathedral

Shortly before lunch time on Friday 2 June 1972 I had a telephone call from the Progressive Party office in Cape Town asking me to go urgently to St George's cathedral in Wale Street. Trouble was brewing: UCT students were holding a demonstration as part of their 'Free education for all' week. They held placards proclaiming 'Education not Indoctrination'. Crowds gathered outside the cathedral. A group of rough-looking men clad in T-shirts, jerseys, or leather jackets and jeans, and carrying lethal-looking batons, were assembling around the corner.

I rushed from the lower end of the city to find that mayhem had been let loose. A few battered and bewildered students, some bleeding, others with clothes ripped open, were sitting dazed on the steps of the cathedral.

Others had sought refuge in the cathedral, where the ruffians entered and again assaulted and manhandled them – some were dragged out by their hair. Other students were being chased up adjoining Queen Victoria Street by baton-wielding thugs. It turned out that the attackers were not merely a group of men who had assembled casually. They were a specially selected posse of policemen belonging to the Special Branch.

The savagery of the attacks and the wanton desecration of the cathedral shocked the citizens of Cape Town. Clive Corder, a senior citizen of the mother city and the chairman of the Council of UCT, decided that as a show of solidarity he would join the students at the cathedral at lunch time on Monday.

Helen and I met there well before the appointed time, to show our solidarity with the students, and to see whether we could help should any difficult situation arise. Indeed, many thousands of Capetonians came to show their solidarity and anger. I acted as an unofficial marshall, trying to get the crowds to stay on the vacant church property adjoining the cathedral. This proved impossible; there were too many people; they spilled onto the streets. In due course the divisional inspector of police announced that the gathering had been declared illegal under the Riotous Assemblies Act, and ordered the crowd to disperse.

Helen and I followed Corder, Archbishop Selby Taylor and others into the cathedral, which was soon filled to capacity. After a brief address by Dean King we all left through a side exit that led us away from Wale Street.

Later that afternoon I went down to the Caledon Street police station, where I presumed the students who had been arrested were being held. The police officer on duty told me that those arrested were being held until they had been formally charged, and in all likelihood would be released on bail. Astonishingly, Dean King was brought out from the cells, and later released on bail.

Later that afternoon I encountered Len Read, the assistant registrar at UCT, walking cautiously down Caledon Street with a small suitcase in one hand. He whispered that he was 'bringing money from the university to pay the students' bail'.

In parliament members debated the events. Helen and Japie Basson (of the UP) spoke out strongly against the brutality of the police, and in favour of the right of citizens, including students, to participate in peaceful demonstrations. Graaff was critical of the behaviour of the police, but ambivalent as far as the rights of the students were concerned. Other members of the UP revealed their ingrained hostility towards the demonstrators.

The following evening there was a mass meeting of citizens at Cape Town city hall, which was filled to overflowing. In an emotionally charged atmosphere Dean King received a hero's welcome. Geoff Budlender put the case for the students. Helen, Dr Marius Barnard and others expressed the feelings of the citizens of Cape Town. Never before or since have I seen these usually phlegmatic people display such unity in anger.

The assault on the students was not over. The next day the action moved from the steps of the cathedral to the steps of Jameson Hall in the heart of the university campus in Rondebosch, where the students held another peaceful demonstration. The police ruffians, using their batons and assisted by fierce police dogs, tried to disperse the protestors from the steps of the hall. Despite the assaults, most of the students stood their ground; they were on university property and had the right to demonstrate in peace.

The assaults only ceased when the university obtained a court order 'restraining the police from interfering with students gathering on the steps of Jameson Hall'.

The assault on the students had taken place a few weeks after the Schlebusch Commission had been appointed by the government, and a few months before it was due to report on the activities of the National Union of South African Students (NUSAS). People feared it was a trap; and certainly the events in Cape Town ripped off the mask of benevolence that the Vorster government chose occasionally to wear.

BOSS steps in

In 1973, following the success of my earlier visit with Helen around Africa, I started to plan another trip of a somewhat different nature. Our previous visit had demonstrated that there were white South Africans who were openly and unashamedly anti-apartheid. I now wanted to demonstrate that there were black, Coloured and white politicians who shared a common opposition to apartheid. Such a demonstration would convey an important message not only to the African states we would visit, but to South Africans at home.

My plan involved a joint venture with Mangosuthu Buthelezi, the president of Inkatha, and David Curry, a senior member of the Labour Party. I discussed the matter with Buthelezi, who indicated willingness to participate. He mentioned that he had received an invitation from the African-American Institute to attend a conference in Addis Ababa later that year. It would be convenient if our African visit could take place immediately after the conference.

As I knew William Cotter, the American head of the Institute, I wrote to inform him of our intentions and ask whether I could attend the conference as an observer. I received a short, and surprisingly curt, response from Cotter: 'I'm afraid it will simply not be possible for you to be invited as all the invitations have already been sent out.'

I phoned Buthelezi and told him of Cotter's response. Buthelezi told me that he had also received a letter from Cotter that cast a very different light on his attitude to the matter. In part, Cotter said, 'You should not travel to the conference in Ethiopia with a white South African, not even such an obvious liberal as Colin Eglin.' Furthermore, in a telephone conversation with Buthelezi, Cotter had indicated that the Inkatha leader's invitation to the conference could be withdrawn if his attendance was perceived as linked to the proposed visit (with Curry and me) to other African countries.

I was angry at Cotter for placing an obstacle in the way of the joint venture – and for his deviousness in giving Buthelezi and me different reasons for doing so. What was particularly ironic was that while a trio of black, white and brown leaders were willing to travel north together – and that certain leaders were prepared to talk with them – white liberals in the US appeared to find this undesirable. Immediate plans for the African visit were stymied.

A couple of months later, in November, the *Sunday Express* carried a story from New York under the headline: 'Eglin Frozen out of Ethiopian Meeting'. The essence of the article was that a South African woman, who had been an ardent supporter of the PP, and was friendly with a person connected to the Institute, was so angry and dismayed at the manner in which I had been treated, that she had decided to reveal the matter to the media.

I phoned Buthelezi and drew his attention to the story. I made it clear that I did not believe the story genuinely emanated from New York.

There the matter rested until a few years later when Gordon Winter, who had doubled as a journalist working for the *Sunday Express* and as an undercover agent for the Bureau for State Security, dealt with it in his book *Inside BOSS*. Winter wrote that at his first meeting with John Vorster, the prime minister had said he was concerned that the PP was making strong attempts to increase its strength within the South African electorate.

Vorster told Winter: 'I have a very good story for you. It is about Colin Eglin. If you pop over to Hendrik's office he will give you all the background on it.'

'Hendrik' was HJ van den Bergh, the head of BOSS. As Winter later revealed, the *Sunday Express* story did not emanate from any 'PP-supporting lady in New York' at all, but had everything to do with BOSS acting on the initiative of Vorster. Winter wrote: 'After being completely briefed by Mike Geldenhuys and Hans Brummer [of BOSS] on the subject of the story I was to write about the African-American Institute, warning Chief Gatsha Buthelezi not to travel to Ethiopia with Colin Eglin, I went back to Van den Bergh's office and gave him a quick run-through of the story I intended mounting.

'HJ smiled as he listened, but then added a note of warning: "To protect us, state in your article that you obtained all your information from a woman in America, who is either friendly with or works with someone in the African-American Institute. Keep it vague but make sure you insert something of that nature to distance the Bureau from you. One other thing, don't break the story until five or six days before the … conference in Ethiopia." I did exactly as I was told …

'Mr William Cotter, the President of the African-American Institute, tried to cast doubt on my story by telling the *Rand Daily Mail* that he could not recall having advised Chief Gatsha to travel to Ethiopia alone. But Colin Eglin did not try to wriggle out of it by using diplomatic gobbledygook. He was honest and said it was ironic that, while black and white leaders were willing to travel to Ethiopia together, "white liberals in the United States should appear to find this joint venture undesirable". Mr Eglin concluded: "How Mr Vorster must be chuckling!" How right he was!

'Eglin was no fool. He knew dirty work was afoot. BOSS told me they had bugged a telephone call at Mr Eglin's home during which he had said words to this effect: "I don't believe Winter obtained copies of all those letters from someone in America as he claims. I fear he got them from someone much nearer home."

This chain of events revealed that Vorster, while professing his commitment to parliamentary democracy, had no hesitation in using the machinery of the state, in BOSS, to undermine his parliamentary opposition.

Preparing for the breakthrough

The process of mobilising the PP for the election scheduled for 1974 began well before the end of the previous year. Gathering a war chest was strongly under way; key constituencies had been identified, and candidates were being sought and, where possible, selected; the party was prepared in terms of organisation and emotion.

From our point of view, the strategic environment had improved tremendously since the previous election in 1970. The NP was still strongly entrenched in power, and electorally it would remain cohesive. Black homelands were being given legal substance, apartheid measures applied and even extended. Yet doubts were starting to creep in about the effectiveness of government policy. Strikes by black workers in Durban in 1973 emphasised the country's dependence on urban black labour permanently settled in the cities. All this undermined Verwoerd's vision of 'self-determination'.

The failure of the government to come forward with a credible policy for the future of the Coloured people also left a gaping hole in its claim to morality – and verligte voices were being raised from within the Nats' Afrikaner base of power.

Obviously, these and related issues were not going to be enough to erode the NP's vote; but they were enough to lend credibility to the need for an effective opposition. In our judgement, there was no doubt that the initiatives the party had taken, as well as our forthright yet down-to-earth approach to certain issues – combined with Helen Suzman's remarkable service record – had established the PP as a party that was relevant.

Despite gaining nine seats from the NP in the 1970 election, the UP was on a downhill track. It remained ambivalent on the dominant issues of race and civil liberties; and was divided over the emergence of verligtes and the formation of organisations such as Verligte Aksie. While the so-called 'young Turks' within the UP welcomed the verligte development, the old guard viewed it with suspicion.

The first outward manifestation of a stirring within the UP came at its Transvaal congress in August 1972, when Harry Schwarz, who led the party in the Transvaal Provincial Council, ousted Marais Steyn, one of Graaff's most trusted lieutenants, as overall Transvaal leader. Furthermore, the UP had dealt itself a serious blow through its involvement with the Schlebusch Commission established by the government in 1972. The commission's mandate had been to investigate NUSAS, the South African Institute of Race Relations (SAIRR), the University Christian Movement (UCM), and the Christian Institute (CI) to determine whether they were engaged in subversive activities.

The PP, through Helen inside parliament and me outside it, opposed the appointment of the commission outright. We argued that it was a McCarthy-type witchhunt that should not take place in a country professing to believe in the rule of law. For its part, the UP appointed four of its MPs to serve on it, and in February 1973 they joined the five NP commissioners in producing a unanimous report that damned NUSAS. The government banned eight NUSAS leaders and declare it an 'affected' – as in the sense of politically dangerous – organisation.

The UP was far from unanimous on the commission and what appeared to be its designed effects. Catherine Taylor and Japie Basson asked critical questions about its rationale. Harry Schwarz called for its disbanding and the appointment of a judicial tribunal. Chris and Marius Barnard, the two heart surgeons who six months before had joined the UP, made it clear that they were at odds with the party in its approach to civil liberties and to participation on the commission.

The English-language press slammed the commission.

The affair added to the tensions growing between the old guard and the 'young Turks'. In January 1974 Schwarz, as Transvaal leader, went to Mhlabatini in Natal where he and Buthelezi, the chief minister of KwaZulu, signed a 'Declaration of Faith' – a joint commitment to provide a blueprint for government by consent, and for racial peace in a multiracial society, stressing opportunity for all, consultation, the federal concept, and a bill of rights.

The old guard was furious with Schwarz, who received extensive praise from the English-language press.

Against this background, my colleagues and I decided to contest the election under two slogans: 'For effective opposition, vote Progressive Party', and 'We have the leaders, you have the votes. Vote Progressive Party.' We decided to contest 23 seats, strategically selected for the maximum impact on our campaign and its ambitions. Of these Houghton and Parktown in Johannesburg, Berea and Musgrave in Durban, and Sea Point and Rondebosch in Cape Town were designated our top priority 'must win' flagship seats.

There were sound reasons why we had chosen Rondebosch – where the PP had not put up a candidate in the previous election. One of them was that Graaff, the previous representative in parliament, had decided to stand in the adjoining constituency of Groote Schuur. This meant that the voters in Rondebosch would not be influenced by loyalty to Graaff or support for an existing UP member of parliament.

The other reason was that large sections of the old Rondebosch constituency, which had been strongly UP, had been transferred to an adjoining constituency while sections of adjoining constituencies, which we anticipated would be strongly PP, had been transferred into the new Rondebosch.

For the flagship constituencies, I was determined to find star-quality candidates. I also made it my responsibility to ensure that the party and its candidates received maximum support from the press. As I had anticipated, the Afrikaans-language press, which had been critical of the government from time to time, was going to close ranks and throw its weight behind the National Party. The English-language press, in the main, had a positive approach to the PP. The *Rand Daily Mail* had no reservations in its support for us. Others, while not abandoning the UP as the major opposition party, expressed to a varying extent the view that South Africa would benefit from the presence of more PP members alongside Helen Suzman in parliament.

Early in December I received a telephone from José Olivier, the wife of Nic Olivier, one of my associates in Synthesis and a prominent *verligte*, with whom I frequently discussed the political scene and the emergence of the *verligtes* as a new political factor. José told me that Olivier had gone to Johannesburg where it was likely he would join the UP and stand for them. She believed her husband would be making a great mistake and would lose much of the credibility he had built up over the years.

I was distressed. Olivier would be a boost for the UP and a setback for the PP in its efforts to attract *verligte* Afrikaners. I tried without success to get in touch with him. Eventually when I did I was too late. Olivier had already committed himself to the UP. As I was not prepared to accept the situation I decided to try to contact Frederik van Zyl Slabbert, a good friend of his, in the hope that he might be able to help me stop Olivier standing for the UP. On Sunday I received a further shock when I saw the *Sunday Times* front-page lead with the headlines: 'Top Afrikaner *verligtes* to support UP' and 'Top professors boost the UP'. The reports claimed both Olivier and Slabbert had turned to the UP in an 'unexpected breakthrough' that would be 'a forerunner of the massive turn in the electoral tide which Graaff said the UP were working at'.

The *Times* made it clear that Olivier had joined and would be a candidate. While to the casual reader it would have appeared that Slabbert had also joined, I sensed there was a degree of ambiguity in the article. When I called Slabbert, he was out. I managed to talk to a very distressed Mana Slabbert, his wife. She told me her husband was in a serious predicament and desperately needed to talk to someone.

Eventually Slabbert and I met at the Jan Smuts Airport Holiday Inn since I was flying back to Cape Town later that afternoon. Slabbert was certainly of the view that *verligtes* should start playing a proactive role in the party political arena; and he was intrigued by the emergence of the young Turks.

When Slabbert had heard that the UP was offering Olivier a safe UP seat in the election, he encouraged his friend to accept the offer. However, while expressing an interest in what was happening, Slabbert had not yet decided to follow the same course even though he had been made a firm offer of the Randburg seat.

During the previous week I had asked Neil Ross, the PP's regional director, to analyse the political situation in the newly delimited Cape Peninsula seat of Rondebosch. As a result of the changes to the boundary, and the absence of Graaff as a candidate, Ross and I concluded that the party would do well, but was likely to lose the seat by about eleven hundred votes. I told Slabbert that Ross and I were of the view that with a candidate of his calibre we could win the seat. I took my courage in my hands and offered him the opportunity of being the PP candidate in the Rondebosch constituency.

If nothing else, he would pin down a large number of UP workers in Rondebosch and help me win Sea Point, the other flagship constituency in the Peninsula. I told him that I needed to know his answer by noon the following Tuesday.

The Rondebosch constituency committee gave me considerable flak for not consulting them before making the offer to Slabbert. I explained the circumstances and said I trusted Slabbert's commitment to the fundamental principles of the PP and believed he could win Rondebosch. The committee endorsed my decision.

On Tuesday, a few minutes before the noon deadline, Slabbert phoned me and said: 'I am your candidate for Rondebosch. I prefer a challenge to a safe seat.'

A night to remember

In Rondebosch the surprise nomination of Van Zyl Slabbert set the campaign alight. Campaign chairman Frank Robb and campaign organiser John Whitehead were there to ensure the enthusiasm was harnessed in the most effective way. In Sea Point I had the benefit of a campaign chairman in charge of each of the four polling districts: Ronnie Abel, Arthur Wienberg, Michael Sher and Peter le Cordeur. Barry Streek was my campaign organiser.

This was the first general election in which the parliamentary and provincial council polls were held on the same day. Sea Point enjoyed an added impetus by having Herbert Hirsch, a dependable and respected resident of the suburb, as its provincial council candidate, and as such a member of the election team. In both Sea Point and Rondebosch the will to win was unbelievable. People flocked to augment the voluntary workforce.

I had the support of a highly motivated and energetic election team – fortunately so, since in addition to being the candidate in Sea Point, I had to carry out my countrywide responsibilities as leader of the party. Because I was the leader of the PP and had David Graaff – son of the leader of the UP – as my opponent, the UP made Sea Point the focal point of its election campaign in the Peninsula.

At one stage Dr Marius Barnard – a distinguished heart surgeon and a personal friend – had been invited by the UP's young Turks to stand against me in Sea Point. He decided not to. Indeed, he became so committed to the Progressive Federal Party (PFP, as the PP became) and what it stood for, that at the final congress of the party in April 1989 he was the only delegate to vote against the PFP's dissolution so that, to-gether with the Independent Party and the National Democratic Movement, it could form the Democratic Party.

It was clear from the outset of the campaign that the NP was as determined as the UP that I should lose Sea Point. The Nats had considered putting up a candidate in the constituency, but backed off when it realised that this would split the anti-Pro-gressive vote. The Afrikaans-language press, led by *Die Burger*, urged Nat supporters to vote for David Graaff. It was also clear that Graaff was flirting with leading Nation-alists in the constituency. This gave rise to two interesting incidents: one to do with *koeksusters*, and the other with Donald Woods.

Carlos Santos, a 'fixer' of sorts who had an uncanny insight into what was going on behind the scenes, got wind of the fact that David Graaff would attend a gathering of Nationalists at the home of a prominent member of the NP in Sea Point. We gave the story to the press, and on the afternoon of the gathering Santos took a reporter and photographer along to wait for Graaff to emerge.

During the meeting, which was addressed by Blaar Coetzee, Graaff must have been alerted that there were people waiting outside. He decided to leave by a back gate, but ran straight into a reporter the wily Santos had positioned there. Asked for an explanation, Graaff said he had been invited by 'a little old lady who used to make *koeksusters* with my granny'. The absurdity ran well in the press.

There was a sequel a few evenings later at a public meeting in the Weizmann Hall, which Schwarz was to address in support of Graaff's candidature. During the meeting, Santos's wife, with a large plate of *koeksusters* held aloft, walked from the back of the hall and politely delivered them to the table on the platform where Graaff was sitting!

Donald Woods, who had done some canvassing for me during the 1970 election, and had assisted me in establishing *Deurbraak* and in organising the Bulugha con-ference, came to Sea Point to help me in the final stages of the campaign. From the time I had been leader of the PP, Woods had taken delight in calling me *Die Volksleier*, and my dear wife Joyce, *Die Volksmoeder*. Ten days before the election he addressed a public meeting that I held in Hout Bay, one of the Sea Point voting dis-tricts. The audience enjoyed listening to Woods, and he enjoyed speaking to them. But not *Die Burger*, which embarked on a week-long tirade against Woods – not for what he said at Hout Bay but for what it alleged he had said at the graveside of Cur-nick Ndamse.

Ndamse, a colleague of mine in Synthesis, was a close friend of Woods who spoke with passion at his funeral earlier that month. *Die Burger*, quoting Woods com-pletely out of context, accused Woods of being a '*boerehater*' – a hater of Afrikaners. Furthermore, as a *boerehater*, he had spoken at a PP meeting in support of Eglin. Afrikaners in Sea Point should vote for David Graaff.

This manipulation of the truth incensed the English-language press. The *Cape Times* published the full text of Wood's funeral address and castigated *Die Burger* in a leader.

The campaign ended in a flurry of public meetings. On the Monday two days before the election, Suzman and I criss-crossed Cape Town so that both could speak at meetings in Rondebosch and Sea Point. The Rondebosch town hall and the Weizmann Hall were filled to overflowing with a total of 2 000 people at the meetings. If attendance and enthusiasm were any measure of success, Suzman and I were on a high.

On 24 April, the day of the election, I received news from around the country indicating that, from a PP point of view, things were going well. There had been no last- minute upsets; election organisation was running smoothly. In our key seats voters were coming in large numbers to the PP tables, and when the polls closed at nine o'clock that evening the figure in our Sea Point campaign office indicated we had won. However, having been beaten by a narrow margin at the previous election, we were taking nothing for granted.

In the UP campaign office not far from ours there were early celebrations; the UP estimated that Graaff had won by about a thousand votes.

Herbert Hirsch and I waited in the Kings Road School hall, the polling station where the four districts comprising Sea Point checked and counted the votes. Suddenly there was a roar from the crowd outside. News had come through that Gordon Waddell, an executive director of the Anglo-American Corporation, who had offered to stand as a candidate for the PP, had won Johannesburg North by a whopping majority of 1 403 votes.

More PP victories followed: René de Villiers, the former editor of *The Star*, won Parktown by 391 votes; Helen Suzman retained Houghton with an increased majority of 3 513 votes; Van Zyl Slabbert won Rondebosch by 1 568 votes; Rupert Lorimer, whom I had persuaded to make a tactical switch from Bryanston to the Orange Grove constituency, to the Progressives' delight had turned a UP majority of 5 166 in 1970 to a PP majority of 742 in 1974!

The question was, 'What about Sea Point?' We had a long wait, as the presiding officer took ill. He was replaced, and the new officer quite correctly wanted to check that the preliminary work was in order before he proceeded with the count. It was completed in the small hours of the morning.

There was a hush as the presiding officer went through the formalities and announced the result: 'For Colin ...' He was drowned out by a tremendous cry of applause and jubilation from the Progs. I had won by 839 votes.

By that time the UP supporters had melted away. A short while later there was further jubilation among the Progressives when the presiding officer announced that Hirsch had won the Cape Provincial Council seat. Day was breaking when Joyce and I returned to our apartment. The telephone rang incessantly. I was exhausted with excitement and could do little more than respond to the callers by saying: 'What a day! What a night!'

My initiatives had succeeded. For the first time, the white voters in significant numbers had turned their backs on apartheid and sent to parliament a viable and energetic party committed to working for a South Africa where all were equal before the law and in which race and colour would no longer be the factors that determined rights and dignity.

Six becomes seven, June 1974

Although the results had been announced by the evening of 25 April, the election was incomplete. Oswald Newton-Thompson, the UP MP for Pinelands, who stood again as the party's candidate for that seat, was killed in an airplane accident while campaigning in South West Africa. A fresh election for the constituency was set for 12 June. Roger Hulley, the PP candidate, had lost the provincial council seat; while he improved the party's position the PP still trailed the UP by 2 554 votes.

In the wake of Newton-Thompson's death, I believed the bandwagon effect of the Progressives' successes in the general election, and in particular its victories in Rondebosch and Sea Point, would enable it to do even better in June: we could win.

The organisational issue was resolved by placing it in the hands of Neil Ross, the regional director of the PP who was widely accepted, even by his political opponents, as having no peer when it came to election co-ordination. He was known as 'Ross the Boss'. The issue of the candidate was more problematic. I had someone in mind – a long shot since he lived in Johannesburg and worked as an employment practices consultant to Harry Oppenheimer. He was Dr Alex Boraine, who had recently distinguished himself as President of the Methodist Church of South Africa.

My relationship with Boraine went back some years. He was intrigued by politics and took the trouble to come to Cape Town for a few days to canvass for me in my election for Sea Point. In this he was joined by Theo Kotze, another Methodist clergyman, who had served in Sea Point but was then working in the Christian Institute.

I phoned Boraine and offered him the nomination. Not unexpectedly he was surprised, but would discuss it with his wife Jenny and with Oppenheimer before responding. A week or so later Alex Boraine became our candidate for Pinelands. His opponent was Annette Reineke, who had recently won the Provincial Council seat in Rondebosch for the NP despite Slabbert's triumphant win in the parliamentary seat. Reineke had been a long-time resident of Pinelands; ironically, in the late 1940s, when I was chairman of the Pinelands Young People's Club, she was my vice-chairman.

The contending parties threw their entire capacity into the campaign. Late on the night of the poll, outside St Stephen's church hall, where 15 years earlier I had held the meeting to report back my reasons for resigning from the UP, the returning officer announced that Boraine had won by 34 votes.

Our six had become seven.

Visit to Nigeria, July 1974

After the drama, my first task was to ensure that our new parliamentary caucus was moulded into an effective political team. This was not difficult: everyone shared a belief in the basic values on which the PP had been founded, and a commitment to building up the party as a vehicle for the promotion of these values. We discussed overall strategy and our priorities for our first parliamentary session at the end of July. Helen's experience and judgement were of immense value. We also managed to raise some money to finance a small parliamentary secretariat.

Before the session, I decided to travel to Africa once more. In Botswana, Zambia and Kenya I could meet old friends and discuss our breakthroughs. In Nigeria I would be breaking new ground. That country's ambassador in Gaborone, whom I knew, issued a visa for me to visit Nigeria and ensured me of an official welcome. My plan was for Helen to come with me to Gaborone, and thereafter for Van Zyl Slabbert to join me in Lusaka and accompany me to Nairobi and on to Lagos.

I saw Slabbert not only as a highly compatible travel companion but also as a new factor in our politics who could convey to our African hosts a refreshing interpretation of developments in South Africa.

Helen and I duly went to Gaborone, and once again I came away swayed by the contrast between the warmth, the generosity of spirit, and the humanity of our Batswana hosts, and the tight-lipped racial bigotry of the apartheid leaders. Slabbert joined me in Lusaka, where we both stayed with Zach and Mona de Beer. Zach, with customary attention to detail, made arrangements for us to meet President Kenneth Kaunda. The encounter was pleasant and friendly. Kaunda was particularly interested in the general election result and the progress made by the PP.

In Nairobi Slabbert and I were the guests of Charles and Margaret Njonjo in their impressive Mathaiga home – not many such homes in Africa could have a guest wing occupied by a professional tennis player, a professor of fine art, and two members of parliament from South Africa! We flew on to Lagos not knowing what to expect.

The promised hospitality materialised. We were met by the deputy chief of protocol and a senior official of the Department of External Affairs. We were official guests of the federal government headed by General Yakubu Gowan; our programme was in the hands of Joseph Iyala, director of the Department of External Affairs.

My first impressions of Lagos were the heat and humidity, and the hustle and bustle of the crowded streets, the vast crowded markets, the variety of newspapers available and the flair for music – minstrels gathering outside the hotels and dance bands playing late into the night. Looking out to sea we saw dozens of ships at anchor waiting for a berth in the antiquated harbour. It all seemed pretty chaotic but it appeared to work, or to work somehow.

At our first meeting Joseph Iyala gave us a summarised history of Nigeria. Prominent was the war of secession by the oil-rich Eastern State, known outside Nigeria as Biafra. A coup had led to the installation of General Gowan as head of the Federal Military Government, and there followed the current post-war policy of reconstruction and reconciliation. Slabbert and I, in turn, outlined political events in South

Africa together with the contrasting objectives for the future of the South African government and the PP. We argued that it was extremely important for us to visit the Eastern State – and were bold enough to say that our visit would not be complete without a meeting with General Gowan.

An hour's flight took us to Enugu where we were generously and lavishly entertained by Oko I Oko, military commissioner for the Eastern State. A couple of the banquets we attended were so lavish that it was difficult for us to believe that we were in 'starving Biafra'. We saw and heard of the progress being made in the implementation of reconstruction and reconciliation, yet sensed a prevailing undercurrent of ethnic and regional tension.

On our last evening in Lagos, Slabbert and I had a busy round of newspaper and radio interviews, one of which carried a full-page article in *The Renaissance* under the heading: 'We will change South Africa without violence'. Next morning after breakfast we checked out of the hotel wondering where we would be sleeping that night, as our flight plans had been disrupted, and took a taxi to a petrol station where AD ('Jim') Blankson was due to meet us at 9 am for our meeting with Gowan.

Nine o'clock – and no sign of Blankson. A quarter past, then twenty past. Still no Blankson. 'Great,' we thought, 'no plane home, and now no meeting with Gowan.'

Blankson's car arrived. He had run out of petrol: 'Get in, the General is waiting for you. Dodon Barracks where his office is located is just down the road.'

General Gowan, a good-looking man of medium build, dressed in his military uniform, received us warmly and put us at ease. Slabbert commented to Gowan that at 32 he was quite young to be a general; to which Gowan responded that Slabbert was quite young to be a professor! Slabbert and I gave Gowan an assessment of the situation in South Africa and the role of the PP.

Gowan outlined recent events in Nigeria, including the war of secession and the earnest commitment of his government to reconstruction. In the same vein as the African leaders whom Helen and I had met on our previous visit, Gowan made it clear that he and his government were not against the whites, but were strongly anti-apartheid. His message to South Africans was that the choice was theirs. Abolish apartheid and be welcomed as part of Africa, or continue as before and face increasing pressure from the rest of the continent.

After an hour with Gowan I suggested he must have other important matters to attend to, and that we should take our leave. He smiled and said that it was hardly necessary to leave because of his commitments; but because we had to get to the airport in time to catch a plane to Madrid on the first leg of our journey back to South Africa. With that he presented us with a new set of air tickets 'with the compliments of the federal government'.

We bade farewell and went outside to meet a very worried Blankson. He did not know how we were going to get through the downtown traffic in mid-morning Lagos in time to catch our plane; he left us and went back into Gowan's offices. A minute or so later, engines roaring, five gleaming motorcycles with presidential outriders clad in white arrived and formed up in front of our car. With sirens blazing our escort cleared a path through the crowded streets, like a ship in choppy seas. The traffic in central Lagos was brought to a standstill as the cavalcade, bearing Eglin and Slabbert, weaved its way to the airport.

Back home the English-language press carried complimentary comments about our visit. Prime Minister Vorster, in the process of attempting his own effort at détente with Africa, was dismissive. PW Botha, Minister of Defence, was furious. He attacked us for throwing ourselves 'at the feet of black leaders in Africa, who allowed gangs of murderers to go for women and children on the Rhodesian and South African borders. These terrorists are not freedom fighters. But Eglin and like-minded people are prepared to sit around a table with these people. We say to them: take it easy. South Africa will deal with you.'

By contrast, Hilgard Muller, Minister of Foreign Affairs, was mildly approving of the PP initiatives. He said he approved of the visits and the patriotism they displayed, and appreciated the goodwill they generated.

12

The Progressive Reform Party
1975

On 25 April 1974, while South Africans were waiting for the final results of the election, Portuguese armed forces led by General Antonio Spinola overthrew the fascist government in Lisbon. The coup ended 47 years of dictatorship, and brought to an end 500 years of Portuguese colonialism. The strategic map of southern Africa was changed, with dramatic effects on the politics and future of South Africa.

The major strategic buffers which the Portuguese colonies of Mozambique and Angola had provided for the South African government would no longer be there. The position of the Ian Smith government in Rhodesia was to become untenable; and Rhodesia itself would cease being a buffer between South Africa and the black states to the north. Overnight the borders of the Republic and of South West Africa became the new strategic frontiers. Independent and hostile black Africa would soon be at the gates of Prime Minister Vorster's South Africa.

With the withdrawal of the Portuguese, white South Africans were on their own on the continent. My concern was that they would develop a *laager* mentality and the country be caught up in a war psychosis. Indeed, much of the politics of the next few years was to be fought against this background. Against this prospect, my message was that white South Africans had to show 'that they were not extensions of Europe in Africa, but that they were Africans – white Africans'. They had to come to terms with Africa.

Time was crucial. I was acutely aware of the need to find common ground with black South Africans on the future of our country. For me the national issue was no longer whether whites wanted discrimination, but how in practice they would get rid of it.

The first session of the newly elected parliament commenced at the end of July. Helen and I shared a front bench on the opposition side of the House, with the rest of our PP team sharing a couple of double benches immediately behind us. Sitting sandwiched between the UP and the NP and facing Vorster and his cabinet colleagues a few metres away, I became very aware that for the next few years my political battles would be waged at close quarters.

It was strange to be back in parliament after 13 years. There was a familiarity about the House of Assembly, the paneled walls, the green leather seats, the Speaker's chair, the secretary's desk, and the officials in attendance, the press and public galleries above. Thirteen years ago I had been a somewhat rebellious backbencher; now I was the leader of a political party that had the responsibility of trying to steer the country in a new direction.

Helen and her six parliamentary colleagues tackled their work and constituency responsibilities with energy and enthusiasm. We were a cohesive and effective team. Added to this, when we were not engaged in the work of parliament we enjoyed one another's company and became friends in addition to being colleagues. We quipped that one advantage of being only seven was that we could convene our caucus in the lift. And the task of projecting ourselves as an effective opposition was made easier by the fact that the UP, the official opposition, was more divided and indecisive than ever before.

On one occasion our team faced a decision on a matter directly related to the stand we had taken on the 'land' issue when we broke away from the UP in 1959. The government introduced a bill to purchase additional land for the Native Trust (then known as the Bantu Trust). In 1936 such land had been promised to 'natives', and indeed, had been the issue on which we left the UP in 1958. So we decided to vote with the government on the bill. Predictably, the UP voted against the bill.

In November the PP held its first national congress since the election. I had decided to propose that we appoint a committee to review aspects of policy, given the developments since the Molteno Commission reported in the early 1960s. My own Sea Point committee wanted to pre-empt this review by asking congress to scrap existing party policy providing for the local option on the use of public amenities, and replace it by a policy in which public amenities would be open to all races. My committee had played a pivotal role in my election as an MP, so I decided to help it draft a resolution to be put to congress. The resolution was passed unanimously and accepted without demur by party formations around the country.

The Argus was prompted to write: 'The party is gearing itself to face up to the changes around it in the vital sphere of constitutional and franchise policy and has bravely made a policy change, underlining the role of its leader … who has chosen for it a small "spearhead" against racial discrimination.'

Before the end of the year the focus of opposition politics shifted back to the struggling UP. By December there were reports of an opinion poll that showed that Schwarz was considered a more effective leader than Graaff. It emerged that Dick Enthoven had initiated the poll and authorised its findings to be made public. In January 1975 the UP suspended Enthoven's membership of the party. This triggered a rebellion, and on 12 April ten members of the Transvaal Provincial Council resigned from the UP.

The following day MPs Schwarz and Dave Dalling, and Senator Brian Bamford, were expelled from the party, and Horace van Rensburg and Enthoven resigned. They, together with a number of UP office-bearers, indicated that they intended to form a Reform Party (RP) under Schwarz's leadership. Within days I received a message indicating that Schwarz would welcome a meeting of the leaderships of the Reformists and the PP.

Schwarz and I, each accompanied by five of our party members, met at the Johannesburg Carlton Hotel on 2 March. It was clear that the RP was seen as an interim stage in the process of opposition realignment; a merger between the PP and the RP was on the cards.

I was aware that Helen, who had borne the brunt of UP attacks in the Transvaal – including those from Schwarz and his young Turks – was not enamoured of finding herself in one party with these erstwhile opponents. She and I were due to address a meeting in the Johannesburg city hall the following evening.

The *RDM* wrote: 'Both the PP leader, Colin Eglin, and its veteran Houghton MP, Helen Suzman, last night committed themselves to achieving a strong *verligte* opposition in South Africa.' Helen in her own inimitable style said: 'I don't seem to be fond of all Reformists who may be contemplating joining us and I'm pretty sure that they are not mad about me. None of that is important. What is of importance is that those of us who come together shall do so on very firm grounds.'

I set out the four principles that became basic to a new *verligte* opposition:

- A belief in the dignity and worth of each individual South African.
- A willingness to come to terms with real power-sharing by all the country's citizens.
- A determination to eliminate race discrimination.
- A total commitment to defend civil liberties and the rule of law.

From then on the process of merging the PP and the RP to form the Progressive Reform Party (PRP) went ahead comparatively smoothly. From the outset Schwarz and the representatives of the RP had stated their willingness to serve under me as party leader. Ray Swart and Slabbert of the PP, and Bamford and Enthoven of the RP, were charged with preparing a working document relevant to the merger.

In the last week of May, Schwarz and I issued a joint statement in which we announced that the national executives had recommended that the two parties merge on the basis of a joint declaration of principles. In our statement Schwarz and I said: 'A turning point has been reached in the history of South Africa's political opposition. For 27 years the story of opposition has been one of increasing fragmentation and division. The old official opposition, divided among itself on important matters of principle, has been unable to give a lead or to rally and unite the forces of opposition. The process of fragmentation has been stopped. The tide has turned. Out of the historic decisions of the executives of the new Progressive and Reform parties, a new effective, combined opposition will emerge – an opposition which will present clear-cut constructive alternatives to the race policies of the Nationalists.'

The national executive decided to offer Schwarz the position of chairman of the national executive on the clear understanding that the position of chairman of the party, which would continue to be held by Swart, was to be the number-two position in the new party hierarchy. Both Swart and Schwarz accepted this arrangement, and with this what might have been a divisive factor in the new party was overcome.

The PRP was formed on 27 July. Long-standing political adversaries came together in a joint belief in fundamental principles and an 'alternative to apartheid'. I identified the need for the PRP to become relevant to black South Africans: 'It is important for us to seek the support of white voters [but] it is equally important that we earn the respect of the millions of black South Africans who are not voters.

'We together with other white South Africans must realise that the peace, the progress and the security of our country and our people will depend in the years to come, not merely on white votes or on statutory authority or on the millions of rands we spend on defence, but on the amount of mutual trust and goodwill and common purpose which exists between white and black citizens of South Africa.'

I went to sleep satisfied that, far from diluting the principles on which the old PP had been founded in 1959, I had helped make these relevant to the needs and challenges of South Africa in 1975.

Vorster, détente and Mandela

During the latter part of 1974 it became apparent that Vorster appreciated the strategic significance of the pending withdrawal of Portugal from its colonies of Angola and Mozambique. He realised that with this strategic white partner departing, it was important for him to reach out to black leaders in Africa. He launched détente. To signal the new direction he gave a major policy speech in parliament in November, talking of peace with black Africa – and asking that South Africa be given 'six months' grace'.

It soon became clear that he and some of his ministers had been making behind-the-scenes contact with leaders in a number of African states. In May 1975 it was disclosed that six months previously Vorster had held a two-day meeting with President Felix Houphouet-Boigny in the Ivory Coast, in September 1974. In February he visited Liberia; and that same month Foreign Minister Hilgard Muller went to Lusaka for talks with the foreign ministers of Tanzania, Zambia and Botswana, and leaders of the Rhodesian ANC.

Later in 1975 the Ivory Coast's minister of information visited South Africa on a fact-finding mission at the invitation of Minister Connie Mulder.

In a parliamentary debate I welcomed the concept of détente but emphasised that if there was no positive response from African leaders, South Africa would be worse off than before. It would result in a whirlwind of raising hopes and then dashing them. Based on my discussions with the leaders of the many countries I had visited, I could state that the key to lasting détente lay not so much in talking to leaders in Africa, but with 'the elimination of race discrimination and apartheid in South Africa'.

I appealed to Vorster to consider the remission of sentences for Nelson Mandela and other political prisoners. This was bluntly rejected by Vorster who replied that he did not consider Mandela and the others sent to jail as political detainees: 'They were sent to prison by a competent court ... They were card-carrying members of the Communist Party who did not have the interests of the blacks or whites at heart, but wished to establish a communist state in the interests of the Kremlin.'

He failed to see an essential pathway to Africa.

Zaire in focus, May 1975

At the end of May I flew to Kinshasa on a four-day fact-finding mission to Zaire. This vast territory – generally known as the Congo – had a long border with Angola, which provided the route for the Benguela railway to the port of Lobito for the transport of copper from Zaire's Shaba province. Its strategic position made events unfolding in Angola as it moved towards independence of special significance to Zaire.

In addition, a close relationship had existed for a number of years between President Mobutu Sese Seko's government in Zaire and Holden Roberto's FNLA, one of the three rival liberation movements in Angola. I wanted to find out more about impending events in Angola as seen from the Zairian perspective, and wished to meet Mobutu, an army officer who had seized power in November 1965.

I became apprehensive when the Sabena aircraft in which I was flying touched down at Kinshasa airport just after midnight *en route* to Brussels. My apprehension increased when I realised I was the only passenger disembarking; that I had no visa; that I could not speak French; and that I did not know who would meet me. I was relieved to see a white-haired man at the foot of the staircase who came forward with his hand outstretched and said: 'You're Colin Eglin? Welcome. I am Larry Devlin. I'll be looking after you for the next few days.'

Devlin explained that he had worked for the US government in Central Africa during the early 1960s. He retired, and returned to Kinshasa as a business consultant. Mobutu was not in Kinshasa at present, he said, but in Gbadolite – a town close to the border with the Central African Republic where Mobutu had been born and to where he moved his presidential office for a few weeks each year. This ensured a serviceable airport, access road, and buildings and infrastructure to support the presence of the president, staff and visitors for his stay in the small town set in the vast rain forest 1 000 km from Kinshasa.

Devlin accompanied me to the government guest lodge, a comfortable air-conditioned bungalow-type of building. The following morning we boarded a Zairian military transport plane for our flight to Gbadolite. At our destination later, Devlin, who spoke French and acted as interpreter, introduced me to the president and we had a congenial and enlightening discussion. The president was less forbidding than I had pictured him: he wore a plain military uniform, tortoise-shell glasses, a neat leopard skin hat and a relaxed smile.

Mobutu asked me whether I had seen the people who had just left his office – a group of whites in European suits. 'They are representatives of the Portuguese government,' he said. 'Perhaps your government should know the irony of the fact that the black government of Zaire is backing the non-Marxist FNLA, while the white regime in Lisbon is backing the pro-Marxist MPLA.'

In spite of the agreement reached between the three liberation movements earlier in the year, there was still no joint government or sign of elections. On the contrary, the Angolan situation had degenerated into armed conflict between the three contenders. The Portuguese were abdicating their responsibility over the colony and preparing to hand over power to the MPLA – which controlled Luanda and its immediate hinterland, but not the rest of the country under the control of the FNLA and UNITA.

Mobutu had met presidents Kaunda and Nyerere on a number of occasions to discuss the implications for the southern African region, which he appeared to understand well. He mentioned that he listened to broadcasts from Radio South Africa. He was not impressed by the South African government's claim that it could maintain enforced segregation and at the same time get rid of race discrimination. To him this was a rejection of the black man's human dignity.

He recognised the economic strength of South Africa and the role it could one day play in the development of the continent. But, he said, the Republic would not be able to do this until it got rid of apartheid and discrimination. As far as formal government-to-government contact was concerned, Mobutu maintained that a prerequisite was a settlement of the Rhodesian and South West African issues. He recognised that South Africa was an independent state and that it would take time to eliminate apartheid, but Rhodesia and South West Africa were different. They represented unresolved problems of the colonial era.

When asked for a message to take back to South Africa, Mobutu's was similar to that given to me by other African leaders: 'Tell the people of your country that we are not opposed to the white people of South Africa. We are opposed to the policy of apartheid.'

Kinshasa was a sprawling city on the banks of the Zaire River, whose population had grown from 400 000 to 2 200 000 in the 15 years of the country's independence. Catholic cathedrals and Protestant churches reminded one that although Zaire was a one-party state and intensely nationalistic – and would describe itself as non-aligned – its economic and cultural involvement leaned strongly towards the West.

One evening on the way back from Kinshasa to Binza, Devlin warned me that since members of the army were poorly paid, they augmented their income by erecting roadblocks and demanding payment from each passenger of a vehicle before allowing it to continue. As I had a South African passport and no visa, and couldn't speak French, Devlin told me to refer any questions and demands the soldiers might make to him. In due course we came to a roadblock and I found myself looking out of the window down the barrel of a gun. Devlin took over and produced a large green and gold embossed visiting card. The blockading soldiers gathered around to examine it, and without further ado removed the barrier and allowed us to pass.

Devlin explained that he had once saved Mobutu's life by warning him of an assassination plot. In consequence Mobutu had made him an officer of the Order of the Leopard – the green and gold card signified that no person could arrest or detain the holder except with the express authority of the president. 'It normally works,' Devlin explained. 'But occasionally I come across someone who cannot read!'

The subsequent disintegration of Mobutu's Zaire was a long time coming.

An advance towards multiracialism

It was the immediate task of the collective leadership of the party to get our fresh message across to the general public and to our party formations and grassroots supporters in particular. We were helped by a supportive English-language press; for its part, the Afrikaans press, which generally supported the NP, understood that the formation of the PRP was a significant event in opposition politics. It had to be content with trying to play off the personalities in the new party against one another.

Of course this made good reading. However, any problems that may have arisen from strong-willed personalities, who for many years had been political opponents, was more than offset by the excitement generated by the formation of the PRP.

During the first year of my return to parliament, I set up the machinery and worked on the process that would enable me to keep in touch with my constituents in Sea Point. I wanted to make sure they came to know me as someone in touch with them – and accountable to them. I would be available for personal advice and assistance. The PRP office was restyled as the 'Citizens Advice Centre' – where voters could obtain general information and, when necessary, discuss problems and political issues with me.

I held regular clinics at which I discussed topical issues: items such as rent control and pensions which were uppermost in the minds of elderly voters. These clinics, while aimed primarily at Sea Point constituents, were often attended by voters from elsewhere in the Peninsula. I was pleased to hear them say that friends had told them I would be able to help them.

On the broader political front, the PRP extended its contacts with Coloured, black and Indian community leaders. We were determined to breach political barriers. In September we convened a summit with the specific object of promoting inter-racial political co-operation. Held in Johannesburg, it was attended by delegations from KwaZulu, Gazankulu, Lebowa, QwaQwa, the Indian Representative Council, the Labour Party, and of course the PRP. This did not reflect the full spectrum of political views, but confirmed the commitment of leaders who had been forced apart by apartheid to work together across racial barriers. After a day of interaction, the leaders of the delegations issued the following statement:

· We, the leaders of organisations and statutory bodies which have been separated from one another by the laws of our country, declare that we will work together for peaceful change in South Africa.

- Because we share a common ideal for our Fatherland, South Africa, and are in agreement on the fundamental issues relating to the future of our country, we have decided to create the necessary machinery in order to examine and articulate our agreement on these fundamental issues.
- We will consult at regular intervals during the next year.
- We will keep lines of communication open, so that immediate consultation between us will take place if the circumstances render it necessary.
- We realise that plans for the future of our country will have to be the outcome of frank discussions and exchange of views between representatives of the various sections of our wider South African community, and to be successful must have broad national assent.

Accordingly, a declaration was made 'of working towards the holding of a convention as representative as possible of all who are South Africans, for the purpose of obtaining a mandate from the people for the constitutional and other proposals which will emanate from the initiative we have taken today. We are agreed that apartheid or, as it is called, separate development does not offer a solution and that any constitutional system must embody a bill of rights safeguarding the rights of both individuals and groups.

'We accept that in one united South Africa, territory and not race must form the basis of government, which should not be racially exclusive.'

Lessons from a wider world

In November 1975 I was one of six MPs who accompanied the president of the South African Senate, Jan de Klerk, and his wife (the parents of the future president FW de Klerk) on a visit to Iran. I took the opportunity to stop over in Zambia, Tanzania and Kenya on my way north; and in Turkey, Greece and Israel on my return south. In the case of Kaunda, Nyerere, and Njonjo – among my previous major contacts in Africa – all showed increasing frustration with the lack of progress on independence for Rhodesia and South West Africa, and the elimination of apartheid.

Nyerere said he would press for South Africa's isolation, adding: 'South Africa is weakening its own case by saying it would lead black South Africans to separate independence instead of acknowledging them as full citizens of South Africa. The government is taking on the mantle of a colonial power.' As for SWA, 'Vorster has no legal right to be there in any case.'

My ten days in Iran could not have been in greater contrast. At that time a close relationship existed between the Vorster regime and the Iranian government under Mohammad Reza Shah Pahlavi. Iran had an embassy in Pretoria, and South Africa had one in Teheran where General 'Pop' Fraser, a distinguished veteran of World

War 2, was the ambassador. There was a substantial two-way trade between the two countries. Iranians would say: 'We are partners, you supply us with gold, yellow gold; we are supplying you with gold, black gold, in the form of oil.'

Given General Fraser's appointment, I had no doubt there was co-operation between Iran and South Africa in the military and armament fields.

We were treated like royalty, staying in the new Hilton Hotel in Teheran where our suites were kept for us even when we travelled to other parts of the country. We had motorcycle and armed escorts, and when we flew it was in the well-appointed aircraft of the Shah's family.

As a foreshadowing of events to come, there were two features of Iran which as a South African I could not help but notice. The first was the vast gap between a small group of wealthy elite and the masses. The Shah had achieved considerable success with his 'white' revolution – a process by which agricultural land was transferred from feudal landlords to small farmers in exchange for funds, which the feudal landlords were required to invest in industrial enterprises.

Nevertheless, the style of living of the elite was outrageously opulent – a house on the French Riviera, a bank account in Switzerland, children educated in England. It all ended suddenly and tragically. In 1978 when the revolutionary regime of Ayatollah Khomeini seized power, bank accounts were frozen, airports and exit points from Iran were closed, and our hosts of 1975 were executed.

The second feature I noticed was that while Iran had the trappings of democracy – in the form of apparently accountable structures of governance – it had a brutally authoritarian regime. In law and administration the Shah was omniscient: his decree was final. His portraits adorned the walls of every building. Monuments to the Shah's father, founder of the dynasty, abounded. Headlines in the media focused on the activities of the Shah. Citizens lived in awe of him and in fear of the secret police. In the end, the Shah and his close family fled to Egypt, which gave him refuge and where in due course he died.

It was my good fortune to be given the opportunity to assess various forms of government across the globe, as in Iran – from where one could draw the lesson of how the prelude to revolution is exacerbated by a gulf between the ruling elite and the majority of the population. In addition to my travels in Africa and visits to the US, I made a number of other productive visits abroad – to South West Africa, Rhodesia, Germany, and early in 1974 to England, the Netherlands, Belgium, France and Israel.

In Rhodesia – labouring under the historical hiatus of its Unilateral Declaration of Independence – I spent two days in 1973; they were neither especially helpful nor encouraging. I met Pat Bashford and members of his Centre Party. They had good intentions but their relatively small political base was under great pressure from the forces of Joshua Nkomo and Robert Mugabe on the one hand, and Ian Smith on the other.

With Smith, while much of the discussion was about South Africa. I sensed no softening of the 'never in 1 000 years' line that he adopted when he declared UDI in 1965. A greater pleasure was that of meeting Sir Roy Welensky, prime minister of the former Central African Federation. He was friendly, blunt-spoken, down to earth, and fascinating when reminiscing about the past. However, with the Central African Federation then only a memory, Welensky had no real vision for a future Rhodesia.

In Germany in October 1972, at the invitation of the federal government, I was able to take in Bonn, Berlin, Hamburg and Munich, and to observe the election for chancellor between Willie Brandt of the Socialist SDP and Rainer Barzel of the Conservative CDU-CSU. All this stimulated my interest in studying further Germany's constitution, the nature of its federal system, and the concept of the free vote in parliament. Aspects such as proportional representation; the division of powers, together with the sharing of finances between the federal government and the provinces; entrenchment of fundamental rights; and the role of the constitutional court became important points of reference in 1991-1996 when I helped negotiate our new democratic constitution.

Top: In discussion with Shimon Peres, then leader of the Israeli Labour Party, in his office in Jerusalem. (Scoop 80 Photographers, Jerusalem)

Bottom: With Van Zyl Slabbert and Alex Boraine in the 'good old Prog days'. (*The Argus*, Cape Town)

Left: With Louis le Grange, Minister of Law and Order (arms folded), on a parliamentary inspection tour of the Angola/South West Africa border, April 1984.

Below: Seated with Harry Oppenheimer, Helen Suzman (partly obscured by gentleman's black hat) and other invited guests at the signing of the Nkomati Accord by President Samora Machel and Prime Minister PW Botha, March 1983.

Above: Outside parliament after my re-election as PFP leader and leader of the opposition, following Van Zyl Slabbert's resignation in January 1986.

Right: In my parliamentary office on a day when things went well.

Above: With the PFP's new leadership team, February 1986: Douglas Gibson, vice-chairman, federal executive; Robin Carlisle, general secretary; Peter Gastrow, chairman of party; Ken Andrew, chairman, federal executive.

Right: Being welcomed by Prime Minister Margaret Thatcher at No 10 Downing Street, June 1986.

Opposite page
Top: Jan van Eck, Colin Eglin and Jasper Walsh, with our wives Eunice, Joyce and Margie, celebrating after Jan and Jasper were elected to parliament at by-elections in Claremont and Pinelands, October 1986.

Bottom: With Alan Paton and my PFP parliamentary colleagues Mamoo Rajab, Pat Poovalingam and Ray Swart after a 1987 election meeting in Durban.

Opposite page
Top: In discussion with General Olusegun Obasanjo and Chief Minister Mangosuthu Buthelezi during a conference in Sitges, Spain.

Bottom: Ji Peng Fei, a member of the National Peoples' Congress and a veteran of 'the Long March', hosting Helen and me at a welcoming dinner in Beijing during our visit to the People's Pepublic of China in November 1987.

Below: With Helen at the entrance to the former Imperial Palace in the Forbidden City, Beijing.

Left: With a community leader during a visit to Crossroads, Cape Town.

Below: The smouldering remains of the squatter camp in Hout Bay after the fire on Christmas night, 1990.

Opposite page
Top: In discussion at Codesa I, December 1991.

Bottom: Joyce and me arriving at Harry and Bridget Oppenheimer's golden wedding anniversary celebration, Johannesburg 1993.

Left: With President Nelson Mandela at the gala banquet held in Joyce's and my honour in Camps Bay at which President Mandela referred to me as '… a respected veteran who holds no punches in his commitment to democratic values', May 1997
(Tina Hirsch)

Below: Joyce and me as members of a group of war veterans and their wives who commemorated the 50th anniversary of the battle of Monte Solé. Taken at the disused cemetery at Casaglia where a hundred civilians were massacred in September 1944. Monte Solé is in the background.

Opposite page
Top: Helen Suzman and Harry Oppenheimer at a reunion of party leaders past and present: Tony Leon, Colin Eglin, Van Zyl Slabbert, Zach de Beer and Harry Schwarz, Johannesburg 1994.
(Times Media Limited)

Bottom: In the chair of an Awepa international conference held in the old Assembly Chamber of the South African Parliament in September 1996. In front: Speaker Dr M Tjitendero (Namibia), Deputy Speaker B Kgisisile (South Africa), Ms Frafjord-Johnson MP (Norway). (Pieter Boersma, Amsterdam)

Above: With Raili after our marriage in St Peter's church in Hout Bay, 8 January 2000.

Opposite page
Top: Leon Wessels, Zach de Beer and Hennie Bester at the gala banquet held in my honour to mark my 40 years in public life.

Bottom: At the University of Cape Town in June 1997 when the degree of Doctor of Laws (*honoris causa*) was conferred on Cyril Ramaphosa, Dr Frene Ginwala and Colin Eglin.

With David Steel (now the Lord Steel of Aikwood), and a former president of Liberal International, and members of the executive committee of the Organisation of African Liberal Parties on the steps of parliament in Cape Town, January 1998. (*Cape Times*, Cape Town)

Top: Welcoming General Obasanjo on his arrival in Gaborone after being released from prison, July 1998.

Bottom: Meeting in Cape Town with Yasser Arafat, president of the State of Palestine, and ambassador Salam Salam El-Herfi.

Top: With Pravin Gordhan at the unveiling of my portrait in the Laureate Room of the Cape Town Club, April 2004.

Above: A cartoon in *Die Burger* when, in October 2003, I announced that I would be retiring at the end of that parliamentary session, 2004. *(Die Burger)*

PART V

Stormy days of opposition

13

Soweto explodes
16 June 1976

In January 1976 Prime Minister Vorster appointed Dr Andries Treurnicht, a leading *verkrampte* (right-winger) and former chairman of the Afrikaner Broederbond, as deputy minister of Bantu Administration and Education. Treurnicht was a proponent of racial segregation and white exclusiveness. It was ironic that his appointment set in motion a chain of events that would accelerate the process leading to the end of apartheid and the creation of a unified and non-racial democratic South Africa.

One of Treurnicht's tasks was to ensure that the policy making compulsory the widespread use of the Afrikaans language as a medium of instruction in black schools was complied with. In the climate of discontent that prevailed in these financially-starved institutions – marked by the poor quality of education, large size of classes, lack of facilities and shortage of books – the new regulations were the last straw.

On 16 June large numbers of secondary school pupils in Soweto stayed out of school to demonstrate; the police moved in; confrontation ensued; the protestors were shot at. There were many deaths. Rioting, arson, and the destruction of property followed. These, together with continuous protests, spread to most of the Transvaal and parts of Natal. In early July the government announced that the use of Afrikaans in black schools would no longer be compulsory, but to no avail.

During the latter part of July, rioting again erupted in Soweto and spread rapidly. By mid-August riots and confrontation with the police spread to the black and Coloured townships of the Cape Peninsula. Further deterioration was inevitable. Adding to the 'unrest' (as it euphemistically became known), between 100 000 and 200 000 workers in Soweto embarked on a three-day strike. Government under normal laws had been replaced by government under the Internal Security Act – and Pretoria threatened even tougher measures. Public gatherings were banned, and thousands of black and Coloured dissidents were arrested. The protests continued.

Two ancillary causes went deeper than Treurnicht's bizarre language bias:

- Young blacks were expressing frustration and anger with the entire system of apartheid.
- Indications were that thousands of young blacks were leaving the country for military training abroad as a response to repression at home.

James 'Jimmy' Kruger, the Minister of Justice, declared that black power would have to be destroyed if race riots were not to become endemic. From that inversion of the causes of the unrest, the crackdown was orchestrated. In these difficult and traumatic circumstances the PRP tried to play a constructive role. We had in fact detected signs of the upheaval: towards the end of May, René de Villiers, our spokesman on black education, reported tension building up in Soweto over the issue of compulsory Afrikaans. I asked him to remain in Johannesburg and monitor the situation closely – a task he tackled with great diligence and sensitivity.

On two occasions, one on 25 May and the other on 11 June, he drew Treurnicht's attention to the situation. On both, the deputy minister brushed him aside, saying there was no need for concern.

On 16 June I called for a special debate in parliament. It took place the following day – and then parliament went into its 'normal' mid-term recess. This gave us no opportunity to debate the issues or to hold the government to account. On 8 September I sent a message to Vorster requesting that parliament be reconvened. I received a short reply from his secretary: 'The prime minister wishes Mr Eglin to know that he sees no reason to reconvene parliament now.'

On Thursday 2 September thousands of pupils from Coloured and black schools on the Cape Flats staged a peaceful protest through the city centre and the concourse of the 'white' railway station. From interviews with their leaders, it was clear that their grievances and objections went far beyond education. They wanted the freedoms and rights enjoyed by whites, an end to police violence and harassment, and the release of all political prisoners and detainees.

That night I decided to convene an emergency meeting of office-bearers and branch representatives of the PRP in the Peninsula. Despite the short notice, there was full attendance when the party members met on Friday. I put it to the meeting that we use the weekend to organise a far larger conclave the following Monday evening, to which we would invite religious, professional, business and community leaders from all racial groupings in the Peninsula. The object was to enable those present to discuss what could and should be done in the agonising situation that had developed and to consider creating the machinery for maintaining direct contact with one another.

The response was overwhelming. Present that night in the Mowbray town hall were teachers, religious leaders, businessmen, politicians, community leaders, and prominent citizens including Cardinal Owen McCann and Sir Richard Luyt, vice-chancellor of UCT. Thanks to Daphne Wilson, a stalwart Progressive since the early 1960s, who had built up and maintained extensive contacts with members of the black community, some thirty representatives from Langa, Guguletu and Nyanga were also present.

Chaired by Hans Middelmann, the meeting was electric. People from the Coloured and black townships spoke their hearts out – and for whites it was an eye-opener. For the first time they heard at first hand of the bitterness and anger of ordinary people of colour, and all present became aware of the vast void in communication between, say, PRP voters and the communities of the Cape Peninsula.

The meeting elected a committee of 14 – the Mowbray Committee, as it was initially called – with Daphne Wilson as the convenor, and immediately went to work. Out of this initiative came a grouping (the Mowbray Inter-Race Group, MIRGE, later MERGE) that was eventually to play its part in the organised resistance movement called the United Democratic Front. But that happened only in the mid-1980s. On 16 September a meeting of 'concerned Capetonians' filled the Cape Town city hall to capacity. I announced that the PRP had decided to call a conference on the elimination of race discrimination: 'Either we work together for peaceful change or we destroy each other in confrontation.'

The following resolution was adopted unanimously: 'We the citizens of Cape Town, speaking amidst the tragedy of continuing disruption and tension in the Cape Peninsula, most urgently appeal to the prime minister to act as a true statesman and national leader to meet the present threat to our country's survival, unhampered by party political considerations. We earnestly believe that the present unrest is the direct result of the government's racial policies, which deny basic rights and freedoms to the vast majority in our country. We urge Mr Vorster to convene a round-table conference with representatives of all races to formulate a policy which all South Africans can support.'

However, the attainment of a just society would take more than a resolution.

Trying to 'save South Africa'

On the eve of the Soweto upheavals – and the reaction of the contending parties to these tumultuous events – a parliamentary by-election in Durban North on 5 May had been won by Harry Pitman, the PRP candidate. The seat had been considered a UP stronghold. This was an indication that voters in the urban heartland of Natal were joining those in the Transvaal and Western Cape in abandoning the UP for the Progressives.

Against this backdrop, while on a parliamentary visit to the West Rand gold mines, Derick de Villiers, a friend and senior UP MP, told me that Graaff was about to call for a united opposition as a key part of a 'Save South Africa' campaign. De Villiers said he hoped that as the leader of the PRP, I would consider Graaff's call seriously.

Complex and far-reaching approaches and negotiations took place over the next year involving Graaff, Theo Gerdener of the then Democratic Party, and me – as well as through a committee of businessmen and academics appointed by the three of us. In essence, the grand opposition coalition came to rest on acceptance or otherwise of what became known as the Kowie Marais Principles – 14 points on which concurrence would need to be achieved before a way forward could be agreed. Marais was a retired judge and a founder-member of the Ossewabrandwag. He proved to be an enlightened committee chairman who presided over the inter-party discussions, and the key points forming the basis of a realigned opposition party may be distilled as follows:

- God is acknowledged as the ultimate authority in national destiny.
- All South Africans have an equal right to full citizenship, in either a federation or confederation, which can only be realised where there is no discrimination on the grounds of race, colour, religion or sex.
- Full citizenship is the basis for loyalty towards the state. Only with this can the state effectively discharge its duty to maintain an orderly society and the security of the country at all times.
- Political rights must be shared by all South African citizens on an equitable and responsible basis, and all systems that could lead to racial domination rejected.
- In a plural society such as that of the Republic, a constitution and an entrenched bill of rights guaranteeing the rights of individuals and minorities are essential. These must be guarded over by a judiciary appointed by an independent authority.
- All citizens have the right to share in the systems of free economic enterprise, which the party is committed to maintain and develop.
- The party stands for democratic government and rejects totalitarian or authoritarian systems such as communism or fascism.
- Except in the case of a duly declared state of emergency or war, every individual has the right to the protection of life, liberty and property, and access to the judiciary.
- The party guarantees the rights of all to maintain their religious, language and cultural heritages, as well to develop them provided this does not encroach on the rights of others.
- All education systems must provide equal educational opportunities for all.
- All inequitable forms of statutory or administrative discrimination are unacceptable in the ideal society for which the party will strive, and will be subject to judicial test.
- The party accepts that certain geographic areas are being developed as economic and political growth points for certain sections of the population. Where the inhabitants of these areas freely elect to proceed towards increasing self-determination, the party will respect their wishes. No compulsory removal of populations will, however, be permitted and the general welfare will be taken into account. There will be no compulsion on anyone to become a citizen of an area other than that in which he is permanently resident.
- These principles, as well as other guarantees, should be incorporated in a constitution to be drawn up after consultation and joint decision-making by all citizens.
- As an inseparable part of Africa, the Republic accepts that peaceful relations with the states of southern Africa, in the first instance, must be brought about and that technological, economic and political co-operation must be encouraged where possible.

By 21 December I was able to respond that 'the principles, which the committee rec-ommends as a basis for an opposition party, are all in accordance with the basic ap-proach of the PRP. However, certain concepts incorporated in the Marais Committee report – institutional guarantees of individual and minority rights, and consultation and joint decision-making by representatives of all – are fundamental not only to those of us who are today in the PRP, but to any opposition party that wants to be-come the real alternative to the Nationalist government.'

Well before that, the bedrock issue had been highlighted as the precise meaning of race discrimination. The PRP believed in equal political rights without discrimi-nation, with voting taking place on a common voters' roll. Protection for individu-als and minorities would be reflected in constitutional and voting structures through the bill of rights; the non-discriminatory provisions of the constitution; and the po-litical environment which constitutional law would create – as it was to do post-1994 through an accumulation of case precedents.

The UP position, most vigorously proposed by the conservative Radclyffe Cadman of the UP, and later folded into that of the PRP, was for 'the separation of power on a race basis at all levels of government'. The consequent breakdown of talks aimed at opposition fusion, and the collapse of Graaff's Save South Africa campaign, evoked strong reactions and recriminations. Graaff and I each gave our own interpretation of what had occurred. I stated that the key issue had been the UP insistence on the separation of power on a race basis 'at all levels of government'. Max Borkum went further and said: 'I can only ascribe the blame for wrecking the talks to Cadman, the leader of the right-wing faction of the UP. It was clear that whenever it appeared that Eglin and Graaff had come to terms, Cadman would interfere. Any consensus that was reached was immediately turned by his intervention into a disagreement.'

Much to Graaff's dismay, Marais and I issued a joint statement. Marais later joined the PFP and was elected as that party's MP for Johannesburg North.

The collapse of Graaff's pivotal campaign was reflected in both tensions within UP ranks and serious party setbacks in the Transvaal municipal elections in early 1977. Owing to internal dissension, it failed to contest any seats in Randburg; and lost con-trol of the Johannesburg municipality for the first time in 31 years – with 11 seats, the UP came third, the NP came second with 15, and the PRP won with 19.

On 19 March Graaff and Gerdener of the DP formally announced their agreement to form a new political party 'on the basis of equal rights for all racial groups in South Africa'. It is worth noting that many elements of the UP had felt it worthwhile talk-ing directly to the PRP in defiance of Graaff; this approach was especially evident among members who were beginning to realise that Gerdener's DP was something of a myth. When, after 24 June, Graaff and Gerdener issued the programme of their new party, I described its policy as 'simply a few steps closer to the Nationalists'.

On 28 June at a congress held on the ice-skating rink at the Carlton Hotel in Jo-hannesburg, the UP disbanded. On the eve of the decision, I had again made an appeal for *verligte* opponents of the Nationalists to join in a unified opposition: 'A grand alliance of South Africans committed to non-discrimination, and prepared to negotiate, will provide not only effective opposition to the Nationalist government but hope and direction to South Africans at a time when the government is leading us to nowhere.'

There were indeed those who came towards us rather than melt into the NRP: Japie Basson, Derick de Villiers, Hymie Miller, Nic Olivier, Graham MacIntosh and Harold van Hoogstraten.

During the next four weeks my PRP colleagues and I held a number of meetings with Basson and representatives from his group. They progressed smoothly – but for a dangerous diversion by Harry Schwarz, chairman of our federal executive, who in August made a speech that the press interpreted as 'advocating a form of partition as the ideal solution for South Africa'. In the *Sunday Times* he wrote: 'Partition is not what I would, in ordinary circumstances, hold forth as an ideal solution … But one must face the facts of life: whites want to stay in South Africa and survive. They do not want to gamble with irreversible experiments. I believe a just partition leading to confederation would give us the answer.'

The speech and article drew extensive coverage in the press and evoked furious reaction within the PRP. After a tense discussion in the federal executive – which happened to be meeting that weekend to finalise the details of the agreement with Basson and his group – the committee issued a statement: 'The PRP does not advocate the partition of South Africa. It believes in the decentralisation of power on a geographic basis to self-governing provinces or states, which will be part of a South Africa in which all citizens have full citizenship irrespective of race or colour.'

Schwarz and Van Rensburg, who supported him, accepted the PRP's rejection of partition, and a crisis was averted. But the incident was not an auspicious prelude to the formation of a unified opposition party.

On the morning of 5 September 1977, at a national conference in Johannesburg, the PRP resolved to form a combined opposition with the Basson group. Out of this was born the Progressive Federal Party (PFP). I was elected leader; Ray Swart chairman; Basson deputy chairman; Schwarz chairman of the federal executive; and Derick de Villiers his deputy chairman. In my inaugural speech, I described the decision as an 'act of faith in ourselves in our ability to motivate our fellow South Africans in a new political movement that would help to shape the course of our country's political history.'

The PFP would adhere to seven basic principles:

· Full citizenship rights for all South Africans without discrimination.
· A new constitution drawn up, negotiated and agreed upon by representatives of all sections of the people.
· The sharing of political rights by all citizens without the domination of one race by another.
· An open society free from compulsory separation or compulsory integration.

- The right of all to maintain and develop their religion, language and cultural heritage.
- Equality of opportunity for all citizens in an economy based on free enterprise.
- The right of every individual to the protection of life, liberty and property, and access to the judiciary in defence of these rights.

As it had been two years previously, when the PRP was formed, my task now was to ensure that the PFP's 17 MPs and two senators blended into an effective political unit. A measure of that growing effectiveness can be construed from the fact of Gerdener's abrupt withdrawal from the PRP. And an even bigger shock came on 5 September, when Graaff announced his retirement from politics. His decision brought to a close an era of opposition politics that started 29 years earlier with high hopes and great expectations. For nearly three decades it combined commitment to public service with a failure to grasp the nettle of race in South Africa – and left behind no particular legacy.

On 30 November, at a general election, the NRP was reduced to ten MPs and surrendered its status as the official opposition to the Progressive Federal Party.

14

Meeting Steve Biko

I had seen at first-hand the stirrings and effects of black power in America. The explosion of Soweto in June 1976, and its subsequent spread, brought such issues home. There were obvious similarities in the philosophical underpinnings of comparable movements in the US and South Africa. At home, the times produced a distinctive figure who for many seemed at the very heart of the ferment.

Donald Woods had been telling me it was important that I meet Steve Biko. The founder and first president of the black-orientated South African Students' Organisation (SASO) and later honorary president of the Black People's Convention (BPC), Biko was the foremost proponent of black consciousness: he was increasingly prominent among the new generation of black leaders. The proximity of Woods's East London home to that of Biko near Kingwilliamstown – and given Woods's strident condemnation of the Nationalists in the columns of the *Daily Dispatch*, as well as his gregarious nature – had resulted in his contacts with Biko developing into a warm friendship. Woods arranged for me to visit Biko during the last week of July 1977.

I was introduced to Biko in his modest office near Kingwilliamstown and was immediately struck by his appearance and personality: handsome, with piercing dark brown eyes, an engaging smile, but thoughtful, direct and firm in manner.

At first we both felt, understandably, a little uncomfortable. However, with Woods in his easygoing way acting as the linkman, we soon developed a relationship that enabled us to speak frankly. We had no difficulty in finding common ground on apartheid and race discrimination as the root causes of the conflict developing in the country. Getting rid of apartheid and race discrimination was the priority.

The discussion that ensued was largely about the process through which this could be achieved. Even here there was a surprising degree of agreement, as Woods was later to write in his biography of Biko: 'I brought the two together and listened throughout to their marathon talk. I felt privileged to do so, because it was a meeting of two unusually sharp minds. After an initial reserve, especially on Steve's side, they got on well, and at the end of their discussion both agreed to stay in contact and to initiate talks between their groups.

'Without revealing details of their conversation, I can say that the general theme was how each in his own sphere could help bring all the elements of the nation together at a conference table. Both stressed the need to do everything possible to avoid violence. Steve said: "When there is violence there is messiness. Violence brings too many residues of hate into the reconstruction period. Apart from its obvious horrors, it creates too many post-revolutionary problems. If at all possible, we want the revolution to be peaceful and reconciliatory, although the actions of the government make it appear as if the Nationalists are trying to provoke the opposite." Each told me separately after the meeting that he had been greatly impressed with the intellect of the other.'

After a beer and a pub lunch in the hamlet of Hamburg, Woods and I were back in the tranquil environment of suburban East London by mid-afternoon.

On 12 September, when I was in Senegal for discussions with President Senghor, I was shocked to hear that Biko was dead. 'Died in detention' was the text of the official announcement. I was grieved at the loss of a talented leader for the country; at the same time I was concerned about the consequences that his death would have on the politics of South Africa and on black-white relationships.

On 19 October we woke up to the announcement that no fewer than 18 largely black organisations had been banned; scores of black leaders arrested; and two major black newspapers, *The World* and *Weekend World*, shut down by government decree. A large number of individuals, including Woods, had been placed under restriction orders.

Woods had reacted very angrily to the death of his friend; and he was particularly angry at the callous reaction of 'Jimmy' Kruger, the Minister of Justice, to Biko's violent death. In the *Daily Dispatch*, Woods flayed the government and Kruger fearlessly and relentlessly. I understood the depth of his revulsion at the injustices of apartheid – so I could understand the extent of his anger at Biko's death in government custody.

Yet by nature Woods was a moderate man with a deep love of South Africa and its people. For the government to brand him as a threat to law and order, and for Kruger to restrict him and deny him the right to continue as editor of the *Daily Dispatch*, was as monstrous as it was stupid.

Meanwhile the public had been learning the sordid details of the last days of Biko's life in detention, revealed by a post-mortem which reported that death was caused by extensive brain damage. Biko sustained at least a dozen injuries between eight and twelve hours before his death. Yet – to the consternation and rage of many members of the public – on 2 December the chief magistrate of Pretoria, Marthinus Prins, who conducted an inquest into the death, ruled that 'no one can be found criminally responsible for Biko's death in detention'.

Later, on 28 February 1978, the attorney general of the Eastern Cape declared 'he would not prosecute any police involved in the arrest and detention of Biko'. As far as the NP government was concerned the matter was closed. However, as far as the wider South African public and the international community were concerned, the implications of the death of Biko remained high on the agenda.

At the time of Biko's death I was preparing for a general election. I resolved that when it was over I would spend a few days in East London. Shortly before Christmas, Woods and his wife Wendy hosted me in their home in the suburb of Vincent. There was some bitterness in Woods's demeanour, but not enough to warp his enthusiasm for life or his sense of fun with friends. He and I decided to play a round of golf at the East London Club where he was a member.

As we drove to the club he told me of the varied reactions of members of the club to his banning. Those who opposed his political views looked at him dispassionately as if to convey, 'Well, you got what you deserved.' Those who knew little or nothing about politics but liked him as a person seemed to have some sympathy – but kept their distance, as if to say, 'You must have done something.' Those who liked Woods but were not clear on the law were careful not to get too close to him. And then there were those who thoroughly approved of Donald's political stance and who reacted to his banning by saying: 'Those bastards.'

At the pro shop there was a discussion whether we could take two caddies with us. In terms of the restriction order imposed on Woods he could only meet with one other person at a time. To be with more would be to create an 'illegal gathering'. Would a round of golf between Woods and me, with two caddies, constitute an illegal gathering?

We teed off with two caddies in attendance. After the game, in the clubhouse, members seemed wary of chatting. Would this also constitute an illegal gathering? Donald and I sat in an alcove off the main lounge to enjoy our drinks at the 19th hole. A number of members greeted my friend warmly – but stood outside the alcove while doing do.

We spoke about our common golfing background. Donald reminded me how, on occasions when we played golf at Mowbray on a Saturday morning, and were walking down the passage to the first tee, Prime Minister Vorster, who had finished playing and was coming off the course, would pass us with his deadpan face, and without glancing sideways would say in his deep-throated voice, 'Hullo, Cor-lin.' Then there was the occasion when Woods wanted to generate some enthusiasm in a young black caddy carrying my golf bag. He asked my caddy if he knew who I was. 'No,' was the response. Woods told him I was a member of parliament and leader of the opposition. 'Ah-ha,' said the caddy, noncommittally. Woods thought he would pile it on and added: 'He agrees with Mandela. And politically he is a friend of Mandela.'

My caddy's face lit up; his eyes opened wide. 'Waah,' he enthused as he picked up my golf bag and walked on with a spring in his step.

Donald concluded the story by saying: 'What I didn't bargain for was that after that every time your ball landed in the rough, which was often, we found it neatly resting on a patch of grass with a clear field in front of it.'

Six days after I bade farewell to Donald, he left South Africa in defiance of his restriction order by crossing the border into Lesotho. Appropriately, during the two days that I spent with Woods and Wendy, neither gave me any inkling of the audacious move they were planning. I simply assumed they were going to spend New Year at home.

On 6 January Donald was reunited with Wendy and his children in Botswana, and six days later they reached London, which was to be their home for many years. He wrote about Biko; a film was made about their friendship; and Biko is remembered to this day.

15

The Nationalist counterattack

Events continued their surprising, at times shocking, course throughout 1977. Thus, in August, Prime Minister Vorster chose to unveil his own government's new constitutional plan. Reflecting his view of 'reform', it posited:

· Three separate parliaments: one each for whites, Coloureds and Indians – each with its own prime minister, cabinet and Assembly. Each would deal with matters specifically related to the race group concerned.
· An executive president elected by a committee of white, Coloured and Indian MPs.
· A council of cabinets presided over by the president and comprising white, Coloured and Indian MPs. This council would deal with matters of common concern for the three race groups, and would be the ultimate executive authority.
· A president's council of white, Coloured and Indian members, with an advisory function.

There was racial ratio built into these structures: four whites to two Coloureds to one Indian. Significantly there was no provision for black participation.

Vorster's explanation was that 'While many blacks had been killed in Africa, striving for independence, the NP was giving it to them, to take, or to leave.' The government favoured representative bodies for blacks – 'but these should be in their own parliament. What we cannot offer the black man is co-participation with them in our parliament.'

The proposed system was roundly rejected by black leaders, by the majority of Coloured leaders, and by the opposition parties in parliament; but the government appeared determined to press ahead. Against this background, the PFP was formed. For my part I was anticipating a journey that would take me to Senegal, the UK, Germany and possibly Sudan. It would be my third visit to Senegal since Helen Suzman and I went there in 1971.

I made my way via Senegal to Geneva, and checked into the Hotel Eiffel, where I was called to the desk to take a telephone call. Who could have known I was in Geneva – and at that hotel?

It was my secretary, Joan Fowle: 'Colin – Vorster has announced an election for 30

November.' I cut short my visit and returned to South Africa.

In Cape Town I found a message from Tertius Myburgh, editor of the *Sunday Times*. When I met him in Johannesburg a few days later, we discussed the coming election and he said I could expect support from the *Times* for the PFP as a unified *verligte* opposition. In great confidence he told me his newspaper had uncovered a major scandal, which he hoped to publish soon and which would have serious implications for the government as well as a dramatic impact on the election.

I waited each week for the revelation. However, while the newspaper and others carried reports about unusual activities conducted by the Department of Information under the direction of Eschel Rhoodie – and raised questions about the funding of the conservative new paper, *The Citizen*– 30 November came and went without 'the big story'.

My full attention had to be on the election. Financial constraints and a shortage of time were factors that persuaded us to contest a relatively small number of selected seats. There would be the existing 17 plus another ten strategically placed around the country. The issue of candidates largely resolved itself. Gordon Waddell, René de Villiers and Dick Enthoven decided to retire from parliament; our remaining 14 would be standing again. In addition, senators Brian Bamford and Eric Winchester were available to contest seats in the Cape and Natal. Ray Swart was ready to stand in Natal, and Zach de Beer decided to return to parliament as MP for Parktown.

I had been having discussions with Jan Marais, founder of Trust Bank and the current chairman of the South Africa Foundation – an organisation dedicated to the improvement of South Africa's image abroad. In the latter capacity he had gained considerable political prominence by posing ten questions, which he said were often put to him – and for which he had no answer – relating to the ridiculous situations that arose through the application of various apartheid measures. He now told me he was keen to go to parliament and would consider standing as a candidate for the PFP.

I told Marais I would try to hold Green Point open for a short time while he made up his mind. Fortunately, however, I pointed out that if anyone else offered themselves as a candidate he would first have to win a party nomination contest. In Durban one weekend I chatted to Ian Wylie, editor of the *Sunday Tribune* and a good friend of mine. In confidence I told him that it was on the cards that Marais would be standing for the PFP in a Cape seat. He was aghast: 'I can tell you confidentially that my newspaper will be carrying a story tomorrow morning that Marais has accepted the National Party nomination for the Pinetown seat in Natal.' He added: 'He's staying just around the corner at the Blue Waters Hotel.'

I phoned Marais and gave him a piece of my mind. Marais, as smooth as silk, said: 'Oh, Colin, I haven't changed my political views. I still have the same objectives. But you must accept that there are different ways of attaining them.'

Marais's duplicity actually served us well. A young *verligte* Afrikaner advocate, Tian van der Merwe, became the PFP candidate in Green Point and won against great odds. He developed into a fine MP and a courageous fighter against apartheid – sadly his promise was cut short in 1991 when he was killed in a motor accident.

As for Marais, he was a fish out of water in parliament with his designer suits, smart shoes, leather briefcase, buffed hair and airs and graces. He was never fully accepted by the hardened political *wildebeeste* who formed the backbone of the NP caucus.

For the PFP, which started out as the PP with seven members of parliament in 1974, and had expanded as a result of two mergers to 17 in 1977, the result of the election was satisfactory although not wildly exciting. We started with 17 MPs and ended with 17.

Before the election Vorster explained that he was going to the country 'to show the unity of white South Africans in their opposition to foreign interference'. What he did not enlighten the electorate on was that he and his cronies had set out to steal public funds in order to purchase influence for his views. The Information scandal – which Myburgh had hinted at – unraveled and destroyed him.

I was able to tell a PFP congress a year later: 'The 1977 election was an attempt to cover up South Africa's biggest-ever scandal. We now know that the election was a phony election, fought on a phony issue, by a government backed by a phony newspaper and receiving a phony mandate.'

In 1977 the English-language press was filled with reports about the flamboyant style and extravagant expenditure of the Department of Information under the direction of Eschel Rhoodie, secretary of the department, and Connie Mulder, Minister of Information and the leader of the NP in the Transvaal. In February 1978 the auditor general Gerald Barrie reported his misgivings about the financial administration of Information. This led to an inquiry by the parliamentary select committee on public accounts. Harry Schwarz served as the PFP's representative; and through him we were able to play a major role in probing the scandal.

There were innumerable rumours that the Nat government was funding *The Citizen*, an NP-supporting English tabloid. Mulder fielded questions on this issue. Eventually on 10 May, in response to a question by Japie Basson, Mulder said: 'The government does not give *The Citizen* funds.'

This eight-word lie was to destroy Mulder's prospects of succeeding Vorster as prime minister when Vorster resigned on 20 September, also as a consequence of his involvement in Info. Mulder was dismissed from the cabinet, resigned from parliament, and was expelled from the NP. Onto the fouled stage of national politics stepped the Cape leader of the NP – PW Botha, sworn in as prime minister after having defeated Mulder into second and Pik Botha into third place in a bruising internal election battle.

South Africa now had at its helm a political leader very different from his predecessors. Strijdom had believed in *baasskap*. The Dutch-born Verwoerd was an ideologue. Vorster was a chain-smoking and rather sinister securocrat. Botha, though, was a political manager – tough, determined and politically streetwise. His bottom line was the survival of the white man in South Africa.

As the events of the next decade would show, Botha would be prepared to make significant changes away from apartheid in the social and economic fields. He knew that there would be political consequences but remained confident that he would be able to manage them in a way that would produce the result he had in mind. There would also turn out to be strict limits to his capacity for change.

My relationship with Botha went back to the early 1950s when, as chief secretary of the NP in the Cape, he would attend political meetings of the UP and the Torch Commando. His function was to ask questions, to make interjections, to harass the speakers and generally to disrupt the proceedings – on occasions not without the use of brute force. Our relationship was civil without being particularly friendly. Indeed, one day towards the end of his term of office, Botha in a relaxed moment said to me: '*Jy weet, Colin – ek en jy, ons ken mekaar. Maar ons hou nie van mekaar nie.*' We know each other, but we don't like each other: that fairly summed up our relationship.

Botha's finger-wagging combative style and his displays of anger concealed the pragmatic side of a political leader who often took steps he considered necessary rather than desirable. His judgement on issues was clouded by an obsession with the concept of the 'total onslaught' on South Africa – the belief that our problems were caused from outside, with Moscow being the main villain. During his 11 years as head of government he was driven not by ideology or dogma, but by his sense of necessity.

It is worth considering the mind of PW Botha. In 1979 he famously stated: 'We must adapt or die.' This encapsulated his approach to policy in the 1980s. Unfortunately for him, and for South Africa, what was needed was not adaptations to apartheid but fundamental change. Some statements by Botha compiled by the satirist Pieter-Dirk Uys reveal the complex, contradictory and often combative character of the new prime minister:

May 1974: 'In the Republic of South Africa under the National Party's leadership, black nations can get freedom without firing shots or revolution.'

November 1977: 'All I want to say to you is watch out what you publish because I am lying in watch for you.'

February 1978: 'I'm not prepared to cut my own throat for the sake of world opinion.'

April 1978: 'We went into Angola with America's knowledge and approval – and they left us in the lurch.'

May 1978: 'Where in the whole world today can one find a society more just than South Africa?'

March 1980: 'It is a sick world in which South Africa has to make its way.'

April 1980: 'If we let Nelson Mandela free, we will set free an arch Marxist supported by Marxists from Moscow.'

September 1980: 'There are attempts to convey the Afrikaner as dishonest. We are no more dishonest than any other nation.'

April 1981: 'As long as there is a National Party government we won't hand over South West Africa to the authority of Swapo.'

March 1982: 'I may know where I want to go, but not how to get there.'

September 1982: 'When you go to bed at night you can't go with hatred in your heart because then you can't sleep. And I'm a good sleeper, ask my wife.'

September 1984: 'The separation of the races happened long before the Nationalist government. God separated the races.'

October 1985: 'The more we reform the more we are condemned.'

April 1986: 'He [Mandela] is keeping himself in jail. The moment he renounces violence, he will be set free.'

May 1986: 'South Africa has the will and the capacity to break the ANC.'

September 1986: 'People must get their perspectives right. If a respectable black man rides in an aeroplane he needs a place to sleep.'

March 1987: 'I detest weaklings in public life. I believe in straightforward and honest politics.'

April 1987: 'As long as I live reform will continue only on the basis of protection for the white man.'

June 1987: 'We will not talk to these people, we will fight them.'

August 1987: 'I try to be a man of peace, but if people tempt me I can become a thunderbird.'

August 1987: 'Unless we can succeed in bridging the gap between the First World way of life and activity in South Africa, and the Third World way of life, political reform will serve us no purpose.'

Ironically, although Botha used the information he held on the machinations of Mulder in order to defeat him, the 'Information scandal' dogged him during his first two years in office. In October 1978 I sent an urgent telex to him calling for a statement on the allegation that vast sums of public money had been secretly used to finance *The Citizen*. I called on him to appoint an all-party commission to investigate the matter. Vorster had been elected president (not then an executive position) earlier in the month, and acting on the instruction of new prime minister had appointed Judge Rudolph Erasmus to head a commission of inquiry into irregularities at the Department of Information. The commission was given one month to report.

As I stated at the time, this was unsatisfactory: 'As the matter to be investigated was the use of funds voted by parliament it was parliament itself, by way of an all-party commission, that should do the investigating. [The Erasmus Commission's] terms of reference were too narrow. As it was the activities of the government that were being investigated, the parliamentary opposition should have been consulted both on the composition and on the terms of reference of the commission.'

In addition, the commission had decided to hear evidence in private.

On 21 November, Schwarz and I met Botha, who was accompanied by Louwrens Muller, Cape leader of the NP and chairman of the NP's parliamentary caucus. We again asked for a parliamentary investigation and for the official opposition to have representation on it. We argued that a full report and all the evidence should be placed before parliament. Botha's response was that he wanted time to consider our request. However, nothing happened.

On 3 December the Erasmus Commission delivered its first report. In it there were references to 'exhibits' – but the exhibits themselves were absent from the copies of the report given to MPs. Then, in an interview with *Rapport*, Erasmus said that except for evidence affecting national security, all evidence would be released to MPs before the next parliamentary sitting in January. He repeated this statement to the *Cape Times*. Yet in early January 1979 Johan Geyser, the commission's secretary, stated that: 'The commission had given serious consideration, whether it should not release evidence before the coming parliamentary session, and had come to the conclusion that no evidence should be released by it.'

Parliament went into recess in December 1977 and prepared itself for the battle looming in January 1978.

Talking to Anna Starcke

In July 1978 I was one of 13 of the 'political elite' interviewed by Anna Starcke – a leading writer on the *Financial Mail* and subsequently a respected political and economic analyst. The latter part of the interview summed up my analysis, concerns and commitment to fundamental change in our country.

Anne Starcke: *Within the realities of the present situation – a white electorate that overwhelmingly rejects your policies, a government that is, at least at the declared official level, moving in the opposite direction of what you believe needs to be done, increasing pressures internally and from outside – how would you define the role of the PFP?*

Eglin: My party, which advocates a form of liberal multiracialism, is not one of the essential poles of power in South Africa. The real poles of power are the white nationalist and the black nationalist groups. At some stage these poles of power will be forced to compromise or else destroy each other and themselves in the process – they will either be forced into conflict that will be completely destructive, or they will be compelled to find some means of getting together and negotiating. The role of a party like mine is to see that this synthesis, this getting together, this compromise, is brought about in the shortest possible time so that violence is minimal.

One has to deal with the reality that the PFP has 17 members of parliament against 135 of the NP, so one's effect is limited. Our role is to try and get white opinion to move so it grasps the political nettle of negotiation earlier rather than later, to see that parliament responds sensibly and constructively to the total pressures in our society instead of responding only to the pressures of the white electorate, and to keep pointing to the need for government to sit down and talk with blacks.

Starcke: *How successful do you perceive yourself to be in these roles?*

Eglin: I don't want to claim it's all the work of the opposition, but, to the extent that very few Nationalists believe in the ultimate success of their policy, we have already succeeded. We have very little difficulty in speaking to Nationalist Afrikaner audiences, especially younger people, and persuading them that the present structure can't last and that the NP hasn't got the answers. They tend not to argue about that. What they do argue about is the form of the alternative. And let's admit it, the opposition has not succeeded so far in presenting the alternative in a way which makes it attractive to the average voter. I believe the PFP has the essentials of an alternative, but it hasn't yet been expressed in a way that captures the imagination. So far our own efforts, together with historical developments, have not yet coincided to crystallise an exciting new deal for the future. One can help to move people, but it is events and history that cause them to start saying, 'Let's re-think in a fundamental way.'

The South West African situation will have a profound effect on whites. If this settlement can be made to work, it will be an experiment in multiracialism actually under the control of the Nationalist government – tremendously important. Likewise, if the whole labour pattern changes, as it well may as a result of the Wiehahn and Riekert commissions [into labour law and influx control], white attitudes are bound to change faster.

I am saying that public opinion, including opinion in the Afrikaner sector, is moving in the direction of our position. I find there are Nationalists right in parliament who are getting frustrated with the government for being so stubborn, who believe it's madness not to start talking. Government of course maintains it is talking – what happens is that when, on rare occasions, Vorster has talks with Buthelezi, he confines the discussion to the implementation of separate development. Now that's no good. Of course Buthelezi doesn't want to discuss that. Vorster should agree to examine with Buthelezi the various options for the future. He should agree to explore and to try to determine what common ground exists.

Starcke: *If it were up to you to start the phasing-in process of transition, how, apart from personal communication with black and brown leaders, would you rate your priorities?*

Eglin: There are four critical areas of equal importance in which one would need to move fast:

Social apartheid – all the apartheid laws in the field of inter-personal relationships including the Mixed Marriages Act, the Group Areas Act, Race Classification, etc. – would go immediately. Planned development programmes would have to be started to redress first some of the crassest imbalances in facilities available in what have been black and white areas.

Economic apartheid – any laws which make it impossible for a black or brown person to move ahead on merit within the economic structure, including the civil service – must go. Here also practical programmes must be started to enable people who have been deprived of opportunity in the past to make use of the new opportunities available. These programmes must include full trade union rights for all.

Education – this is a top priority. This is so important that if the money isn't readily available one should contemplate deficit budgeting to get it off the ground, because the very effect of this development will be to stimulate economic growth and that way one can recoup the outlay in due course.

Finally, the pass laws – we should start immediately with the phasing out of these laws. While population influx must continue to be carefully monitored to ensure a balance in the provision of facilities, the pass laws as such must go a lot faster than most whites realise.

Starcke: *All of these measures, particularly if introduced concurrently – as you say they should be – require an immediate and ongoing financial commitment vastly in excess of South Africa's present budget. When discussing education, housing, homeland infrastructure, etc., with government members, they always agree that the need for faster development is there. Then they ask, 'Who's going to pay for it?' Where would you get the funds?*

Eglin: If it's been possible over three years of comparative recession to increase our defence budget from R700 million to nearly R2 billion, then I believe that in times of increasing growth it should be possible to find the same amount of money for education and other services. Defence has been so thoroughly established as the government's top priority that if the government decided next year that another R500 million was needed I have no doubt whatsoever that the money would be found. I believe that expenditure on education and housing is in the end going to be as decisive for whites' security as military hardware, and that it should be seen as such.

Secondly, if we have the correct internal political climate, funds from abroad will not be a problem, both in the form of private investment and as long-term government loans. The problem for a PFP-type of government would not be one of shortage of funds – the problem would be how fast the funds can be converted into buildings and institutions and facilities in order to train people, to keep pace with higher expectations.

Starcke: *Mr Eglin, a basic fear of businessmen, be they Afrikaans- or English-speaking, centres around the feeling that black leaders and their followers have a scant understanding of the economic system, that everything would be wrecked in the cause of a utopian political ideal.*

Eglin: I believe that a young modern group of blacks is emerging with a fairly sophisticated appreciation of the difference between the various economic systems. But we will delude ourselves if we think that the decision on a private enterprise system versus a collective economic system will be made by a sophisticated evaluation of the merits of the two systems.

It's going to be decided by the pressure from the economic have-nots who, becoming political haves, use their political power to get a fairer share of the economic cake as rapidly as they can.

That's why the time factor is of such importance. The longer the white man waits to come to a real negotiated accommodation with the black man, the more difficult his position is going to be and the more the scale within the changing society is tipped towards a radical, socialist, Marxist type of economic system as opposed to a better balanced system of a free enterprise and public-sector economy, one which I happen to believe would be to the best advantage of all concerned. The best hope we have of achieving this balance in the future is for our political system to become rapidly more responsive to the requirements of the have-nots. Only by sharing political power and economic opportunity will we be able to prevent the destruction of the essential free enterprise thrust in the total economic system.

Starcke: *Something puzzles me, Mr Eglin: Despite your concern about the time factor, about the urgency for action required and the fact that you – your party – is impotent now to accelerate change – despite all that I sense a basic optimism in you. On what do you base that?*

Eglin: I believe that we in South Africa will talk with one another before we will destroy one another. I don't think people go in for self-destruction. I think they posture, they push their luck as far as they can, and they try to assert their authority for as long as they have it. But they also adapt when they realise their position becomes untenable. Already whites have come to realise that unless we can get rid of discrimination in the economic field we are doomed economically. The same is now happening in the social field – whites are beginning to realise that restrictive laws originally introduced to protect their identity have in fact become a danger to their identity.

They haven't yet reached a stage where they realise that restrictive laws in the political field are also a danger to their future survival, but they will. The trend is there. And I have to believe they will reach that stage soon, because the time factor will determine what kind of society we get thereafter.

Fine-tuning opposition policy

With our recently acquired status of official opposition, the political events of 1978 gave every opportunity for the PFP to demonstrate its *bona fides*. One valuable initiative of our Eastern Transvaal region – on a proposal by its chairman Peter Soal – was to invite Dr Nthato Motlana, chairman of Soweto's Committee of Ten, to address a conference on the theme 'Negotiating for the Future'. The committee had arisen as a consequence of the Soweto upheavals and the jailing or exile of so many young black leaders. It represented, in effect, adult support for the children, and Motlana, a medical doctor who would count Mandela among his patients, rose naturally to a senior position.

At the conference, Motlana expressed disagreement with aspects of PFP policy, such as a qualified franchise and the protection of minorities. He called for majority rule in a unitary state, yet qualified both concepts: 'I do not use the words "black majority rule". In any majority party in South Africa, a Colin Eglin might well be a prime minister elected by a majority of blacks.' Later he amplified: 'Majority rule in a united South Africa is the maximum bargaining point at a negotiating table. What finally emerges from that negotiating table might well be a federal system. That could be acceptable to me so long as it was not a race federation, and so long as South Africa was not balkanised. I do not necessarily exclude federalism – as long as South Africa remains one country.'

At the same conference I said: 'A simple fact, which those of us with white faces have to accept, is that the days of exclusive white decision-making are over. Negotiation is the only way to ensure not only national unity, but national survival as well.' I went on to invite Vorster to take part in a national convention to formulate a new constitutional system for South Africa. I said that to be effective such a constitution had to include all major interest and power groups. There could not be a convention in the real sense of the word unless the government, a key power group, was included.

The conference drove home to many whites the importance of listening at first hand to the views of black leaders. When the PFP was formed in 1977, I announced a commission to examine prospects and policies for the party. Van Zyl Slabbert was chairman, and its starting point had been the 14 Kowie Marais Principles and the seven guiding principles that flowed from them. Since then party policy had changed in emphasis, due to the prevailing political environment, but not in substance.

Therefore a number of specific matters needed to be re-examined. Foremost was the issue of the franchise. Whatever the merits of the qualified vote may have been in the early 1960s, political attitudes and constitutional realities called for a revision in favour of a universal adult franchise. Other burning issues were the extent and form of the federal components of our constitutional proposals, not least provisions for safeguarding minorities and details of the composition and functioning of a national executive.

At the PFP federal congress in November 1978, Slabbert submitted a substantial report on the relevant issues. While it noted that its suggestions on the mechanism of drafting a national constitution were negotiable, there were certain non-negotiable principles:

· There had to be full and equal citizenship rights for all South Africans without any form of discrimination.

- Political rights would be shared by all citizens without the domination of one group by any other, and all would enjoy an open society free of apartheid.
- The right of all to maintain and develop their religious, language and cultural heritages had to be protected.
- There would be equality of opportunity for all citizens in the economy.
- Every individual had the right to the protection of life, liberty, property, and access to the judiciary in defence of these rights.

On the issue of domination and the franchise the commission stated: 'Whereas a system of proportional representation prevents the exclusion of any significant political group from representation in government, it does not necessarily prevent the domination of one group over others, or a majority or a minority imposing its will on the rest. The problem of domination is the major political problem in South Africa.

'Debate on this issue has quite erroneously and irrationally focused on the system of franchise to be implemented. The committee feels that it should be made quite clear that the threat of domination is incidental to and not a consequence of the system of franchise in operation. It all depends what the structure of government is within which the franchise is exercised.

'The preoccupation in South Africa with linking the franchise to domination is a direct consequence of our experience of the winner-takes-all majority form of government in a Westminster parliamentary system. Thus the Afrikaner Nationalist movement, through the numerical preponderance of its supporters, was able to mobilise on an ethnic basis and capture control of power and impose its will, not only on those participating in elections, but also upon those excluded from the process.

'In short, the present system of government is tailor-made for group domination in a plural society.'

The problem was to determine what the minimal constitutional preconditions were that would eliminate the possibility of one group dominating all others. The committee decided that it was 'particularly appropriate' to give prominence to the advantages of a federal government that decentralised certain powers to lower levels of government. The view was that not only should there be separation of the legislative, executive and judicial arms of government, but, as important, that the 'winner-takes-all or first-past-the-post form of election is conducive to domination and that a system of proportional representation is particularly effective in countering winner-takes-all politics'.

The committee also proposed a minority veto to be effective in different spheres of governance – in short, a method of government by consensus with deadlock-breaking mechanisms.

The committee's recommendations were accepted by the congress and became PFP policy. The task of promoting them as a realistic alternative to apartheid lay ahead.

London to Lagos

Before the 1979 session kicked in, I caught a flight to London on a journey that was to take me to New York, Washington, Dakar, Banjul (Gambia) and Lagos. First I was to be a guest of the British government, and a 'greeter' from the Foreign Ministry would meet me on my arrival at Heathrow. I was one of the last to leave the aircraft, and on the tarmac I saw two gentlemen wearing dark overcoats and bowler hats. When I stepped down, the greeters moved forward. One put out his hand and with relief and anticipation said: 'Colonel Elgin, I presume?' Colonel Elgin I was, and Colonel Elgin I have been ever since – whenever I need a boost to my ego.

Cold, wintry and gloomy London was in the grip of a fuel crisis made worse by a coalminers' strike. During the day it was overcast and raining, with rain giving way to snow.

To conserve fuel, central heating was cut back. By night advertising lights were switched off; shop display windows, usually so bright, were illuminated by candles. Leicester Square, Piccadilly Circus and Oxford Street had a ghostly look. I encountered the British attitude to their rulers when the Sunday newspapers published pictures of prime minister James Callaghan clad in a coloured floral shirt and bathing trunks, enjoying a holiday in the sun on a beach in Guadeloupe. Such accountability!

Most politicians were out of town; nevertheless the Foreign Ministry arranged for me to meet David Owen, the Foreign Minister, and Margaret Thatcher – then leader of the opposition. Owen, young and oozing self-assurance, was one of the four foreign ministers of the countries comprising the Western Contact Group which had come to Pretoria for discussions on the South West Africa issue. He was very well briefed. Then it was on to the Houses of Parliament at Westminster to see Margaret Thatcher. She was at her desk hard at work, and from her appearance drawing some pleasure from the general discomfort of the Labour government.

When I met her then, and on subsequent occasions, I noted her sharp mind and most definite views; and was fascinated by the way her voice rose in pitch as she expressed something about which she felt strongly. On this occasion the focus was on Ian Smith and the situation in Rhodesia. 'Isn't it wonderful?' she exclaimed. 'Smith is through!' I was not at all sure what she meant by 'through' and when I probed she said: 'He is through the drift. Dennis [her husband] has been in Rhodesia and tells me that agreement has been reached with Bishop Muzorewa and Edison Sithole, and that things are coming right.'

I said I had no first-hand knowledge of recent events in Rhodesia and would be chary of coming to conclusions until I knew to what extent Muzorewa and Sithole (moderates alike) represented the black people of that country. What neither of us knew just then was that the person who would really be 'through' was Thatcher herself: Callaghan returned, was forced to call an election, his Labour Party lost, Thatcher's Tories won – and she broke through several barriers to become the new prime minister! This was to have a marked influence on the later debate over sanctions on South Africa.

In New York the mood vis-à-vis my country was shifting marginally. I met ambassador Donald McHenry – the US Deputy Permanent Representative to the United Nations – who was convener of the Contact Group comprising the US, UK, France, Germany and Canada, all of whom were represented on the powerful UN Security Council. The group was an attempt to adopt a common attitude on the SWA issue and play an intermediary role in seeking to resolve differences between South Africa and the UN on the issue. Its linkage with South Africa (which insisted that it, not the UN, had jurisdiction over the former German colony) was through the respective countries' ambassadors in South Africa.

McHenry introduced me to UN ambassador Andrew Young, and the three of us discussed the election of Botha as prime minister and developments in South Africa. McHenry and I had met on occasion when I was in the US and he was in South Africa; I found him both intelligent and sound in his judgement. While understandably opposed to apartheid, he equally understood the complexities of the South African situation. Chester Crocker, former Assistant Secretary of State for African Affairs, later wrote in his book *High Noon in Southern Africa*:

'Western diplomacy appeared to have stemmed, at least for now, the tide of Soviet influence symbolised by Angola's alignment with Moscow and the strong Soviet influence within Swapo and the African National Congress. The imaginative leadership of our UN ambassador Donald McHenry played a key role in these events.'

I also had a brief but satisfactory meeting with Kurt Waldheim, secretary-general of UN, and Brian Urquhart, the long-serving under-secretary in charge of UN peacekeeping operations. A general view of Western opinion was thus firmly in mind when I flew on to Dakar in Senegal. Senghor made a point of introducing me to Abdou Diouf, his prime minister and in due course his successor. In Dakar, too, I called on the Gambian high commissioner to discuss a meeting I hoped to have with President Dawda Jawara when I was in Banjul – as I hoped to be in a few days.

However, the day before I left for Banjul, Callaghan called the general election that would see him ousted from power; and, as it happened, a group of British MPs in Gambia at the time had to cut short their visit, flying back to the UK. One consequence was that protocol officials received me rather frostily when I arrived at Banjul airport. From their perspective, I claimed to be an MP, I had a visa for Gambia issued in London – yet I was travelling on a South African passport. The British MPs had rushed back to London the day before, so what was I still doing in Gambia? Was I an imposter?

I was questioned by the authorities and explained that I was a South African who had visited Gambia some years previously. This seemed to confuse them still further.

I recalled that when Helen Suzman and I were in Banjul in 1971 we had been looked after by a foreign service officer named McDonald, who was very tall and had a beautiful set of large white teeth. I somehow communicated this information. The official in charge picked up a telephone, dialed a number and spoke. A few minutes later the tall McDonald, with white teeth gleaming, entered the room. From being an imposter I found myself a guest of the Gambian government, enjoying the comfort of a room in a guest house overlooking the Gambia River. The smiling McDonald arranged my meeting with President Jawara.

After leaving Banjul and changing planes at Accra, I arrived at the new Murtala Mohammed Airport on a Nigerian Airways flight late on a Saturday afternoon. My understanding was that Dr Lawrence Fabunmi, who was now in Lagos in charge of the legal and consular section of the Foreign Ministry, would be around to assist me. However, no one met me, and I joined the passengers queuing up at passport control. When my turn came, the official on duty, having taken one look at my South African passport, sent me to the back of the queue. When I reached this official again, he handed my passport to a military major, head of the airport security section.

The major instructed me to wait and went off with my passport. While he was away an announcement came over the intercom: 'Will the Honourable Colin Eglin report to the internal enquiry counter.' *At least someone knows I'm here*, I reflected, and set off. I met an official from the protocol department who apologised for being late, then asked for my passport to see me through immigration and customs. His face fell when I told him my passport was in the hands of a security major. 'Now we have a problem!' he said.

We wandered back to find the major with my passport containing an entry visa issued by Ruda Mahommed, the Nigerian high commissioner in Botswana. The protocol official gave the major a long explanation; but he merely shook his head and asked who I was; why I was coming to Nigeria; what were the arrangements for my stay; and who in Nigeria would vouch for me?

I replied as best I could – which was not good enough for the major. I had to wait while he dealt with other would-be visitors. Between telephone calls, he dispatched luckless people to immigration detention barracks and directed that they should be put on the next plane to the country from whence they had come. A number of times I heard the major mention my name on the telephone and end the conversation with a curt: 'That is not good enough.'

After four hours a tall man with flowing robes and headgear arrived. He was the deputy chief of protocol, with instructions from the Foreign Ministry: Eglin was to be granted entry to Nigeria and placed in his care. The major – recognising a superior authority – endorsed my passport and said: 'I hope I haven't inconvenienced you.' It was time for being gracious, and I replied: 'No major, I realise that you were only doing your duty.'

I was assigned a driver called Christopher who took me to the official guest house on Victoria Island, on the far side of downtown Lagos. Christopher turned out to be a joyful driver: with all the windows of the car open to let in cool air, and with reggae music blasting from a cassette player, he waltzed his car through the traffic, hooting at cars in both directions. I leaned forward: 'Christopher, do you like driving?' 'No, Sah,' he replied, 'I love it!'

My temporary home on the island was not far from a beach where on Sunday afternoons crowds sometimes assembled to witness the execution by gunfire of persons convicted of murder, armed robbery, and other violent crimes. As I filled in a registration form, I felt an arm around my shoulder. It was Dr Fabunmi, my Nigerian friend who from his office in the Foreign Ministry had eventually persuaded the major to allow me to enter Nigeria. 'Hello, Colin,' he said cheerfully. 'Welcome to Nigeria. I thought I should come here to deal with any further problems you might have.'

In my bedroom I read a local newspaper and listened to a programme of music and comment that exposed the evils of apartheid and extolled the virtues of the armed struggle. The telephone rang. I was surprised to be greeted by name by a man with an African accent. He said he would like to talk, and I explained I was out of the city at the government guest building. 'No problem,' he said. 'You're in room B2 and I am in room C3 on the floor above you.'

'You're welcome to come down,' I replied.

I opened the door to a young black man wearing a white T-shirt, cut-off denim jeans and sandals, and carrying an open bottle of beer in one hand. We looked at each another, and I said: 'You're not Nigerian, you're a South African. Come inside, but before you do how about getting me a bottle of beer?' He complied, and we sat down to chat.

He had left South Africa in 1976 and was now in Lagos where he was helping to ensure that weapons got through to Swapo and Umkhonto we Sizwe (MK) cadres in Angola. MK was the armed wing of the ANC. I had to answer his questions about what was going on 'at home'. Eventually I broke in: 'It's all very well for you to sit here in Lagos and send arms to the cadres in Angola. When are you going to join them in engaging the South African army?' 'One of these days,' he said, 'I'll go south and if I come across one of those *boere* in the bush, I'll kill him with my AK-47.'

'And what will you do if by chance you come across me?'

'No, now that I've met you I wouldn't want to kill you.'

'How will I be able to stop you?'

'Just call out my name.'

'Yes, but I don't even know your name,' I said.

'Well, I won't give you my surname because I don't want to run the risk of prejudicing my family back in South Africa. But you can use the name by which I am known here in the struggle.'

'And what is that?'

'It's Cheerful!'

I said to myself: 'I mustn't forget "Cheerful!" Who knows – it might come in handy one day!'

Dr Fabunmi took me to meet the director of the Nigerian Institute for International Affairs, a post he had held before entering the foreign service; and then on to the Foreign Ministry to meet the secretary for foreign affairs and senior members of his department. I also had appointments with the US ambassador and UK high commissioner. Each gave his perspective on the progress Nigeria was making towards returning to democratic government and civilian rule under the leadership of Lieutenant General Olusegun Obasanjo who took over as the head of the Federal Military Government after the incumbent Brigadier Murtala Mohammed was assassinated in February 1976.

The next morning there was no motorcycle escort as there had been when Van Zyl Slabbert and I left Lagos in 1974. However, Dr Fabunmi drove me to the airport in a Foreign Ministry vehicle, and was kind enough to see me right to my seat in the aircraft. When next I heard from him he was in Warsaw as the Nigerian ambassador in Poland. We kept in touch sporadically over the years, and in 1991 I dined with him once more in Lagos.

But in Cape Town in 1979 I barely had time to prepare for the no-confidence debate which, as leader of the opposition, I would lead. With Botha in the saddle and the Information scandal building to a climax, I expected a rough year in politics. I did not anticipate how rough it was going to be.

Paranoia and corruption

By early 1979, parliamentary politics were in tumult. The catalysts were several. There was Botha's aggressive style; his attempts to get the Information scandal behind him with the minimum of damage to himself and his cabinet; his anger at further and continuing revelations in the press. The official opposition kept the matter at the forefront of the agenda. There was diplomatic conflict between South Africa and the stance taken by the Western Contact Group on a settlement of the SWA issue, and talks aimed at a resolution appeared stalemated – but Info was on everyone's mind.

Vorster had been newly elected as state president, but under a darkening cloud that led to the refusal of the PFP to congratulate him, and an attempt to impeach him for breach of the constitution. By February, Frans Esterhuyse in his weekly column in the *Argus* wrote that relations between government and the opposition had reached a new low: 'On the one hand the prime minister, PW Botha, indicated that he might shut his door to the leader of the opposition, Colin Eglin. On the other hand a number of PFP MPs, some reacting with interjections of "disgusting" and "disgraceful", walked out while the prime minister spoke … The issue about which the government seemed to be hypersensitive was that of collective cabinet responsibility in the Information scandal and opposition allegations that members of the cabinet knew what was going on but refused to admit it.'

On 6 February Botha, in response to the motion of no confidence which I had introduced for the PFP, offered to resign if the opposition could show that he or his cabinet had been aware of the irregularities that led to the Information scandal. On 16 March, under considerable pressure, he gave the Erasmus Commission a mandate to investigate the funding of *The Citizen* and to report back within two weeks. As before, on the appointment of the commission, we asked to be present at the hearings and to give evidence. We also asked for those giving evidence to be cross-examined and for the evidence and exhibits to be made public.

Our request was to no avail, and we were restricted to a 72-page submission.

On 2 April the commission found that no member of the present cabinet knew of the funding of *The Citizen* by the state, or of any other Information department irregularities. However, while Vorster was no longer a member of the cabinet and fell outside the commission's remit, Erasmus found that he had early knowledge of *The Citizen* project. In parliament I stated: 'Total exposure and deep surgery are required to rid South Africa of the Information scandal. What is clear is that Vorster and Mulder knew about *The Citizen* and other irregularities before the 1977 election, and withheld this information deliberately …

'It is also clear that the present prime minister, PW Botha, and the Minister of Finance, Senator Owen Horwood, were involved in one way or another in a method of budgeting and transferring of funds which the commission regarded as an irregularity from a technical, constitutional and audit point of view.'

Later that afternoon I received a message asking me to come to the House as Pik Botha, the Minister of Foreign Affairs, would be referring to me in the course of the debate. I took my seat in the House. Botha commenced by stating that at a meeting late on the afternoon of 27 February, he had given Japie Basson and me, together with Vause Raw of the NRP and John Wiley of the South African Party (SAP), confidential information on developments at the UN on the issue of UN Resolution 435 dealing with the Swapo-SWA issue. He accused me of telephoning the US ambassador at the UN, Don McHenry, leader of the Western Contact Group, and of giving him precisely that confidential information. Eyes ablaze, and in his best theatrical manner, Botha delivered a personal attack on me that must surely have been the most vicious and venomous ever seen in the South African parliament.

In his words: 'You took confidential information and conveyed it to strangers so as to make my negotiating situation more difficult. When a minister gives confidential information to another member, he cannot traffic with the enemy, and as a citizen of South Africa one cannot go over to them and feed them information and use this House for engaging in the politics of the enemies of South Africa.

'There has been no previous example of such an abominable, blatant, arrogant breach of confidence against a member of the government as that of the leader of the opposition. If I were you I would crawl into a hole in the ground and stay there. I should never come out again.'

I could scarcely believe my ears. What was particularly shocking was not the ferocity of Botha's attack, but his assault on my integrity. Part-way through the tirade, amid a chorus of jeers from the Nat benches, I claimed the parliamentary right to give a personal explanation. This was a tactical blunder. I should have realised that in the couple of minutes allotted to me in terms of the rules, I would be unable to give an adequate response to Botha's emotional and unsubstantiated onslaught. I should have allowed him to finish his speech, studied his allegations in a dispassionate manner, and dealt with them substantially at the next available opportunity.

Once I had gathered my composure, I asked myself: why this avalanche of abuse, and why now? Yes, I had phoned McHenry – who to my knowledge was far from being an enemy of South Africa. But no – I had not conveyed any confidential information to him; I had not prejudiced Botha's negotiations in any way; I had not phoned McHenry secretly or recklessly; I had not phoned him after the briefing with Botha, but after a meeting with the German ambassador who as a representative of the Western Contact Group gave us a different perspective on the issue.

There was nothing sinister in my call to McHenry – and I had discussed the matter with Basson beforehand. Now I believed that as leader of the parliamentary opposition I had a right and responsibility to get a clearer understanding of the issue. I believed McHenry was the person most likely to contribute to this. The following morning, at our request, Basson and I met Pik Botha privately and explained the position of the Contact Group. Botha appeared to appreciate our interest but said he was already aware of the group's perspective.

A few days later, on 7 March, UN Resolution 435 was debated in parliament, and Botha made no mention of my telephone call or of his subsequent meeting with Basson and me. In the course of the debate I welcomed the stand taken by PW Botha on the latest proposals for a settlement in SWA, and stated 'that I was satisfied by the fact that the prime minister had left the door open for negotiation … We as the official opposition will support the government in any means it takes in order to bring the settlement back onto the rails.'

After Pik Botha's attack, Zach and Helen were outspoken in defending me and slamming Botha for his behaviour. Basson was distinctly guarded in his support. For their part, NP members continued their orchestrated attempt to discredit me. In this they were joined by Vause Raw and John Wiley.

In New York McHenry described the attack by the Foreign Minister as 'a totally distorted presentation'. An official note was handed to the South African ambassador in Washington, which read in part: 'The Minister of Foreign Affairs referred, by implication, to the United States and to Ambassador McHenry as being among South Africa's enemies, an allegation which is totally unfounded. We categorically reject the allegation of improprieties … Mr Botha's remarks … could affect the negotiations over SWA/Namibia.'

I was unhappy; not because I was under pressure, but because I had allowed the issue in the debate to slip out of the PFP's hands. More than this, I had let down many PFP members who had faith in my ability to handle difficult situations. I reached the conclusion that there were two reasons for the outburst: PW Botha's determination to deflect the debate in parliament, the press and indeed in the country away from the Information scandal and government's involvement in it; and that the prime minister wanted to punish me for not accepting the findings of the Erasmus Commission.

Shortly before the ten-day Easter recess, I was talking to Ormond Pollak, parliamentary correspondent of the *Natal Mercury*, when my door opened and an ashen-faced Joan Fowle asked whether she could interrupt since she had something urgent to tell me. A strange man had called and said: 'This is Scorpio. Tell your boss we have had enough of him. We are going to do to him what we did to Turner.'

A year earlier Rick Turner, an anti-apartheid activist, had been shot dead through the window of his Durban home. Joan contacted the office of Colonel Kerneels Mouton, the police officer in charge of parliamentary security, and he said he would assign a police guard to my Clifton apartment. Joyce and I prepared for what we hoped would be a relaxing break at the Oppenheimers' stud farm near Magersfontein, a few kilometres south of Kimberley.

That night at about 12.35 Joyce and I were woken by a shot being fired and the sound of breaking glass. Two more shots followed. I went to the front door, without putting on the light, and found a bullet hole at head height in the glass panel of the door. I called the Camps Bay police and Colonel Mouton. When two constables arrived a few minutes later, I opened the front door to find that the landing had been blocked with flower pots, a dustbin and loose plants pulled from a nearby garden. Within an hour half-a-dozen police officers, including Mouton and the chief of the CID of the Western Cape, arrived on the scene.

Next morning Joyce and I went to the airport to catch our plane to Kimberley. I first issued a statement: 'This is a despicable act of political thuggery which is a discredit to South Africa. When you take into account the details of the threat which was made to me over the telephone in my parliamentary office last Friday, then I believe Pik Botha must be apportioned a share of the blame for his unbridled, unjustified attack on me. His allegation that I am hand-in-glove with an enemy of South Africa is despicable in motive and must create the very climate which encourages political thuggery of the kind that took place at my home last night.'

The political climate became even more tense. In Johannesburg, Horace van Rensburg of the PFP received a telephone call, threatening: 'Eglin will not escape death next time. You will be the next in line!'

By the time Joyce and I returned home after Easter, the police had arrested two suspects. One was a 22-year-old university student, Bryan Hack; the other a 29-year-old businessman, Arnold van der Westhuizen. They were charged with attempted murder and granted bail of R100 each.

When parliament reassembled in April, I decided to use the debate on the prime minister's vote to refute Pik Botha. But the following day I was criticised in the press for spending too much time on the 'McHenry affair' and not enough on the government and the Information scandal. I realised that as far as the public was concerned, Pik Botha had created a perception that was not going to be easy to dispel.

Prime Minister Botha continued the attack on me. One bizarre allegation was that I had used CIA facilities during my visits in Africa. The Nats and their supporters tried to project an image of the PFP as a whole that was radical and unpatriotic. Suzman was criticised for sending a telegram in her personal capacity to the prime minister asking for clemency for Solomon Mahlangu, an MK operative sentenced to death for an attack

186

in Johannesburg. De Beer was accused of suggesting that overseas investors should not invest in South Africa. As a result of a short story that Dave Dalling had written for *Punch*, he was accused by finance minister Horwood of using the story as a 'thinly disguised but carefully planned device to attack and try to discredit the Afrikaner'.

In the mean time the politics of government moved on. The Wiehahn Commission, appointed two years previously, tabled its report recommending far-reaching reforms in the labour field. These included the registration of black trade unions, abolition of job reservation, the establishment of an industrial court, and a national manpower commission. A week later the Riekert Commission recommended significant reforms for urban blacks, the promotion of home ownership, the lifting of the curfew on blacks in white areas, the scrapping of the system of random arrests of blacks under the pass laws, and greater opportunities for black trading in white areas.

At the same time, the nation was witnessing the unfolding of Prime Minister Botha's grand strategy. A white paper on defence recommended the development of a 'total national security strategy' to counter 'the total onslaught' against South Africa. A bill was introduced designed to prevent anyone publishing material relating to the alleged misappropriation of state funds without first getting the permission of an advocate general, who would conduct his inquiries in secret. After heated debate, certain offensive clauses were dropped.

On 4 June the Erasmus Commission presented its final report on Info. It exonerated PW Botha and Owen Horwood – but amazingly reversed its earlier findings on Vorster, and now found that he had indeed been aware of irregularities relating to Information and had to bear responsibility for them. That day he resigned as state president, and Marais Viljoen was sworn in as acting state president.

The duplicity of the government over seven years stood revealed. Many individuals and institutions played their part in uncovering the scandal. They included Gerald Barrie and Anton Mostert through their investigations. The Erasmus Commission played its strange part. Parliament provided a platform for questioning and debate, and the PFP shouldered the major responsibility for this consistent probing.

However, no institution deserves greater mention than the English-language press. The *Sunday Express*, with Rex Gibson as its editor and Kit Katzin as its chief investigative reporter, broke the story. The *Rand Daily Mail*, with Allister Sparks as its editor, and Mervyn Rees and Chris Day as its main investigative reporters, conducted its exposés with tenacity and skill. When one takes into account the awesome powers wielded by government at that time, the courage, skill and tenacity of the press must rank as the finest exercise of investigative journalism in the history of our country.

16

A question of leadership

At the end of July, parliament went into recess. I decided that I needed to take stock of my position as leader of the party – I knew the McHenry affair had had a negative impact on my effectiveness and authority. This, together with the concerted effort by PW Botha and the NP to paint the PFP as unreliable and unpatriotic, was a matter for concern. In these circumstances it was inevitable that the issue of party leadership would come up for discussion within the party and speculation in the press.

In a strong reaction to an article in the *Financial Mail* which suggested that the PFP might have to elect a new leader before the end of the current session, the PFP caucus issued a unanimous statement: 'Any suggestion that Mr Eglin's position as leader of the PFP is in doubt is entirely without foundation. The caucus is firm in its belief that his character and integrity remain untouched by the government's smear campaign and that he continues to be the right man to lead the official opposition.'

What I wanted to know was, to what extent had my effectiveness been damaged? And to what extent was the damage retrievable?

I was aware – even before the McHenry affair became a factor – that my position as leader was not as strong as it had been in the early 1970s, the heyday of the Progressive Party. There were a number of reasons. At each of the two mergers – with Harry Schwarz's Reform Party in 1975, and with Japie Basson's group in 1977 – my position as leader had been diluted. My continuing leadership was a condition of the mergers rather than the outcome of the freely expressed wishes of those joining together.

There had been an acknowledgement of my leadership qualities in the establishing of the PP as a viable political party, and in the negotiations that led to the formation of the PRP and the PFP. There was also recognition of my role in ensuring that the PFP had a clear-cut strategic mission and practical policies. However, while I had done well in defining the party's position on political issues, there were occasions in parliament when I had not done as well.

Quite understandably, the emergence of Frederik van Zyl Slabbert contributed to the leadership debate. Young, intelligent, articulate, and an Afrikaner committed to basic liberal values, Slabbert was seen increasingly as a man of the future. I shared this view and would have been comfortable had he become leader when it was time for me to go. But I was well aware that Slabbert did not see himself as having a career in politics, less still if he was locked into the position of party leader.

In addition, Slabbert and I were close friends. He had repeatedly told me I was the person he wanted as leader – and I was certain that he would have told me otherwise, had that been his position. Nonetheless, the issue would not go away. The party made a very poor showing in the Swellendam and Randfontein by-elections; in both it came last, polling only 378 and 681 respectively, and suffering the humiliation of being beaten by the NRP, with 2 640 and 1 415 votes. A view widely held in the party was that the McHenry affair contributed to this defeat.

Coincident with this, Slabbert allowed his name to go forward as a contender for the vacant post of vice-chancellor of UCT. This immediately raised the energy level of those PFP members who had set their minds on his becoming leader – and without Slabbert there was little prospect of a change. I was aware of the lobbying in the upper echelons of the party, yet what concerned me more were reports of unhappiness at the grassroots level, and a concomitant decline of morale and enthusiasm.

By the time our federal executive committee met on 29 July, the issue of the PFP leadership featured prominently in both the English- and Afrikaans-language press. I had been in politics long enough to know that when the press repeatedly attributed their reports to unknown 'senior members of the party' it was not thumb-sucking. Although leadership was not on the agenda, I asked each person present to state his or her frank and truthful attitude on the matter. Somewhat to my surprise, Zach turned what would have been an informal discussion into a formal debate by moving a vote of confidence in me as leader. He was seconded by Kowie Marais. Gordon Waddell followed, putting his case for a change and stating that, with Slabbert available, it should be made.

The discussion continued until late afternoon. Listening to it was a harrowing experience, but I found it extremely useful. Most of the old Progressives, including Helen Suzman, Ray Swart, René de Villiers, Ivor Sparg, Max Borkum, Thelma Henderson, Rupert Lorimer, Peter Soal, Malcolm Wallace, Andrew Savage and Joel Mervis came out in strong support of my continued leadership. Slabbert expressed his confidence in me as leader. Many of the new generation supported a change.

Horace van Rensburg, Dave Dalling and Douglas Gibson were forthright in their calls for a change. Japie Basson, Tian van der Merwe and Herbert Hirsch – while expressing their concern – wanted the issue to be decided by the party at a national congress. At one stage Suzman, who was not convinced that Slabbert was committed to a future in party politics, asked him what had happened to his candidature as vice-chancellor at UCT. Slabbert replied that, if I stood down as leader, he would not be available for the vice-chancellor's post. However, if I again made myself available as leader, he would give consideration to the vice-chancellor's post if it was offered to him. This reply confirmed, rather than removed, Helen's doubts about his commitment to party politics – but strengthened the determination of his supporters not to lose him.

Late that afternoon a vote was taken on the motion 'that a change of leader in the party is desirable'. The result was 25 for; 19 against; and three spoilt papers. No announcement was made when the meeting was adjourned; the members felt I should have time to consider my future.

The following morning I told the executive that I had given careful consideration to my position, and would consult my local constituency committee and make a comprehensive statement at a report-back meeting that I had arranged for 6 August. A special national congress would be held on 3 September.

I suppose my own pride was a factor in determining my decision. I had led the party through tumultuous times; I was still its leader. If there was to be a change of leadership, I wanted to be part of that decision and I wanted to manage the change with dignity and concern for the party's interests.

On Monday the *Cape Times* carried the following report: 'Smiling and cracking jokes as he spoke to pressmen, Mr Eglin said he appreciated the way in which members had spoken out – at his request – on the leadership issue. "I would not have wanted it any other way," said Mr Eglin, who began the discussions himself on Saturday. He made it clear, however that he would not take any snap decision on his future.

'"In terms of the party's constitution, I will be leader until nominations are called for at the congress. Whether I will be available is something I must consider."'

I set about consulting members of my constituency committee and other members of the party. It was clear there was considerable support for a change of leadership; however, a significant number of members believed that the choice of leader should be left to congress and that I should allow my name to go forward as a candidate.

Helen, who throughout this difficult period had been one of my strongest supporters, stated that only a congress had the right to elect a party leader, and both Slabbert and I should allow this choice.

Within a few days I made three related decisions:

- I would not make myself available for re-election as leader at the congress. In spite of pleas by Helen and others, the reality was that if I were re-elected as leader, I would find myself in a well-nigh impossible situation. I would have to oppose a rampant NP machine with a divided party of my own and a questioning English-language press. This would damage the PFP's ability to be an effective opposition.
- I would endorse Van Zyl Slabbert as the person to succeed me. I could trust him to continue to build on the basic liberal values he and I shared, and which were fundamental to any effective opposition. The sooner party members rallied around him the better it would be for the party.
- I would not resign as MP for Sea Point. I believed that I still had a role to play in the party and in the country's political life, as an opponent of apartheid and a champion of liberal values. In addition, the members of the PFP and the constituents of Sea Point were unanimous in wanting me to continue to represent them in parliament.

I was not going to allow the Bothas – PW and Pik – to have the satisfaction of seeing me removed from parliament.

I announced my decisions at an emotion-laden meeting in the Sea Point civic centre on 3 August. I also decided I should meet Slabbert to discuss the situation, and invited him to my home for dinner and a discussion. When I mentioned this to Joyce I received an icy look, and she said: 'I'm not having Slabbert to dinner in my home.'

Embarrassed, I phoned Slabbert to say that dinner was off, and explained the circumstances. He was taken aback; he liked Joyce and had great respect for her. A few days later Joyce told me she had changed her mind: I could invite him to dinner and she would be a good hostess.

Slabbert came to dinner, and after Joyce retired we did some serious talking. The next morning Joyce said: 'Judging by the number of empty wine bottles in the kitchen, you and Van Zyl must had had quite a session last night – or should I say early morning!'

The Scorpio trial

The shooting at my Clifton flat was to have repercussions that affected my understanding of what faced anyone who made himself visible in his opposition to the ruling regime. A few weeks after the arrest of Van der Westhuizen and Hack, I was called to the chambers of the province's attorney general, Abraham Lategan. There I was told that the government had made a further assessment of the shooting, and its opinion was that, since I was leader of the opposition – and the threat prior to the incident was made at my parliamentary office – there were constitutional implications.

The state had decided that Van der Westhuizen and Hack – with one David Beelders, currently living in Windhoek – would be charged under the Terrorism Act. Beelders was being charged as the head of Scorpio, a group responsible for a number of acts of violence against individuals and organisations in the Peninsula who were known to be liberal opponents of the government.

After a trial lasting a few weeks, Hack was found not guilty; Beelders and Van der Westhuizen were given sentences of seven-and-a-half and six years respectively. They served their sentences in Pretoria Central, a prison where white political prisoners were held.

Six years after the trial I received a call from Beelders, who had been released from jail. He said he felt he owed it to me to come and speak to me. I agreed to see him at my quantity surveying office, and he told me there were three matters on which he would like to say something.

The first was that he wanted to thank me for the manner in which I had given evidence at his trial 'straight down the line', uncoloured by any prejudice. The second was that while he was opposed to the political views of the leftist prisoners also held in Pretoria Central, he had to say that they were very intelligent and articulate and simply ran rings around the warders.

The third point, which he emphasised as the most important, was in two parts. He did not deny that he had committed the offences on which he had been found guilty – but said that in view of the publicity those actions attracted at the time, he thought I should know he was not the only one involved. He believed the authorities had decided to make someone the scapegoat, and had chosen him.

He told me of his shock when – while in a house in Windhoek, 2 000 km from Cape Town – a car pulled up at the front gate and two security policemen, who had arranged protection for him while he carried out activities for Scorpio, arrested him and took him to Cape Town. He said it was clear that the new government under Botha wanted to bring the curtain down on Scorpio, and at the same time do it in a manner that would prevent the unlawful involvement of the security police becoming known to the public.

I was fascinated. When I recalled my earlier experiences with BOSS, I realised that what I had been told pointed to the tip of an iceberg of duplicity and deception committed with the full knowledge of the NP government.

All this formed part of the background against which the PFP congress to effect a change of party leadership took place. It was held on 3 September 1979 in the President Hotel, Johannesburg, and was attended by some four hundred delegates. Zach recused himself from the leadership contest, and after a welcome address by Ray Swart I delivered my valedictory address. I reviewed the year's achievements and thanked the party for giving me the opportunity of playing a role as leader. I called on the delegates 'to bring down the curtain on the past and to meet the challenge of the future'. Slabbert was unanimously elected leader.

In his acceptance speech he made generous remarks about the role I had played in moulding the PFP into the official opposition. He added that he saw me as his political tutor – but, more importantly, stated: 'My policy and principles are precisely the same as my predecessor's as clearly defined in the party's constitutional proposals.'

The party would continue to promote the interests of all South Africans, irrespective of race or colour; totally reject any form of forced segregation; repudiate any form of partition in its constitutional proposals; see South Africa not as a collection of nations but as one plural society with a diversity of cultural and ethnic groups sharing a common destiny; and regard patriotism not in terms of privileged white South Africans under pressure, but as embracing all in a feeling of common loyalty.

Slabbert's election was supported by the rank-and-file of the party and welcomed by the English-language press. I was elected party chairman.

Slabbert threw himself energetically into his new task by conducting a nationwide 'meet the people' campaign. His first real test came in a by-election in the Edenvale constituency where Nic Olivier, who had joined the PFP with the Basson group in 1977, had lost his seat to the NP in the general election later that year. Now, in a by-election, Brian Goodall, the PFP candidate, won the seat, polling 6 029 votes to the NP's 4 867 and the NRP's 2 503. This victory enhanced Slabbert's position as leader, and demonstrated that the PFP, and not the NRP, was the real opposition in parliament.

This was the first time the NP had lost a by-election since it came into power on 26 May 1948.

17

New directions

Freed from the responsibilities and duties of party leadership, I tackled parliamentary and constituency work energetically. Over the next six years the politics of our country was going to unfold against a multi-faceted tableau of action and reaction, concession and oppression, hope and desperation. PW Botha started moving government policy away from Verwoerd's rigid racially based ideology. His commitment was to ensure that white South Africans remained in control of their destiny.

South Africans witnessed the fascinating and at times extraordinary spectacle of the Botha government making reformist moves in the social, economic and political fields, while at the same time ratcheting up the state's security apparatus and strengthening its military power. On the other side of the spectrum pressures for fundamental change were increasing in intensity and broadening in character.

The formation of the United Democratic Front (UDF) in May 1983 reflected the growing populist dimension of the struggle: increasing violence in the townships reflected growing frustration and determination. Sanctions of all kinds confirmed South Africa's growing isolation and a hardening of attitudes against apartheid in the international community.

When parliament opened in February for its 1980 session, I no longer qualified for a seat on the front bench. Zach generously gave up his seat in the second row to save me from being relegated to a backbencher. Slabbert asked me to be the party's spokesman on constitutional development and Coloured relationships, and I found myself back in touch with people at grassroots level.

In Sea Point the issues concerning the voters were pensions for the aged, security for flat-dwellers as rent control was phased out, petty crime and anti-social behaviour in the streets, and amenities for Coloureds and blacks. I dealt with these issues on a case-by-case basis at 'voters' clinics', through information sheets and intervention with the police and other authorities. Many local PFP-orientated bodies called on the Cape Town city council to open municipal amenities to all – and it did so in defiance of the National Party-controlled national and provincial governments.

In Johannesburg I joined my PFP colleagues in supporting the Indian community of Pageview in its fight against the destruction of their homes and businesses under the Group Areas Act.

The community destruction in the Cape took place against the background of a tremendous housing shortage on the Cape Flats. This affected blacks as well as Coloureds. We warned that the crisis was becoming explosive. I held meetings with the chief labour officer in an attempt to stop the eviction of black residents from the single quarters of Langa, and called on the authorities to stop the demolition of squatter shacks before alternative accommodation was available.

In the Cape, apartheid took on an added dimension of cruelty. In terms of an official Coloured labour preference policy, no more blacks were to be allowed to settle permanently in the Western Cape; and to the extent that additional black labour would be needed, it would be allowed on the basis of an annual contract. This restriction resulted in a freeze on the construction of new houses for blacks – a policy that had the unforeseen consequence of helping to smash influx control itself.

A vast spectrum that included businessmen, industrialists, farmers, economists and opposition politicians all pointed out that the policy was both wrong and unsustainable. In May 1983 – in a dramatic turnaround from its Coloured preference policy – the government announced that a huge new black township was to be developed at Khayelitsha ('Our Home') on the Cape Flats. It was said at the time that PW Botha had been taken by helicopter to assess the housing and squatter situation on the Flats. Having done so, and with the minimum of consultation with town and regional planning authorities, Botha pointed to the map and said: 'That is where it is going to be.' And with that Khayelitsha was born, and the Coloured labour preference policy put to rest. Pragmatism had trumped dogmatism.

The effects of apartheid endured, of course. There were bizarre and cruel examples, many of which were inevitably reported abroad to the detriment of the Botha government.

- St Dunstan's was an organisation for the welfare of war-blinded ex-servicemen, of which I was vice-chairman. It held an annual reunion dinner for its members and their wives living in Cape Town. One year, in the absence of a venue that could accommodate such a mixed gathering, the Coloured and white war-blinded veterans and their wives were forced to segregate in two adjoining rooms in a District Six restaurant. The doors between the rooms were folded back and the British ambassador, patron of St Dunstan's, stood and looked alternately from one room to the other to address his sightless audience.
- An elderly Afrikaner of humble background – who with some pride told me that he was one of two gatekeepers at the entrance to Groote Schuur, the prime minister's residence in Rondebosch – came to see me on a personal matter. He had been told by the official who gave him his weekly pay packet that from the following month all employees would have to produce their identity documents when receiving pay.

  He took his ID from his pocket and without saying a word handed it to me. I saw that printed on it was the letter 'K' – meaning *Kleurling* (Coloured). In Afrikaans, he slowly and heavily said that if they realised he was Coloured he would lose his job. Instead of being a gatekeeper he would have to sweep the leaves from the driveway. I assured him I would do my best to help, and asked him to see me again in a week's time. He took his ID back and shuffled off with his head bowed and shoulders bent.

When he didn't return as arranged, I drove to the entrance at Groote Schuur and asked about him. The gatekeeper on duty told me that his elderly colleague had been found dead. He had committed suicide.

- I was asked to take care of a young black American lawyer who had attended a reunion of Rhodes Scholars in Grahamstown and would be passing through Cape Town on his way home. He turned out be an engaging two-metre tall former college football star from Los Angeles, with a fine Afro hairstyle. On the way from the airport I told him he would be staying in our home for the night. He said that was great, but I shouldn't have troubled: I should have put him up in a city hotel. I told him that this was not easy; in terms of apartheid law hotels in the city were closed to blacks.

After our guest had met Joyce, been introduced to our daughters, and settled down to a welcoming drink, he said that he would like to call a cab and take Joyce and me to dinner and a show. I replied that this, too, was not easy: apartheid would not allow us to travel together in the same cab, nor to dine together in a restaurant, nor to go together to a show. The former Rhodes Scholar shook his head in disbelief.

One issue that I took up with government – and with which I was unexpectedly successful – was that of persuading the authorities to grant old-age pensions to priests and nuns. I had been shocked to learn that they were debarred from receiving state pensions. The given reason was that they had taken a vow of poverty. In reality, I suspected the truth had far more to do with the '*Roomse gevaar*' ('Catholic threat') attitude of the Dutch Reformed Church.

I held a series of discussions with Dr LAPA ('Lapa') Munnik, Minister of Health and Welfare, in which I pointed out that any drunken layabout, who had never worked or served the community, qualified for a pension.

From June 1982, priests and nuns became eligible to receive old-age pensions, although they had to be five years older than other categories of persons to qualify. I received many letters of thanks. Among these was one from Archbishop Denis Hurley, president of the Southern African Catholic Bishops' Conference, written in his charming personal style, which included the following: 'Dear Mr Eglin – You should be the most prayed-for man in South Africa once the good elderly Sisters get busy on you.'

The Tricameral constitution, 1980-1984

In March 1980 PW Botha started a process of constitutional development through which he intended to bring Coloureds and Indians into the parliamentary system in a way that would not impinge on the overall political control of the whites. A bill to create a Coloured Persons Council consisting entirely of members nominated by the government was proposed. Angrily, I described it as 'a shameful and cynical measure', 'a slap in the face for the Coloured people', and 'a callous breach of faith'. (In August, in the face of concerted opposition in parliament and rejection by significant leaders of the Coloured community, government abandoned the proposal.)

The previous May, an all-party parliamentary commission – chaired by Alwyn Schlebusch, the Minister of Constitutional Development – proposed in an interim report that the Senate be replaced by a President's Council (PC) consisting of white, Coloured and Indian members nominated by government – and having advisory powers only.

Slabbert, Basson, Dalling and I – representing the PFP on the commission – issued a minority report rejecting the proposed council. For us a related issue was whether, once the PC had been established, members of the PFP would serve on it. The party caucus met and resolved that PFP members could not serve. In June 1980, the Republic of South Africa Constitution Bill, which made provision for the creation of the PC, was tabled. Slabbert opposed it vigorously and reiterated our caucus decision on non-participation.

Basson, in defiance of the council decision, announced that he was prepared to serve on the PC. Slabbert immediately suspended him from the caucus. Basson subsequently resigned from the PFP, was duly nominated to the PC by State President Botha, and rejoined the NP.

By the time parliament resumed on 23 January 1981, members of the PC had been appointed; Schlebusch had been elected to the new position of vice-president and chairman of the PC. The Senate was abolished. Twelve new MPs were nominated to parliament by the political parties according to their electoral strength. Nic Olivier, head of the PFP's research department, was the party's sole new MP.

The PC was formally inaugurated on 3 February, representing Botha's first tentative steps towards constitutional reform. The initiative for taking the process forward now lay with the PC and, in particular, with one of its committees chaired by Denis Worrall, which had been charged with recommending a new constitutional framework. While the Worrall committee was considering its mandate, Botha announced a general election on 29 April 1981. This was a year-and-a-half earlier than required in terms of the constitution. We assumed that Botha wanted endorsement of the changes he had made and a mandate to take the process further.

The PFP decided to contest the election on a broad front, nominating candidates in 77 seats compared with 27 in 1977. We fought a vigorous campaign, focusing on security and social welfare, and linking the security and welfare of whites with those of blacks. We successfully exploited a statement by Lapa Munnik – that a pensioner could live comfortably on R20 a month – and won 26 seats, a gain of nine. In Sea Point I won comfortably with an increased majority.

On 30 May Worrall's PC committee, in an interim report, recommended a constitutional structure that combined the racial concept of Vorster's 1977 proposals with elements of jargon in vogue in political science circles at that time. Whites, Coloureds and Indians were to be included, blacks excluded. Within a few days, Worrall resigned from the PC to become the South African ambassador to Australia. This was typical of Botha the political manager: in selling a reform package, he did not want to be dependent on an English-speaking Nationalist whose reason for being a Nat was quasi-intellectual rather than fundamental. Botha preferred to be supported by Chris Heunis, who had taken over from Schlebusch as Minister of Constitutional Development. A straight-line Afrikaner Nationalist, Heunis had served as Botha's MPC in George for a number of years.

The multi-party constitutional commission, now led by Heunis and on which Slabbert, Dalling and I served as PFP representatives, started working in earnest. Heunis was an interesting chairman. He was intelligent, and willing to listen to and engage in debate, but he tended to be domineering when seeking to get his own way. While skilful in analysing situations and conceptualising solutions, he was less so in expressing these lucidly or succinctly. His concepts were often overwhelmed by a distracting flood of words – a form of language that came to be known as 'Heunis-speak', a euphemism for nonsense.

It was notable that few of the submissions to the committee were in line with the Verwoerdian concept of separate development. In overwhelming numbers they envisaged a constitutional solution within a single South Africa. I was surprised and pleased by the strength of submissions that argued in favour of political representation based on the voluntary association of citizens rather than on statutorily defined racial groups.

The outcome – presided over by Heunis – was a new Tricameral constitution, a refinement of the Vorster proposals supplemented by some of Worrall's ideas.

Parliament would consist of three separate Houses, one each for whites, Coloureds and Indians. Each House would have authority over what was termed 'own affairs' in matters which, in terms of the constitution, were appropriately vested with each group. Legislative authority over 'general affairs' would lie in decisions of the three Houses voting, but not debating, jointly. Each House would have its own cabinet with executive authority over its 'own affairs', while executive authority over 'general affairs' was assigned to a cabinet consisting of white, Coloured and Indian ministers – appointed and presided over by an executive state president.

The PC would continue – though now its members would be nominated by the political parties and not appointed by the president.

Two facts remained dominant and crucial:

- Black citizens were excluded from all of the constitutional structures. There had been provision for an advisory black council, constituted out of homeland formations, but it was soon scuppered – chiefly by the opposition of Mangosuthu Buthelezi.
- Every decision on 'general affairs' at any joint meeting in the three Houses, or by the cabinet, the PC or the body electing the state president, would have a built-in majority of white representatives. Thus the legislated numerical composition of the three Houses was biased and ensured a preponderance of white members.

The old apartheid constitution had been based on domination by exclusion; the Tricameral constitution relied on domination by co-option into segregated structures.

Even before the RSA Constitution Bill was placed before parliament, a significant political event took place as a consequence of the Botha 'reforms'. For some they went too far – and in February, 22 members of the NP caucus refused to support a motion of confidence in Botha. A week later they resigned from the NP to form the Conservative Party (CP), an old-style apartheid body.

On the other hand, in January 1983, the 'Coloured' Labour Party, in an unexpected about-turn, decided to participate in the proposed Tricameral parliament – although it rejected its provisions! A week later the South African Indian Council followed suit. These decisions were crucial to the success of Botha's constitutional gamble, since they meant that despite widespread opposition within the respective communities, the Coloured and Indian Houses would have sufficient members to make them function. They represented a triumph for Heunis, who had worked long and hard to persuade those affected to participate.

At the other end of the political spectrum the United Democratic Front (UDF) – comprising 320 community, labour, women's and student organisations – was formed to oppose the Tricameral constitution.

The UDF developed rapidly into a cohesive movement that not only opposed the Tricameral parliament, but played a major role in mobilising South African citizens of all races in opposition to apartheid.

Eventually, on 9 September 1983, after a gruelling series of debates in parliament, the bill establishing the new constitution was approved by 119 votes to 35. The PFP and CP opposed the bill, but the NRP sided with the government.

Botha announced that, before enactment, a referendum of white voters would be held on the new constitution. It was set for 2 November 1983. The question put to voters was simple: 'Do you approve of the Republic of South Africa Constitution Act of 1983, Yes or No?'

The PFP campaigned for a 'No' vote with the intensity of an election campaign. We based our approach on the glaring defects of the Tricameral constitution – but were unable to compete with the NP slogan that it was 'a step in the right direction'. Sectors of the English press bought this line – including the *Financial Mail* and the *Sunday Times*. The result of the referendum, in which there was a 76% turnout, was

65,95% in favour and 33,53% against.

This of course was a disappointment for the PFP – and also a blow for Slabbert. He found it difficult to accept that many PFP supporters had abandoned him and the party's principled opposition in favour of a misconceived 'step in the right direction'.

Nonetheless, on 13 July 1984 the all-white parliament met for the last time. During August 1984 elections were held under the Tricameral constitution for the Coloured House of Representatives and the Indian House of Delegates in which there was an extremely low voter turnout. On 3 September the new constitution came fully into effect and in consequence Botha was inaugurated as state president – combining his functions as head of state, head of the executive, chairman of the cabinet and commander-in-chief of the armed forces. In addition he controlled the National Intelligence Agency and the secretariat of the State Security Council.

Rev. Allan Hendrickse, leader of the Labour Party, and Amichand Rajbansi, leader of the National People's Party – and chairmen of the ministers' councils of their respective Houses – were appointed to the Botha cabinet as ministers without portfolio. No other persons of colour were appointed; but with the various bodies in place, the Botha-Heunis process of constitutional restructuring was complete.

Ironically, the creation of the Tricameral parliament had far-reaching consequences very different from those anticipated by those white voters who voted 'Yes' at the referendum. The deliberate exclusion of South Africa's black majority, more than any other action by the NP government, led to massive anti-apartheid mobilisation and a sharp increase in the scope and intensity of pressure, internal and international, against the government.

Who would have thought, when a triumphant Botha was inaugurated as executive president in 1984, that within six short years the leaders of the NP – the party that had banned the ANC and imprisoned its leaders – would have unbanned the liberation movements, released the political prisoners, and begun negotiating a non-racial constitution? Who would have thought that ten years after the Tricameral parliament was born, in the chamber specially built to house it, Robben Island Prisoner 46664 would be addressing the non-racial parliament as the president of a democratic South Africa?

At a congress held in November 1984 the PFP resolved to open its membership to all races in spite of the Prohibition of Political Interference Act. Seven months later, in June 1985, the ANC for the first time opened its national executive committee to all races – appointing five white, Coloured and Indian persons, including the communist Joe Slovo.

Finding the facts in Zimbabwe

In 1980 Rhodesia was poised for independence as Zimbabwe, and I went on a four-day fact-finding mission to witness change at first hand. There were obvious comparisons – and warnings – to be absorbed.

Understandably, the mood in Salisbury – later renamed Harare – was dominated by the approaching hour of independence, midnight on 17 April, when Prince Charles would officiate at the relinquishing of British sovereignty. The streets and buildings were being decorated in red, black, white and green bunting, and with the flags of the new Zimbabwe. Among the majority of whites, still reeling from the shock of Robert Mugabe's landslide victory at the recent election, there was calm mixed with apprehension. Yet the prevailing mood was festive – and it was difficult to realise that only three months before Rhodesia had been the target of sanctions and international ostracism, and that thousands of its citizens were involved in a bloody bush war.

I met a number of people playing leading roles in the transition, as well as private-sector leaders in commerce, industry, mining, agriculture and education. From my discussions I gathered that Mugabe had been making moderate and conciliatory statements, consulting extensively with the private sector, and that he had appointed Dennis Norman, a highly respected figure in the farming community, as Minister of Agriculture.

Then as now the 'land issue' was at the forefront of thinking and concern. The Mugabe government was committed to a land resettlement programme for 100 000 refugees, the 600 000 people displaced by the war, and the many landless rural peasants. Mugabe had stated he was anxious that resettlement be characterised by the productive use of land – and that where land was being used efficiently by commercial farmers, it would not be affected by resettlement schemes.

In the aftermath of the war, the attainment of independence and Zanu(PF)'s victory in the first free election, black Zimbabweans had high expectations. White Zimbabweans had doubts and reservations – but were prepared to be hopeful, and wanted to be helpful.

Over a year after independence, in October 1981, I returned to Zimbabwe with PFP colleagues Ray Swart, Tian van der Merwe and Graham MacIntosh. The new country had by then broken off diplomatic relations with South Africa, though we were well received by members of the government. We met cabinet ministers including Joshua Nkomo, a minister without portfolio and leader of the ZAPU party, Simon Munangagwa, Minister of State in the prime minister's office, and Dennis Norman.

The secretary of finance and the governor of the Reserve Bank provided us with insight into their perspectives on the financial position, and our group also established contact with many of the leading personalities in the private sector.

While we observed many changes in the political arena, I sensed there had been very little progress in the socio-economic field. This was reflected in the style and tone of government statements. Black Zimbabweans were becoming frustrated that so many expectations remained unfulfilled. The process of land settlement was slow, despite the fact that a government committee had reported that 1,2 million hectares were available for resettlement, and a private-sector analysis had put the figure at 4 million hectares.

The ruling coalition of Mugabe's Zanu(PF) and Nkomo's ZAPU was under strain and risked coming apart at the seams – a potentially dangerous situation aggravated when a large cache of arms belonging to ZAPU was found on a farm outside Harare.

At this stage, though, in spite of real concerns and frustrations there was still underlying hope for the future. Mugabe appeared to be trying to heal the divisions of the past and to deal rationally with the pressures being put on him. MacIntosh was so impressed by what he had witnessed that on our return he wrote an article under the heading: 'Zimbabwe a Miracle of Reconciliation'. I wrote an article that was far less effusive: 'Zimbabwe's fears and hopes for the future'.

It was evident that what happened to our immediate neighbour in the north would have profound implications for negotiations and future prospects in South Africa. We were to maintain our contacts and observations over the decades.

Perspectives from abroad

From 1980 to 1985 the number of my visits and range of my activities outside South Africa increased. I was fortunate enough to have the opportunity of seeing great areas of the world – and not just as part of my political work. Some were taken as a break from politics. Joyce was able to accompany me on a number of these trips to Africa, Europe and the Near East.

But of course many visits abroad were purely political in nature. I have described a few of my experiences in Zimbabwe, but many other places – including West Germany and Taiwan – drew my attention. Joyce was with me in September 1981 when a complex route took us to Senegal, Turkey, Greece and Israel. This was her first visit to Senegal and, having heard so much about the country from me, she was looking forward tremendously to seeing it for herself.

The focus of my visit was a meeting with President Abdou Diouf, who had taken over from President Senghor on his retirement a year earlier. While it lacked the personal warmth that had developed between Senghor and me, it was cordial and, from my point of view, extremely helpful. Diouf was clearly going to adopt the same approach to South Africa and apartheid as that of his predecessor.

At the end of the visit we were due to leave Dakar at midnight, touching down at Nouchat, the capital of Mauritania *en route* to Paris, where Joyce and I were to catch a connecting flight to Athens. Before we departed, Babaca Gaye, a Senegalese entrepreneur who had been most considerate to me in the past, invited us to have dinner with him at the airport restaurant. It was a cheerful occasion restrained only by the fact that we had to converse through an interpreter. At one stage I said to Gaye: 'Why have you been so kind and generous to me on my various visits to your country? After all, you don't know me well. You are Senegalese. I am a South African. You are Muslim, I'm a Christian. You are black and I am white.'

Gaye broke into a broad smile: 'Do you remember some years ago, when you and that lady [Helen Suzman] came to Dakar? Well, when you went to Paris to get your visa, the local office of Anglo-American helped you with your arrangements. A friend of mine, who worked in that office, told me that you were coming to Senegal and you were a good friend of Mr Harry Oppenheimer.'

He paused to laugh: 'I decided that any person who was a good friend of Mr Harry Oppenheimer was good enough to be a friend of Babaca Gaye.'

It is against such warm memories that one needs to set our experiences in Turkey. An eerie atmosphere dominated our stay. The country had just emerged partially from a period of military government and instability. A civilian administration was in place, there was a prime minister and a cabinet – but the final power still rested with the military. Joyce and I were shocked when, for example, we walked round a corner to be confronted by fierce soldiers patrolling with sub-machine guns at the ready. In the concourse at the airport and in other public places there were placards with photographs of 20 people who were 'wanted'. When, one by one, these individuals were seized, a rough black X was marked across their faces on the poster.

When I went to meet Prime Minister Turgut Ozal, the building teemed with armed military personnel. I couldn't make up my mind whether they were there to protect the PM from outside intruders, or as a constant reminder as to where the real power lay. I got the impression that the latter was the case.

Ozal and I were joined in our discussions by Husnu Dogan, head of the government's foreign investment department. Ozal, who had a background in economics, was relaxed and genial, and forthcoming in discussing the government's attitude and policy on foreign investment and involvement in prospecting and mining. His belief was that the time had come for Turkey, which had in the past frowned on such investment, to open up the country to foreign capital. He explained that for too long Turkey had been suspicious of outsiders; for too long it had relied on exporting its labour to Europe as its only significant means of acquiring foreign currency. The new approach was for Turkey's mineral resources to be developed, and for this to happen foreign investment and know-how were essential.

Joyce and I went on to Istanbul, and after two days flew to Israel. Here I had a brief meeting with General Moshe Dayan, and a longer discussion with Shimon Peres.

But perhaps, during this period, the visit that left the strongest impression on me was to the UK in June 1983. It came by way of an invitation to me and Helgard van Rensburg and Leon Wessels – two National Party MPs of the younger generation – to attend, as observers, what had been termed the Second Trans-Atlantic Meeting. This was one of a series of gatherings of representatives of the Bow Group of the UK's Conservative party and the Rippon Society of the US Republican party.

The meeting commenced with a formal dinner in London's Park Lane Hotel addressed by Sir Geoffrey Howe, chancellor of the exchequer in Margaret Thatcher's cabinet. We were accommodated in a number of colleges of Oxford University; the discussions were held in the Oxford Union, and focused on Conservative-Republican liaison, US-UK relationships, and the dominant issue of the time – the Cold War. I realised that to these northern hemisphere politicians, Africa was relevant only in that it impinged on their strategic interests in the struggle between the USSR and the West.

On one Sunday, the day of our departure, I persuaded my two colleagues that instead of going directly to London we should rent a car and drive to the capital via the Chiltern hills. We would see something of the English countryside and have lunch in a traditional English tavern in the historical and architecturally interesting town of Great Missenden. The countryside was, of course, beautiful, but in Great Missenden our plans went awry. We arrived a few minutes after two and found to our dismay that the pubs had all closed their doors. We ended up having a Chinese meal.

Over the noodles our discussions inevitably returned to South African politics. To my surprise, Van Rensburg and Wessels, probably because they were a long way from the rigid discipline of the NP caucus, started asking me questions about the details, and the implications for the future, of PFP policy. They sensed that Botha was taking a reformist path, and were interested in how far I believed that process would have to go.

Thus: 'Group Areas? How far must reform be taken?'

I replied: 'The Group Areas Act will have to be scrapped in its entirety.'

'The Pass Laws?'

'They will have to go as well.'

'And the vote? Do you mean a vote for all South Africans on a common voters' roll?'

'Yes,' I said. 'I understand your concern about your rights as a citizen and your rights in the language, cultural and religious fields. However none of these rights will be protected by depriving the majority of the citizens of South Africa of their right to vote, or by exercising the vote on the basis of separate racial voters' rolls. The protection of your rights lies in a constitution that is negotiated and agreed to by all South Africans, and in the development of a non-racial and democratic South African society.'

Of guarantees, I said: 'There are no absolute guarantees in politics. However, I believe the route I have outlined is the best way to protect rights. There is no other way.'

When in 1986 the NP-dominated parliament voted to repeal the pass laws, I received notes from Van Rensburg and Wessels: 'Remember Great Missenden!' That became the regular greeting between us as slowly apartheid laws in the social and economic fields were scrapped. But the real 'remember Great Missenden' from Van Rensburg and Wessels was reserved for 22 December 1993, the day on which parliament adopted South Africa's new democratic constitution, which made provision for all South Africans to have full voting rights on a common, non-racial voters' roll.

By this time Van Rensburg was chairman of the House of Assembly, and Wessels was the Minister of Labour in the cabinet. Both voted for the new constitution and for full voting rights for all on a common voters' roll!

At war with our neighbours

During the early 1980s there was a marked increase in armed conflict in South Africa and the southern African region as a whole. MK had ratcheted up its activities under the banner of the armed struggle. The Botha government had adopted an increasingly strong-armed militarist response to the challenges to white South Africa's political authority.

On the one hand these activities included armed attacks on military, security and strategic targets inside South Africa; bomb and land mine explosions resulting in civilian casualties; cross-border insurgent raids; and the emergence of terrorism as a factor in South African politics. In 1983 alone there were no fewer than 42 explosions and attacks within the borders. On the other hand the struggle faced the destructive power of the government's military and security forces; there were deaths due to police shooting, the deployment of the army in black and Coloured townships, and attacks by South Africa's conventional land and air forces on targets in neighbouring states.

All this resulted in increased violence and loss of life, and a significant destabilisation of the entire region. Apart from the continuing conflict along the Namibia-Angola border, at various times South African forces attacked targets in Zambia, Botswana, Mozambique and Lesotho, and crossed the border into Swaziland to abduct ANC members.

In April 1982 I visited Gaborone soon after Pretoria's forces had conducted a cross-border raid into Botswana. I found President Quett Masire – usually relaxed and genial – in an extremely angry mood: 'South Africa is trying to turn my country into a Lebanon!' He was adamant that the Botswana government would not permit his country to be used as a base for armed attacks on South Africa; but equally adamant that Botswana would uphold the international law on the right of asylum for political refugees.

I did not envy his situation. His predecessor, Seretse Khama, had once said to me that he was afraid Botswana, with its long border with South Africa, would be sucked into the vortex of an armed conflict certain to develop in southern Africa; a prophetic warning.

That same year, on 9 December, South African armed forces conducted a massive raid into Lesotho, attacking and destroying 12 houses in Maseru, and killing 41 people among whom were women and children. The government claimed its forces had struck premises and killed members of the ANC's armed wing in exile, while the ANC claimed that those killed were refugees and that it would respond with a retaliatory attack. The UN Security Council unanimously condemned the raid as a premeditated aggressive act.

I was concerned that white South Africans, under the impact of Botha's propaganda campaign, increasingly saw this escalation of internal violence and regional instability not as a result of domestic policy but as a consequence of hostile foreign forces engaged in a 'total onslaught'. I believed the PFP should persuade white South Africans that, whatever the external factors, the prime cause of the conflict was the denial of fundamental human and political rights to the black citizens of South Africa.

I issued the following statement to the *Cape Argus* after the Maseru raid: 'South Africans, whether they are supporters or opponents of the government, would do well to ponder deeply about the event and its implications for the future of our country and its people. We would be wrong if we saw the Maseru raid in isolation. We would be doubly wrong if we evaluated its importance merely in [its] immediate stated security terms. For the Maseru raid has wider implications for the future ... of staggering dimensions.

'Such strikes have become a feature in regions of the world, where because of the nature of the internal issues, the conflict and strife generated by these issues has spilt over international boundaries. This in turn has resulted in the countries in such regions becoming enmeshed in a spiral of increasing violence and counter-violence, with internal issues becoming more and more internationalised and the region as a whole becoming increasingly infected by a process of destabilisation.

'Our region, southern Africa, is such a region. Our country, South Africa, is such a country. We can respond to these external factors by tightening our security network, by increasing our military might, by mobilising our young men, and by occasionally knocking the hell out of targets in neighbouring states when the heads of our security apparatus believe that these targets are being used as bases for terror attacks ... But if this is our total response to the situation that is developing then we in South Africa are dooming ourselves to a future of increasing violence, increasing destabilisation and, what is more, to a future of increasing division, polarisation and bitterness within South Africa.'

I said that we had to deal with the external forces – but even more, we had to deal with the internal factors. Why had young black South Africans left the country in such numbers? Why were they now working from outside to overthrow the established system inside our country? Why was there such significant support inside South Africa for their objectives although not for their methods?

The policies of apartheid and the consequent repression had fuelled the fires of political militancy while frustration, even despair, had stoked the climate of violence. A commission set up by Chief Buthelezi had found that 99% of blacks believed that unless conditions improved within the next decade, escalating violence would be inevitable. At least half of those surveyed believed more young people would leave 'for military training'.

Yet in June 1985, three years after the assault on Maseru, South African armed forces crossed into Botswana. Houses were destroyed and 15 people killed. President Masire and his foreign minister were beside themselves with grief and anger, and said they would have to find ways of getting reparations from South Africa.

Mozambique, decolonised and independent, was another country that suffered as a consequence of the anti-apartheid military struggle. But here, for a time, developments looked more propitious. On 16 March 1983, in an unexpected and dramatic diplomatic move, Botha and President Samora Machel signed the Nkomati Accord – in effect a peace treaty and non-aggression pact overtly directed at peaceful co-existence between South Africa and Mozambique. I was one of a group of politicians, businessmen, mayors, administrators and civic leaders taken by air to Nelspruit and then by motor coach to Nkomati on the South Africa-Mozambique border to witness the signing of the accord.

It was a grand occasion: two presidents, cabinet ministers, bemedalled army generals, top officials, national flags, guards of honour, national anthems, presidential handshakes and military salutes in the heat of the African sun in an open field near a railway station. It amounted to a welcome and surprising respite from the spiral of violence and counter-violence, cross-border raids, military retaliation, armed conflict and destabilisation. Internationally it was seen as an important breakthrough, and paved the way for President Botha to embark on a successful eight-state visit to Europe.

The next year, Ray Swart and I joined Helen on a visit to Maputo at the invitation of Aquina de Braccia, the head of the Africa Studies Department at the Eduardo Mondlane University and a close friend, confidant and advisor of President Machel. We had discussions with cabinet ministers and other officials. We addressed students and staff at the university, and answered questions on the PFP's position on the political situation.

In spite of the Nkomati Accord, we found there was still considerable tension between the two countries. South African military forces surreptitiously continued to support Renamo – the armed opposition to the ruling Frelimo party. Maputo remained the home base for many exiled ANC activists, and South African forces still raided them. Our discussions understandably centred on the political, security and economic relationships between Mozambique and South Africa, and the damage caused by the conflict.

A number of government members were at pains to ask us to use any influence we might have to persuade Portuguese settlers, who had left Mozambique at the time of independence and were now living in South Africa, to return to help get the economy going again. We were assured that factories and businesses that had been nationalised, and the property that had been confiscated, would be returned to their former owners. The reasons were obvious enough.

Maputo, in the main, was a depressing experience. In the old 'concrete city' abandoned high-rise apartment buildings were in a state of decay. Factories had closed down, and the shops were dreary with little merchandise on display in the windows. Peeling paint and rotting garbage were everywhere. Beyond the tree-lined curve of the bay were a roadstead silting up and a harbour scarcely used. The sprawling black townships – said to have doubled their population since independence – were scarred by overcrowding, makeshift shacks, unemployment and poverty.

We soon became conscious of how much the development of Mozambique was going to depend on good political and economic relationships with its powerful neighbour, South Africa. That was the whole point of the Nkomati Accord; but it was in doubt soon enough.

Our host, De Braccia, had spent some years in exile in Algeria before returning to southern Africa to take part in the Mozambique liberation struggle. He gave us considerable insight into the personality, character and thinking of his president. Tragically, on 19 October 1986, he, Machel and a number of his close associates were killed when the aircraft in which they were returning from Malawi to Maputo crashed on South African territory.

Subsequent commissions of inquiry, appointed by the South African authorities, have declared that South Africa was not responsible in any way for the accident. The findings never dispelled suspicions widely held in Mozambican liberation circles that the crash was the result of 'dirty work' by South Africa.

Helping to build the city

Throughout my involvement in politics I appreciated being able, as a quantity surveyor, to keep in touch with the real world of building economics. It helped me avoid acquiring political tunnel vision. I enjoyed working alongside the architectural, design and town-planning component of the industry. Although quantity surveying deals primarily with financial control and cost management, I developed a feel for design and planning.

Here are four projects in Cape Town and the Peninsula in which I became involved.

Marina da Gama. In 1971 Bernard James and Partners were appointed quantity surveyors to the new Anglo-American project near Muizenberg. As originally envisaged, it included a deep-water yacht marina as well as a shallow-water residential marina, and I worked closely with prominent architects and town planners such as Revel Fox, Michael Munnik, David Jack and Michael Lowe.

The deep-water phase was abandoned at an early stage, but gradually the overall conceptual plan developed. A model was made and taken to Johannesburg for the approval of the Anglo-American board. To the distress of the project team, Anglo turned down the proposed design. With some diffidence I asked whether I could make an input. The problem as I saw it was that the design of the houses could have been of a suburb anywhere in the country – not of a marina close to the sea in the Western Cape.

I argued that the residential structure consisted of roofs with walls under them, whereas the appropriate design from an aesthetic, functional and historical point of view was that they should consist of walls with roofs between them. I also said that the colour of the roofs should not be red but dark-gray or black, matching old thatch.

Walls with roofs between them won the day. The new design was developed, the board of Anglo approved, and Marina da Gama went ahead. Swampy wasteland was turned into an attractive township for convenient and relaxed waterfront living.

The New Parliamentary Precinct. The Parliamentary Committee on Internal Arrangements had to consider, among other matters, plans for developing the site of the old Marks Building to provide parliament with additional office space. Parliament Street, an important access road from De Waal Drive to the city centre, ran between the parliamentary complex and Marks. During the months when parliament was not in session it was open to the public, but during the first half of the year, with parliament in session, the road was closed to all vehicular traffic and as a public thoroughfare.

I put forward a suggestion that Parliament Street be fully closed as a public thoroughfare and should be pedestrianised and developed as an integral part of the parliamentary complex. As for the Marks Building, I suggested it should be retained, subject to internal upgrading and modernisation. I was sure Capetonians would acknowledge parliament's needs and would soon develop alternative year-round access routes to the city. So it proved, and additionally Stal Plein was developed as an underground parking area with a generous paved forecourt to parliament and Tuynhuys at ground level.

Granger Bay and the Waterfront. In the early 1980s I raised the issue in parliament of the ineffective use being made of valuable land belonging to the South African Railways and Harbours parastatal. Over the years transport patterns had changed, and while in the past railway stations and (to an extent) harbours had been the focal points of urban economic activity, with the development of motor vehicle and air transport – and containerisation – the relationship between the city and the SAR and H had changed.

Granger Bay to the north-east side of the old harbour remained undeveloped, and with the construction of the Duncan Dock and the container berths the old harbour (consisting of the Victoria and Alfred basins) was only partially used. In addition the oil tanks in the 'tank farm' in the disused quarry adjoining the Alfred Basin were being decommissioned.

I put forward a case that these three areas should be used for an integrated development that could provide first-class residential, commercial, recreational and fishing industry facilities, as well as a new hub for Cape Town's tourism industry.

Quite apart from these economic considerations it could, to an extent, reintegrate the city with the sea, a feature that Cape Town, which was previously known as the Tavern of the Seas, had lost with the construction of the Foreshore and the elevated concrete freeways along its seaward perimeter.

I had meetings with both Prime Minister Botha and Gene Louw, the administrator of the Cape Province, at which I asked them to take the initiative in establishing a committee comprising representatives of the central, provincial and city governments, as well as from the private sector, to get the ball rolling.

By 2005 the Waterfront at the Victoria and Alfred basins had developed into one of South Africa's major tourist attractions; the development of the old tank farm as a yacht marina and residential area was well under way; and there was a modest canal linking the Waterfront with the new Cape Town International Conference Centre.

Garden Piazza at Cape Town Station. In the mid-1980s, in line with my argument that land occupied by South African Railways in the centre of towns and cities would have to be used more cost-effectively, I put the case for the future redevelopment of the Cape Town railway station concourse. I envisaged the present low-rise concourse building, while retaining a concourse at ground level, being replaced by a taller structure of, say, six storeys, with two lower wings leading out to Adderley Street at each end.

The rectangle of land enclosed by these buildings on three sides and by Adderley Street on the other could be developed into a user-friendly 'garden piazza' that would retain the greenery of lawns, but would introduce garden pathways, flowerbeds, and perhaps some water features. My suggestion drew some public attention, as well as some criticism. I did not press it further at that stage, but hoped a 'garden piazza' would feature when the redevelopment of the station concourse takes place at some time in the future.

Meeting the ANC in Lusaka

In October 1985 a PFP delegation consisting of Slabbert, Boraine, Peter Gastrow and me went to Lusaka to meet members of the executive committee of the ANC. At the time we were planning the visit, we were unaware that a group of businessmen, led by Gavin Relly, chairman of Anglo-American, would be making a similar visit a few weeks before us. My colleagues were already in Lusaka when I landed there on my way back from a visit to Europe. I was met by the ANC's dapper international relations officer, Thabo Mbeki, who whisked me through the airport, avoiding immigration and customs formalities, and took me to join the others at their hotel.

From there we were taken to a house in a suburb of Lusaka where we met Alfred Nzo, Thomas Nkobi, Gertrude Shope, Simon Makana and Mac Maharaj. With Mbeki, these were the members of the ANC executive committee. Our programme for the next two days consisted of discussions under the joint chairmanship of Nzo and Slabbert, and of informal personal interaction over meals and during the evenings. Thanks to the helpfulness of Vernon Webber, head of Anglo in Zambia, his home provided an agreeable venue for relaxed discussions over a glass or two of 'Uncle Harry's whisky'.

The talks ranged from an assessment of the current political situation in South Africa; the primary objectives of the ANC and the PFP; and strategies for getting rid of apartheid as a prelude to establishing a democratic non-racial South Africa. We found much common ground, particularly on the primary need to get rid of apartheid. Where we differed was on the methods of achieving this, and particularly on the use of violence. But we developed an understanding of each other's point of view, discussed prospects for keeping in touch in future, and agreed to issue a joint statement.

Mac Maharaj and I were sent off to do the drafting. After a relaxed couple of hours of discussion in a quiet corner of a Lusaka sports club, Maharaj and I reached agreement. The statement read: 'Apartheid lies at the heart of the present crisis. Both sides share the urgent need to dismantle apartheid and to establish a united, non-racial democratic South Africa. Both are deeply concerned to conserve the human and natural resources of our country and to remove one of the most potent factors affecting the stability of the whole South African region. Areas of difference were discussed in a frank and cordial atmosphere.

'In particular, there were differences on the role and centrality of the armed struggle in bringing about fundamental change.

'On the question of a national convention as a basis for devising a constitution for a united, non-racial, democratic South Africa, the PFP explained its position that such a convention could only take place once certain conditions were met. The ANC stated that it does not consider that there has come into being at the present moment a climate under which it can begin to consider a negotiated resolution of the crisis. At the same time, the ANC does not rule out for all time either a convention as a means of devising a constitution, or negotiations as a means of resolving the crisis.

'Both believe that one of the urgent issues is to secure the unconditional release of Nelson Mandela and all political prisoners and detainees.'

At the conclusion of our meetings the delegations went to State House where we briefed President Kaunda on the nature of our discussions and the areas of agreement and disagreement. As we flew out of Lusaka I recalled Nzo's poignant words: 'And so we say farewell to you as you go back to South Africa – our wonderful country – while we stay right here.'

During our flight to Johannesburg we exchanged thoughts and impressions. We were amazed at how well-informed the ANC was about what was happening in South Africa, and how eager to know details of the unfolding political scene. Then there was their passion for South Africa: they were certainly not agents of Moscow engaged in the 'total onslaught' to which Botha constantly referred. Their desire was to be 'home one day'.

At the airport on our return we held a press conference at which Slabbert outlined the nature of our discussions and the conclusions we had drawn from our Lusaka experience. We were encouraged to believe South Africans could still negotiate out of their problems.

Botha's response was that 'any discussions of this nature are unwise and disloyal towards the young men who risk their lives for the safety of South Africa'. Slabbert's counter was stinging: 'Mr Botha claims that his opposition to our talks was because the ANC was violent and communist. Yet his government was prepared to deal with the communist regime in Mozambique and with organisations like Renamo and Unita, which were involved in violence within their own countries. Yet when we talk to the ANC to find out their alternatives to our young men losing their lives, we are called disloyal … When it suits the government to do so it deals with the communists, but when we wish to talk to the ANC, who have some communists among them, we are unwise. The real issue is not violence or communism as such, although I am deeply opposed to both. The real issue is: how serious are we about a peaceful solution? We will talk to any organisation or group that can play a role in bringing about such peace. With whom is the State President prepared to talk to do the same?'

The world and Mr Botha

During an extended visit to the US in mid-1985, I had detected a markedly sharp hardening of attitudes towards South Africa and an increase in calls for economic sanctions. Indeed, emotional responses to my country went beyond disinvestment and sanctions into the wider sphere of rejection and isolation. On the long flight home I meditated on the situation, and decided to request a meeting with Botha at which I would tell him what I had seen, and put to him the immediate steps I believed he needed to take to turn the situation around.

Botha agreed to see me. Armed with a sheaf of notes, I went to have my say, to tell him of my concern. I said that in my opinion the trend would not be reversed as long as the image created by negative events overshadowed government's reforms. Indeed, instead of making a positive impact, reforms were being seen as measures to make apartheid more bearable and manageable. They failed to signal fundamental change.

I believed the time had come for government to make a declaration of intent, saying that it was resolved to do away with apartheid – and by this I meant repeal all discriminatory legislation with deliberate speed. The declaration should be crisp, clear and unambiguous, and each element of intent should be reinforced by a commitment to specific action. The pass laws and influx control had to go. South African citizenship had to be restored to those whose citizenship had been stripped away by parliament; indeed, parliament could be reconvened for this purpose before the end of the year. And Botha should commit his party to a process of negotiation.

I urged Botha to give substance to this intention by releasing Nelson Mandela.

Botha listened with surprising patience. He asked some probing questions but did not respond in any substantive manner to my request for Mandela's freedom. Speaking in Afrikaans, he said he had '*begrip vir die man*' ('an understanding for the man'). Mandela had been in prison for 20 years – and that was a long time. He, Botha, would never justify the actions that led to this incarceration. 'However, sometimes I wonder what I would have done had I found myself in the same circumstances that he was.'

The upshot was that, 'Yes, I could contemplate releasing Mandela … But – ' looking at me firmly and speaking with emotion – 'you must understand that I have a responsibility towards my *volk*. I will never negotiate with Moscow.'

It came home to me that while Botha saw Mandela in human terms, when it came to Mandela the political leader he saw him as an agent of Moscow – not as a South African fighting for the freedom of his people. I wondered what more I could do, and what else would have to happen before Botha realised that the source of South Africa's agonising problems was not Moscow but apartheid.

I felt better for at least having had my say. Shortly after the meeting Botha wrote to me thanking me for our discussions and for 'very interesting notes'. A week later, on 15 August, addressing a Nationalist congress in Durban, Botha made what became known as his disastrous 'Rubicon speech', all the more disastrous because of the high expectations that had preceded it. Prompted by the possibilities, the enthusiastic Foreign Minister Pik Botha had arranged functions to which selected political and community leaders were invited to listen to a ground-breaking speech by the president. Then – at the crucial historical moment – Botha, far from setting the NP government on the road away from apartheid, stuck vigorously to a racially based agenda and regaled his audience with the dangers of the 'total onslaught'.

And yet … Botha was a complex and at times contradictory man. In January 1986 he announced that legislation would be introduced to restore South African citizenship to all persons deprived of it. And six months later the pass laws were repealed.

However, he did not start the process of negotiating a new non-racial constitution, nor did he release Mandela. Instead, by June 1986, he declared a nationwide state of emergency.

But well before that, my own relationship with my party was to change yet again. I had some forewarning of this when Slabbert and I travelled to Australia and New Zealand to hold discussions with their respective senior political leaders. Since we had also received invitations from the UK's Foreign Ministry to attend a conference at Ditchley Park, north of Oxford, Slabbert decided to make our 1985 visit down under part of a partial round-the-world trip.

In Australia we discovered that South Africa was receiving considerable public attention. One reason was that Malcolm Fraser, the former prime minister, had recently been appointed co-chairman of a seven-person Commonwealth Eminent Persons Group to travel to South Africa to ascertain whether it could assist in resolving the political impasse. I ran into flak from the Australian press for saying that as Fraser was seen as a very controversial figure in South Africa, he was perhaps not the most appropriate person to head the mission.

When we arrived at our Australian hotel – after an exhausting Cape Town-Johannesburg-Perth-Sydney flight – Slabbert and I decided to go downstairs to a cellar restaurant for a snack and a glass or two of some good red wine. We found a table in a relatively quiet corner, while in the adjoining room Australian youngsters were enjoying a disco. Slabbert remarked: 'On waking up in the morning a young South African would say to himself: "I wonder what future there is going to be for me in South Africa?" Or: "I wonder if I will be conscripted to do military service on the border?"

'On the other hand a young Australian waking up would say: "I wonder what the waves will be like on Bondi Beach?" Or: "I hope I didn't make my girlfriend pregnant last night."'

Slabbert then stunned me by saying he was considering resigning from parliament and as leader of the PFP. I knew he was frustrated at the slow rate of change in South Africa, and deeply concerned that valuable time was being wasted by the Botha government. Yet I had detected nothing in his public statements – or in *The Last White Parliament*, a book he had recently written – that suggested he was contemplating resigning.

On the contrary, in his book, while discussing the Tricameral parliament, he wrote: 'Participation in the tricameral system is necessary because I believe that evolutionary constitutional change is both possible and desirable.'

As best as I could – late at night after 17 hours aboard a plane and a couple of glasses of wine – I tried to put the case against his resignation. His response was that he had been in parliament for close on twelve years, six as leader of the opposition, and had not succeeded in getting Botha to accept the basic changes he believed in. I shared his concern about the time factor, but said I believed that international and domestic pressures – including the work that he and the PFP had been doing in parliament – had helped to destroy the credibility of apartheid. This had created an environment in which the rate of change was bound to accelerate. My suggestion was that Slabbert should have a frank face-to-face discussion with Botha on the issue of South Africa and its future.

In the morning Slabbert told me he had spoken to Jenny Nothard, his secretary in Cape Town, and asked her to try to arrange an appointment with Botha immediately after he returned from abroad.

Our trip was illuminating. In Sydney we saw John Howard, the leader of the Liberal Party, who only two months previously had become leader of the opposition. He was interesting and engaging without being impressive; we did not know at the time that we were talking to the man who in due course would oust the Labour Party and go on to be prime minister of Australia for three terms.

That evening we met a large number of expatriate South Africans in the home of one who had relocated to Australia. We were warmly and enthusiastically received, and they all wanted to hear about political developments in South Africa 'from the horse's mouth'. However, a suggestion that they pitch in some funds for the PFP provoked a nil response.

In Canberra we had an excellent meeting with Prime Minister Bob Hawke. We went on to Brisbane, and in the town of Ipswich we met Foreign Minister William (Bill) Hayden.

We got around. Granted, we were in the country for only three days. However, I could not help but feel that Australians – perfectly comfortable with a whites-only immigration policy and not overtly sensitive to the plight of their own Aboriginal minority – condemned apartheid in a peripheral rather than a fundamental manner. I sensed that calls for sanctions and boycotts against South Africa were a means of expressing disapproval of apartheid – but I doubted whether many Australians saw them as a means of compelling white South Africans to hand over political power to a black majority.

In Wellington, New Zealand, Slabbert and I had an agreeable discussion with Prime Minister David Lange whose Labour Party had defeated Robert Muldoon's ruling National Party a year previously. Lange was a large man who had undergone surgery to reduce the size of his stomach. While he had strong views on apartheid, Africa was not the focus of his attention. His priority was to stimulate the sagging New Zealand economy, the key to which was to modernise the production of frozen lamb for export and find new markets, especially in the Near and Far East, to replace the traditional one in the UK which was shrinking as a result of the phasing out of Commonwealth preferences.

It was interesting to get a Pacific Ocean perspective on international affairs. Slabbert departed for engagements in the US and then on to the United Kingdom. I stayed to enjoy the scenic delights of South Island by going down to Canterbury and on a six-day coach tour. I left with an impression of majestic snowcapped mountains, glaciers, rivers and lakes, plains and rolling hills covered with millions of snow-white sheep nibbling away at green grass – and newly constructed modern 'refrigeration units' in which the nibbling sheep were converted into frozen lamb. There was no evidence of poverty, or of great wealth. An agreeable land in which to live: but how dull without the challenges of harnessing dormant talents and human potential!

I stopped off in Auckland for a day before going on for a three-day stay in Hawaii, and then on to the UK where I met Slabbert again. We travelled from London to Ditchley Park for three days of talks on matters relating to economic development in Africa and enjoying world-class British hospitality. Then Slabbert and I returned to what would ultimately be our different political fates.

After he had his meeting with Botha, Slabbert called me in Cape Town. 'It was as I thought it would be,' he said. 'I could make no progress with Botha. He won't agree to the minimum steps which I believe are essential if we are to save South Africa from the consequences of apartheid.'

With Christmas soon upon us, Joyce and I went to our holiday home in Hermanus and Slabbert to Swaziland, where his wife Jane's parents lived, and where she managed a thriving design and weaving business.

18

Slabbert resigns, I am recalled

During the first week of January 1986 Slabbert asked for my comments on a document he had prepared setting out a proposed plan of action for the PFP. By the time I had finished, I was filled with despair at what Slabbert intended – and disbelief that a person as adept as he was could have produced such a flawed and fanciful scheme.

Briefly, his proposal was that all PFP MPs resign from parliament and then contest their seats again – on the basis that those re-elected would not take their seats until the government had repealed the Population Registration Act.

I told him that I believed his plan was unworkable and would achieve nothing of value for either the country or the party. On the contrary, it would divide and weaken us, leaving us with fewer seats and less influence than before. I suggested that he get Nic Olivier's opinion, and he said he would. A few days later he told me that Olivier's reactions were similar to mine, and he had decided to drop the plan.

The annual no-confidence debate was scheduled to begin on 3 February and run throughout the week until the Friday. In the preceding week, the PFP's parliamentary caucus had its customary pre-session meetings to discuss the political situation, and, guided by Slabbert, to decide the issues it would deal with in the debate. As usual Slabbert was skilful in analysing the political situation, and lucid and compelling in putting forward the strategy we should adopt. There was nothing in his words, or his demeanour, to suggest that he was about to resign.

On the afternoon of the debate, Slabbert introduced the motion and analysed the political situation with great skill. He listed the failures and contradictions in government policy; he put the questions that government had to answer; and warned that its policies were taking South Africa down a dead-end road. He set out the required alternatives.

By Friday, the focus and the speculation of the public and media were on Botha, not on Slabbert and how he was to wind up the debate. The PFP MPs were in an upbeat mood.

At about 8.30 that morning, as I was meeting with some foreign visitors in my office, Slabbert put his head around the door and said he would like to see me. Once I had said farewell to my visitors I went to Slabbert's office where, without preliminaries, he told me he would announce his resignation from parliament that afternoon, at the conclusion of the debate. I was surprised but saw no point in arguing with Slabbert at that stage. I simply said I was sad to hear him say this, and was concerned about the consequences for the party. I added that I hoped he had told Helen Suzman; he said he would do so immediately.

A short while later Helen came to see me. She was fuming. I don't think I had ever seen her so angry. She lashed out at Slabbert, noting that he had told her that he had served in parliament for 12 years: 'I reminded him in no uncertain terms that I had been there for 26 years – 13 of them on my own.'

In the early afternoon the PFP caucus was summoned and told of the decision. Slabbert said it was final: it could only be changed in the unlikely event of Botha announcing a fundamental change in government policy. When the House of Assembly met at two-fifteen the atmosphere was electric.

In his speech Botha did not, of course, throw race-based policies overboard. Instead, he came out fighting in their defence; and accordingly Slabbert, after a withering response, announced his resignation from parliament: 'I wish to conclude on a more personal note and without acrimony and bitterness. This is my 12th year in parliament, five of which I spent as an ordinary member of parliament, and I am entering my seventh as leader of the official opposition. Particularly in my latter capacity I have often asked myself what the role of an opposition must be in a complex and conflict-ridden society such as ours. Even now, with clarity of conviction, I can answer that an opposition must question the actions of government, which we have done. It must expose the contradictions and shortcomings of government, which we have done. It must protest against injustice and the erosion of civil liberties, which we have done. It must define alternatives to the policy dead-ends in which government leads us: that we also have done.' He paid 'sincere tribute' to his PFP colleagues.

Then he went on: 'There is, however, another aspect of opposition which has a momentum and life of its own and which is independent of these very important political functions I have just mentioned. That aspect is political leadership in opposition. This too has to be judged, but on different grounds, and the most important judge is the person himself. He has to decide when the tension between analysis and practice is no longer bearable for him; in other words he has to decide when the moment has arrived to go. The magic moment for any political leader is to find the right time to go …

'I have decided the time has come for me to go. I have done my share and I believe it is time for someone else to have a go at it.'

The Nationalists were taken aback.

At a special caucus meeting after the debate I was asked, as chairman of the PFP, to act as leader until the federal council could decide the issue the following Saturday. I knew my life was again going to change.

The emotions generated by the departure of the leader they had admired and trusted were soon manifest in PFP ranks. Members outside the parliamentary caucus were bewildered, while within the caucus there were a few members who, being close to Slabbert, took his resignation stoically and with understanding. For the rest, reactions ranged from anger to disbelief and disappointment.

Slabbert sent me a letter, asking me to read it for him at the next caucus meeting. He addressed his colleagues: 'I take leave of you under very painful circumstances and have gathered from various sources how angered and upset many of you feel. Perhaps the time will come when the anger will have subsided and we will be able to talk politics with one another again.

'Whatever else you may think or feel about my actions, I wish to assure you that there was not the slightest doubt in my mind that my resignation was a political statement and not an act of self-indulgence. I knew that it would have repercussions for yourselves and for the party, but this was going to be inevitable, whether I did it immediately and at short notice, or whether I dragged it out over a period of three months, seeing deputations asking me to reconsider ... [Best] wishes for your continued performance in the House.'

Slabbert's letter did not help to mollify feelings. For most of the caucus, their leader had abandoned them.

There was much conjecture about what Alex Boraine was going to do. He was a close confidant of Slabbert and had been chairman of the party's federal executive throughout the period of Slabbert's leadership. His immediate response did not help anyone to understand the rationale behind the precipitate resignation, for without supporting or criticising Slabbert, Boraine told the media that he would decide that week both on his candidacy for party leadership – and on whether he too would resign.

He added: 'What I am certain about, however, is that there must be a radical rethinking within the PFP about what it means to be an opposition party.' This was tantamount to Boraine telling PFP members that under a new leadership they should do things that they had failed to do during the six years for which Slabbert and he had held the two top leadership positions in the party.

For a week my function was essentially one of damage control, and seeing that the parliamentary team kept a grip on the situation and were effective in the debates. Boraine did resign. In parliament I would later comment: 'I have been too close to Dr Slabbert to join in any public recrimination over his decision to abandon parliament. His actions may well have hurt many of his friends. But let me say that I, for one, would not mind enduring the hurt and damage if his dramatic move would drive home to this stubborn and shortsighted government the desperateness of the situation that is developing in South Africa.

'I want to express my appreciation for Dr Slabbert's work in parliament and in particular his efforts to make the debates in this House relevant to the realities of a South Africa of 30 million people.' Then I turned on the government: 'The PFP may have a temporary setback, but it is not the PFP, it is the government, and regrettably with that the country, that is in deep trouble. Once again the leader of the NP and the head of the government has "blown it". In a brief ten minutes the state president dealt a crushing blow to the process and prospects for negotiations in South Africa.'

I knew that the members of the federal council were giving consideration to the issue of the new leader. From conversations I had, requests I received, and rumours I heard, I sensed there was strong support for me to be elected once more. It was a daunting prospect: I had rather enjoyed a political role without the duties and responsibilities of leadership. The Nats would taunt me about the manner in which I had lost to Slabbert. Nevertheless there was a crisis in the party, which had to be dealt with. I agreed to stand and the federal council unanimously elected me as leader.

I did not see this as a commitment without end. Once the party was functioning effectively, it would be time for me to decide whether to step down. Meanwhile I would give the position all I had. I had concerns but no doubt in my ability. As I saw it there were three immediate tasks:

- To help party members to overcome the trauma of Slabbert's departure.
- To spell out a strategic mission for the party that would be credible and of value to the country in seeking a peaceful solution to its problems.
- To ensure that party members, public representatives, personnel and formations worked in a cohesive and goal-orientated manner to fulfil our strategic goals.

At this time of difficulty, I was greatly encouraged by Harry Oppenheimer who, writing in the *Sunday Times*, said straightforwardly: 'The resignation of Dr van Zyl Slabbert has subjected the PFP to a severe and undeserved ordeal. There is surely no precedent for the sudden resignation of an admired and trusted political leader in a manner which could not fail to do great harm to the party he led.

'Colin Eglin has now resumed the leadership. There is no one better equipped in this time of trouble to maintain unity and build up the party's significance. I feel a deep debt of gratitude to him. When, seven years ago, he was replaced as leader he accepted the situation with a dignity that was beyond praise and simply buckled down … [His] qualities are essentially those of a good soldier. He is calm in time of stress, he has excellent judgement, and he is a man of courage whose reliability and loyalty to this party have been tried in the fire … He deserves the support of all who are looking beyond apartheid to the building of a just, free South Africa of which all of us, black, white and brown, can be proud.'

Since there was no way I could justify Slabbert's resignation on political grounds, I decided to deal with it, as indeed Slabbert had done, on an extremely personal basis. My view was that his decision was one that every leader had to make for himself. Once he had lost belief in the relevance of what he was doing – and with that had lost both the desire and the will to lead – continuing as a captive of circumstances would be like living in an emotional hell.

While Slabbert had performed brilliantly in parliament, I knew he was never entirely comfortable operating within the parliamentary system, which he found too restrictive and ritualistic. As I expressed it in an interview, he had seen his role as a leader in terms of a time span and also in terms of political goals; and it seemed that the time had run out, and the goals had not been achieved.

The issue of why Slabbert resigned became more complex and controversial when Botha revealed the full text of the conversation he and Slabbert had had at their meeting on 25 November. The meeting was not confrontational, and the differences between Slabbert and Botha were no greater than one could have expected at the commencement of exploratory discussions. At no stage did Slabbert lay down any markers that would define reasons for his resignation. On the contrary, Slabbert told Botha that the time was ripe for an initiative and that he had some thoughts on this which he would like to discuss with an appropriate group in the government.

Botha identified the group as a cabinet committee under Chris Heunis. He invited Slabbert to put his proposals to the group. Botha further said that, if necessary, he would attend such a meeting if his schedule permitted him to do so.

Slabbert's response was that he would very much like to do this and that he would contact Heunis the following morning. Botha replied that he was seeing Heunis later that day and would tell him what had been decided.

The meeting concluded with Slabbert saying: 'Mr President, many thanks,' and with farewell pleasantries.

I believed the party should put the issue of Slabbert's resignation behind it. My strategic vision for the PFP was that it should use the parliamentary system, for all its flaws, to persuade the government and the voters to abandon apartheid and start a process of negotiation – towards a new non-racial and democratic system. However, it was imperative that it reached out to those citizens compelled by law to act outside the system to achieve their own objectives.

The PFP could only be effective if it brought into the parliamentary arena and into the minds of the white voters the needs, hopes, anguish and, at times, anger of the disenfranchised. It would be a Pyrrhic victory for the PFP if it persuaded whites to abandon apartheid and start negotiation – but black citizens turned around and said they were not prepared to negotiate.

I used Suzman as an example. In terms of ritualistic parliamentary politics she didn't need to reach out beyond its parameters – but in terms of Helen being effective in the interests of the country, she did. She went to prisons like Robben Island, Modder B and Pretoria Central. She saw the farmworkers in the potato fields at Bethal. She observed a treason trial in Delmas. She spoke to displaced people and those in squatter camps. She made it her job to intercede. This was what made her an effective politician, changed the lives of thousands, and earned her the respect of many more.

I continued to thump out this strategic message, and was ably supported by Peter Gastrow, the young MP for Durban Central, as party chairman, and Ken Andrew, the MP who had scored a stunning victory over the NP in Gardens in 1981, as federal executive chairman. Robin Carlisle, a member of the President's Council and a real mover and shaker, had been appointed to the newly created post of secretary-general. To assist me with our outreach function, Peter Soal, the MP for Johannesburg

North – who had a remarkable flair for ferreting out information and establishing person-to-person communication – was appointed to head up 'special projects'.

These, of course, were the years of 'unrest', of crisis. Individual party members and formations initiated outreach programmes, reinforced in some regions by the establishment of UMACs (Unrest Monitoring and Action Committees). The function of these committees was to monitor incidents of social disorder, manifested in violent protest, arson, police brutality, arbitrary arrests, and the demolition of squatter homes. The relevant UMAC would intercede with the authorities (where possible) and keep PFP members and the party's leadership informed so that we could raise such matters in parliament – or directly with cabinet ministers.

Another indication that the party was in good shape and functioning was that in June it launched the Progressive Trust for a new South Africa, which under the chairmanship of Tony Bloom announced that it had already received pledges of R7 million to promote party recruitment and initiate national negotiations for a new constitution.

In September, at a successful federal congress, I was re-elected leader, together with the others who held senior positions at federal level. My overall strategic objectives were endorsed. It was clear from the agenda of the congress and the tenor of the debates that the party had indeed settled down post-Slabbert and was moving into readiness for the election due to be held in the first half of 1987.

PART VI

The era of negotiation

19

The Eminent Persons Group

At a meeting in Nassau, Bahamas, in October 1985, the Commonwealth Heads of Government appointed seven prominent citizens to form an Eminent Persons Group (EPG), whose prime purpose was to promote political dialogue in South Africa, coupled with the cessation of violence. There were concerns.

The ANC-in-exile and its supporters were suspicious that the appointment of the EPG by prime minister Margaret Thatcher would delay the imposition of sanctions. A letter from the Botha government to the EPG reflected its own suspicions. Pretoria was prepared to view the initiative 'constructively' and hoped the EPG would be 'equally constructive'; that it would confine itself to promoting peaceful political dialogue; that it would be unbiased and discourage violence – and avoid action or comment 'which might be interpreted as encouragement to those promoting or supporting violence'.

The letter indicated that the group could visit the Republic to acquaint themselves with prevailing circumstances there and in the southern African region. It highlighted 'progress' already made in South Africa, as well as the government's reform programme.

The EPG comprised seven prominent persons from Canada, India, Tanzania, the UK, Nigeria and Australia. Its co-chairmen were Malcolm Fraser of Australia, and General Olusegun Obasanjo, former head of state of Nigeria. In February 1986 they and Dame Nita Barrow, one of the members, made a preliminary visit to South Africa. The whole group visited South Africa from 3-17 March, and held meetings with the state president and several cabinet ministers as well as with leaders of political parties, churches, trade unions, the private sector, the UDF and, in Pollsmoor Prison, with Nelson Mandela.

The EPG and the government maintained a low profile throughout the visit, and no press statements were issued.

Before arrival in South Africa, the EPG met Oliver Tambo, president of the ANC, and his colleagues in Lusaka at the request of Commonwealth leaders Mugabe and Kaunda.

The EPG returned to South Africa from 13-19 May for discussions mainly on the issue of ending violence as a prerequisite to the steps outlined in the EPG's possible negotiating proposals. Hopes of a breakthrough ran high when, on 15 May, Botha said he was prepared to negotiate with South African citizens, provided they did not resort to violence to attain their political goals or call on foreign agents to support them.

The next day I decided to take an initiative that was to make an impact on my personal relationships and activities over two decades. I wanted to make contact with General Obasanjo, whom I had learned was staying at the Newlands Hotel in Cape Town. From all I had heard and from my experiences in Nigeria in 1979 – when Obasanjo, then head of the military government, had initiated the drafting of a new democratic constitution and prepared for an election that would see political power handed over from a military to a civilian government – I thought of him as an attractive and most interesting figure.

I phoned the hotel and was put through to Obasanjo. I explained who I was, told him I had visited Nigeria in 1979, and said that I wished to meet him. Without formalities, Obasanjo said: 'Certainly. Come around to the hotel later this afternoon.' In his hotel suite – aware of my wartime rank of corporal – I addressed him then and in the future as 'General'.

Obasanjo was of medium height, stockily built, and clad in flowing pale-blue cotton robes and matching hat with its crown flopping forward. He had a broad smile: 'Take a seat. Would you like some tea?' And the afternoon's conversation commenced.

He had been extremely impressed by Mandela, whom he found well-informed and alert. Mandela showed no bitterness towards his captors, and said Buthelezi was a friend. I subsequently learned that Obasanjo had also met senior members of the South African armed forces, and impressed on them that South Africa could not win a purely military conflict. Obasanjo's frank and thoughtful intervention made a profound impact, and was an important factor in the political changes that took place in the military establishment.

I did my best to give Obasanjo my analysis of the political situation. I said that while the government had made reforms in the economic and social fields, and was realising that policies based on apartheid were not providing a viable political solution, it baulked at any policy that provided for the sharing of political power with the black majority. I spoke of the efforts the PFP was making to encourage negotiation, and said that I was worried that time was running out for a negotiated solution. Obasanjo said a one-man-one-vote policy should be the objective, but would not be achieved overnight. It needed a process, and the sooner a process commenced the greater were its chances of being carried through peacefully.

While I was with Obasanjo, Botha was addressing the President's Council. We heard part of his speech on radio: it was the old, hard-line PW. When Obasanjo and I parted later we expressed the hope that we would meet again, and concurred that we were less optimistic than earlier about the prospects of the EPG succeeding.

Two days after the EPG's departure, on Monday 19 March, South African land and air forces launched attacks on alleged ANC targets in Gaborone, Lusaka and Harare.

The prospects of the EPG succeeding had become close to zero. The Commonwealth was shocked. There were angry denunciations of the raids from Europe, the US and the UN.

Given the scale of the attacks and their serious political consequences, I asked Phillip Myburgh, the PFP spokesman on defence, and Peter Soal, who ran special projects, to travel to Gaborone, Lusaka and Harare. Their mandate was to inspect the sites of the attacks; and to discuss the situation with representatives of the affected nations, and where practical with the ANC. They were to assess the political implications.

Myburgh and Soal visited Gaborone where President Masire received them warmly. He was angry at what had occurred, and at the fact that Pretoria had not made use of diplomatic channels to notify his government in advance. He said the targets had no military or security significance, and suggested that South Africa was punishing Botswana because it had refused to sign an Nkomati-style accord.

In Lusaka they held lengthy discussions with President Kaunda, who told them that the camp bombed by the South African Air Force was for refugees in transit under UN control. It was 'a downright lie' to say that diplomatic channels had been used to warn his government of this kind of attack. The PFP men also met Oliver Tambo, who told them that the ANC had an information centre in Lusaka but there had been no ANC presence in the area that was attacked.

In Harare Myburgh and Soal made contact with Nathan Shamuyarira, who sent the Director of Information to show them the city office building that had been badly damaged by explosives, and a completely demolished suburban house. The office had housed the ANC's information centre, and the house had been the home of the ANC's representative in Harare for the past six years. Later Shamuyarira also told them that the buildings had no military or security significance, and denied any diplomatic contact to warn them of reprisals if the ANC was not removed from Zimbabwe. He said Zimbabwe supported the ANC but did not allow them to operate against South Africa from military bases on its territory. The attacks had put relations between Zimbabwe and South Africa under tremendous strain.

Myburgh and Soal returned to South Africa with a very clear impression that the raids had been conducted more for political than for security reasons, and had been aimed more against Botswana, Zambia and Zimbabwe than against the ANC. My conclusion was that the militarists inside the Botha government did not want talks with the ANC at any price, and had won the day.

A few months later I had breakfast in Obasanjo's suite in London's Dorchester Hotel. He was cheerful until the discussion turned to the EPG mission. At one time its members had high hopes of achieving a breakthrough, but these had been dashed by the raids. He told me that although the EPG would be disbanded, he would continue to take a personal interest in South Africa and would be available whenever South Africans thought he could be of assistance.

Circumstances would bring the General and me together in a number of interesting and challenging circumstances over the next two decades.

20

Worrall makes his move

While I was in London in September 1986 Denis Worrall, at that time South African ambassador to the UK, contacted me to discuss the political situation back home. Worrall and I had known each other for many years. When he, like me, was in opposition we often rubbed shoulders. When he joined the NP we crossed swords, and when he wrote articles for publication in the Afrikaans press under the presumptuous title of '*Engelse Mening*' ('English opinion') I got angry.

Now Worrall took me into his confidence. As ambassador he had been finding it increasingly difficult to defend government policy; and the 'Rubicon' speech had made it well-nigh impossible. We parted without having taken his dilemma further. I returned to Cape Town to prepare for the PFP federal congress and to start the work of preparing the party for the election early in the new year. Worrall, while not forgotten, slipped to the back of my mind.

Early in January Mervyn Smith, a keen PFP supporter, came to talk to me on what he said was a confidential matter. He was aware that the party had started the process of finding candidates and putting them in place in appropriate constituencies: could I try and keep the nominations for a winnable seat open, since a public personality of political significance was likely to become available? He was not able to give me the person's name and, hard as I pressed him, gave me no hint of who it might be.

Worrall contacted me from Johannesburg. Would it be possible for me to come to that city as there was a matter of some importance he would like to discuss with me before he returned to London in a few days. I flew to Johannesburg, went to the Holiday Inn Airport Hotel as arranged, and asked reception to inform Worrall I had arrived. I was sent up to room 112.

As I got out of the lift and looked around to find room 112, I noticed a familiar figure scurrying down the passage towards the exit staircase. When Worrall emerged from his room I asked: 'Was that Piet Koornhof?' Worrall, slightly embarrassed, replied: 'Yes – we were just having a friendly chat.'

Worrall said he was contemplating resigning as ambassador and returning to South Africa to take an active part in politics. How would I respond to the suggestion of him standing as a PFP candidate? I told him that the reality was that, should he be nominated, it was most unlikely it would be in a safe opposition seat. My advice was that he return to parliament via a seat he won for himself. I further suggested he stand as an independent, and I was sure that the PFP would at least consider standing back and not putting up a candidate to oppose him. There were two seats currently held by the NP that could be so contested – Port Natal and Helderberg, the former held by Stoffel Botha, the NP leader in Natal, and the latter by Chris Heunis, the NP leader in the Cape Province. Our meeting ended inconclusively with Worrall and me agreeing we should keep in touch.

There were times – usually on the pavement in Cape Town – when I would come across Jannie Momberg, an ardent Nationalist and chairman of the party's Stellenbosch branch. We usually exchanged a few pleasantries and moved on. But more recently he had begun telling me that he too found it increasingly difficult to justify the South African government's policies to those he met on his travels abroad. He had been especially bruised by the roasting he had received when, at the 1985 NP congress in Port Elizabeth, he had proposed a motion that the Group Areas Act be repealed. He found it particularly difficult to move all the way from the NP to the PFP, but should someone like Worrall, who at that stage had no party affiliation, resign he would give serious consideration to joining him.

I said that if I heard of any such development I would get in touch with him.

Over the next few days I picked up much gossip in newspaper circles that Worrall could be contemplating resigning. I became convinced the Sunday newspapers were going to carry a story on the matter the following weekend. I discussed the situation with Barry Streek, the political reporter for the 'morning group'. I said I would be calling Worrall to tell him that I believed it would be in his best interests to issue a personal statement outlining his intentions rather than reacting to newspaper speculation. I asked Streek whether – if Worrall decided to make such a statement – he would ensure that it was carried prominently in the *Cape Times* on Saturday. Streek agreed.

I then phoned Worrall in London and told him that an article about his possible resignation and return to politics was about to appear, and suggested he prepare an appropriate response. However, should he wish to pre-empt the situation, Streek was standing by to handle the release of a statement to the morning newspapers.

I also told Worrall of Momberg's comments, and suggested I should tell Jannie about the situation that was developing so that he could prepare a statement of support.

When I tracked Momberg down I simply said: 'Jannie, your moment of decision has arrived!' I told him what was about to happen, and that Worrall expected a call from him. The next day, as Botha prepared to open parliament, the *Cape Times* carried a report on Worrall's possible return to politics. Botha was furious.

One day later Worrall announced that for some time his government had known that it had been his wish to return to South Africa and public life: 'I believe that this is the time for bridge-builders within all communities … to make their voices heard.' Momberg's response was that he would resign from the NP and support Worrall.

Three months later Worrall stood as an independent candidate in the Helderberg constituency, with Momberg as his campaign manager, and came close to scoring a dramatic victory over his opponent, Chris Heunis, by reducing his previous majority of some three thousand votes to a bare 39.

It was two years later that Worrall, together with Wynand Malan and Zach de Beer, was elected a co-leader of the newly formed Democratic Party (DP). In the 1989 election Worrall was re-elected to parliament, where he served for five years before retiring to go into private business. For his part Momberg had helped Worrall form the short-lived Independent Party, which merged with the PFP and Malan's group to form the DP.

Momberg, too, was elected to parliament in 1989. He served as an enthusiastic DP member for two years until he and four colleagues resigned from the DP to join the ANC. In 1994 he was returned to parliament as an ANC member, and went on to become one of that party's whips. He left in 2001 to become South African ambassador to Greece.

He took it with good grace that on one occasion I introduced him as 'a politician who moved briefly through the DP on his way from the NP to the ANC'. It was something of a pathfinding career.

The setbacks of 1987

By the time parliament reassembled at the end of January 1987, preparations had begun for the election for members of the House of Assembly – the House for white representatives in the Tricameral parliament. The election was set for 6 May. Regional formations of our party were on election alert and had commenced the process of selecting candidates. This presented no real problem; almost all the 26 sitting PFP members were offering themselves for re-election.

At our national head office Robin Carlisle, who was in charge of overall election organisation, described our campaign as 'turbocharged'; Joan Hemming, who had experience as a marketing executive in Johannesburg, was marketing director; Dermot Judge, a professional in public relations, handled our PR; and Ken Andrew, chairman of the executive committee, was PFP co-coordinator. My responsibility, with a small committee, was to develop the strategic thrust of the campaign. Opinion surveys taken a few months before May showed that PFP support was holding compared to the 1981 election. Further, on an important issue such as political power-sharing, with which the PFP was identified, 67% of English white voters and 59% of Afrikaans white voters accepted this as inevitable.

However, the marketing consultants found that the PFP faced image problems. A strong voter perception was that the PFP could not be trusted to manage the country. It was seen as too radical, selling racial justice at the expense of security. The challenge was to market the party and me in a manner that would change this perception to a positive one.

I had put it to the party that the earlier concept of a *verligte* alliance – of individuals in one party – should be extended to an alliance of parties that might differ on aspects of policy, but share a commitment to get rid of apartheid and the NP government. The election was an opportunity to start the process of alliance politics in the belief that, properly managed, it could transform the fragmented opposition into a force for change. I encouraged the party to take three relevant decisions on key issues:

- The emergence of three independents as candidates. There was Worrall, Wynand Malan, and Dr Esther Lategan, a prominent Stellenbosch sociologist. In line with my earlier discussions with Worrall we decided not to nominate candidates in the three seats in which the independents intended to stand. We would have been hard-pressed to sell our strategic mission, to get the NP government to dismantle apartheid, if we were seen to be fighting the independents, who had broken ranks with the NP precisely because they would not dismantle apartheid.
- How we were to deal with the New Republic Party (NRP). This was particularly relevant to Natal where, in 1981, the NRP had won seven of its eight seats. Traditionally there was no love lost between the PRP and the NRP, and our assessment was that the NRP would not do well; nevertheless, it held the balance of votes in a number of marginal seats that in three-way contests would, in all likelihood, go to the NP.

  After discussing the issue with Ray Swart and others in Natal, I met Bill Sutton, the leader of the NRP in Cape Town. With very little haggling we agreed to put to our parties a proposal of an electoral alliance whereby we would not oppose one another in certain agreed seats – and concentrate on fighting the NP. On balance I felt this was the correct decision given the temper of the times and the realities of constituency-based politics.
- The third issue to consider was whether to refrain from opposing NP candidates whom we considered to be *verligtes* and who could help change attitudes within the NP. The decision was taken not to oppose Sam de Beer in Geduld, Leon Wessels in Krugersdorp, and Albert Nothnagel in Innesdal.

Nothnagel remained a *verligte* thorn in Botha's side until he was shunted off as South African ambassador in the Netherlands. De Beer and Wessels, while not as outspoken as we had hoped, were both to make constructive contributions in the negotiations on a new constitution and the transition to democracy.

In February, with election preparations in full swing, Horace van Rensburg – the PFP member for Bryanston – announced his resignation from the party. His given reasons were that the party was soft on security, naïve about communism, seemingly unpatriotic, and that it pandered to the ANC, and was anti-Afrikaner. This attack on the PFP was like manna from heaven for the NP's propaganda machine. It set the scene for the beginning of the NP's electoral onslaught on the PFP, which increased in intensity and viciousness right until polling day.

The Nationalists launched a massive advertising campaign against the PFP. A major theme was developed in a large ad with the banner headline: 'Over your dead body would you vote for the ANC – So why should you vote for the PFP?' Then there were 'corroborating' extracts from statements by communist leaders such as Leonid Brezhnev in 1973 and Vladimir Lenin way back in 1917: 'Our aim is to gain control of the two great treasure houses on which the West depends – the energy treasure house of the Persian Gulf and the mineral treasure house of the middle and southern Africa' (Brezhnev). 'We must hate – hatred is the basis of communism. Children must be taught to hate their parents – if such are not communists. If they are, then the children need no longer worry about them. Children should be present at the executions, and should rejoice in the death of the enemies of the proletariat' (Lenin).

We reiterated our assessment that apartheid was the root cause of the country's problems; and the solution lay in scrapping it and negotiating a non-racial future.

The election results were an immense disappointment to us. As the early tallies started coming through it became clear that the NP's fierce election campaign had damaged not only the PFP but shifted the whole white electorate to the right. The Conservatives, contesting an election for the first time, won 23 seats – two more than the number of MPs who had defected from the Nats to form the CP in 1982. The NRP was all but wiped out, with only one seat in the Natal midlands.

Of the three independents Malan retained his seat in Randburg; Worrall almost defeated Heunis; and Lategan did creditably in Stellenbosch. Our PFP total was reduced to 19 seats compared to 26 in 1981, and we lost our status as the official opposition to the CP.

A few days before the election I had met the NP Transvaal leader, FW de Klerk, who asked me about my party's prospects. I replied that the opinion polls showed that the PFP was holding up fairly well, but he could relax. We would not be taking over the government. Given the hairstyle that both Botha and I sported, I added: 'However, you can be assured that both the state president and the leader of the official opposition will be bald!'

Alas, Andries Treurnicht, the CP leader, had a fine head of dark brown hair. The PFP was almost back to where it was in 1977. Our efforts to 'turbocharge' politics had backfired miserably.

Slabbert goes to Dakar

I tried to recover from the exhaustion of the election. But there would be serious consequences for the party, and the situation would require frank examination and reappraisal. The loss of a quarter of its seats in parliament, the loss of its position as official opposition, and relegation to third place after the NP and CP, would have a serious impact on the party's effectiveness. While I was sure the hard core would remain defiant and resolute, morale among members and supporters had suffered a severe blow.

The vision of the PFP as a growing force for change in the dwindling time available to South Africa had been dashed. Despite our vigorous campaign, the NP propaganda machine had managed to brand the PFP as weak on security, soft on communism, naïve about the ANC, and not to be trusted with the future of the country.

As leader I would have to carry the responsibility for the drubbing – and as leader my effectiveness had been impaired. I nonetheless remained convinced that the key message the party had tried to put to white voters – that in the South African situation it was imperative to begin negotiations – was correct, and the PFP must retain it if it was to be true to itself.

As far as my own future was concerned, I knew it would be necessary to find someone else to lead the party into the next election. Meanwhile I had a role to play helping to get the party back on track after the 6 May buffeting.

Sooner than I had anticipated, an event took place that impacted further on the embattled PFP. A few hours before parliament adjourned for its mid-year recess, Gastrow asked to see me in the lobby behind the House of Assembly. He told me that he would be going as one of a group invited by Slabbert to visit Dakar in Senegal where it would meet the ANC for discussions. The purpose of telling me was not to seek my permission but merely to advise me what he was going to do.

I was even more surprised when it emerged that other MPs and prominent members of the PFP were also involved. I told Gastrow that, knowing there would be repercussions for the party, I was surprised that he (as chairman) had not consulted me. In the circumstances I trusted that Gastrow would present the PFP's policy and approach to fundamental change in South Africa.

Within a day or two, news of the Dakar visit and the names of its participants appeared in the press. They included Gastrow and Pierre Cronjé, both PFP MPs, Pieter Schoeman, a PFP member of the President's Council, and a number of other prominent PFP members, some of whom had served as MPs. Not one had discussed the matter with me. They must have known that holding discussions with the ANC under the leadership of Slabbert, who had resigned as leader, was bound to have repercussions. I was also disappointed that Slabbert did not feel that he could, or should, confide in me.

The group, comprising businessmen, academics, clerics, artists, politicians, professional people and journalists – many of whom were Afrikaans-speaking – duly met the ANC for three days of discussions. At the conclusion the two groups issued a joint declaration outlining the nature of the talks, the issues that had been identified, and the conclusions reached.

The Dakar visit received great publicity in the media and, as might have been expected, was fiercely attacked by Botha and the NP. Botha was also quick to seize on the fact that among the participants were public representatives and prominent members of the PFP – and to trot out the oft-repeated taunt that the PFP was soft on the ANC.

There was fierce debate in PFP circles, including its parliamentary caucus. While there was acceptance of the fact that holding discussions with the ANC was a sensitive political issue, there was no significant disagreement in principle with the PFP having such meetings. However, there was concern that senior members of the PFP had made the trip under the aegis of Slabbert, who had generated great tensions through his precipitate resignation. There was criticism of Gastrow, Cronjé and Schoeman, members of the parliamentary caucus, for not having consulted either the caucus or me before they committed themselves to this sensitive political venture.

On 27 July I issued the following statement: 'We recognise that the process of exploring ways and means of ending violence and of starting negotiation would not be without risks. It will at times involve talking to other South Africans with whom we disagree on many issues. Yet frank and direct talking must take place if there is to be a prospect of peace. It is against this background that I am satisfied that the PFP members who took part in the recent conference at Dakar, and who stated to the ANC delegation the PFP's attitude, both on violence and on constitutional alternatives, made a positive contribution to the well-being of this country and its people.'

I thought that with the issuing of this statement, the debate inside the PFP on the Dakar issue had been put to rest. This was not to be. Harry Schwarz proceeded to raise the issue in parliament. He distanced himself from the PFP members who had taken part in the discussions, emphasising that they had not gone to Dakar in their capacity as PFP members. He went on: 'Throughout the election campaign, I said that I was not prepared to negotiate with someone who had an AK-47 on the table. I said it during the election campaign and I say it now.' He referred to people who said the ANC was 'a killing machine', and said the 'ANC must stop killing people'. He concluded: 'One can be against apartheid without playing *voetjie-voetjie* with the ANC.'

Tensions flared up again. The resulting debate in caucus revealed the fault lines that had been opened within its ranks by the 'soft on the ANC, weak on security' campaign.

Gastrow, Cronjé and Schoeman expressed sincere regret to the PFP caucus for not having discussed the proposed visit properly or timeously with me as leader; and the caucus issued a statement: 'The Party is totally opposed to violence as a political instrument and is committed to exploring ways and means to ending violence and encouraging the process of negotiation. While the party is opposed to apartheid and will continue to strive to bring about democratic government in South Africa in accordance with Western liberal principles, its policies differ in many respects from those of the ANC.'

The NP and the Afrikaans press were quick to point out that the statement did not criticise Gastrow, Cronjé and Schoeman; nor had it endorsed my opinion that the PFP members who had taken part in the Dakar conference had made a positive contribution.

A clash between the PFP and the government took place when General Magnus Malan, the Minister of Defence, announced that he had decided to exclude Gastrow – the PFP's spokesman on defence – and Cronjé from all future confidential defence briefings and visits to sensitive military areas. The caucus reacted angrily and I was deputed to try to get Malan to reconsider. When he refused, I informed him that until he reversed his decision members of our caucus would not be accepting invitations from either him or his department.

Members of the caucus were in a tense and fractious mood.

Involvement with international liberals

Before the Slabbert debacle in 1986, I had travelled in Europe for a busy round of meetings, the first of which was that of the steering committee of Liberal International under the chairmanship of Senator Giovanni Malagodi, president of the Italian senate and the president of the organisation. The agenda established the theme and prepared the working papers for a congress to be held in Pisa later in the year. Although not a member of the committee, I had been invited to attend since LI was concerned with the situation in South Africa. I had attended two previous congresses when the PFP was an observer, but this was to be the first time I experienced the functioning of LI at close quarters.

Malagodi was one of the wisest and most erudite of the leaders I met during my next 15 years of active membership in LI.

When the PFP became a full member of LI, I was elected as a vice-president, a position I held until 2003 when I stood down at my retirement from parliament. My involvement was like opening a window of fresh air to the outside world. It constantly reminded me that economic, political and human freedom was not only intertwined but indivisible. In the modern world no country could be an island unto itself; and whether assessed in terms of war, poverty, disease and violence, or peace, progress, development and health, South Africa, like it or not, was part of an increasingly interrelated world community. Included in the institution's focus was the increasing importance of the impact of globalisation on the developing world.

In 1987 I put forward the name of my friend Olusegun Obasanjo as a recipient of a Liberal International Peace Prize for that year. Obasanjo was in prison, and Nigeria was under the military rule of Sani Abacha, a dictator; Obasanjo's wife Stella accepted the Peace Prize on his behalf, at Oxford, at a congress marking LI's 50th anniversary.

A few years later in Copenhagen I was pleased to propose Helen Suzman as the recipient of the LI Peace Prize for 2002. I enjoyed being in Budapest with members of Helen's family when she received the award and responded with a typically feisty speech about developments in South Africa.

The African connection to the international liberal community was very real. At a congress in Reykjavik in 1996, a group representing liberal parties in Africa met to discuss the state of liberalism in Africa and the role that LI could play on the continent. The consensus was that although there was goodwill towards Africa, LI was very Eurocentric and primarily preoccupied with issues relevant to the developed world. If liberalism was going to grow in Africa, Africans would have to do it for ourselves. We decided to form the Organisation of African Liberal Parties (OALP), composed of LI members, which would focus on liberalism in Africa. The Reykjavik Declaration announcing our intentions was signed by Senegal, Ghana, the Central African Republic, Malawi, Zambia and South Africa.

At the first meeting of the OALP in Lilongwe (Malawi) the following year, President Bakili Muluzi was elected president for a year to be followed Maitre Abdoulaye Wade of Senegal. I found myself secretary-general; and representatives of the OALP met on occasion in Cape Town and Dakar. The number of members grew, and for a few years the organisation played a useful linking and supporting role among its member parties. However, there were practical difficulties.

One of these was not uncommon in African organisations – a chronic shortage of funds. Keeping effective lines of communication open, let alone personal contact, between countries spread around Africa proved extremely difficult. Added to this was the Francophone and Anglophone divide which had to be bridged by duplicating the number of people holding office and ensuring that communications were in both French and English.

After a couple of years under the presidency of Wade, it was decided to close down the OALP as a separate organisation and to fall back on LI and its congresses, executive meetings and workshops for the back-up needed to develop liberalism in Africa. During the 1990s and the 2000s, LI expanded from its predominantly Western European base; and with this broadened the scope of the debate within the organisation. After the end of the Cold War and the fall of the Berlin Wall, political parties from former Eastern European countries started joining as either observers or full members.

There were new members from Latin and South America. Contacts were developed with political parties in Southeast Asia. While Africa continued to be represented, the growth of liberal parties on the continent was slow and sporadic: in most countries they had to contend with the coercive pressures of the ruling party.

Following a successful workshop which the Liberal Democratic Party (UK) had organised in Mombasa, I discussed the idea of setting up an African Liberal Network (ALN) with the Libdems' international relations office. Unlike the OALP, the Network was not to be a top-heavy money-hungry organisation but rather a vehicle for communication to and from a central office and through which affiliates could communicate with one another. In July 2003 a number of African parties belonging to LI met in Johannesburg, and resolved to form the ALN – setting out their commitments and objectives in what became known as the Johannesburg Declaration.

The ALN is still in the formative stage. It provides a useful link between liberal parties in Africa, and has supplemented this by arranging workshops with political organisations concentrating on women and youth.

In October 2003, as my retirement from parliament approached, I stood down as vice-president of LI; and at a congress in Sofia, Bulgaria, in May 2005, the organisation did me the honour of making me a Patron. On the same day, the honour was also conferred on Lord Steel – David was a long-standing friend who had been the leader of the UK's Liberal Party, the president of LI, and the first chairman of the Scottish parliament. He had deep roots in Africa and a great love for its people.

Edging towards disinvestment

During the 1970s anti-apartheid activists in the US and South Africa put pressure on American firms operating in the apartheid state to apply a code of employment practice embracing non-racialism, black advancement and social responsibility, known as the Sullivan Code. While the application of the code resulted in improved labour conditions in a number of US-owned firms operating in South Africa, it had little or no effect on bringing about political change.

In the 1980s, though, the domestic pressures in America shifted away from the Sullivan Code to disinvestment. This involved Americans disposing of shares they held in South African companies, disposing of affected business assets, and ceasing to do business in the country. US universities were in the forefront of the disinvestment movement, while the black lobby used as leverage the threat of boycotts of the products of those US companies that chose to remain.

The PFP was opposed to sanctions against the South African economy. While they could be seen as an expression of moral outrage against apartheid and a symbol of support for the oppressed, the party did not believe they would assist in bringing about fundamental political change. On the contrary, given the 'total onslaught' syndrome prevalent among whites, this form of economic pressure, apparently a response to domestic pressures in the US rather than a carefully worked-out strategy for bringing about change, was more likely to harden white attitudes.

Blacks in South Africa were divided. Some, like Bishop Desmond Tutu and Reverend Allan Boesak, were calling for sanctions; others such as Chief Buthelezi opposed them. The difference in approach to disinvestment between, on the one hand, the exiled and those activists in the country who would not be directly affected, and on the other those workers and their dependants who would lose their jobs and employment benefits, was demonstrated by events in East London in 1991.

At that time – after their unbanning – the ANC exiles had returned to South Africa, political prisoners had been released, and political activists unbanned. Yet the ANC insisted that sanctions and disinvestment remained in place until the Nationalist government had agreed to a new non-racial constitution. As a consequence of continuing labour disputes and work stoppages at its assembly plant in East London, Mercedes-Benz announced that it was considering shutting its plant and withdrawing from South Africa.

The ANC leadership now living in South Africa – alert to the traumatic and negative impact that such a withdrawal would have on the economy of East London – dispatched two of its senior members, Joe Slovo and Steve Tshwete, to the city to talk to the workers and persuade Mercedes-Benz not to close operations and leave. Labour relations improved at the car assembly plant; Mercedes stayed on and, two years later, the Nationalist government agreed to a new constitution.

Sanctions and disinvestment impeded the growth of the economy – but except where they were directed against the government itself, they made little or no contribution to the end of apartheid. I had many discussions on the subject with businessmen both in the US and in South Africa; and in August 1986 I was invited to speak at a conference in New York on 'The Disinvestment Dilemma'.

The thrust of my talk was that there was a positive role for US companies in bringing about peaceful change in South Africa, and if they wished to play it they should remain invested in South Africa. I questioned whether economic disengagement was indeed a viable political strategy for change, and said: 'To me apartheid is evil. It is degrading. It is a danger to the security of all who love South Africa. I am concerned with fashioning a strategy which, in a real and practical way, will rid my country of apartheid and allow my people to live in peace and freedom in a non-racial and democratic South Africa. To me as a South African "getting rid of apartheid" is not a useful slogan: it is a deadly serious political objective.

'Although external factors are relevant, fundamental change cannot simply be imposed from outside. It must come primarily from the forces generated within the society. Indeed, external factors are most effective when they strengthen the internal dynamic. They are at their least effective when they retard the internal dynamic and weaken the forces of change within the society.

'There are those who, looking at South Africa, say "there is no change" or "nothing is happening" or "things are getting worse"; and they then proceed to fashion a cataclysmic revolutionary strategy as the only way of forcing change.

'In spite of the apartheid laws, the South African scene is not static. Indeed, the violence that is occurring is that of a society in a state of uneasy transition. Although blacks share a common opposition to apartheid they are far from united on the instruments and the methods by which they should attempt to get rid of it. In spite of 30 years of National Party rule in South Africa, 20% of white voters at the time of the last election in 1981 voted for the non-racial policies of the PFP. In the universities, the churches, the press, in organisations and institutions around the country, in commerce and in industry, there are white South Africans who work openly and unashamedly to promote non-racial principles.'

I conceded that there were 'ugly, right-wing parties and movements – but there is also evidence of a rethinking and challenging taking place among younger people from traditional Afrikaner homes. A fundamental – organic – process of structural change and modernisation is taking place. In spite of the laws of apartheid and the intentions of its protagonists, the thrust of this process is not towards apartheid but away from it.

'The process was initiated and is being propelled by an expanding economy. It is being reinforced by a host of factors – emotional, educational, moral and political … It involves the migration of people from the rural to the urban areas, the bringing together of Third and First World South Africans in a new productive entity.

'But there is another parallel and interlocking process that is taking place. This is the process of statutory change – the changes in the laws. There have been changes in the apartheid laws and practices. Some of these changes have been significant, but to date none has addressed the key issue of political power, which, in a constitutional sense, remains firmly in the hands of whites.'

Nevertheless, I had 'yet to hear anyone advance a valid argument for why economic recession, combined with social instability leading to black-white conflict, should cause a beleaguered white group to move in the direction of reform. Damaging the South African economy will not bring down the Botha government, but retard fundamental change and with this weaken the economic muscle blacks are starting to use.'

I pointed out that the net effect of economic sanctions would mean that by the end of 1987, 50 000 employment opportunities would have been lost and the gross domestic product adversely affected to the extent of some 2% (or R2 billion). In 14 years' time, two million employment opportunities would have been lost, and GDP would have remained static in real terms. There would be considerable social and economic deprivation. Change away from apartheid required an expanding, not a contracting economy!

I was able to refer to three positive developments:

- The constructive interaction taking place between representatives of employer organisations and trade union leaders. This was occurring at local, regional and national level, and related primarily to labour and economic issues; nevertheless, the interaction was developing a momentum that could make an important political impact.
- The model effect of what was known as the 'Indaba' in Natal – an all-race negotiating and debating forum with its sights set on future solutions to apartheid.
- The growing consensus on the issue of fundamental change developing among a wide spectrum of leaders in the private sector.

With hindsight, I would not have urged differently.

21

The De Beer-Eglin team renewed

Frustration still ran high among members of the PFP parliamentary caucus as the 1988 session began. As an opposition we were fragmented, displaced by Treurnicht's Conservative Party as the official opposition. Among parties generally opposed to apartheid, the NRP lingered – with only one MP; it was swiftly fading. Wynand Malan's recently formed National Democratic Movement (NDM), with three MPs, was quietly establishing itself as relevant. Worrall's Independent Movement, although it had no MPs, was active in holding public meetings, recruiting members, and attracting considerable press attention. Worrall appeared to be gaining support among voters who, while dissatisfied with the Nationalists, were not disposed to supporting the PFP.

We were also hurting from the defection of three MPs.

After some soul-searching at a two-day meeting in September 1987, the PFP federal council decided where the party should place itself in the spectrum of South African politics. I announced our mission statement, placing us in the centre, rejecting violence, and committed to negotiation: 'The party will strengthen the middle ground in South African politics, vigorously demonstrating its commitment to being a determined custodian of liberal values, and engaging those on both sides of the rapidly polarised political scene and persuading them to talk.'

This was acceptable as a starting-point. However by January 1988 the party's forward planning had to take account of the fortunes of Malan and Worrall. I felt that although Worrall appeared to be gaining support at the expense of the PFP, this was not having a great impact on the hard core of seats represented in our party's parliamentary caucus. It was being felt in those constituencies where we had lost in the last election and which had no direct representation in parliament.

Frustrated PFP members, seeing the political tide going out, called for an alliance of opposition parties – a possible merger of the PFP with Malan and Worrall. The federal executive advanced the date of the next federal council meeting to 20 February, and put on the agenda a review of the white political 'market', options for the PFP, and options for the reconstruction of a liberal opposition.

I made it clear at the meeting that I supported co-operation between parties opposed to apartheid and would consider the concept of a merger, as in the past. However, I was not prepared to abandon the core principles of equal rights, individual freedom and the rule of law; or to destroy our painstakingly constructed organisational base and infrastructure.

The federal council decided that the PFP would participate in the House of Representatives (for Coloureds) and the House of Delegates (for Indians), the two other Houses in the Tricameral parliament, to fight apartheid and replace the Tricameral system itself with democracy. There were two immediate consequences.

One was that I met Allan Hendrickse, leader of the Labour Party in the House of Representatives, to discuss co-operation. Given the fact that his party was fragile and under attack from the UDF, Hendrickse was cautious. Nevertheless we 'agreed on a sound basis for co-operation between the PFP and Labour on matters of common intent'.

The other consequence was that two members of the House of Delegates, Mamoo Rajab and Pat Poovalingam, joined the PFP to become members of its parliamentary caucus, though as MPs they would have to sit in a separate House. Both were respected members of the Indian community in Natal: Rajab as a prominent businessman, and Poovalingam – a member of the former Liberal Party way back in the 1950s – as one of the founders of Synthesis in the 1970s. Both enriched our discussions and broadened our political perspectives.

In March the federal council met again to review the situation. It resolved 'to appoint Eglin, De Beer and [Errol] Moorcroft to find a facilitator to negotiate co-operation between the anti-apartheid opposition parties … to bring together those who belonged together'. At this stage prospects of a closer relationship between the PFP, Malan, and Worrall's Independent Party (formed on 17 March), were not promising. Worrall, who led the Independents, had never been close to Malan and, while not attacking the PFP in public, had remained demonstrably aloof from it. At a meeting in Pretoria, Malan had made derogatory comments about Worrall and ruled out co-operation with the PFP.

Over the following months, the Eglin-De Beer-Moorcroft committee held a number of informal discussions with Worrall and Malan but made no progress in negotiating any formal co-operation arrangement.

Earlier in the year I had informed a couple of my close colleagues that since I did not believe I was the person to lead the PFP into the next election, presumably to be held in 1989, I intended standing down when I considered it appropriate. One of my main considerations was whether there was a person committed to the same basic principles as mine who would be capable of keeping the party intact and motivated by those principles. Following a discussion I had with Bobby Godsell, a keen PFP member and a rising star in Anglo-American, and a subsequent exchange of letters between Harry Oppenheimer and me, it appeared that Zach de Beer might be available as just such a leader should I stand down.

I was surprised at first to hear that Zach might be available; he had returned to parliament in 1977 only to resign in 1979 to concentrate on his career in Anglo-American, where he was an executive director. When I subsequently discussed the leadership with Zach he told me he would certainly consider taking over should I indeed wish to stand down. He was chairman of the party's finance committee and had been playing a valuable role in the party's federal structures. Members respected him, and I had no doubt he had the qualities required to lead the PFP at that time.

In addition, I was aware that since Zach had not played a leading role during the last few turbulent years he was not as associated with the PFP's image problem as I was. This being so, it might be easier to achieve some form of realignment between the PFP, Malan, and the Independents, with Zach at the helm of the Progressives.

On 15 June – with the end of the parliamentary session in sight and a general election lying ahead – I wrote to Ken Andrew, chairman of the federal executive, informing him that I had decided I would not be available for re-election as leader. I added that should questions be asked, I would not be resigning from parliament or from the PFP. At the federal congress on 3 August, De Beer was elected leader of the party and I was elected party chairman.

The De Beer-Eglin team had returned to the helm. Our history went back to the election in Maitland in 1953, which had blossomed into the formation of the Progressive Party in 1959, which, while changing form, had endured successive triumphs and disappointments as the PP, the PRP and the PFP for 35 years.

As Zach was not a member of parliament I was elected PFP parliamentary leader. I accepted on condition that this was to be for one parliamentary session only. But there were surprises in store.

On occasions, sitting on the patio of my apartment watching the Atlantic rollers crashing down on Clifton's First Beach, I would reflect on my two-and-a-half years as a second-time leader of the PFP.

They were tough, unrelenting years. Tough not so much in the physical sense, but because, while the clock of South Africa was ticking towards a point of no return, my colleagues and I in the PFP were trying, with a degree of desperation at times, to get our message across to a white constituency held in a state of fearful political paralysis by Botha's propaganda machine. Tough because we had to deal not only with a belligerent and domineering opponent in Botha, but because we had the whole apparatus of the state arraigned against us.

I was disappointed that at times I had not performed as well as I should have. I had been unnecessarily brusque in dealing with some people; I was aware that in some quarters I was known as Mr Gruff. I felt I had not dealt with certain issues as crisply and persuasively as I should have done.

However, I remained convinced that the main message I had tried to get across – the urgent need to get rid of apartheid and set in motion a process of negotiation with all representatives of all sections – was the correct message, given the situation in which South Africa found itself. I was proud of many of my PFP colleagues, members and supporters who had stood by their principles in difficult times. I was disappointed with the few who seemed concerned more about the perceived image of the PFP than about the principles on which it had been founded.

Feeling somewhat battered and bruised, I was unaware that in less than three years a leader of the NP – the party that had vilified the PFP for calling for the end of apartheid, for the release of Mandela, for the unbanning of the ANC and the Communist Party, and for the beginning of negotiations on a non-racial constitution – would be doing all these things to the acclaim of the world and with the support of the overwhelming majority of white South Africans.

The PFP itself may not have been on the side of fortune: but as the future would show, politics and its entanglement with history was a process – not an event.

Saving the Sharpeville Six

When the time came for the Nationalists to negotiate, the event was preceded by a moratorium on the death penalty, which was later declared, by the Constitutional Court, to be unconstitutional. Historically South Africa was a hanging nation. Against this uncompromising background, six members of MK were tried and found guilty of killing a black local councillor in Sharpeville, and they were sentenced to death in 1986. The date for their execution was finally set for 18 March 1988.

Given the political circumstances of the councillor's murder (part of an uprising against those perceived to be doing the government's dirty work) and the negative consequences that this multiple execution would have, Botha was under great pressure domestically, and even more so internationally, to grant the Sharpeville Six a reprieve. In the UK the Thatcher government, which was resisting applying sanctions on South Africa, was in the forefront of foreign governments pressing Botha for clemency.

On 17 March, against the background of my own aversion to the death penalty and my concern about the consequences for South Africa should the hangings take place, I decided to seek an urgent meeting with Botha. I received a prompt and positive response from Botha – and immediately phoned Helen Suzman, who as an outspoken abolitionist held strong views on the issue, and asked her to join me in meeting the president. I knew that she had not spoken to Botha for 22 years – not since September 1966 when Botha had accused her 'and her friends' of being responsible for Verwoerd's murder.

Helen said that, in spite of her anger against Botha, she would accompany me. As we walked across the paving to Tuynhuys where Botha's offices were situated, I noticed that Helen's legs were pumping the ground like pistons, a sure sign to those who knew her well that there was trouble brewing. So as we entered Tuynhuys I said: 'Helen – now behave yourself. Remember there are six lives at stake.'

Helen was polite and at her persuasive best with Botha, who was joined by Kobie Coetsee, Minister of Justice and the cabinet secretary. He received us courteously. I explained that our purpose was to try and persuade him to use his presidential prerogative to grant a reprieve to the Sharpeville Six and that I, followed by Helen, would like to present the case from our personal perspectives.

Before I did so, Botha told us that the signing of the executive order for carrying out an execution was one of the most unpleasant and difficult duties he had to perform in his capacity as president. He said he had tried to find a procedure that would enable him to avoid doing so, but that whatever procedure was followed the final decision and the signature on the executive order had to be that of the president.

My case related largely to the political circumstances in which the killings had taken place. I spoke not only of the negative consequences for South Africa should the death sentences be carried out, but also of the positive impact that granting a reprieve would have on the political situation. I put it to him that somehow the spiral of violence had to be reversed – and I believed that such an act by him could help do this.

Helen in her usual forthright manner set out the reasons why capital punishment was barbaric and wrong, and why it should be abolished. In the light of Botha's personal opening remarks on signing an executive death order, I felt Helen was hitting some appropriate buttons. She said she understood that Botha was an admirer of the late Dr DF Malan, the former prime minister. Botha acknowledged this was so: 'He was my political tutor. He was an inspiring leader.'

Helen went on to ask Botha whether he recalled that in 1942 two members of the Ossewabrandwag (an anti-Smuts Afrikaner group of militants) had planted a bomb in the post office at Benoni, killing two people; they had subsequently been found guilty of murder and sentenced to death. She asked Botha whether he recalled that Malan, who was leader of the opposition at that time, had raised the matter in parliament with Prime Minister Smuts and had asked for the death penalty on these men to be lifted. Malan had argued: 'South Africa already has enough martyrs. It doesn't need two more.'

Helen then said to Botha: 'South Africa has enough martyrs; it doesn't need six more.'

With that she handed Botha a sheet of paper, saying, 'Here's a copy of the page from *Hansard* which I've just quoted. I thought you might like to have it.'

Botha listened patiently and attentively. He explained to us that he made it a general rule not to interfere with decisions of the courts. As far as the death sentence was concerned he made two exceptions: one was a murder committed in a fit of passion such as a three-cornered love relationship; and the other was in the case of *stamgevegte* (tribal faction fights). There was also a tradition that the president would not interfere with the decisions of the courts unless there were indications from the judges of other factors which he could take into account. In the case of the Sharpeville Six there were no such indications at the original trial or when the appeal was heard.

Botha told us he was aware that an urgent application was being made that day to postpone the execution for four weeks so that new facts could be put before the court. These new facts 'could affect his final decision even if the court upheld the death sentence'. Helen and I left satisfied that we had done our best. We noted Botha's serious approach to the matter and couldn't help feeling that he was hoping further evidence would emerge to justify his granting a reprieve.

On 12 July the Six received an indefinite stay of execution in order to pursue an appeal. On 23 November Botha granted the Sharpeville Six their reprieve from death.

The log jam breaks up, 1988

Neither the turmoil in South Africa nor the activities of parliament stood still while the PFP responded to the Slabbert resignation, the electoral setback, the defections and early stages of the opposition realignment. My colleagues and I had to be proactive against the background of the deteriorating situation. We had to deal with the issue of external pressures, growing civil unrest, and Botha's response.

We called for the lifting of the state of emergency, which the government reimposed each year. We attacked the Joint Management Security System, a parallel control mechanism that took authority and accountability from the normal organs of state and vested them in a Joint Management Council (JMC) responsible not to elected representatives or the cabinet but to the State Security Council. With a steady flow of information reaching us from the party's monitoring committees around the country, we raised the issue of the heavy-handed and often brutal behaviour of the security police in dealing with anti-apartheid activists.

In the Cape Peninsula we called for the government to cease demolishing squatter shacks and instead to deal with the housing crisis in a constructive and sustainable way. In the other provinces we called on the government to stop forced removals. At question time in parliament, with Helen in the vanguard, we peppered cabinet ministers with questions. On the tenth anniversary of the student uprising in Soweto I called for 16 June to be declared a public holiday dedicated to reconciliation.

In parliament, too, there was the issue of black economic empowerment – which I first raised when addressing the UCT Graduate School of Business on 'The Role of Business Now' in June 1976, and to which I would return during the constitutional negotiations in 1993-1994. I urged the business sector to take up the challenge and see that blacks were brought into the economy in a meaningful manner, 'not just as employees, not just as managers, but as partners and as co-owners of the economy of South Africa'.

I warned that if this did not happen, black South Africans would use their growing political power to attack the free enterprise system and replace it with one they 'perceived to be more effective in meeting their needs and aspirations'.

Our pleas and protests and questions often fell on deaf ears. Amid the escalation of violence the country appeared to be in the grip of political stalemate.

Yet, in 1988, there were indeed signs of movement – some subtle, some more overt – that I sensed could be a portent of greater things to come. The most important related to the war in Angola and with it the issue of independence for Namibia. Following the military setback at Cuito Cuanavale suffered by the South African forces in a pitched battle with Angolan forces – reinforced by Cuban military personnel and equipped with Russian armaments – representatives from South Africa, the US,

Cuba and Russia met in June 1988 on a number of occasions in London, Cairo and Brazzaville in attempts to reach agreement on ending the conflict.

In July 1988 the four countries signed a 14-point agreement on independence for Namibia and the related issue of the withdrawal of Cuban forces from Angola. In August a joint declaration heralded the formal cessation of hostilities in Angola. Although the Namibians were not represented in these discussions, given the international nature of the dispute over the status of Namibia, it was clear that independence could not be delayed for much longer.

On 18 July, on Mandela's 70th birthday, in a surprising leading article *Die Beeld*, a pro-government newspaper, urged the famous prisoner's release. In October, in another surprise move given the traditional conservatism of white sports administrators, representatives of the ANC and the South African Rugby Union met in Harare to discuss the 'normalisation' of sport and how to get South Africa back into international sport.

In November Harry Gwala of the ANC and Zephania Mothopeng of the PAC were released from prison. In December Mandela was transferred from Pollsmoor Prison to the Victor Verster Prison complex at Wemmershoek, near Paarl. The political log jam was beginning to break up.

The concern of world powers

As a consequence of my Liberal International contacts, I held an intense round of talks in London and was enabled to see the situation in South Africa as reflected in foreign concern. My most significant discussion was with prime minister Margaret Thatcher. In addition, I met people such as Sir Geoffrey Howe and Lynda Chalker, Minister of State at the Foreign Office; and staffers and researchers at Chatham House, headquarters of the Royal Institute of International Affairs.

Howe and Chalker – both members of the Thatcher government – had a particular concern that they were coming under increasing pressure, internationally and domestically, because of their opposition to sanctions. I could give them no comfort.

My meeting with Thatcher at 10 Downing Street was arranged by Robin Renwick, later Sir Robin, the UK's ambassador to South Africa. I found her to be extremely well-informed on the politics, the personalities and the interactive processes taking place in our country. In appearance and manner, she was exactly the Prime Minister Thatcher I had seen on television, heard on radio, and read about in the press. She wore a royal blue tailored suit and a darker blue blouse and white pearl necklace. Her coiffure was immaculate; and a black handbag hung from her left arm as her right stretched out to me.

During our discussion she was friendly and relaxed. She had a no-nonsense approach to the issues we addressed; her comments and questions were direct and to the point; she was quick to pick up and respond to the points I made; and she was strong in her opinions and forthright in expressing them.

We focused on South Africa, the impact of international pressures, the role of the PFP, and the prospects for change. Thatcher was most positive in wanting to help South Africa solve its seemingly intransigent problems. At one stage she turned the conversation to Chief Buthelezi and the Zulus. It was clear she admired Buthelezi's political leadership and was fascinated by the Zulu people. She raised her voice and pronounced in an exultant way: 'The Zulus are not just a people, they are a nation!'

Later she said pointedly: 'Your party doesn't believe in one-man-one-vote, does it? It doesn't seem to have worked elsewhere in Africa.' I had started to respond by giving her an outline of the PFP's franchise policy when she interposed: 'Of course, I'm referring to one-man-one-vote in a unitary state.' I responded that while the PFP did not support unfettered majority rule, it believed it was fundamental that all citizens had the right to vote and enjoy a direct say in the central parliament: 'The vote and access to parliament are to all South Africans "a badge of citizenship" and have become a fundamental issue on which no black leader can compromise.'

I departed not necessarily agreeing with all that Thatcher had said, but nevertheless impressed: here was a formidable political leader. Nevertheless, I was concerned that she did not appear to recognise the centrality of universal franchise in resolving South Africa's political crisis.

As it happened, I flew from London to Lisbon where I attended a luncheon of the Lisbon-South African Chamber of Commerce – addressed by Chief Buthelezi. To my surprise his speech dealt precisely with the issue of the franchise in a future democratic South Africa. Some key points in his address were: 'Wherever democracy is found anywhere in the world, there is one state with one sovereign parliament resting on universal adult franchise. Anything less than this is less than genuine democracy.

'The present constitution rests on racial distinctions which are entrenched in it. I will have nothing to do with a constitution resting on cornerstones of race distinctions. Unless we have a race-free constitution, we will not have a race-free democracy, and unless we have a race-free democracy, political violence can only spiral upwards.'

When I wrote from South Africa thanking Thatcher for our meeting – bearing in mind her high regard for Buthelezi and her reservations about the franchise – I enclosed a copy of his address on which I had marked the passages dealing with the franchise. I received a polite acknowledgement from Mrs Thatcher's secretary.

In Portugal I attended a conference in Sintra, some thirty kilometres from Lisbon – an attractive and historic town nestling against the wooded slopes of a mountain and at one time the summer resort of the monarchy. The meeting of leaders of liberal and centre parties had been jointly convened by the Portuguese prime minister, Prof. Anibal Cavaco Silva, and the West German minister of economic affairs, Dr Martin Bangemann. The prospects and problems of the world economy were addressed – especially the advent of the high-technology revolution and its global impact.

I became ever more aware that with the political demise of the USSR – and the failure of the communist and other highly regulated economic systems to generate growth or provide prosperity – we were entering a new era of economic development. Protectionism, state intervention and administered prices were no longer going to be the essential features of balanced growth. The emphasis was going to be on free trade, market forces, and an open exchange of scientific knowledge and technology. A significant feature of the discussions was the repeated focus on the unity of the world economy and the inter-relationship between the developed and developing world. With the Cold War coming to an end, the political centre was gearing itself to play a more significant role in world affairs.

The Sintra conference was one of a number of meetings, seminars and workshops in which I took part in the late 1980s and early 1990s, and which were held under the aegis of the International Academy for Development in Freedom. Participants generally came from Europe and Africa, and discussions focused on the liberal response to the challenges of development and democracy in the rapidly changing international climate.

In the course of the meetings, I was in touch with Carmo Jardim whom I had first met in Cape Town. She was the daughter of George Jardim, a Portuguese settler in Mozambique who had attempted to stage a coup against the Portuguese administration in the mid-1970s and subsequently become a supporter of Renamo, the opposition to the Frelimo government. Carmo was an attractive young woman with a remarkably adventurous spirit. She had a pilot's licence, and while still in Mozambique had flown supplies to various Renamo outposts in the hinterland. Her recreation in Portugal was sky-diving.

Although she and her father lived in Portugal when I met her, she retained an interest in developments in Mozambique and maintained contact with Alfonso Dlakama, the Renamo leader, then in exile in Europe. On one occasion, in discussion with a high-ranking Mozambican diplomat, I mentioned that I was in contact with one of Jardim's daughters. Far from being shocked he showed a keen interest in using this contact. As a consequence I wrote to Carmo, enclosing a copy of the ambassador's visiting card, and conveyed to her the main points of his viewpoint as follows:

- If you are in any position to help bring an end to the conflict in Mozambique, anything you could do would be welcome.
- The Mozambique government is anxious to secure reconciliation with those who left the country in the post-1970 era.
- The government would be pleased to see Jardim back in Mozambique. Your father at one stage owned the Grand Hotel in Beira, and the hotel is available to the Jardim family again if they wish to return.
- My contact would be most interested in talking with you should he pass through Lisbon; but in the meanwhile, if you have any inclination to contact the present Mozambique government, you can do so through the present Mozambique ambassador in Lisbon.

I did not have an opportunity of following up my letter to Carmo, but learned that some former residents of Mozambique had indeed been in touch with the Mozambican embassy in Lisbon. Furthermore, dramatic internal events had shifted my attention to the issues of conflict resolution and reconciliation in South Africa once more, to which developments in Mozambique would perhaps be pertinent – but were peripheral.

Enter the Democratic Party

Once Zach had settled in at the helm of the PFP a series of informal discussions took place between Worrall, Malan and him on the issue of opposition realignment. Consensus developed on the desirability of the creation of a single opposition party.

During this period of debate and interaction a fresh element was emerging in the ranks of the opposition. Known as 'The Fourth Force' it consisted of *verligte* Afrikaners opposed to apartheid and disillusioned with the NP. They wanted a role in the political arena but did not feel completely at home in any of the three existing opposition parties. The group included people such as Prof. Marinus Wiechers of Unisa, Prof. Sampie Terblanche of the University of Stellenbosch, and Dr Wimpie de Klerk of RAU – a former editor of *Die Vaderland*, and a leading political analyst and a brother of FW de Klerk, leader of the NP in the Transvaal. Another was Hilda Burnett, a former officer commanding the SADF's Women's Military College at George.

This Fourth Force gave added impetus to the concept of realignment and the formation of a new political party to end fragmentation of the opposition. It would also provide a political home for the growing constituency of *verligtes*. In the light of this evolving consensus, Zach, Worrall and Malan appointed a small interparty committee to ascertain whether there was common ground on issues of critical importance in taking further the process of realignment. It comprised David Gant and Jannie Momberg of Worrall's Independent Party (IP), Esther Lategan and Jannie Hofmeyr of Malan's NDM, Tian van der Merwe, and me as chairman. A series of meetings commenced in December 1988.

We kept in touch with our respective leaders, and on occasion the committee met the leaders collectively. There was considerable common ground on the principles on which the new party would be founded, and on such key issues as policy and strategic mission. But there were problems of structure, including the emotive one of leadership.

Malan wanted a complete break with the past. This was easy for him, with only himself and two MPs who had defected from the PFP, and a party only recently formed and without a national organisational structure. It was not so easy for the PFP, a long-established party with a significant membership, a nationwide organisation, 16 MPs and scores of municipal councillors. But I believed the problem could be overcome.

Another obstacle had nothing to do with realignment *per se*, but was simply the fact that there was no love lost between the IP and Malan. Their representatives on the committee constantly sniped at each other and gave the impression that the parties would prefer not to merge. My suggestion was that the committee adjourn and that the reluctant parties try to sort out their differences. Once they had done so, they should contact me and the committee could resume. The matter appeared to hover in mid-air.

Yet the following Sunday morning I read a prominent report in the *Sunday Times* based on a statement by Gant, to the effect that at a bilateral meeting the Independents and the Malan group had decided to take a joint initiative on the issue of realignment and the formation of a new party. They had decided that Worrall and Malan would be the co-leaders and De Beer the chairman.

For Worrall and Malan to have done a deal of this nature when their parties were supposed to be in three-way negotiations with the PFP was bad enough. But to feed this to the press was to destroy the trust essential to the success of the negotiations. To make matters still worse, a Monday newspaper carried a report that the IP 'might suspend its unity talks role'. The article went on to quote a party spokesman to the effect that 'the party's leader Denis Worrall was poised to suspend unity talks in Cape Town if the PFP refused to accept the IP's leadership and the party's executive proposals'.

The committee assembled later that day and decided that in the climate that had developed over the weekend, there was no point in taking negotiations further. The divisive issues that had come to the fore as a result of leaks and statements to the press were now in the public domain and could only be resolved at leadership level.

Fortunately, the impasse was broken. Two days after the suspension of the three-party talks, I went to Johannesburg as one representative of the three parties, each headed by its respective leader, together with members of the Fourth Force led Wimpie de Klerk. We all met in the Parkwood home of Louis Luyt.

Luyt – better known as a rugby administrator and a flamboyant businessman – was a surprise entrant on the political scene, but had apparently offered his services as a facilitator to Zach, Worrall and Malan. De Klerk, who had agreed beforehand to chair the meeting, had done some preparatory work in drafting guidelines for the procedure and nature of the decisions we could take. He also annexed a draft press statement we could issue depending on progress. Given the number of issues to be resolved and the emotionalism involved, he was of the opinion that it would be inappropriate to announce that a new party had been formed 'finished and *klaar*'.

However, he suggested that we state a few key points to maintain momentum and stimulate expectations. The month of January should be used to work through the important outstanding issues systematically, and if all went well we would be able to complete our work and hold the founding congress of a new party in February 1989.

The discussions were amicable. There was little tension, though we all realised a difficult time lay ahead when we had to work out details acceptable to the four elements present. That afternoon we issued a statement outlining our agreement and our intentions.

The PFP, IP and NDM would cease to exist, and a new party yet to be named would be born. Afterwards I went home with Zach and during the evening he and I spent hours talking with some nostalgia about the people, the events, the trauma, the good days, the bad days, the fun days, the successes and the disappointments that were all part of our long association with the PFP and the PP before it.

We realised that the new party was going to be different, yet somehow we were satisfied that the values on which the older parties had been founded and their strategic mission would live on as the core elements of the new party.

As planned, discussions between the four entities got under way in January. Step by step the essential elements of the new party, its policies and strategic goals, structures, management and membership were put in place. Parallel to this, Zach was meticulous in keeping the members of the PFP's federal council, parliamentary caucus and other party formations informed of the steps being taken and the progress being made.

While there was no conflict over the choice of a new name for the party, the issue that nearly derailed the talks was that of the leadership. Worrall, and Malan in particular, persisted with the proposals they had agreed between themselves at a Cape Town steakhouse. Although the PFP did not favour the idea of having co-leaders, we put forward a proposal that Zach, Worrall and Malan should in fact jointly lead the party.

Worrall and Malan opposed this, and at one stage Malan threatened to withdraw from the talks. Eventually he said he would agree to the co-leader proposal as a temporary arrangement lasting only six months. It was agreed that at the first congress of the party – to be held within two years – a single leader should be elected.

The leadership issue, so dominant during the negotiations, evaporated as time moved on. In 1990, after FW de Klerk had made his dramatic announcement unbanning the ANC and releasing Mandela, Malan resigned from parliament and as co-leader of the new party. When the next congress of the Democratic Party (DP) was held in 1990, Worrall appeared to have lost interest and was not available for election. Zach de Beer was elected leader of the DP.

On the day before the DP was due to be formed I, as chairman of the PFP, had the doubtful pleasure of presiding over a federal congress at which the PFP decided to dissolve and become part of the new party. For those who had made so many sacrifices for the PFP, it was a moving and nostalgic experience. This was particularly so for the 'fifty-niners' such as Helen, Ray Swart, Max Borkum, Zach and me – and a few others present – who had helped found the Progressive Party 30 years before in November 1959. We all made brief farewell speeches.

Ray took us back to the founding years from 1959-1961. Helen and Max Borkum spoke of the lonely years of 1961-74. Zach told the old PFP members to go forward with faith in the new party since 'the ground rules by which the former Progressives intend to play the game in the DP have been clearly established'.

When the issue of dissolution was put to the vote only one dissenting hand was raised: it was that of Marius Barnard.

The next day in an auditorium at the Johannesburg College of Education some 1 600 people came to attend the DP inaugural congress. For many delegates the faces they saw, the names they heard, and the people they met were new. The excitement generated by the newness was heightened by the expectations and the uncertainties of what lay ahead.

In a brief address to the delegates I said: 'Yesterday saw the closing of a chapter in the history of three political parties. Today sees the opening of a new chapter not just of a new political party, but also in the history of our country. We are present at a turning point in the history of our nation but we do not merely want to be part of history, we must be part of the future. Our country is one of great potential. Ours is a people of great promise. We in this new DP have a duty to ensure that the potential is realised and that the promise is fulfilled.'

The DP's colours and logo were launched. Messages and telegrams were read out. Prof. Wiechers outlined the party constitution. Wimpie de Klerk spoke of our principles and policies, and Zach, Worrall and Malan each gave a short address. Key personalities were introduced, and De Beer, Worrall and Malan were confirmed as co-leaders. Within the space of five short hours the DP's show was on the road.

On 30 April, three weeks after the founding of the DP, Helen Suzman announced that she would be retiring from parliament at the election to be held later in the year. Friend and political foe alike joined in paying tribute to her memorable and courageous 36 years of service to South Africa. I knew that for me parliament would never be the same without Helen.

22

The advent of De Klerk

On 18 January 1989 I was a member of a small multiparty committee of parliament meeting under the chairmanship of FW de Klerk to consider the timetable and work programme for the coming session. The meeting was held in a committee room in the new assembly building of parliament overlooking Stal Plein, the paved square where Tuynhuys, the building housing the presidential offices, was located.

During a short break in the proceedings, a member, looking out the window, drew attention to the fact that an ambulance was pulling away from the entrance to Tuynhuys and proceeding up Roeland Street towards Groote Schuur Hospital. The rest of us joined him, wondered why the ambulance had been there, and then went on with our meeting.

Later we learned that PW Botha had been taken to hospital following a mild stroke earlier that day. Botha returned a few days later; but understandably the country was rife with speculation as to whether he was capable of carrying out his presidential duties, and in the event of him not being capable, as to who might succeed him.

Two names were being bandied about. One was Barend du Plessis, the Minister of Finance, one of the younger members of the cabinet. He was seen as a *verligte* by nature, if not by conviction. The other was De Klerk, as Minister of Education and Transvaal leader of the NP. His political background was impeccable from the Nat perspective: he had been reared in the teachings of the Gereformeerde Church and the politics of the NP, in which spirit his father had served in the cabinets of both Strijdom and Verwoerd. He was perceived as part of the party establishment and someone who could be relied on to take the orthodox party view on political issues.

On 2 February Botha told the NP caucus that while he would continue in office as State President, he was resigning as leader of the NP and that the caucus should proceed to elect his successor. De Klerk beat Du Plessis by eight votes. In consequence he became NP leader and heir apparent to the ailing Botha.

De Klerk was a lawyer by profession, and had been elected to parliament in a by-election in Vereeniging in 1972. When I returned to parliament in 1974 – at that time as leader of the PP – I followed De Klerk's speeches and actions and his rise within the ruling party structures with great interest. Over the years I developed a good relationship, though not a close friendship, with him. He was affable and sociable. He enjoyed a round of golf and relaxing with his companions at the 19th hole. He smoked too much but was a competent parliamentarian and skilful debater, being one of the few Nationalists prepared to use parliament as a forum for debating issues rather than a platform for blowing his party's trumpet and denigrating his opponents.

Of course De Klerk was conservative. Although not obsessed by race, he saw separate development, as he called apartheid, as a means of solving South Africa's racial problems, and believed that 'own affairs' was the building block on which any future constitution and society should be built. Nonetheless, his style was very different from that of Botha. There was no finger-wagging or verbal broadsides. Whereas Botha's decisions and actions appeared driven by instinct and emotion, De Klerk allowed his to be shaped by analysis and logic. I saw him as belonging to a new generation of Afrikaner nationalist leaders. While well-versed in the history and tradition of the Afrikaner, he lacked the militant intensity of his predecessors, all of whom had taken part in the struggle during the 1930s and 1940s for the cultural identity, economic parity and constitutional self-determination of the *volk*.

A few years earlier, in a break at a committee meeting that De Klerk and I attended, I asked him how it was that on occasions in parliament he was able to quote from speeches I had made as far back as 1958. De Klerk explained that when I returned to parliament in 1974, his party whips told him to mark me and generally to follow me in debates. In order to do so effectively he had read every speech I had made in parliament since 1958.

I responded: 'That must have been tough on you. But I trust that reading my speeches will stand you in good stead some day in the years ahead.'

On a more recent occasion, while travelling in the same aircraft from Johannesburg to Cape Town, De Klerk and I got talking about current political issues. At one stage he asked me: 'Colin, why do always say that I am *verkramp*?' I responded that I did not always say he was *verkramp*: 'My indictment is worse than that. I have watched you carefully over the years. I realise that you aspire to be State President of South Africa one day. My indictment is that in spite of your obvious political aspirations I do not know whether you are *verlig* or *verkramp*.'

'Well,' he said, 'I am *verlig* in terms of my definition of the word. But perhaps if you were the leader of the NP in the Transvaal with Andries Treurnicht [of the CP] breathing down your neck you might also sound like a *verkrampte* at times.'

I have often wondered whether the course of our history would have been different if Botha had resigned both as leader of the party and as state president. That this did not happen created a unique opportunity that comes to few political leaders and countries. Had De Klerk been elected state president in such circumstances, he would surely have found himself defending existing policies and run the risk of being seen as perpetuating the old regime. It would certainly have made it more difficult for him to break the traditional mould of NP politics.

Fortunately for him and the country, De Klerk had seven months before being encumbered with the responsibilities of the presidency. This gave him time to take a long, hard look at the political situation in South Africa and to assess in its historical perspective the presidential role that he was destined to play. It enabled him to put space between himself and Botha, so that when he became president he was seen to be his own man.

During this interregnum, tension began to build up between Botha and De Klerk, and within the NP, as the parties geared up for the 6 September general election. The situation came to a head on 14 August when the cabinet confronted Botha and demanded his resignation. Botha duly resigned and De Klerk became acting state president.

Meanwhile, despite the fact that the state of emergency had recently been extended for another 12 months, Botha and Mandela actually met for the first time in Tuynhuys on 3 July. Mandela followed up the meeting with a statement in which he said that only dialogue with the ANC would bring about peace.

The September election saw the CP, with 39 seats, holding its position as official opposition. The DP, led by the troika of De Beer, Worrall and Malan, did comparatively well to win 33 seats, and the result showed that the DP had managed to shed the negative 'soft on security' image that had plagued the PFP in 1987. The NP, while retaining its hold on government, lost ground for the first time in decades, losing 16 seats to the CP and 11 to the DP.

De Klerk's reaction to the result reflected a fundamental shift in the political landscape. Two years earlier, after the general election, Botha had succeeded in isolating the PFP and declared that the voters had shown overwhelmingly that they were determined to fight the enemies of South Africa. Now De Klerk had isolated the CP and brought the DP into the political mainstream by declaring that more than two-thirds of the voters had voted for reform! Botha's foes had become De Klerk's friends.

On 11 September, just days after the election, a ground-breaking event took place in Cape Town. More than thirty thousand citizens, led by the mayor Gordon Oliver, Archbishop Desmond Tutu, Reverend Allan Boesak and other religious, civic and business leaders, marched through the streets in silent protest against the heavy-handed manner in which the police dealt with peaceful protests. My parliamentary colleague Tian van der Merwe and I were in touch with Adriaan Vlok, the Minister of Law and Order, throughout the morning, seeking to ensure that the march took place without police intervention. Apart from any other consideration, past experience had shown this invariably led to violence.

Vlok told us that in terms of the emergency regulations he could not consider giving permission for the march unless the organisers first asked permission in writing. We put it to the minister that, given the issues involved and the mood of the citizenry of Cape Town, it was unrealistic to expect the organisers to seek permission. He declined to say yes or no: Van der Merwe and I felt he was playing for time.

As the morning drew on and crowds began to gather at St George's cathedral – from where the march was to start – the nature of the decision facing Vlok and the government changed from whether it would give permission, to whether it would ban a march already in the making. Later, dispensing with formal procedures, De Klerk permitted the march. Massive, orderly and solemn, it was an impressive demonstration of the feelings of the ordinary people of Cape Town.

The right of citizens to peaceful protest was established. In due course this right was written into the bill of rights in the new South African constitution.

On 20 September, having been sworn in as state president, De Klerk announced his intention to review discriminatory legislation; to consider the release of political prisoners; to end the state of emergency as soon as possible; and to put forward a far-reaching set of constitutional proposals.

From then on, the pace of reform accelerated. More political prisoners were released. The security police were reigned in. There were no more bannings and detentions. No longer could the police wield rawhide whips against peaceful protestors. De Klerk also announced that the National Security Management System would be abolished. The beaches were declared open to all races.

In December De Klerk and Mandela met for talks on the country's future. The stage was set for a great moment of history.

Fundamental change at last

It was warm and windy on Friday 2 February 1990. Parliament was due to be opened by the state president – a ritual re-enacted time and again since the first parliament of the Union of South Africa was opened in 1910.

There was a whiff of political expectancy in the air. Since De Klerk had taken over as acting state president, following Botha's resignation, and increasingly since his inauguration as state president on 20 September following the NP victory at the general election earlier that month, there was a sense that the South African political scene was changing. Speculation in the press and discreet leaks from the president's office suggested something important was about to happen: that De Klerk's speech was not going to be merely another 'opening of parliament' routine.

Yet political analysts, myself included, were sceptical. De Klerk was by nature conservative; and while he had proved a skilful debater, at no time since his election to parliament in 1972 – nor during his nine years as a cabinet minister for Botha – had he suggested that he had the potential to be an initiator of change, let alone a reformer.

On the day before the opening of parliament, I addressed a lunchtime meeting of the Institute of Citizenship. My subject: 'Prospects for the Parliamentary Session'. Much of my talk focused on what I believed De Klerk *should* do and say – lift the ban on the ANC, release Mandela, scrap the Group Areas Act, and inaugurate the process of normalising South African politics.

I concluded by saying: 'These are the things that De Klerk should do. However, we are all mindful of De Klerk and the NP – we have been let down in the past. Don't expect too much from President de Klerk tomorrow!'

On Friday morning, while cabinet ministers, MPs, members of the diplomatic corps and invited guests were making their way to the parliamentary buildings – where troops from the various formations of the SADF were already in ceremonial positions – other people drawn from the citizenry of Cape Town were converging on Greenmarket Square, an historic gathering-place three city blocks from parliament.

From there, under the aegis of the anti-apartheid UDF and led by such prominent Capetonians as Archbishop Tutu and Allan Boesak, there were to be marches through the streets of Cape Town to coincide with the 11 am opening of parliament ceremony. Banners already in evidence proclaimed 'Unban the ANC', 'Release Mandela', 'One man one vote' and 'Down with the racist parliament'.

At ten-fifteen, 45 minutes before De Klerk was due to commence his address to parliament, Peter Soal put his head round my office door. Peter, who was puckish by nature, with an uncanny ability to ferret out information, had a broad grin. 'Would you like to read what De Klerk is about to say?' he asked. And with that, he handed me a faxed copy of *the* speech.

Copies had been given to members of the media 'strictly embargoed until delivery at eleven o'clock on 2 February 1990'. The embargo was honoured, but apparently this did not prevent a copy of the speech, which had been sent overseas, being transmitted back to South Africa and a small circle of interested persons.

I speed-read the speech with increasing incredulity. Here was De Klerk the conservative, the Afrikaner nationalist, the man I could not evaluate as being either *verlig* or *verkramp*, presenting a package of measures that were going to fundamentally transform our politics. I read key sections of the speech again. I said to Peter: 'Difficult to believe. I wonder whether FW fully understands what he is doing? Does he realise that South Africa will never be the same again?'

We wandered down to the Assembly, tense with expectancy but buoyant in the knowledge that much that we had been fighting for since 1959 was about to take place.

Precisely at eleven o'clock, as the last notes of *Die Stem*, played by the South African navy band outside parliament, echoed through the chamber, the sergeant at arms called out in stentorian tones: 'Mr Speaker!' and the presidential party, led by Deputy Speaker Helgard van Rensburg and flanked by the gold-braided and bemedalled generals of the security forces, entered the chamber.

As my seat was on the aisle, De Klerk had to walk past me to take his seat to the right of the Speaker's chair. I watched as he walked away from me across the carpeted floor of the Chamber: a small figure with a slight stoop. Then he rose to the Speaker's podium and spoke quietly and confidently.

He dealt with the suspension of the death penalty, and the pending revision of the law relating to it; the economy; social conditions; and international relations. He then said: 'The focus now has to fall on negotiation. Practically every leader agrees that negotiation is the key to reconciliation, peace and a new and just dispensation. However, numerous excuses for refusing to take part are advanced. Some of the reasons being advanced are valid. Others are merely part of a political chess game. And while the game of chess proceeds, valuable time is being lost.'

Tensions rose. He went on: 'Today I am able to announce far-reaching decisions in this connection. I believe that these decisions will shape a new phase in which there will be a movement away from measures which have been seized upon as a justification for confrontation and violence. The emphasis has to move, and will move now, to a debate and discussion of political and economic points of view as part of the process of negotiation.

'The steps that have been decided on are the following:

- The prohibition of the African National Congress, the Pan-African Congress, the South African Communist Party and a number of subsidiary organisations is being rescinded.
- People serving prison sentences merely because they were members of one of these organisations or because they committed some other offence which was merely an offence because a prohibition on one of the organisations was in force, will be identified and released. This does not affect prisoners who have been sentenced for other offences such as murder, terrorism or arson.
- The media emergency regulations as well as the education emergency regulations are being abolished in their entirety.
- The security emergency regulations will be amended to continue to make provision for effective control over visual material pertaining to scenes of unrest.
- The restrictions in terms of the emergency regulations on 33 organisations are being rescinded. These organisations include the following: The National Education Crisis Committee; South African National Students Congress; United Democratic Front; Cosatu; Die Blanke Bevrydingsbeweging van Suid Afrika.
- The conditions imposed in terms of the security emergency regulations on 374 people upon their release are being rescinded, and the regulations which provide for such conditions are being abolished.
- The period of detention in terms of the security emergency regulations will be limited henceforth to six months. Detainees also acquire the right to legal representation and a medical practitioner of their own choosing.'

He concluded: 'Implementation will be immediate and, where necessary, notices will appear in the *Government Gazette* from tomorrow.'

Members of the right-wing CP were furious. Members of De Klerk's own party listened to their leader's announcement in stunned silence. Old time anti-communists in the Nationalist ranks blanched when De Klerk included the Communist Party among the organisations to be unbanned. Members of the PFP, together with some members of the Labour Party from the House of Representatives, greeted the announcement with approving 'hear-hears'.

As I listened to De Klerk, my mind went back almost thirty years – to Monday

29 March 1961, when the same NP that today was unbanning the ANC and the PAC introduced the Unlawful Organisations Bill precisely to ban the ANC and PAC.

When De Klerk's speech was over, I sat back in my bench for a while before going up to my parliamentary office to ponder on the significance of the occasion and read the *Hansard* of the debate that had taken place thirty years before. I recalled being in the Assembly on that day, and the turmoil and strife prevailing in the country. FC Erasmus, the Minister of Justice, had introduced the Unlawful Organisations Bill, to the acclaim of other Nationalist members, in their determination to crush mounting black resistance.

I recalled Sir de Villiers Graaff as leader of the opposition criticising the legislated repression yet concluding: 'I will support this bill ... I want to go further ... I am prepared to assist the government to the maximum of my ability ...'

First there had been silence, then anger among both Nationalists and the UP when Jan Steytler, leader of the Progressive Party that had been formed only ten weeks before, moved that the bill be rejected outright. There had been my own trepidation when I stood up to second Steytler, since I was conscious of the importance of the occasion and the ugly mood of the overwhelming number of members of the House.

As I finished reading from the parliamentary record of that debate, I was filled with a deep sense of history – and of achievement. The wheel of authoritarian banishment politics had gone full circle. I had been in parliament and opposed the banning of the ANC and PAC by a NP government in 1961; today, thirty years and many traumatic events later, I was in parliament to hear a leader of the NP unbanning the ANC and the PAC. For me, De Klerk's speech was a vindication of my years of opposition to apartheid, and to the authoritarianism of successive National Party governments. With great fondness and pride I thought of my colleague Helen Suzman, who for 13 of the darkest years of apartheid had alone championed the cause of liberal democracy and the rule of law. Helen had retired; how she would have loved to be present on this historic occasion.

The sound of cheerful voices in the corridor outside my office broke my train of thought. There was a knock and my colleague Tian van der Merwe's head appeared: 'Come and join us in the staffroom. We're going to open a bottle of champagne that we have kept on ice for just such an occasion!'

Joyce and I were determined to be present when Nelson Mandela emerged from prison after 27 long years. On the morning of Sunday 11 February we drove to Wemmershoek and parked our car at the side of the road outside Victor Verster Prison. Mandela was due to be released at eleven o'clock. There was a delay of an hour, partly owing to formalities that had to be completed and because, it was said, Mandela wanted to shake hands with – and thank – the prison staff who had looked after him over the past three years.

The crowd was in a festive mood. This was the day they had been waiting for, but never dared believe would dawn. Eventually the doors opened and Mandela, with his wife Winnie at his side, stepped out, a free man. The cheers of the crowd were interspersed with cries of 'Viva Mandela' and 'Amandla' as a smiling Nelson and Winnie, with clenched fists aloft, walked down the road and away from prison.

Joyce and I made our way back to Cape Town and later that afternoon joined the crowds on the Grand Parade outside the city hall where Mandela was going to make his first public speech in 27 years. He appeared on the balcony to tumultuous and prolonged applause. He spoke clearly and firmly with the distinctive Mandela accent that was soon to become recognised by people around the world.

This had been a day worth working and waiting for. We slept soundly that night.

I was fascinated and excited by what De Klerk had done. But like so many other South Africans and South Africa watchers around the world, I was intrigued and inquisitive. What had moved the conservative NP leader, with his background and upbringing, to lead South Africa in such a radically new direction? Did he appreciate the full implications of what he was doing? Did he have a clear-cut political objective?

After much reading, reflection, analysis, and discussion with people both close to De Klerk and distant from him, I reached my own conclusions.

De Klerk must have known that although under pressure his government had the military power, the economic resources and the electoral support to carry on for a number of years without making any fundamental changes to the political power structure. However, his logical mind and analytical approach would have told him that the effort of maintaining the *status quo* would bring a heavy cost: not only in terms of cash, but in international isolation, lives lost, resources wasted, racial tension, internal conflict, and, perhaps most important of all, the loss of the opportunity of finding a peaceful solution to South Africa's problems. That cost was rising, and in due course would become unacceptably high.

De Klerk, as State President, must have engaged in serious analysis of the South African situation, and could well have come to see clearly the problems facing the country and the possibility of solving them. The crux of the matter was not that white South Africans were facing a 'total onslaught' masterminded by the communists in Moscow; but that it was necessary to come to terms with the fact that the majority of South Africans were being denied basic human rights.

The prospects of finding a solution together with black South Africans must have appeared brighter to De Klerk following Botha's and his discussions with Mandela. He would have grasped Mandela's public commitment to a peaceful solution; become aware of the discussions between representatives of the ANC and emissaries from the South African government; and of the Harare Declaration in which the liberation movements committed themselves to a process of negotiation.

The result of the recent election must have warned De Klerk that his electoral power base was shrinking, and if he was going to move forward he would have to do so without much further delay. The question facing him was not whether he should move forward, but how he should do so. No doubt, too, De Klerk looked down the long dark tunnel of Botha's approach to South Africa's problems, and saw no light at the end.

Botha's approach of incremental economic and social reform combined with government dictating the pace of political change would not satisfy black aspirations, but would lead to a repeating and escalating sequence of reform, resistance, repression and violence.

To succeed, the situation required not only a fundamentally new direction in policy, but that the new policy had to be presented and packaged in such a way that there could be no doubt it was fundamental. It was based on an assessment that he could achieve more for the white minority, and indeed for the country, through negotiation than by trying to impose his will on the black majority.

The 2 February speech embodied a package of steps that openly and almost triumphantly declared it was taking South Africa in a new direction. It was not so much a renunciation of past policies as a commitment to work out a new future through negotiation. The immediate objective was to normalise the political situation so that the process of negotiation could take place.

A question often asked at that time was whether De Klerk was fully aware of the consequences of what he did on that day. I have no doubt that – in terms of the fact that there could be no going back and that South Africa would in future be very different from the past – De Klerk was fully aware.

However, from speeches he made and discussions that took place during the negotiation period, it appeared that De Klerk still believed that race-based building blocks could be part of the structure of a new constitution, and racial vetoes an integral part of power-sharing. The next couple of years would show that getting rid of race-based laws and structures was not going to be the consequence of negotiation, but actually a prerequisite for negotiations to take place at all.

Whatever his reasoning, motivation or expectations, the important thing was that on 2 February 1990, De Klerk got it right.

All eyes on Mandela

The world had waited for decades to see and hear Mandela, and now his every action, statement and movement was scrutinised. South Africans had heard and read about him – yet he had been invisible for 27 years, though from behind prison walls he had inspired millions of South Africans and supporters around the world to fight for the liberation of the country. What kind of person he would emerge as would be a crucially important factor in the future of our people.

There was also great public interest in the release of political prisoners in general and the return of the exiles. White South Africans faced the fascinating – and perhaps unnerving – prospect of encountering these men and women as real people and not as the characters presented by government propaganda. 'What's next?' was the question of the day. What process would have to be put in place to defuse antagonisms? To what would it lead? What if it failed?

I was in a fortunate position. I was not tied down by the duties and responsibilities of party leadership, yet was generally recognised as an experienced politician and a senior parliamentarian. In addition, I was acknowledged as a committed liberal. I had a long-standing personal and working relationship with Zach de Beer, who after September 1990 was sole leader of the DP. Over the years Zach and I had spent many hours, often late at night, analysing the political situation and discussing strategies for the way ahead. In recent times Zach had shown less interest in strategising and, recognising this as one of my stronger suits, often sought my opinion and advice.

He showed his trust in my judgement by giving me a free hand to express myself on political issues and to explore alternatives of both policy and strategy. In the next few years I made full use of the opportunities our relationship provided.

I knew that the issue of a new constitution – its content, drafting, ratification, implementation and concomitant transformation of government structures and transfer of political power – was going to dominate South African politics. The immediate focus was on creating the conditions for constitutional negotiation. The initiative for this had shifted from parliament to the interaction between the ANC and De Klerk's government.

Parliament's main function now was to give legislative effect to any agreements reached between the parties. This involved repealing the vast array of apartheid laws and the laws inhibiting freedom of speech and political action.

The first relevant event was a series of meetings over 2-4 May 1990 between government and the ANC at Groote Schuur, the state president's Cape Town residence. Apart from their symbolic significance, the talks were ground-breaking. They led to the issuing of a statement known as the Groote Schuur Minute: 'The government and the ANC agree on a common commitment towards the resolution of the existing climate of violence and intimidation, from whatever quarter, as well as a commitment to stability and to a peaceful process of negotiation.'

The Minute went on to deal with the establishment of a working group to make recommendations on the definition of political offences, the release of political prisoners, the granting of immunity, and the return of exiles. Government undertook to review existing security legislation and work towards lifting the state of emergency. Both government and the ANC agreed to establish channels of communication to curb violence and intimidation, and agreed that the aims of the statement should be achieved as swiftly as possible.

The era of repression and resistance was over. Negotiation had truly begun. Two days after the Minute had been issued, PW Botha resigned from the National Party in protest against De Klerk's reform proposals. Effectively, he disappeared from the political scene, languishing in retirement at his home in Wilderness near George.

The next important meeting was held in Pretoria in August 1990 against a backdrop of increasing violence and intimidation, especially in Natal. In addition, tensions had risen between the government and the ANC when it was revealed that senior members of the Congress – including Mac Maharaj, Ronnie Kasrils and Pravin Gordhan – had been engaged in clandestine anti-government activity under the code name of Operation Vula. Nonetheless, the Pretoria Minute recorded that 'the ANC had suspended the armed struggle and the South African government had committed itself to suspend the state of emergency as early as possible and to give urgent consideration to the repeal of the Internal Security Act'.

Both delegations expressed concern at the level of violence, and committed themselves 'to do everything in their power to bring about a peaceful solution as soon as possible'.

The third formal meeting between the ANC and government was held in Cape Town in February 1991 and concluded with the DF Malan Accord, signed by De Klerk and Mandela. It recorded that the meeting had received the report of the working committee set up to deal with matters raised in Pretoria, and to identify problem areas and generally to assist in taking the negotiation process further.

The task of creating the conditions for negotiation was nearing completion. The time had come to give consideration to the form, structures and methodology of the process.

After De Klerk's 2 February speech and until the formal constitutional process began in November 1991, I attempted in my speeches and actions to address the issue of the conditions essential to transformation. In the week after Mandela's release, speaking in parliament, I asked De Klerk to have the day on which Mandela would be released named the Day of National Reconciliation; and asked him to take account of the emotional ties that black South Africans had with the anthem *Nkosi Sikelel' iAfrika*; and to gain an understanding of the constitutional proposals in the Freedom Charter and the spirit of the slogan 'the people shall govern'.

Later I called on De Klerk to lead a national campaign against violence – quickly becoming the greatest threat to the negotiation process. I urged him to start this campaign by convening a national summit on violence attended by leaders of all sections and interests in South Africa. Whether my requests were effective, or merely my timing was right, three days later in a television address to the nation he announced that he was calling a two-day national summit of political, church, labour and business leaders and academics on ways and means of addressing and assuming co-responsibility for ending the orgy of violence and intimidation sweeping the country.

Anticipating the lifting of sanctions and the normalisation of South Africa's trade relations, I urged the government 'to produce a comprehensive plan of action ... to get the economy moving forward'.

While the private sector was the primary engine of growth and productivity, the government had a vital role to play in the field of job creation, overall productivity and economic expansion – not as a competitor or an interventionist manager, but as a co-operative, creative and reinforcing partner of the various elements that formed the private sector.

I called on the government 'to do all in its power to bring outsiders into positions of power and influence inside the process of government and to do this before South Africa had a new constitution'. Later I took it upon myself to say: 'The DP believes the period of transition ahead should be used to broaden the base of government unity. It is time to build mutual trust, promote co-operation and confidence, prepare people for non-racial democracy, and break down the barriers that years of apart-heid have erected.'

In responding to the repeal of the Land and the Group Areas acts, I said: 'The re-peal in itself will not end the intense controversy that has surrounded this legislation for decades.' The iniquities caused by the laws would not go away: 'These iniquities are either going to be tackled by the government in an imaginative way in consulta-tion with the affected people, or they will remain a political issue dividing our nation and bedevilling our politics for decades to come.

'It is not good enough for those who have [disseminated] apartheid to repeal their discriminatory laws. In the interests of peace and constructive politics they must undo the damage they have done to the fabric of our society.' There was a need to create the machinery to redress undesirable imbalances in the ownership and occu-pation of land.

In November 1991 it appeared that the NP and ANC were deadlocked over the mechanisms for drawing up a new constitution. The ANC wanted an elected Con-stituent Assembly to do this, while the NP wanted an all-party conference to draft the document. The DP, which was not involved in negotiations at that stage, had argued the case for a national convention, representing all sections of the people. However, the party had not argued that representation had to be achieved through an election based on universal adult suffrage.

I had come to the conclusion that a Constitutional Assembly (CA) elected on the basis of universal adult suffrage would, in fact, be the only effective way of ensur-ing the representivity of the assembly and legitimacy of the new constitution. At the same time I felt that a multi-party congress (MPC) could play an important role in the preliminary stages. At a special conference of the DP in Sea Point on 15 Novem-ber 1991, I put forward a proposal that would combine an elected CA with a multi-party congress.

Realising that there would be an interlocking relationship between the process of negotiating a new constitution, and the transition to that new constitution, my pro-posal made provision for the constitutional changes required for a Government of National Unity (GNU) to be in place while the drafting occurred.

In essence, I suggested the establishment of a multi-party conference comprising representatives of all existing political parties and movements. It would have the fol-lowing functions:

- To establish the basis for moving ahead to a new democratic era.
- To decide on the constitutional principles on which to base a new constitution.
- To determine the composition, powers and functions of the elected Constitutional Assembly to draw up the constitution.
- To determine the composition, powers and functions of the multi-party GNU that would function while the Constitutional Assembly drew up the new constitution.

- To decide on the practical provisions for the transitional GNU and the bill of rights.

During the term of the MPC, existing government structures would remain in place – but government and parliament would have to pay attention to pressures from extra-parliamentary factors. At the end of this phase, parliament would have to pass legislation to give effect to the main agreements reached, including setting up a CA and a transitional GNU.

In a second phase, the establishment of the CA would be on the basis of universal franchise and proportional representation, and it would have the following functions:

- To draw up a new democratic constitution within two years based on the principles agreed to by the MPC.
- To endeavour to take decisions on the basis of consensus – though where this was not possible, to decide on the basis of a positive vote of 70% of the members.

Then the new constitution would be submitted to the voters by way of a referendum. Upon approval, it would come into effect and a new government and parliament would be elected in terms of the constitution.

The DP conference voted overwhelmingly for my proposals. The *Cape Argus* said that 'the DP's dramatic shift to an elected body to draw up the new constitution had boosted the chances of a negotiated compromise'. Subsequent events showed that the roles played by the Convention for a Democratic South Africa (Codesa, the multi-party negotiating forum) and the Constitutional Assembly were remarkably similar to the DP proposals.

It was soon realised that to make constitutional provisions for a GNU and a bill of rights during the transitional period, the MPC would in practice have to draw up a transitional constitution; and that to form a GNU there would have to be an election. It was decided that members of the National Assembly (400) and the Senate (90) elected to the transitional parliament would double up their function by serving both as members of the legislature and as members of the CA to draw up the constitution on the principles agreed to by the MPC. Upon adoption of the new constitution by the CA and its certification by the Constitutional Court, the new basic law would come into effect. However, to provide continuity the GNU and the elected legislature would remain in place until the next parliamentary election.

The proposals adopted by the DP, apart from helping to unlock the negotiating process and move it forward, helped to establish the DP as a creative and constructive player in the transition.

Namibia gains independence

In parallel – and in some contrast – with the fundamental changes taking place in South Africa, Namibia was finally moving rapidly towards its own independence. In November 1988 in Geneva the South African government, Angola and Cuba had signed their agreement on the cessation of hostilities in Angola and on freedom for Namibia. As PFP spokesman on foreign affairs, I had welcomed this 'as the best news South Africans have heard for many years'. Now, as independence approached, I thought back to the many people who had helped me to understand the issues and emotions prevailing during the nation's protracted birth.

There were my contacts with people who had Swapo connections; there was Dirk Mudge, leader of the anti-Swapo Democratic Turnhalle Alliance (DTA); Clements Capua, the Herero leader; business and professional people; and newspaper editors and journalists. None came to mind more than my friends Hans Berker and Bryan O'Linn.

They were advocates, passionate about Namibia, and both had earlier been members of the liberal Namibia Patriotic Front. Hans was of German extraction, calm and measured in his manner. Bryan, of Irish-Afrikaner parentage, was emotional and excitable. They would go on to become judges of the high court in Namibia – and Berker appointed as the first Chief Justice. He would play an important role in guiding the drafters of the new constitution on matters relating to the judiciary, the rule of law, and the judicial process.

An election for a constitutional assembly to draw up and approve the new constitution – and, having done so, to become the first legislative assembly of independent Namibia – was due to be held on 1 November 1989. I was one of a group of South Africans invited to monitor the election. In Namibia it soon became clear that our hosts were the DTA: we attended briefings and meetings in Windhoek, and a major DTA rally in Katatura township.

We suspected that the DTA election campaign – as well as our visit – was being heavily funded by the South African government using taxpayers' money. We were certainly generously looked after. It was only a year later that in response to probing questions in parliament PW Botha admitted that over the years his government had given R100 million to opposition parties in South West Africa-Namibia.

The election was won by Swapo with 42 seats; the DTA managed 21; and four other smaller parties came in with a combined total of 10.

The next visit I made to Namibia was with a group of MPs to attend the independence ceremony and celebrations in Windhoek on 21 March 1990. It was a great occasion. Windhoek was festooned with the new Namibian flag, and Namibians were in an exuberant mood. The presence of government leaders and dignitaries from around the world emphasised the significance of the event. In the Windhoek stadium, where FW de Klerk, newly elected as South African president, sat among the dignitaries, the crowd became more subdued as midnight approached. There was a hush as the South African flag was lowered, followed by a roar of approval as the Namibian flag was raised.

Sam Nujoma was sworn in as president, and the troops marched past in salute. Everything was so orderly, so peaceful, so necessary – and so inevitable.

By contrast there was the money wasted, the resources squandered, the communities disrupted, and the lives lost as the South African government tried to prevent the Namibian nation enjoying its freedom. Now Namibia was free, while South Africa was still moving in that direction, not without its measure of problems and challenges.

Getting to know the ANC

My Democratic Party colleagues and I – in anticipation of becoming involved in the constitutional negotiating process – made considerable efforts to get to know the African National Congress, its philosophy, objectives, policies and personalities. We did this partly on a collective basis through meetings and conferences, partly individually by studying statements by leaders such as Mandela, and through direct and personal contact with ANC members.

I studied such foundation documents as the Freedom Charter, adopted by the Congress of the People in 1959; the statement of the National Executive Committee on the 75th anniversary of the ANC in January 1987; the OAU's Harare Declaration of August 1989; and the ANC's constitutional guidelines issued later that year.

At the time of the Groote Schuur meetings in May 1990, a couple of my DP colleagues and I drove out to the Lord Charles Hotel in Somerset West in the hope that we could meet and speak to some members of the ANC delegation who were staying there. We did so: and our meetings and greetings were warm and friendly. Subsequent discussions were informative and stimulating.

It was a great experience to talk once more with Reverend Beyers Naudé (Oom Bey), the courageous DRC dominee who had broken with the conservatism of his church, and again to meet Alfred Nzo, secretary-general of the ANC, who had hosted Slabbert and me when we went to Lusaka in 1985. I was especially pleased to encounter Walter Sisulu, a doyen of the liberation struggle and a long-term prisoner on Robben Island; as well as Joe Slovo, chairman of the South African Communist Party and chief of staff of Umkhonto we Sizwe – seen by most white South Africans as a sinister and dangerous agent of Moscow.

Our visit confirmed that in the days ahead we would be dealing with concerned fellow South Africans and not the dangerous subversives portrayed by years of propaganda.

April 1990 took me to a conference on the island of Bermuda, convened by former US senator Dick Clark as part of a programme of the Aspen Institute to help members of the US Congress to inform themselves of the issues at stake in South Africa. In addition to 17 congressmen, there were 16 South African participants. Ten of us represented political parties or interest groups; the other six were experts in their fields, and were to participate as 'resource persons'.

Each of us representing a South African political entity was called on to identify the key issues facing the country and outline proposals for the future. I left the beautiful Atlantic island wiser and better informed; for one thing I had strengthened my personal relationships with South Africans such as Gerrit Viljoen, Minister of Constitutional Development, and Oscar Dhlomo, secretary-general of Inkatha. I had come to know Murphy Morobe of the UDF, Dikgang Moseneke of the PAC, and Cyril Ramaphosa of the National Union of Mineworkers and the ANC – each of whom was to play a significant role in the constitutional talks. And I had become a friend of Dr Mamphela Ramphele, the companion of the late Steve Biko who went on to become vice-chancellor of UCT and later a managing director of the World Bank.

In 1990, too, I was a member of a DP group that met cadres of the ANC to discuss regionalism in the new South Africa. A vast difference was revealed between ANC and DP thinking on the related issue of decentralisation of power. The ANC believed in a highly centralised system of government with powers vested in the central government, and regional and local authorities having only delegated authority – and essentially functioning as the administrative and delivery arms of the centre.

We on the other hand aimed at achieving the maximum degree of decentralisation through a three-tier system of government in which each level – national, provincial and municipal – would have powers and functions defined in the constitution. In a developing country such as South Africa, we believed there would be overlapping powers in certain fields; that there would have to be mechanisms for co-ordination between the three tiers; and that all divisions of governance would have to share revenue collected nationally to ensure the provision of basic services. I appreciated the ANC's open approach to discussion and analysis, yet realised that on the issues of decentralisation and federalism, tough negotiations stared us in the face.

These were certainly the years of political cross-pollination. In October 1991 I formed part of a DP delegation led by Zach to the first conference of the Patriotic Front (PF), a loose alliance of parties and organisations opposing apartheid. Held in Durban and drawing some five hundred delegates, it followed an agreement between the leaders of the ANC, PAC and Azapo on the need to find common ground on key negotiation issues.

Early in the proceedings Ramaphosa, as chairman, informed De Beer that there had been objections to the presence of the DP at the conference. While he made it clear that he did not agree, he suggested that to avoid unnecessary acrimony or disruption, the DP should stay on as observers with full speaking but no voting rights.

We were startled, since at a recent meeting between the ANC and DP leadership the Congress had gone out of its way to tell us it wanted the Democrats to attend and persuaded us to accept the invitation. De Beer, not wanting to precipitate a row on the floor, agreed to Ramaphosa's proposal.

The conference enabled us to understand the strategy the ANC intended adopting, and to make personal contact with individuals who would become key players in the negotiations.

After months of intense discussion between the affected parties, the first formal meeting of the constitutional negotiating process was held at the World Trade Centre in Kempton Park, near Johannesburg, on 29 and 30 November 1991. The main function of the meeting was to make arrangements for the first plenary session of the negotiating structure – known as Codesa (Convention for a Democratic South Africa) – due to begin on 21 December. A steering committee was appointed which in turn set up sub-committees to deal with various facets of the arrangements.

A key issue was the basis on which Codesa would make decisions. The recommendation was that there should be 'sufficient consensus'. Although this term was never formally defined, it was understood to mean there was sufficient agreement among the participants to enable the process to proceed; conversely, that the degree of disagreement would not prevent Codesa from continuing its work. During the life of Codesa (and its successor, the Multi-Party Negotiating Forum) there were occasions when the application of the phrase was disputed. Nevertheless, it remained intact as an invaluable procedural tool.

I was appointed convener of a six-person sub-committee mandated to produce a draft Declaration of Intent to be put to the next plenary session. We immediately asked the political parties that wished to do so to submit their own proposed drafts. The task of synthesising the documents and the debates to produce a single document fell largely to Valli Moosa and me. I took the task very seriously, realising that the Declaration of Intent was going to be the founding document of the negotiating process itself. I felt part of history in the making.

There were three intermediate attempts before the final draft was presented at the plenary on 21 December. The Declaration of Intent was accepted with acclaim and signed by the leaders of all parties present except for President Lucas Mangope of Bophuthatswana – who said that he could not sign without the approval of the homeland government – and the leader of the Ciskei Bantustan. Nor was it signed by Mangosuthu Buthelezi, who was notably absent.

Six months later, at the next plenary, Buthelezi and his Ciskei counterpart signed the declaration after it had been amended to satisfy them that the phrase 'undivided South Africa' did not exclude the possibility of a federal system. Mangope never signed. As a federalist, I believed that Inkatha and the Ciskei had withheld their signatures more for tactical than for substantive reasons.

My sub-committee was also confronted by another unanticipated issue. Inkatha and the KwaZulu government insisted that in addition to their two delegates the Zulu king should be represented personally at Codesa. Dr Ben Ngubane of the Inkatha Freedom Party and I were appointed to try to find a mechanism for resolving the issue. All compromises were rejected by Ulundi, and in due course Ngubane and I had to report to the sub-committee that we had made no progress.

The issue of the Zulu king remained unresolved and a bone of contention for many months – with Buthelezi threatening to withdraw from Codesa if the king was not accorded personal representation. The Codesa management committee believed that the Zulu monarch was adequately represented by the delegation from his KwaZulu government, and that additional representation would have caused problems in relations with other delegations at Codesa. In the event, Buthelezi did eventually personally withdraw from Codesa while KwaZulu and Inkatha remained active participants.

Codesa's first plenary session on 21-22 December was historic. The leaders of all the parties and organisations, together with their delegations, were seated in the cavernous conference hall, which had been appropriately decorated. On the rostrum were Chief Justice Michael Corbett; the two presiding officers, Justice Ismail Mohammed and Justice Piet Schabort; and representatives of various religious denominations who opened the proceedings with prayer.

Present in the visitors' bays were ambassadors and dignitaries, and leaders from South African civil society. Needless to say, the media were there in large numbers. My sense was that the occasion was more than the commencement of a process: it was the signing of a peace treaty that would end a conflict that had raged in and around South Africa for close on forty years.

The DP occupied seats in two front rows of a central block, with the NP delegates to the right and the SACP delegates behind them. Helen Suzman, who, although she had retired from parliament, was a member of the DP delegation, delivered a brief address later in the day which had a great impact on the meeting and affected the future composition of Codesa. She observed that only ten of the two-hundred-odd delegates were women, and demanded a greater role for women in the negotiating process. In her pointed and telling manner she said: 'As with racism, so with sexism; you can enact legislation but despite this, racism and gender discrimination exist.' When Codesa reassembled a few weeks later, every delegation had at least one woman member, and women and men alternated in the chair of the negotiating councils.

Two events at the plenary were of special significance. One was the signing of the Declaration of Intent. This was on the agenda. But the other, a furious clash between Mandela and De Klerk, was not.

The Declaration of Intent contained a commitment to 'regular elections on the basis of a common voters' roll'; and, dramatically, this changed the power relationship between the National Party government (NPG) and the ANC. Prior to the signing the NP could approach the negotiations as the dominant force, but it then had to concede that its dominance was transient and realise it had to approach the talks on the basis that it was going to be a political minority in the new national architecture. From then on its strategy was directed to beefing up the power of the minorities rather than trying to maintain majority power for itself. It could delay – or even obstruct – the process, but the reality was that the ANC was in the driver's seat.

The Mandela-De Klerk clash occurred towards the end of proceedings. Both were to make closing speeches, and both wished to speak last – and De Klerk succeeded in his claim that as State President he was entitled to do so. Mandela spoke in a conciliatory, embracing and positive manner. De Klerk, who followed, was also conciliatory and positive. However, at one stage he departed from the general style of his address to attack the ANC for allegedly having broken the DF Malan Accord.

As De Klerk said this I looked at Mandela to see his reaction. His usually relaxed face became taut; I nudged Zach and said *sotto voce*: 'Here comes trouble.'

Although technically the business of the plenary was done, Mandela decided otherwise. Without waiting for the chairman he marched to the podium and proceeded to berate the president: 'I am gravely concerned about the behaviour of Mr de Klerk today. He has launched an attack on the African National Congress, and in doing so he has been less than frank. Even the head of an illegitimate, discredited, minority regime such as his, has certain moral standards to uphold. He has no excuse, because he is a representative of a discredited regime, not to uphold moral standards ...[No] wonder the Conservative Party has made such serious inroads into his power base. You understand why.

'If a man can come to a conference of this nature and play the type of politics which are contained in his paper, very few people would like to deal with such a man. We have handled the question of Umkhonto we Sizwe in a constructive manner. We pointed out that this is one of the issues we are discussing with the government. We had bilateral discussions but in his paper, although I was with him, I was discussing with him until about 8.30 last night, he never even hinted he was going to make this attack. The members of the government persuaded us to allow them to speak last. They were very keen to say the last word here. It is now clear why they did so. And he has abused his position because he hoped that I would not reply. He was completely mistaken. I am replying now.

'We are still prepared to have discussions with him if he wants, but he must forget that he can impose conditions on the ANC and, I daresay, on any one of the political organisations here. This type of thing, of trying to take advantage of the co-operation which we are giving him willingly, is something extremely dangerous and I hope this is the last time he will do so.'

The audience listened to Mandela in stunned silence.

De Klerk replied briefly. He was firm and remained committed to what he had said earlier, but was not combative and left the door open for reconciliation. The bemused and concerned delegates left the plenary wondering whether the negotiating process was going to unravel even before it had started.

The following day, reconciliation between the two leaders took place. However, the incident made everyone aware that beneath the surface there was a serious element of mistrust between the negotiators.

The Kempton Park meeting went on to agree that the structure of Codesa would consist of a plenary, a representative management committee, a small daily management committee, and five working groups in which each party would have two members and two advisors. Each group would deal with specific aspects of the negotiations; and there would be a secretariat.

The first working group was to consider the creation of a climate for free political participation and the role of the international community. The second would address the constitutional principles and the constitution-making body. The third would deal with the issue of an interim government; the fourth, the future of the homelands; and the fifth with time frames for negotiation and the transition.

Denis Worrall and I were the DA's representatives on Working Group 2, with Prof. David Welsh and Tony Leon as advisors. Other delegates who would play significant roles in the group were Ramaphosa and Valli Moosa of the ANC with Albie Sachs and Frene Ginwala standing in as delegates during the lengthy absences of Ramaphosa; Slovo of the SACP; Gerrit Viljoen and Tertius Delport of the NP; Ngubane of Inkatha; and Rowan Cronjé of the Bophuthatswana government.

The primary task of Working Group 2 was to make recommendations on the constitutional principles and the constitution-making body, and as the principles would be binding on the new constitution, it was clear that this group would deal with the critically important issue of how political power, and the structures in which it was vested, were going to be exercised.

From the outset I came to terms with the fact that the real negotiations were between the ANC and the Nationalists. Any small player had a greater chance of success if he put forward proposals in a manner that enabled the big players to 'own' them. Neither the ANC nor the NPG would see DP proposals as part of a political power ploy. My belief and hope were that the constitutional explorations conducted by the PP and PFP over many years would stand me in good stead.

I also soon realised that I had a lot to learn.

The impact on white politics

The commencement of democratic negotiation had a profound impact on parliamentary politics. De Klerk had removed the issue of apartheid, and an element of fresh debate was how precisely to replace it – after all, it had been the dividing line between political parties for the past 40 years. Of course the objective was a new non-racial democracy, but, combined with this, what needed to be done to remove the legacy?

The ANC had been brought in from the cold as a key player in a normalising society. Inevitably, the electoral position of the DP would be affected. Although the impact of the changing political environment did not show up in our voter support base until the 1994 election, it did so much earlier at leadership and caucus level. This was hardly surprising. The DP had only been formed nine months before De Klerk's speech, and had done so out of the desire of three disparate political parties – and the *verligte* Fourth Force – to unite and bring an end to apartheid as soon as possible. To a large extent this unifying factor had been removed on 2 February.

In the months that followed an avalanche of events pushed our original mission to one side:

- Malan resigned from parliament and as co-leader of the DP on the grounds that his political objectives had been achieved by De Klerk's announcements.
- Members of the Fourth Force withdrew from active participation in party politics.
- De Beer was elected sole leader of the DP.
- Worrall, one of the former co-leaders, stayed on in parliament but his political ardour waned as his interests turned towards a post-parliamentary career in the private sector.
- Harry Schwarz accepted an invitation from De Klerk to become South African ambassador to the US.
- Some members of the parliamentary caucus, individually or in groups, felt that the DP had fulfilled its mission, and began to look for a new political home for the future.

Rumours and parliamentary gossip were that some members of the caucus had been talking to the ANC. The atmosphere was neither tense nor unpleasant; however, having experienced the unravelling of the PFP in the mid-1980s after the resignation of Slabbert, I sensed new fault lines starting to develop. These became a full-scale fracture when five DP members defected to join the ANC in April 1992. I later learned that in all 12 members had met Mandela to discuss joining the ANC. Mandela had advised them not to do so at that stage – but rather to stay in the DP. Seven followed his advice, but the others believed the time had come for them to identify with and join the ANC.

Since the ANC did not want to be represented in the Tricameral parliament, its five new members had to occupy their seats in the Assembly as independents.

The NP, at leadership and caucus level, had been coping well with the doubts and tensions that must have arisen from the radical changes to its policies: there were no outward signs of dissent or dissatisfaction. In October 1990 the party opened its membership to people of all races. As apartheid laws were repealed one after the other, market research showed that the NP was gaining support among Coloureds and Indians. However by-elections in two white constituencies, Virginia in December 1991 and Potchefstroom in February 1992, where the NP lost to the CP, revealed a massive and irrevocable shift of support from the Nationalists.

The day after his party's defeat in Potchefstroom, De Klerk announced that a referendum of white voters would be held on 17 March for the NP to secure a mandate to continue negotiations. In De Klerk's words: 'Our [the NP's] credibility was seriously eroded. I realised that something had to be done to tip the scales back in the NP's favour.'

The question put to whites at the referendum – to which they had to vote 'Yes' or 'No' – was: 'Do you support the continuation of the reform process that the State President started on 2 February 1990, and which aimed at a new constitution through negotiations?'

The DP had no hesitation in mounting a vigorous campaign in favour of the 'Yes' vote. On a few occasions De Beer, contrary to the opinion I had expressed to him, appeared on city hall platforms with De Klerk. I did not believe such joint rallies would bring in any additional 'Yes' votes. DP supporters would vote 'Yes' in overwhelming numbers without De Klerk telling them to do so; conversely, NP voters were unlikely to be persuaded to vote 'Yes' by the participation of the DP leader as a speaker at these meetings. In addition I believed that exposing DP supporters to De Klerk in such joint ventures would blur the identity of the DP to its disadvantage.

On the day De Klerk announced the white referendum, I was chatting to Joe Slovo, with whom I developed a good personal relationship. I had learned to appreciate his intellect, his wit, his directness and, as time went on, his remarkable political acumen. He was one of the few on the ANC's side who seemed to understand the processes going on in both black and white politics. Slovo told me the ANC was in a quandary. It believed that in the interests of negotiation, De Klerk should get his strong mandate to proceed; however, the ANC could not be seen supporting or getting involved in any way in a whites-only referendum.

Later that afternoon I left Joe with his quandary in Kempton Park and flew to Cape Town. Early the next morning I was woken by the bedside phone ringing: 'It's Joe here. Joe Slovo. I've been thinking all night about the referendum. I think I've found the answer to my quandary and have drafted a statement to be directed to the white voters.' He went on to explain that the statement could not go out in the name of the ANC – but it could do so in the name of Codesa. It could not call on white voters to say 'Yes' in the referendum – but it could say 'there can be no turning back'!

Bleary-eyed, I thanked Joe and asked him to put a copy of the statement on my desk at the World Trade Centre for me to look at later that morning. On my arrival I glanced at the statement – but since I had a heavy schedule of meetings, did nothing more about it until later. I thought Slovo's statement was brilliant in its concept and powerful in its message. My problem was that Joe had written it in the jargon and idiom of the struggle, which made it more appropriate for members of the liberation movement than for white voters. Without altering the basic message, or its thrust, I made 11 alterations, which I thought appropriate. Then I phoned Joe and read the revised statement. There was a moment's silence at the other end of the phone. Then, 'That's brilliant,' he said. 'The changes are just what was needed.'

The statement in its amended form was adopted by the Codesa steering committee and immediately released to the media.

The result of the referendum was that a resounding 69% of white voters voted 'Yes'. As far as they were concerned the negotiations for a new constitution should proceed. As for the CP, the fact that it was gaining support at the expense of the NP did not mean it would grow: in August 1991 five of its MPs defected to form the ultra-conservative Afrikaner *Volk*sunie, of which little has since been heard.

The Hout Bay squatter saga

The political drama inevitably had its social component. It was after all the continued migration of poor people from mainly rural areas into the relatively prosperous Western Cape, with its promise of a better life, that had precipitated the collapse of the pass laws and influx control. Yet during the 1970s and 1980s, Hout Bay – with its fairly isolated location between the western side of the Table Mountain range and the Atlantic Ocean, its distance from commercial and industrial areas, and its limited employment opportunities – did not experience the crisis in housing for blacks or the related problem of squatting affecting the rest of the Cape Peninsula.

But pressure for black housing inexorably built up in the Peninsula. Hout Bay itself changed in character from being a small fishing harbour and village with a hinterland of farms and smallholdings to that of a significant harbour with a fish-processing industry, a tourist magnet, and a built-up residential area with shops and commercial facilities. As it did so, the black housing crisis spilled into the area.

The problem was aggravated by the fact that no housing was available for blacks, since no provision for this had been made under the pretext that there was no significant influx. Then black migration to the Cape escalated with the repeal of the pass laws in 1986; after that blacks were no longer prevented from seeking work there, and black husbands were not prohibited from joining their wives and families, or bringing them to live with them.

The squatter problem caught up with Hout Bay with a vengeance in the late 1980s. Pockets of economic 'immigrants' started to build shacks on unattended private and public land. These enclaves were often in areas that were ecologically sensitive. Residents, developers and environmentalists were concerned at what was happening. Tensions increased in 1990 when a court judgement declared that the squatters who had established their homes could not be evicted unless alternative sites were made available to them. As MP for the area, I became heavily involved in attempting to defuse the strains and resolve the problems.

Many of the white residents, while concerned about what was happening, recognised the problem, which could not be wished away or solved by angry rhetoric. Certainly, squatting aroused fierce passions. At one stage 350 property owners threatened to boycott payment of their property rates unless the squatters were removed. I appealed for calm and a rational approach.

The issue centred on affordable housing and available land. I suggested that the existing dwellings on the remaining smallholdings in the area be upgraded; that land be identified for site-and-service schemes; and that adequate accommodation should be offered by employers in the area.

The response from a vociferous group of protestors was that no blacks should be allowed in Hout Bay, and black squatters should be moved to a site somewhere in the Cape Town municipal area on the far side of the Peninsula. My position was that, whatever the difficulties, the solution had to be found within Hout Bay itself.

I raised the matter with Sam de Beer, the Minister of Housing, as I believed the Hout Bay situation had national as well as local implications. He was sympathetic but seemed loth to take any action.

The matter came to a head on the night of 25 December 1990, when a fire, driven by a raging south-east wind, swept through the squatter camp that housed the families of employees of the fishing industry. I went to the site the next morning to find complete devastation. Metal frameworks of furniture and smouldering remains of timber posts and beams were the only evidence that this area had been home to hundreds of people. I asked a policeman who appeared to be guarding the site where all the people were, and he told me they were at the Anglican church hall, adding that he and his colleague had been sent to the site to prevent any squatters from returning.

I found the displaced families huddled with what remained of their possessions in a small hall. At the local police station I asked the commander why the police were preventing the squatters from returning to their burnt-out homes. His reply was that he had instructions from the owner that the land was private property and anyone who entered should be arrested and charged with trespassing. I was shocked and appalled. I was aware that the owner, when he purchased the site, had agreed that the squatters could use a portion of the land until alternative accommodation was found.

I contacted this man, a prominent citizen of Camps Bay, who explained that earlier that morning he had been phoned by people in the Hout Bay area putting him under pressure to agree that since the fire had forced the squatters to vacate the site, their right to return had lapsed. In the circumstances he felt he was no longer under any obligation to provide land for them.

I said that apart from the moral issue, and the human plight of the squatters as a result of the fire, I found his argument untenable. I told him I believed that if fire was used as an argument for preventing the squatters from returning, a tense and potentially explosive situation would develop in Hout Bay. I appealed to him to rescind his decision and allow the squatters to return in terms of his original agreement.

After further discussion he agreed to do so; but as the issue of finding an alternative site for the squatters in Hout Bay had dragged on for some months, he needed to know when the issue would be resolved. I took a deep breath and told him I would ensure resolution within six weeks. On this basis he agreed to the squatters' return.

Both he and I knew we would face the wrath of the people who believed they could use the fire as a lever to get rid of the Hout Bay informal settlement.

The next morning I phoned De Beer's office, to be told he had gone overseas on holiday and would only be back in office in the new year. I was unwilling to let the matter stand over until his return, so I decided to put the issue before De Klerk. Knowing that the president normally went to his holiday home in Hermanus over the Christmas and New Year period, I drove down to the seaside resort.

I knew De Klerk was a keen golfer, and thought he might be enjoying a round at the local club that morning. At the golf club I had a look at the scoreboard: my hunch was correct. De Klerk was playing golf and was due back in the clubhouse at 12.30. I returned to the club promptly at 12.30 to find that De Klerk had come off the course and was sitting with some friends in the lounge. I approached one of his aides to ask if he would mind breaking away for a few minutes to see me on an urgent matter.

De Klerk did so. I told him of what had happened at Hout Bay, of my undertaking to the owner, and my attempt to contact De Beer. Although not *au fait* with the details of the squatters' situation, he recognised a problem and told me that he would consider the matter and contact me within a day or two.

True to his word, De Klerk dropped in at my Hermanus retreat a couple of days later to tell me he had made arrangements for De Beer to contact him immediately on his return to South Africa and before he returned to his office. This was good news: at least something was happening.

A day or two later, in January, I was at the club once more. Sam de Beer had a holiday home in the nearby village of Vermont – and he too was a keen member of the golf club. The scoreboard told me he was playing that day and was due off the course shortly. So he was, but he seemed less friendly than usual. His opening comments were: '*Colin, ek het gedog jy was my vriend, maar jy het my gedrop!*' ('Colin, I thought you were my friend, but you've dropped me!')

As he stepped off the aircraft from Europe he had been given a message to phone De Klerk, who told him of my conversation and my concern at the delay in resolving the Hout Bay issue. De Klerk had made it clear there should be no further delay.

On 21 January, less than four weeks after I had given my undertaking to the owner of the land, De Beer's office announced that a portion of land in Hout Bay owned by the Regional Services Council had been allocated for the resettlement of the squatters. This land was a prime site on the slopes of the mountain above the council's office and a nursery plant, and adjoined a well-developed white housing estate.

One major hurdle had been overcome. The next was to get the squatters to move voluntarily. A difficulty was that they were scattered around the valley and had no formal body to speak for them. Although not a squatter himself, Dick Meter, a UDF activist who lived in the harbour area and was the chairman of the Hout Bay Action Committee, often fulfilled the role of spokesman. Meter, however, had been arrested and was being detained by the security police.

I thought there was a good chance I could persuade Adriaan Vlok, as Minister of Law and Order, to have Meter released, not only because of the role that he could play in resolving the squatter issue, but because in my opinion he was by no stretch of the imagination a danger to the state. I put my request to Vlok; Meter was released.

A three-person team visited every squatter shack, one representing the Regional Services Council, one the Hout Bay Ratepayers Association, and one the squatter community. Each shack was numbered, and the names of the inhabitants listed. Meetings were held to explain details of the proposed resettlement. After some weeks the process was completed, and with the agreement of the squatters the resettlement process began.

The land needed to be prepared, and basic services installed for about three hundred families comprising 2 400 people, whose status would change from that of 'squatters' to 'permanent residents'. A few months before the resettlement was complete, I approached Robin Renwick, the UK ambassador, for a grant towards building a modest community hall. His response was prompt and generous: R40 000 to build a practical and useful amenity in the new township to be called Imizama Yethu.

Reactions among white residents varied. Those who had campaigned for the removal of the squatters were angry. Those from whose property the squatters had been removed were pleased, and were able to get on with plans for development. The white community as a whole – while naturally concerned that a new township on the slopes of the mountain might lead to a large influx of unemployed black people from outside Hout Bay, leading to an increase in crime and what was seen as anti-social behaviour – by and large accepted the situation as a reality. The white Ratepayers Association and the black Residents Association formed a liaison committee.

Sadly, years later, the new inhabitants had still not been given ownership of the land promised to them as a condition for agreeing to move to Imizama Yethu. Shacks had proliferated and spread beyond the confines of the original site, and estimates put the population of Imizama Yethu at between ten thousand and sixteen thousand.

The good news was that in 2003 Niall Mellon, an Irish developer with property interests in South Africa, who drove past Imizama Yethu on his way to work each day, decided to take action to rebuild the self-made shacks as proper houses. He launched the Niall Mellon Township Challenge, which involved 700 Irish volunteers coming to the Cape each year to build brick houses for the community. In addition to giving their time and labour, each volunteer had to raise R35 000 – part of which paid for their flight to South Africa, with the remainder contributing to buying building materials.

Thanks to Mellon's initiative, the efforts of the Irish volunteers, and donations from various companies, Imizama Yethu's residents enjoy many of the benefits of having become the owners of well-built, weatherproof homes.

PART VII

Return to a welcoming world

23

Rejoining the world

During the first few years of the 1990s, the number and scope of my international visits and engagements – already numerous – increased tremendously. In 1987 Helen and I had journeyed to China and I had felt that the beginnings of that nation's economic reforms looked like capitalism to me. My feeling was that China, with its vast natural resources, huge manpower, intense work ethic, educational facilities and potential market would be a major force in coming years.

There were lessons to be learned from the Chinese response to rural development, mass housing, community-based education, population planning and care for the aged. China, after all, had managed to provide basic food, clothing and housing for one-fifth of humankind. The scale of our problems fell into perspective.

My first visit to China left me fascinated with the country: its people, its culture, its history, its scale, its problems and its achievements. I became an avid reader of books and journals on China. I kept in touch with the contacts I had made through the Chinese Association for International Understanding (CAFIU), the organisation that hosted Helen and me. In the ensuing years I visited the vast country on a number of occasions, on three of them with Joyce, and on one joined as well by Jan Steyn, former director of the Urban Foundation, and his wife Ann.

With Joyce and the Steyns I sailed up the Yangtze River into two of the three gorges and on up a tributary of the Danning River. I visited rural development schemes, agricultural collectives and Special Economic Zones. There were discussions with academics, community and workers' leaders, managers of industrial enterprises, Communist Party functionaries, and government leaders at national, provincial and municipal level.

Twice I was invited to the Zhongnanhai, the walled government complex adjoining Beijing's Forbidden City, for talks with members of the central Politbureau. The first was in 1988 with Hu Qili, a member of reformist Zhao Ziyang's government. The second was in 1989 with Soon Ping, a member of the hardliner Jiang Zemin's government, which took over after the events in Tiananmen Square in June that year.

On my return to South Africa, in addition to addressing audiences on my general impressions of China, I always made a special point of telling businessmen and industrialists of the emerging economy I had seen and pointing out the opportunities that would arise for doing business with China once South Africa got rid of apartheid.

That had been before the advent of De Klerk. I had previously been abroad as a member (however liberal) of a pariah nation. Now, in the 1990s, what a pleasure it was to travel abroad and talk about South Africa. No longer did foreigners inquire with morbid inquisitiveness about events in the apartheid state. No longer did they have a distant sense of outrage at what the South African government was doing, and pity for the people they saw moving at increasing speed towards a South African apocalypse.

The morbidity had given way to hope and a positive approach to our future. Pity had given way to respect for a people that had overcome the obstacles of the past and was moving towards a new freedom. Of course there were questions; there were doubts. But there was hope and encouragement.

For a couple of years I continued to attend conferences of the Friedrich Naumann Stiftung at Sintra in Portugal. I continued to be a regular participant at meetings and congresses of Liberal International. Having temporarily deserted the US in favour of China, I resumed travelling to the States again. And Europe beckoned.

The Association of Western European Parliamentarians Against Apartheid (AWEPAA), a voluntary association drawn from legislators in West Europe with its headquarters in Amsterdam, invited me to Luxembourg to brief a conference on developments at home. I did so, and was subsequently invited to participate in a number of similar conferences in various European cities over the next few years. I was pleased when a stage was reached in the South African negotiations enabling AWEPAA to change its name to Awepa – the Association of West European Parliamentarians for Africa.

A short while after the ANC and PAC were unbanned, Tony Leon and I, who were attending a small conference in Geneva convened jointly by the World Council of Churches and the UN, were surprised to find the ANC delegates objecting vociferously to the presence of the PAC. The entire first day of the conference was wasted as the ANC and PAC delegates locked horns. It took a threat from the convenors to call off proceedings entirely to get the two liberation movements to sit down together. An indication of a surfacing conflict over the spoils of power? Perhaps.

In the 1990s, too, Africa began to focus on the implications of the emergence of a free South Africa. What would it mean for the continent? General Obasanjo, although not involved in party politics in his own country, Nigeria – for long periods party politics were not permitted there – remained deeply committed to promoting democracy and development on the African continent. He had initiated an internationally funded organisation called the Africa Leadership Forum (ALF) which brought leaders, academics and activists together at conferences and workshops where they could analyse relevant problems facing Africa, search for solutions, and agree on programmes of action.

Obasanjo worked long and hard to arrange a pivotal conference drawing in a number of significant African leaders, from government and civil society, to meet and commit themselves and their governments, institutions and people to aim at achieving certain development goals.

The result was a three-day forum in Kampala in May 1991, attended by a number of presidents and ex-presidents, 27 heads of government, and about five hundred delegates. The South Africans invited were Alfred Nzo of the ANC, a representative of the PAC, Alex Boraine of Idasa, and me. Discussions took place in four working groups, each of which dealt with one of four crucial issues: security, stability, development, and co-operation in Africa.

At the conclusion the delegates adopted the Kampala Document, which called for the creation of a Conference on Security, Stability, Development and Co-operation in Africa on lines similar to those of the 'Helsinki Conference' on security and co-operation in Europe.

The Kampala meeting was followed by a conclave of OAU ministers and a summit of African heads of state in Abudja later that year at which 'a link between security, stability, development and co-operation in Africa' was acknowledged. The compelling message to Abudja of the Kampala Document was that 'the stability and security of each African country is inseparably linked to the security of all African countries', and that the continent could not make any significant progress on any front without 'a lasting solution to problems of security and stability'.

Ten years later, the Kampala Document played a significant role in the formulation of the treaty constituting the new African Union (AU) that replaced the OAU, and in shaping its New Programme for Africa's Development (Nepad). What struck me at Kampala was not only the remarkable display of African unity and purpose, but also the important role played by the leaders of civil society.

Two men reinforced my positive impressions of their capacities. One was Obasanjo himself, leading not only by convening the conference but also in keeping it focused on its objectives. Then there was a masterful display of chairmanship by former president Nyerere of Tanzania and, in particular, his off-the-cuff closing comments. This was vintage Nyerere: creative, humorous, direct and self-critical.

Seeing and listening to Nyerere at close quarters, I realised why he was considered one of the outstanding personalities of Africa in the latter 20th century. In October 1999, on the occasion of Nyerere's death, I had the privilege of paying a tribute to him in South Africa's National Assembly. My conclusion: 'Julius Nyerere played an important role as one of Africa's statesmen. He was a true son of Africa. A leader who has helped to shape the history of the continent he loved, and to change the lives of the people who live on it.'

While in Kampala I received news of the tragic death of my friend and colleague Tian van der Merwe. While he was driving into Cape Town from the airport an approaching car jumped the strip separating the two carriageways and crashed head-on into him. He was a diligent and courageous MP. As DP spokesman on law and order he pulled no punches in exposing and condemning the brutality of the security police. Had he lived, he would unquestionably have made an important contribution to South African politics.

24

The negotiations: progress and deadlock

At Codesa, when Working Group 2 started its work in 1992 the atmosphere was relaxed and congenial. Hopes of reaching consensus were high. Since the members felt that the matters referred to them were of a fundamental nature, they agreed not to set up sub-committees but to deal with their assignments in plenary sessions where the parties could be fully represented. To assist in its various activities, an eight-person steering committee, of which I was a member, met before each plenary.

Parties were requested to make written submissions on each issue to be considered; and these were usually amplified by a verbal presentation followed by questions, answers and discussion. The first area of disagreement was that of the constitutional principles. The dispute was not so much about substance but about the different perspectives that the ANC and the other negotiators held on the extent to which the principles should shape the final constitution.

The NPG approach was that, considering that the constitution would be drawn up in terms of the constitutional principles agreed at Codesa, and because the ANC would be the dominant player in the constitution-making body, the principles should be specific and detailed. The ANC, on the other hand, argued that Codesa, not being an elected body, should not bind the Constitutional Assembly (CA), which would be an elected body. In the circumstances the principles should not be spelled out.

As the DP realised that the constitutional principles would be a central feature of the constitution-making process, my colleagues and I put a special effort into drafting and debating the principles. In the event, the issue was resolved neither by firm debate nor by sloppy compromise, but by what I have termed 'the chemistry of negotiation'. By the time the elected CA was required to comply with the constitutional principles drawn up by Codesa, the basic principles were to a large extent 'owned' by all the political parties.

One issue to which our working group particularly applied its mind at an early stage was that of minority rights. Here my DP colleagues and I differed sharply with those who saw minorities as statutory, defined racial groups, as well as with those such as the ANC who saw democracy as simple majority rule. The DP recognised that to the extent that groups were recognised constitutionally, they had to be the product of voluntary association and not of statutory classification.

I presented our approach under the heading: 'The Meaningful Participation of Political Minorities'. *Inter alia* I stated: 'The DP sees both political minorities and political majorities as the product of citizens associating voluntarily to express their individual rights on a collective basis. Individuals forming political minorities have no claim to special rights, nor do individuals forming majorities have a divine right to rule over others.

'Representative parliamentary democracy would only work if political minorities have a real prospect of becoming a political majority from time to time – a form of power-sharing by rotation. The DP believes that the political pressures generated by the urge of political minorities to play an effective role has to be accommodated in an organic and holistic way by bringing the constitutional provisions and all the structures of government into account. The central government must not be the only instrument for exercising power.'

I went on to deal with the constitutional mechanisms to give political minorities access to power. There should be:

- a multiplication of the number of sites, national, regional and local, at which power could be exercised, so that minorities at one site of power could be a majority at another;
- a bill of rights guaranteeing all citizens equality before the law, freedom from discrimination, and freedom of association, speech and political mobilisation;
- checks and balances that, in addition to preventing the abuse of power, would distribute power away from a single central authority; and
- special voting majorities giving minorities a meaningful say on matters dealing with language, religion and culture, fundamental rights, and the constitution itself.

On the constitutional structures to give minorities access to power, I suggested a two-chamber parliament with one house elected on the basis of proportional representation and the other elected through the regions (provinces), as well as:

- a judiciary that was non-racial and impartial, and judicial appointments that would be made from minorities as well as majorities;
- a public service as well as parastatals, boards and commissions that would reflect the non-racial, non-sexist and democratic character of the state, and where individuals, whether from majorities or minorities, would be able to exercise aspects of power;
- a range of executive structures operating at national, regional and local level within the powers laid down in the constitution; and
- the emergence of executive governments that were broad rather than narrowly based. The DP believed that while South Africa was in a process of transition, and developing democratic conventions and cross-cutting interests, it would be

necessary to make provision for shared executives drawn from parties with proven support.

On the role of civil society, I said that power and influence should not be exercised solely through political and constitutional structures, but throughout the structures of civil society – labour, business, religion, sport, cultural and community organisations. A vigorous civil society was an important agency for spreading power more evenly.

My conclusion: 'The DP believes that by shifting the nature of our politics away from the struggle for dominance at a central source of power and by encouraging a multi-party approach to politics, we would be able to do justice to the meaningful participation of political minorities without doing violence to the rights of citizens who form political majorities.'

Federalism was bound to be hotly debated – and it was.

The Bantustan policy of the NP and the race federation of the former United Party had given federalism a bad name and a racial connotation. Since it was anathema to the ANC, I tried to avoid using the word when advancing my arguments, preferring to use the more cumbersome if less repellent phrase, 'constitutional decentralisation'. Once the concept of federalism could be viewed free of racial connotations, the case for having three tiers of government – each with legislated powers and functions – became much more acceptable.

My belief was that, whatever the ANC ideologists might have wanted, the nature of South African society, and the geography of the country combined with pressures at grassroots level for recognition for some form of regionalism, would persuade the ANC to move from its centrist position to one with a federal component.

While consensus was developing in our working group around the concept of a three-tier system of governance, there was none on the rights and powers of the tiers or on the power relationship between the subordinate tiers and the centre. However, we made progress on a number of other constitutional principles, some of which had their origin in the Declaration of Intent adopted by Codesa. These were to set in motion the process of drawing up and establishing a constitution to ensure that:

- South Africa would be a united, democratic, non-racial and non-sexist state in which sovereign authority was exercised over the whole of its territory.
- The constitution would be the supreme law, and would be guarded by an independent, non-racial and impartial judiciary.
- There would be a multi-party democracy with the right to form and join political parties and with regular elections on the basis of universal adult suffrage on a common voters' roll; and in general the basic electoral system would be proportional representation.
- There should be a separation of powers between the legislature, the executive and the judiciary, with appropriate checks and balances.

- The diversity of languages, cultures and religions should be acknowledged.
- All would enjoy universally accepted human rights, freedoms and civil liberties – including freedom of religion, speech and assembly – protected by an entrenched bill of rights and a legal system that guaranteed equality before the law.

Dominating every other issue was that of power. The elected CA would be empowered to draw up a new constitution and to determine who, in terms of that constitution, would achieve political power – and how it should be exercised.

The sides were poles apart. It was clear to me that assessments of relative electoral strength would prove a dominant factor in determining attitudes to decision-making procedures. Those against the ANC were for strong and binding constitutional principles, and decisions subject to effective minority vetoes. The ANC approach was for less detailed principles, and minimum limitation on the powers of the elected authority.

At a critical stage, the NP's chief negotiator Gerrit Viljoen withdrew from the talks and resigned from parliament. At the same time Cyril Ramaphosa, the ANC's negotiating heavyweight, returned to head its team in the sensitive Working Group 2. These changes were to have a significant bearing on the course of negotiation.

Viljoen was a man of considerable presence, stature and authority as a senior member of the cabinet and a confidant of De Klerk. His place was taken by Tertius Delport, the deputy minister of Constitutional Development, who had been Viljoen's number two.

Delport had had a successful academic career and had a sound knowledge of constitutional issues, but he lacked the status and the gravitas of his predecessor. Added to this, he was not given a full ministerial position when Viljoen moved on. Roelf Meyer, the Minister of Defence, represented the NP in Working Group 3 and was promoted to head Constitutional Development.

The shuffling of Ramaphosa and Delport made for fascinating political theatre but failed to break the deadlock between the ANC and its opponents.

The five working groups were due to report to a Codesa plenary on 15-16 May. The plenary duly met but promptly adjourned for five hours to give the members of Working Group 2 an opportunity for a last-minute attempt to reach agreement. The specific issue was once again the percentage of votes required for the CA to take decisions on a transitional constitution. The ANC suggested 66,7%; the NP insisted on 75%. I attempted to break the impasse by proposing 70% but no-one would compromise.

Essentially, the NP insisted on a Senate with the power to block any decision of the National Assembly. The ANC countered this with a proposal that 50% of the votes cast at a referendum would be sufficient authority to adopt the new constitution.

When the plenary met again, Working Group 2 said it was unable to reach agreement and that in the circumstances there was no report to consider. The ruling was that as reports from the working groups had to be seen as part of a package of recommendations, if there was to be no agreed report from Working Group 2, no report could be adopted at the plenary.

Later in the afternoon, while delegates were discussing the way forward, Zach asked me to speak on behalf of the DP. I was angry at the manner in which the ANC and the NP had put their own interests ahead of the interests of the people; so I decided to be blunt and with Mandela and De Klerk present, to be personal. In essence this is what I said:

'Of course we're all disappointed at not having a report from Working Group 2 before us. Millions of people around South Africa share our disappointment. But being disappointed is not good enough. After all, we are the collective leadership of South Africa. What are we going to do about it? I look at the galaxy and the talent of the leadership that is here, and say we should take the first urgent steps to resolve the impasse.

'A basic lack of mutual trust of one another is hampering us in finding a solution. Unless the participants in Codesa, by their behaviour themselves, and by their behaviour one towards the other, start to develop a sense of mutual trust, of trust that we each are committed to a genuine democratic and non-racial South Africa, we are never going to reach agreement on the crunch issues that are before us.

'It is not good enough to say: "Well, we hope one day the working group can find a solution." I believe that while we're assembled here, and in particular while the leaders are assembled here, we've got to see whether we can break out of the impasse. I don't believe that the issues that divide us are so great that, quite frankly, the De Klerks and the Mandelas and others that are assembled here today cannot resolve this impasse.'

My words seemed to have made an impact. Soon after the plenary adjourned, I met Mandela in one of the corridors. He stopped me and said: 'Colin, that was a powerful intervention. You have given us all something to think about.'

The following day the *Weekend Argus*, under the headline 'To the Rescue', reported that De Klerk and Mandela had had a dramatic late-night meeting to rescue Codesa from the brink of failure. It carried a photograph of them shaking hands, with me in the background, and the caption: 'Mr Colin Eglin, who was to play a crucial role in bringing the two leaders together, looks on.'

Hennie Serfontein, in *Vrye Weekblad* (a dissident Afrikaans publication), commented that as a veteran parliamentarian I had played a 'glittering role' in concentrating the minds of Mandela and De Klerk. They had re-evaluated their opposing positions as a result. Indeed, the following morning Mandela and De Klerk each made short conciliatory speeches, and the atmosphere at Codesa – now reaching the end of its second round – became more relaxed, and the delegates appeared in a more accommodating mood.

The plenary, on its final scheduled day, considered the reports and recommendations from Working Groups 1, 3, 4 and 5, and a report of progress made from Working Group 2. However, as Working Group 2 had not been able to agree on a recommendation, the plenary decided that none of the reports should be adopted. The administration was instructed to collect and collate the records of proceedings of the working groups so that these would be available when Codesa met again to take the process further. Thus, while the negotiating process was still intact, the latest round of talks ended on a disappointing note.

Perhaps we had been too optimistic and too impatient.

Dark clouds over the talks

The plenary over and Codesa deadlocked, delegates returned home and MPs – a little weary and uncertain – returned to Cape Town to resume their parliamentary duties. After some reflection I decided to ask De Klerk to meet me so we could review the proceedings of Working Group 2 and I could express my opinion of what went wrong.

I made two points. Firstly, I thought the president had made a tactical error in having Tertius Delport take over as the government's negotiator in the group. I was of the opinion that Meyer, who had done well in Working Group 3, and who had been appointed Minister of Constitutional Development in the place of Gerrit Viljoen, would have the status and authority to go eyeball to eyeball with Ramaphosa. Secondly, for negotiations to succeed, particularly ones such as ours which involved talking with and making concessions to 'the enemy', the leaders of both sides had to be able to demonstrate to their supporters that they had won something.

At that stage I believed De Klerk could demonstrate to his support base that he had won on a number of issues; Mandela, on the other hand, was not in the same position. In a sense the government had won too much and the ANC too little. I suggested that De Klerk's group had been too keen on winning, too greedy for its own good. On reflection, De Klerk responded by saying that perhaps for negotiations to succeed we should try to go for a win-win and not a win-lose situation.

I recalled that Ken Andrew and I had taken part in workshops, part of a future-planning exercise named the Mont Fleur Scenarios after the conference venue near Stellenbosch where they took place. Various scenarios for South Africa's development had been posited – negative as well as positive. Among those that could lead to stasis or further breakdown, one (the so-called 'flamingo' scenario) envisaged the creation of a growth-orientated democracy.

In essence, government would adopt sound social and economic policies and observe macro-economic constraints. It would curb corruption and raise levels of efficiency. In the social sphere there would be well-targeted investments leading to a decrease in violence and giving people confidence that many of their social needs would be met in the longer term. The outcome would be significant improvements in social policies and increased confidence in the economic sphere. To my ears, De Klerk's 'win-win' suggestion was a political variant of the flamingo scenario.

He thanked me for speaking frankly. What I did not realise then was that South

Africa retained a terrifying potential for violence – and that episodes of this would come close to destroying the difficult yet constructive labours of Codesa.

A mere four weeks after I had been reassured by De Klerk's position, on 17 June in Boipatong, a township south of Johannesburg, a group of Zulu migrant workers brutally and indiscriminately massacred 48 residents ranging in age from old men and women to young babies.

The massacre, on top of the continuing violence – especially in Natal, the Zulu heartland – was the last straw for the ANC. Brushing aside the fact that De Klerk had immediately expressed his shock and revulsion at the attack, and said his government would not rest until the perpetrators had been brought to justice, the ANC issued the following statement:

'The NP government pursues a strategy that embraces negotiations, together with systematic covert actions, including murder, involving its security forces and surrogates … [The] Boipatong massacre is one of the most chilling instances of the consequences of the actions of the De Klerk regime … [The] ANC has no option but to break off bilateral and Codesa negotiations. It will keep the situation under continuous review.

'The response and practical steps taken by the De Klerk regime to [our] demands will play a critical role in determining the direction and speed with which *bona fide* negotiations can take place …'

The brutality at Boipatong had destroyed the tenuous trust between the ANC and the government. Letters and memoranda that passed between Mandela and De Klerk did nothing to defuse the situation. The ANC made a number of demands that could not possibly be met then. At one stage the NP did soften its stance on some of the issues that led to the impasse in Working Group 2. The ANC's response was that this did not go far enough, and announced that August would be a month of 'rolling mass action', which would continue until the government met its demands.

Rolling mass action took the form of general strikes, worker stayaways, protest marches and demonstrations, all of which gathered momentum. There was no visible sign of the NP government giving in to the ANC demands, or of the ANC abandoning its new tactics. Like many others in South Africa, and indeed around the world, I was deeply concerned at this turn of events. In retrospect I felt that perhaps we had been too optimistic, too hurried, and in a sense too closeted.

We had been focused on the formal negotiating process, keen to make rapid progress; and there was the reality of our growing involvement with one another. Perhaps we had not paid sufficient attention to the necessity of taking the citizens whom we claimed to represent along with us. Even while the negotiations ran their course at Codesa, continuing violence had been undermining the faith that people had in what we were seeking to achieve. Moreover, as mutual blaming and recrimination of the ANC and the NP had shown, this had helped destroy the trust essential to the success of our venture.

There had always been the danger of a gap developing between leaders who were negotiating with 'the enemy' and their constituents who were not included in the talks – and had been conditioned to 'fight it out'. There had always been a fatalistic expectation of a widening civil war: perhaps this was how it would begin.

The gulf between De Klerk and his white constituency had manifested itself in the humiliating defeat of the NP at the hands of the CP in the Potchefstroom by-election. It was this that prompted De Klerk to call a referendum to consolidate his support base and strengthen his hand at the negotiating table. Aware of the disaffection of his own constituency, it was Boipatong that not only prompted Mandela to suspend the ANC's involvement at Kempton Park, but initiated the call for rolling mass action to consolidate his support base and strengthen his hand.

So what rolling mass action was for the voteless, the referendum was for the voters. However diverse these responses to the situation, they did enable ordinary, otherwise excluded people to participate in history by making their views a factor to be taken into account by the negotiators.

I said at the time: 'Carefully directed mass action could strengthen the negotiating process by focusing the public's attention on key issues, broadening the base of public participation, ensuring that negotiators had secure support bases, and by producing a creative balance between the parties at the negotiating table.'

I warned: 'There is always the risk and danger of mass action getting out of hand, of becoming violent and of developing a momentum of its own and finally of becoming an end in itself. In these circumstances, mass action could end up undermining, instead of underpinning, the negotiation process.'

I travelled to Ulundi, the KwaZulu capital, for a meeting with Buthelezi at which I hoped to focus on the deteriorating general situation and, in particular, on the violence that was escalating as a consequence of the hostility between the ANC and the Inkatha Freedom Party. Buthelezi was his amiable and charming self. He asked, as he always did, after 'Joan' – he never could get Joyce's name right – and we discoursed for a while on earlier days. When we reached Codesa, he did not hold back in repeating his disapproval of the ANC withdrawal.

I said that I was deeply concerned by the hostility between the ANC and the IFP, and believed it to be the major cause of the violence, and that it was having an extremely negative impact on the prospect of further negotiations. A joint appeal by Mandela and Buthelezi would help reduce the level of conflict. Buthelezi said he shared my concerns but was quite emphatic that the fault lay with the ANC. Mandela and he had been old friends, he added. I said I was soon to hold a meeting with Mandela and asked whether he would have any objection if I raised the matter of his relationship with the former prisoner. Buthelezi said that he would welcome it.

A few days after my meeting in Ulundi, I joined Mandela in his office in Shell House, the ANC's Johannesburg headquarters. This was the first occasion on which I had met him in this way; I felt privileged, and would have been overawed had it not been for the warmth with which Mandela made me comfortable and put me at my ease.

I outlined my understanding of rolling mass action as part of a negotiation process, but expressed my concern at the danger of it escalating and replacing negotiations altogether. Mandela appeared to accept this analysis, but stated firmly that 'rolling mass action is necessary strategy, but negotiations remain the objective of the ANC'.

I told him of my discussions with Buthelezi. Mandela confirmed that he and Buthelezi had been friends who had fallen out over differences of policy and strategy. He did not commit himself further, and because I felt it would be inappropriate to take the matter any further then I was left with the impression that he would seek to find an occasion to try and restore his relationship with Buthelezi.

For many months after our meeting, whenever I met Mandela, he would ask how 'our friend Buthelezi' was getting on.

A truly remarkable man.

An unexpected and horrifying event occurred before the two leaders could resolve their differences. On the morning of 11 April 1993 South Africans were shocked at the news that Chris Hani, the charismatic general secretary of the South African Communist Party, a member of the ANC's national executive committee and a commander of Umkhonto we Sizwe, had been shot dead outside his home in Boksburg.

Many people had seen Hani as a future national leader and an important link between the veterans of the struggle and the new generation of young South Africans. Given the climate of tension and mistrust that prevailed as a result of the ongoing violence, the uncertainties that surrounded the negotiating process, and Hani's popularity as a dynamic leader of the younger generation – as well as the political and racial overtones of his murder – South Africa sat on a powder keg for several days. De Klerk condemned the murder and said that the government would do all in its power to track down the perpetrators and bring them before the courts. The nation was shocked still further when Clive Derby-Lewis, a prominent right-wing politician, who had served in the Tricameral parliament as a Conservative Party member, together with his wife Gaye and Janusz Walus, a South African of Polish origin, were arrested and charged with Hani's murder.

However, many blacks still saw De Klerk's government as part of the problem. His intervention was not enough: it was the firm stance of Mandela in a televised appeal for calm that made the critical difference. While the atmosphere remained tense and preparations for the resumption of negotiations remained on hold, South Africa endured and survived the critical days during which our history could have taken a very ugly turn.

The case against Gaye Derby-Lewis was withdrawn. Months later Clive Derby-Lewis and Walus were found guilty and sentenced to life imprisonment.

I was one of the DP representatives who were part of the crowd of 90 000 South Africans who paid tribute to Hani at a moving funeral service in the FNB stadium outside Johannesburg. Although I had heard and read much about Hani and in particular about his leadership qualities, I regretted I had not come to know him personally. We had both taken part in Codesa, and served on different committees exploring the route to democracy. We greeted each other occasionally when we happened to meet in the corridor, which served the nearby offices of the SACP and of the DP. On one occasion, shortly before his death, I came across Hani and his SACP colleague Ronnie Kasrils, engaged in serious conversation. I said jokingly: 'I get worried when I see you two communists in a huddle. I hope you are not planning the downfall of my party.'

'No,' said Hani, 'you don't need to worry. I have a high regard for the role that you Progressives played in opposing apartheid.'

More generous than some of his colleagues, I thought to myself as he moved on.

It was only in June of 1993 that a summit between Mandela and Buthelezi finally took place. It focused on the issue of violence, and resulted in the two leaders making an undertaking in respect of joint rallies, free political activity, and the strengthening of the peace accord – the essential basis of the Codesa talks in the first place.

Nonetheless, the breakdown in negotiations continued throughout July and August, and well into September. Apart from testy memoranda between them there was no public evidence of true communication between the ANC and the NP government. The international community was concerned at the situation, and the UN Security Council, at a meeting on 8 July, passed a special resolution 'requesting political parties to return to negotiations'. Cyrus Vance, a former US secretary of state, was sent to South Africa as a special representative of the secretary-general to try to break the impasse. His visit was followed by observer missions from the UN, the European Community and the OAU.

With the economy suffering, business leaders offered to help to get the negotiations restarted.

Abruptly, the breakdown ended almost as suddenly as it had started. Ironically, just as the rupture had been precipitated by a massacre, the resumption of talks was triggered by another. On 7 September several hundred ANC supporters, led by SACP member Ronnie Kasrils, split away from an ANC crowd lawfully demonstrating at a stadium outside Bisho, the capital of Ciskei. They broke through a gap in the fence surrounding the stadium and attempted to march on the capital.

Members of the Ciskei army reacted by firing on and killing 28 marchers and wounding many more. Yet another massacre had shocked South Africans – and jolted the ANC by forcing the realisation that indeed there was the risk of violence getting completely out of hand. In the aftermath of Bisho, the ANC reduced their demands to three realisable issues – the release of political prisoners; the banning of the public display of dangerous weapons; and removal of the fencing of migrant worker hostels.

A few days later De Klerk and Mandela met and signed a 'Record of Understanding' in which the ANC and NP reiterated their commitment to negotiations. Although the Record of Understanding revealed no victories for either side on constitutional issues, the government's agreement to the ANC's non-constitutional demands was sufficient to permit the masses who had participated in the rolling mass action to feel their actions had been effective, and the ANC had after all been the victor in the showdown with the NP.

Over the next few weeks there was a vehement rejection of the Record of Understanding by a group of leaders with Buthelezi in the forefront. Once again the negotiations which the ANC and NP had agreed to recommence would be put on hold.

25

Getting negotiations back on track

Most South Africans breathed a sigh of relief when the Record of Understanding was signed. Its details were less important than the fact that negotiations could resume. Little did they anticipate that another six months would elapse before a new Multi-Party Negotiation Process (MPNP) would meet to take the debates forward.

The DP welcomed the Record – a view not shared by a significant group of leaders, including Buthelezi, Mangope of Bophuthatswana, 'Oupa' Gqozo of Ciskei, the CP, the Afrikaner Volksunie, and the Afrikaner Freedom Foundation, who all rejected the Record of Understanding outright.

Buthelezi was especially vehement in his rejection. He was opposed to the concept of an elected Constitutional Assembly, and livid at the inclusion of clauses relating to the carrying of dangerous weapons and the fencing of workers' hostels, both of which he believed were directed at the IFP and its Zulu supporters. Zulu men were traditionally martial and carried weapons to signify their manhood.

Buthelezi was also angry with the NP and ANC for having reached agreement in 'bilaterals' on matters which should have been subject to negotiation, discussion and agreement in multi-party forums. He said: 'The signing of the Record of Understanding by Mr de Klerk and Dr Mandela has served notice on us that [they] think that they can decide upon the parameters of negotiations unilaterally and then get us to fill out the flesh of the body politic they have decided on. We say no to this.

'This agreement is the peak of a much deeper and broader agreement between the government and the ANC on how to share South Africa. The carefully selected words of this agreement should be read in the light of a broader understanding of what is happening, and of what are their plans for our future.' With measured anger Buthelezi added that the signatories had agreed to a future strategy of 'ethnic cleansing'.

A few weeks later, the parties and organisations that had rejected the Record formed the Concerned South Africans Group (Cosag); they formally withdrew from the negotiating process and committed themselves to oppose the Record of Understanding.

The next few months were characterised by a flurry of bilaterals aimed at speeding up the process by finding as much common ground as possible before multi-party talks began. Those who wanted negotiations to proceed met Cosag to find ways of bringing the latter back to the table. The parties also held workshops and conferences in which they revisited strategies and policies relating to both the transition and the constitution. I took the unusual step of writing to Zach de Beer expressing my concern at the manner in which the DP was handling the process. I pointed out that while the other parties appeared to have internal structures, representatives and staff focusing on the issues, the DP seemed to be drifting. Zach, who must have been taken aback by my crisp comments, responded that while he did not necessarily agree with my criticisms he had decided to appoint me as the DP's chief negotiator with responsibility for leading our team. Ken Andrew would assist at this level, and support staff would be sought. I was grateful to Zach.

One of our first tasks was to prepare updated position papers on the constitution-making process, the transitional government, and the electoral system. These would be debated at the DP's national congress in November. The congress endorsed the proposals, the main features of which were: an elected constitutional assembly to write the new constitution on the basis of those principles agreed by a multi-party negotiating forum; a multi-party transitional government created within the framework of the existing constitution which would be modified to provide adequate checks and balances; a bill of rights with no racial elements; and an electoral system based on a combination of constituencies and party lists, resulting in proportional representation.

My team had therefore been given an updated platform on which to enter the next round of bilateral and multi-party negotiations. In the course of these talks the DP modified its stance and agreed it would be preferable to have a transitional constitution rather than a transitional government on the basis of the existing constitution (however modified). We remained adamant that the functions of the transitional government and those of the constitution-making body should be completely separate.

The transitional constitution finally agreed by the Multi-Party Negotiating Process (MPNP) met the DP's demand for the separation of government and constitution-making. It also met the NP's concern for constitutional continuity, and the ANC's insistence that the Constitutional Assembly be elected. Provision was made for members elected to the transitional government to serve also as members of the Constitutional Assembly which would draft the final democratic constitution.

The refusal of Cosag to return to the table remained a major obstacle. While it had been clear all along that the ANC and NP would be the main players, it was realised that for the new constitution to enjoy the loyalty of all South Africans, the process which led to it had to be inclusive. To leave out the Zulus represented by the IFP – and Afrikaners represented by the CP, and the other hard-line white parties – would be to court disaster. Instead of the constitution being a unifying factor it would be a source of division and escalating ethnic tensions. The onus for resolving the problem was on the NP and ANC; but I did not believe the DP should stand aside and do nothing.

I made a point of keeping in touch with Buthelezi. I realised he had become increasingly sensitive in recent years to his uncomfortable position between the Nationalists, who tried to use him, and the ANC that wanted to destroy him.

Buthelezi responded warmly, sending me copies of speeches and statements. He wrote: 'It was wonderful to have you with us and to talk as of old about our great concerns about the future of our country. I always say that however we are demonised by other political parties and the media – I always argue that we are closest to the Democratic Party as representing democratic liberal values. Our discussion brought this home so strongly. Thanks for taking the time to come. I just feel that I should keep you informed of my doings so that you can hammer me as a friend if you feel I need hammering, or support me where you feel I deserve your support.'

Violence continued in spite of the efforts of the various political leaders and the structures of the National Peace Accord. Buthelezi had led marches of Zulus brandishing 'cultural weapons' in defiance of the peace accords. His IFP deputy, Frank Mdlalose, after a Johannesburg march, read out a petition 'on behalf of the Zulu nation': 'We protest at the way the affairs of the state are conducted to accommodate the destructive way of the ANC/SACP alliance in its clearly intended termination of the Codesa negotiation process by leaving Codesa without a quorum and by taking to street-corner mass action.'

At a Chaka Day rally King Goodwill Zwelithini denounced the Record of Understanding as an attempt 'to wipe us off the face of the earth as Zulus'.

I felt it was time for me to have another discussion with Buthelezi. On 8 January 1993, accompanied by James Selfe, the DP's head of research, I went to Ulundi. Somewhat to my surprise Buthelezi was accompanied by six of his cabinet ministers. The meeting followed a familiar pattern with Buthelezi reading a lengthy statement: 'All my political instincts tell me that we will yet again suffer from the consequences of a weak government capitulating to ANC demands for a transitional process, and steps and timetables which will lead them to monopolistic power politics or finally even perhaps the seizure of power. I believe that Mr de Klerk is sacrificing the power of the South Africans on which he should be relying.'

The first matter I raised was my concern at the extent of the ethnic mobilisation that appeared to be taking place among Zulus. Buthelezi responded by saying that to the extent that this was happening, the blame lay with the ANC whose provocative behaviour was evoking a response on what seemed an ethnic basis. If the ANC stopped its provocation, the Zulus would stop responding.

Taking a deep breath and hoping for the best, I then told Buthelezi that while the DP would support Inkatha's proposal for a federal dispensation for KwaZulu-Natal, it would not support any move to structure that unit on an ethnic basis. We believed that rights and privileges, including voting rights, should be enjoyed on a non-ethnic, non-racial basis. As I spoke I sensed that Buthelezi's features and those of his colleagues were hardening. 'You white liberals,' he said. 'You fight with us all the way until the stage is reached when we can get our Zulu state, and then you turn against us.'

I responded that given the population of KwaZulu-Natal the state might well have a prominently Zulu character; however the DP believed that all its citizens should have equal rights, irrespective of race or ethnic origin. There was a tense, awkward pause before I moved on to outline our federal proposals – and with this the mood became more relaxed. Our meeting ended with a useful discussion on the federal concept and its relevance in South Africa.

On the following 4 March representatives of the former Codesa parties, and the IFP and PAC, met in the World Trade Centre at what was called a Negotiation Planning Conference (NPC). The steering committee had asked me to be the provisional chairman until it was formally constituted and could elect a proper chairman. I enjoyed this short-lived experience.

The NPC called for the resumption of negotiations; but since the Cosag members were completely dismissive of Codesa, it resolved that the new negotiating body would be known as the Multi-Party Negotiating Process. A sub-committee of which I was a member was assigned to take charge of the arrangements for the first meeting of the process group in April. Representatives from 26 parties, and of traditional leaders, duly met on 1 April and resolved to establish the MPNP.

The constitutional negotiating process was finally back on the rails.

Weaving the democratic fabric

The Multi-Party Negotiating Process agreed that the Codesa format of five working groups functioning independently with no political co-ordination was not appropriate to drawing up the transitional constitution. The task required a more systematic and co-ordinated approach. The MPNP decided on four structures:

- The plenary consisted of ten members from each party, including its leader. It would be the highest decision-making body.
- The negotiating forum would comprise two members and two advisors per party.
- The negotiating council would be the primary negotiating body and consist of the chief negotiator, plus one advisor, per party. Seven technical committees of experts would furnish advice and draft texts of the sections of the transitional constitution based on deliberations in the council.
- A planning committee of ten would be responsible for the overall co-ordination and activities of the MPNP, and decide on priorities for debate and the mechanism to be used in the resolution of disputes. Members of the committee who chaired its meetings in rotation were Ramaphosa, Meyer, Slovo, Gordhan, Zam Titus, Frank Mdlalose, Benny Alexander, Chris de Jager, Mike Webb and me.

I enjoyed the work and responsibilities of being at the hub of the negotiating process. I had known the MPNP was about politics and power; it was also about people.

Alexander left the committee soon after it was formed; Mdlalose resigned when the IFP withdrew from the negotiations; and in due course De Jager and Webb followed suit. We were assisted by three individuals, Fanie van der Merwe, Mac Maharaj and Ben Ngubane, who together functioned under the title of 'the secretariat'.

Van der Merwe was a canny Afrikaner, a director-general in the government's Constitutional Affairs ministry. He had played a highly confidential role in enabling Mandela – during the final three years of his imprisonment – to communicate with Oliver Tambo in London. Maharaj had been imprisoned on Robben Island, was a member of the ANC's executive council, and had recently commanded the ANC's clandestine Operation Vula. Ngubane was a respected member of the IFP and a confidant of Buthelezi. Like Mdlalose he resigned when the IFP withdrew from the MPNP.

When deadlock occurred it was referred to the secretariat. Van der Merwe and Maharaj, in a quiet and unassuming manner, would in due course report back either that the problem had been solved or on the process for dealing with it. A remarkable symbiosis developed between the bald Afrikaner civil servant and the hirsute Operation Vula commander. They approached problems from contrasting political backgrounds, but reported as one. They even spoke like each other.

I became directly involved in constitutional matters, interacting with advocates Arthur Chaskalson, Dikgang Moseneke, Zac Yacoob and Bernard Ngoepe. Subsequently Chaskalson, Moseneke and Yacoob were appointed judges of the Constitutional Court, with Chaskalson as its first president and Moseneke later as vice-president. Ngoepe became Judge President of the High Court in the Transvaal.

The technical committee drafted texts of the transitional constitution – based on discussions in the negotiating council – for the subsequent consideration of the negotiating body, and as a result a new dimension was added to the process: for party negotiators to be successful they would have not only to debate issues with one another, but also take into account the personalities of the members of the technical committees who did the actual drafting.

As negotiations proceeded the concept evolved of having a single elected body structured so that its members could carry out the functions of both a transitional government and a Constitutional Assembly. The DP accepted a single elected body – but insisted that if one of its functions was to be the transitional government, it should function within a constitutional framework defining the separate functions of government and constitution-making; and should provide for checks and balances, a comprehensive bill of rights, an independent judiciary, the separation of powers, and the devolution of authority to the regions.

This framework could be achieved through either significant amendments to the existing constitution or a new transitional constitution. The latter route was chosen and became the main focus of effort in the following months. A helpful piece of the transformation jigsaw puzzle had been put in place earlier when a technical committee under the chairmanship of the DP's Ken Andrew proposed a Transitional Executive Council (TEC) to act as an executive watchdog before a transitional government was in place.

The multi-party process went hand-in-hand with bilaterals between the NP group and the ANC, and I presume more frequent interaction between Ramaphosa and Meyer. Progress was also facilitated by the ANC making a significant concession by agreeing to a constitutional principle that government be structured at three tiers – national, regional and local. Each level would be democratically elected and have powers and functions entrenched in the constitution.

In June 1993 the negotiating council considered that sufficient progress had been made to set 27 April 1994 as the date for South Africa's first democratic election under the transitional constitution. This decision – and the appointment of a commission to demarcate voting regions, effectively the basis of new provinces – raised the temper of right-wing protest against the whole concept of a non-racial constitutional dispensation. Protest meetings and rallies were held. Delegates at the World Trade Centre had to run a gauntlet of right-wing protestors on the road to the centre.

One Friday morning my colleagues and I received the news that about three thousand armed right-wingers – having brushed aside the former military boss General Constand Viljoen, who tried to persuade them to turn back – were marching on us. The spectacle I witnessed from a vantage point on a mezzanine landing overlooking the glass-fronted entrance hall was truly remarkable, more like a scene from a Steven Spielberg movie than a negotiating forum.

On arrival outside the centre, the right-wingers pushed past two flimsy cordons of police who did not resort to using their firearms. Some suggested that this passive behaviour indicated sympathy with the protestors; but I was prepared to accept that it was out of concern for a bloodbath if shooting started. The invaders crowded against the glass door, which had been closed as a security measure. Suddenly a gap appeared in the crowd and a makeshift armoured vehicle burst through, smashing the doors and opening the way for the roughnecks to pour into the entrance hall.

In marched bearded Eugene Terr'Blanche, leader of the Afrikaner Weerstandsbeweging – the AWB, the most militant opponents of a non-racial political deal – complete with slouch hat and lookalike swastika badge emblazoned on his khaki uniform. Six bodyguards, members of his Ystergarde (effectively his Stormtroopers), dressed in black uniforms with silver insignia on their epaulettes, accompanied him.

Tension mounted as Terr'Blanche and his men shoved towards the staircase leading to the conference hall. At the foot of the staircase, after a few words with his bodyguards, Terr'Blanche, accompanied by two of them, turned left and marched down a corridor. A journalist standing near me on the staircase asked the bodyguards what was happening and where Terr'Blanche had gone. The reply: *'Die leier het gaan pis.'* ('The leader has gone for a piss.')

Terr'Blanche returned and signalled to his followers to follow him up the staircase. By this time, the members of the MPNP had moved to their respective offices and caucus rooms. Terr'Blanche and his supporters went on to occupy the empty conference hall. For a while the corridors echoed to the lusty singing of patriotic Afrikaner anthems, emotional speeches and loud applause. But gradually the turmoil subsided as word got around that Terr'Blanche and company wanted to meet representatives of the MPNP to discuss their way out of the World Trade Centre. This bluster was rather like the dog that chased a double-decker bus and, having caught up with it, didn't know what to do.

In due course Terr'Blanche withdrew. The CP negotiators did not conceal their sympathy with the invaders. One of their leaders was heard to say to the police: '*Moenie skiet nie. Hulle is ons mense.*' ('Don't shoot. They're our people.')

I was filled with a deep sense of shame, anger and outrage. Ramaphosa was enraged: 'The right-wingers were trying to drag the country into a state of barbarism and hooliganism. They acted in the name of Afrikanerdom. They have disgraced Afrikaners today. The image of Afrikaners, and many of them are peace-loving people, lies in tatters in the mud.'

Despite this violent interruption and the three-week recess that followed, the constitutional principles were approved and the first draft of the transitional constitution was published before the end of July. From then on it was up to the parties to consider the draft; for the negotiating council to debate it section by section and revise it in the light of the debate; and for the revised draft to be published – and the entire process of debate, revision and publication to be repeated until the final document was ready for approval at a plenary meeting of the MPNP.

Parallel to the negotiations, progress was made on the finalisation of the functions and composition of the Transitional Executive Council, the Independent Electoral Commission (to monitor the election), and the demarcation of provincial boundaries. Parliament, for its part, had outstanding legislation to pass, as well as the new legislation required to give effect to decisions made by the MPNP.

Cosag would not go away. In October, its member parties regrouped as the Freedom Alliance (FA), and, together with the representatives of Bophuthatswana and Ciskei, determined to maintain their boycott of the negotiations. Strenuous efforts were made to persuade the FA to return, but to no avail. With time running out, the MPNP decided it had no option but to proceed with the finalisation of the transitional constitution despite the absence of the new alliance.

A fierce debate flared over whether a single ballot paper or two separate ones should be used in the election of members of the National Assembly and of the provincial legislatures. The NP, IFP and DP and others – essentially the federalists – argued for separate votes on separate ballots. The ANC-SACP and its allies wanted a single vote. Slovo had some members close to tears when he told them that a two-ballot paper system would favour the wealthy and well-educated and discriminate against poor and illiterate voters. (In the 27 April 1994 election the two-ballot paper system was used, and caused no problems. The poor and the illiterate demonstrated that they knew where and how to vote!)

One issue that troubled me would have repercussions that continued well into the

21st century. It concerned a constitutional clause that stated that an MP would lose his or her seat in parliament if he or she 'ceases to be a member of the party which nominated him/her as a member of the National Assembly'. This meant that an MP would be prevented from leaving his party – on, say, a matter of conscience – because of the prospect of losing his livelihood. It would place enormous, indeed coercive, powers in the hands of the party bosses and prevent the free expression of views on national issues. It was contrary to the spirit of the transitional constitution.

It appeared that, despite opposing views, the NP and the ANC had agreed to the election taking place on the basis of party lists and not on the basis of constituencies. The DP had submitted detailed proposals of a constituency-based system with additional MPs to be nominated to ensure proportional representation. An additional worry was that, combined with a party list system, the anti-defection clause would stifle open debate in parliament and prevent MPs from effectively holding the executive to account. They would be agents of their political parties rather than representatives of the people.

The debate on these related issues and their impact they had on our nascent democracy would continue for many years.

On 18 November 1993, two days before the date set for the completion of the transitional constitution, a number of important issues remained unresolved.

The reality of what was in truth a two-sided negotiating table revealed itself when, late in the night of 16 November, Mandela and De Klerk met and decided how the issues would be dealt with. This became known as the 'six-pack agreement'.

Nonetheless, in a committee dealing with the judiciary, the DP demonstrated that a determined small player could not be ignored. The DP's Tony Leon protested that the element of the 'six-pack agreement' on the method of appointment of judges would politicise the Constitutional Court. Before the day was out, the ANC agreed to amend the system: although still not perfect, the DP acknowledged this as acceptable.

In the early hours of the morning of 18 November the exhausted members of the MPNP adopted the transitional constitution, which included 34 constitutional principles, a section that dealt with the Constitutional Assembly, and the method for the adoption of the final constitution. It was a momentous occasion for all South Africans. For those of us who had been negotiating for almost two years, there was a double celebration. Ramaphosa had just turned 40, and we partied through the night.

Showdown in Mmabatho

The first meeting of the multiparty Transitional Executive Council (the watchdog TEC, proposed by Ken Andrew's committee) was held on 7 December. It was the formal beginning of transitional government under which the National Party continued to enjoy its status under the existing constitution – it remained the majority in parliament – but was divested of absolute power. South Africa would now be governed by a government that could not act on its own: it had to do so in tandem with the TEC.

The council – which had two members from each of the MPNP contingents, including Andrew and me from the DP – met in Pretoria on a weekly basis. The management committee consisted of Ramaphosa, Meyer, Slovo, Gordhan, Zam Titus and me, assisted by the Van der Merwe-Maharaj team as the executive secretariat, and met almost continually. Administration was handled by Theuns Eloff and Gill Hutchings of a representative private-sector body, while Gordhan, Titus and I chaired the TEC and its management committee on a weekly rotating basis.

The bond forged by mutual understanding at the World Trade Centre strengthened further as we shifted from negotiation to executive action. Notable absentees from the TEC were the right-wing parties as well as Bophuthatswana, Ciskei, and the former Cosag members who had regrouped as the Freedom Alliance.

The partners to the negotiations shared in the subordinate structures of the TEC – and the spheres of authority were law and order, stability and security, defence, intelligence, local and regional government, foreign affairs, and the status of women. We moved swiftly and decisively.

We stopped the Development Bank of South Africa from making a loan of R216 million to the Bophuthatswana homeland. We instructed the police to dispatch security staff to strife-torn northern Natal. We took steps to compel the KwaZulu government to supply us with information on alleged police hit-squads. We demanded that the law and order ministry restructure its 'internal stability' division.

These crisp decisions, taken at the very commencement of our term of office, conveyed to government and the civil service the clear message that the TEC meant business and intended asserting its authority.

As 27 April grew closer, reports coming to us indicated a likelihood of country-wide industrial action in the form of strikes, demonstrations and picketing. This could easily get out of hand and undermine the election. Accordingly we called on employers and workers to resolve their disputes in the national interest; and the trade unions decided to hold back their demands until after the election.

The TEC also had to deal with matters left unresolved by the MPNP. One was the new national flag, which the management committee referred to a two-man sub-committee comprising Ramaphosa and Meyer. Week after week, looking slightly sheepish, they said they had nothing to report. On the absolutely final deadline they smiled and introduced us to Fred Brownell, the State Herald. He unrolled the new South African flag.

The members of the management committee stood and applauded. Next day all the members of the TEC on being shown the flag also stood and applauded. The flag, as required by the constitution, had arrived. Asked about its symbolism, Brownell replied that apart from the colours having an African feel, the magic resided in the fact that every person would see exactly what they wanted them to mean. It was a brilliant concept.

The major cloud over the election was the stated non-participation of the Freedom

Alliance parties. All had their different reasons. The IFP demanded a more federal arrangement – especially for KwaZulu-Natal. The CP and General Viljoen (leader of the Freedom Front) demanded greater protection for the Afrikaans language and culture, and a degree of self-determination in the form of a *volk*staat. Bophuthatswana and Ciskei were holding out for some form of recognition as autonomous states.

The matter came to a head when the Independent Electoral Commission reported that it could not complete its arrangements unless there was certainty about whether the inhabitants of Bophuthatswana and Ciskei would be recognised as South African citizens and vote in the election. The reality, of course, was that this would indeed be the case.

Lucas Mangope, chief minister of Bophuthatswana, was contacted in his capital, Mmabatho, and informed that his 'subjects' would be recognised as South African citizens and had to be allowed to vote. Would he assist? In truth it did not matter: by March Mmabatho was in a state of insurrection. The civil servants were on strike, and stoppages spread to other sectors of the community. There were incidents of looting and damage to property. The police were unable to cope with the situation.

Mangope contacted General Viljoen and requested armed volunteers to assist in restoring law and order. He may have had a mutinous army in mind, but memories of the invasion of the World Trade Centre were fresh.

Viljoen at that stage saw in an independent Bophuthatswana a possible constitutional model for a future Afrikaner *volk*staat and was only too willing to assist. He called on various commandos loyal to him to gather their arms and come to Mangope's rescue. Terr'Blanche, naturally, as leader of the far-right AWB, saw an opportunity to mobilise his own men and enter the fray. Neither Mangope nor Viljoen had anticipated Terr'Blanche's intervention – and made it clear to him that his irregulars were not welcome and should withdraw. When, in fact, some South African troops did arrive, Terr'Blanche's men starting pulling out. A fatal incident then took place.

A car in which three AWB militants were leaving Mmabatho became separated from the main body of vehicles. A couple of Bophuthatswana police stopped their car, ordered them out, and threatened to shoot them. The three were on the ground pleading for mercy when one of the policemen opened fire, killing them all in the full view of the world's press. The gruesome sight shocked newspapermen and television viewers around the globe. It also shocked right-wingers out of their romantic illusion that they could achieve their political objectives by force.

It certainly shocked Viljoen, who a few months previously had called the young men under his sway to perform military training. It reinforced his recent decision to register his new party, the Freedom Front (FF), with the IEC with a view to taking part in the election – and strengthened his resolve to attempt to achieve Afrikaner self-determination through democratic means. After that day in Mmabatho he never veered from this course. In retrospect, the march on Bisho had set a precedent for the demise of the 'independent' homelands. A few functioning casinos were left.

At about nine o'clock on 13 March, the night of the Mmabatho killings, two helicopters took off from Waterkloof air base heading for Bophuthatswana. One was conveying Pik Botha, George Meiring (head of the defence force), Fanie van der Merwe and Maharaj to Mangope's farm home to tell him that the South African government no longer recognised him as the president of Bophuthatswana. The other was taking Ramaphosa, Meyer and me (I was chairperson of the TEC that week) and a couple of staff members to the South African embassy in Mmabatho. There, with Dr Tjaart van der Walt, the South African ambassador, we were to wait for the first group to complete their mission to Mangope.

When they returned and reported I imagined how Mangope felt betrayed by the South African government that had backed him through thick and thin, and supported him in the face of international rejection.

We proceeded to make arrangements for the TEC and the South African government to take over authority in Bophuthatswana. Was this a takeover of an independent state by a foreign country? Was it a coup?

On balance it was the latter. We decided that, save for the change at the top, where we appointed Van der Walt and TR (Job) Mogorro as joint administrators, the administration of Bophuthatswana could remain in place for the meanwhile.

Back at Waterkloof in the early hours of the morning, Fanie van der Merwe, with a twinkle in his weary eyes, said to me: 'Colin, I never thought I would live to see a good liberal like you, the defender of constitutions, taking part in a coup!'

I returned home to Clifton later, by which time Joyce, having abandoned a weekend in Hermanus, was also there.

By Monday I was back in Pretoria and received news that was going to change my personal life. Joyce had collapsed in a competition at the Mowbray Golf Club and been rushed by ambulance to City Park Hospital. A short while later Zach, who had been called in to assist medically, called me to say that Joyce was seriously ill and under heavy sedation. I immediately returned to Cape Town.

In hospital, with her eyes half-closed and the mere suggestion of a smile, Joyce whispered: 'Hello, love.'

A few days later she was diagnosed with multiple myeloma, a cancer of the spinal bone marrow. That night I wept quietly for my life-loving lover and companion of 44 years.

26

Towards a 'new history'

That politicians have a private life is no secret; what does generally remain concealed is the depth of passion, support and commitment that arises in the best of these relationships. Without them, few public lives can survive the stresses of decision and responsibility that become their lot. Joyce's diagnosis would prove fatal within a few years – and I shall summon my resources to give the essential details in the course of my narrative. But I ask my readers to allow us the essential privacy of devoted life-partners as I detail the public events that shaped South Africa's future, and how, as a participant, I wrestled with the commanding issues of each day as it arose.

By March 1994 the TEC was in full spate; the agenda for council meetings usually ran to ninety pages. Work was mainly related to the election or the removal of obstacles to the election, or the demand for policy decisions outside the Electoral Commission's terms of reference. The TEC also had the responsibility of dealing with the legal implications of the ousting of Mangope, and of ensuring that the public services in Ciskei and Bophuthatswana ran effectively.

We remained seized with the issue of violence and concerned that the Freedom Alliance parties were still staying out. In fact, though, as a result of untiring efforts by De Klerk and Mandela, and international pressure, Alliance parties started coming on board. The Freedom Front would participate. Even Buthelezi – as the result of a formal undertaking that there would be international mediation on outstanding issues – did so at the last moment. Until the final week before 27 April it was touch and go. Then the IFP signalled its willingness, and millions of stickers with the IFP's name and logo had to be printed and stuck on the existing ballot papers.

It was an election very different to the nine I had fought since first standing as a candidate in Pinelands in 1958. It was not a 'whites only' election. Indeed, it was more than an election: it was an endorsement of South Africa's new democratic constitution and a celebration of a miracle of political reconciliation. With apartheid no longer the dominant issue, the basic question was: who did the people want to lead them under the new constitution? For the majority it was seen as a choice between Mandela and the ANC, or De Klerk and the NP.

For someone like me, accustomed to parliamentary elections in a constituency, taking part in an election on the basis of proportional representation was an unusual experience. A candidate did not become an MP because of special skills and attributes, or support in a constituency. He became one by virtue of the number of votes cast for his party on a nationwide basis and of the position he held on the list of the party he represented. The contest was centralised, and relied heavily on opinion polls, newspaper and television advertisements, and public relations events. For the first time there were television debates along the lines of the presidential debates in the US.

The DP ran an efficient, albeit modest election campaign. We were competing against two big parties and big names. De Klerk and Mandela had recently been jointly awarded the Nobel Peace Prize. What we hoped was to hold our own among white voters, and – based on the result of the 1989 'whites only' election – to win 4% of the votes which would translate into at least sixteen seats in the new National Assembly.

On 27 April I rose early. I wanted to be one of the first to vote. I parked my car and walked along Main Road to the voting station at the Green and Sea Point civic centre. I passed the usual mix of people up and about at that early hour: black, white, Coloured; businessmen, typists, shop assistants, municipal workers, newspaper vendors and layabouts. Near the civic centre I saw people queuing to cast their equal votes. Freed of the insidious impact of discrimination, all were South Africans – not 'us' and 'them'.

Voting was an enriching and satisfying experience. In its glow I reflected on the characters of those with whom I had been privileged to work to reach this day. I would miss them: the remarkable twosome, Fanie van der Merwe and Mac Maharaj; Zam Titus, a lawyer from Transkei, modest, self-effacing, strong in his commitment, generous in his relationships, a stickler for detail; Pravin Gordhan, a qualified pharmacist, agent in Operation Vula, a member of the SACP and one of the cleverest people I had ever worked with.

Roelf Meyer and Cyril Ramaphosa – whose names were always coupled together – had oiled the wheels of negotiation. They complemented each other but were different in style and personality. Ramaphosa drove the process; Meyer eased the pain of surrender. And Ramaphosa was astute enough to concede Meyer enough to fulfil that task. He was a highly competitive leader prepared to go up-front, giving and taking. Meyer left the impression he could get more from Ramaphosa by holding back and talking to him in private.

Particularly close to my political and private soul was Joe Slovo, most remarkable of them all. Charming and intelligent, he was a creative lateral thinker with a deep human understanding. It was he who produced the draft of the 'no turning back' statement issued by Codesa at the time of the 'whites only' referendum on reform. He proposed that all meetings of Codesa and the MPNP should be open to the public. And he insisted on 27 April 1994 as the date for the election, focusing minds and energies.

Through an article in a South African communist newspaper, he broke the deadlock on power-sharing. His approach was summed up in a letter to Constand Vil-joen: 'The biggest threat to general Afrikaner aspirations comes not from us, but from those who hanker after a past that can be no more. You can make it possible for us to share a new history.'

Slovo's interventions often shaped debate at the World Trade Centre, and it was not surprising that his ANC colleagues often deferred to the views of 'Comrade Joe'.

I had many off-the-record discussions with him. Once I commented that the ANC would not gain ground among white voters as long as it had the albatross of the Communist Party around its neck. 'That may or may not be,' he responded. 'However, they should be grateful for the influence that the Communist Party has had on the ANC in years gone by. It helped to move the ANC from being a black party to becoming a multiracial party. It helped the ANC to change from being primarily a nationalist party to being a party with a sense of social concern.'

When Slovo learned that Joyce was suffering from multiple myeloma, the same condition from which he suffered, he never failed to ask after her.

The ANC was deeply fortunate to have had Comrade Joe on their team.

Consequences of the democratic election

The election was a triumph for democracy and a massive endorsement of the negotiations. Although sporadic violence continued during the run-up to the poll, especially in northern Natal, it did not disrupt the voting. Certainly there were a few administrative problems, such as the late arrival of ballot papers and the late opening of voting stations. However, these were not serious enough to have an impact.

A surprisingly large number of South Africans – 22 million of them – turned out to vote, most of them for the first time. At some voting stations the turnout was so heavy that many had to stand patiently in queues that snaked across the open veld to make their precious mark. Other stations had to be kept open after the official closing time to give voters waiting outside their turn.

The counting of votes under the supervision of the IEC went relatively smoothly, except in northern Natal where the possibility of irregularities with ballot boxes was a concern. Even there the Commission, after discussions with representatives of the participating parties, was able to declare a result acceptable to all.

When the IEC was able to announce the final result on 5 May it showed that the ANC with 62,56% of the votes had sufficient to ensure its presidential candidate would be elected – and it would qualify for an executive vice-president and 18 members of the cabinet. However, it was short of the 66,7% that would have enabled it to adopt the final constitution on its own.

The NP with 20,39% was entitled to an executive vice-president and six members of the cabinet. The IFP (10,58%) could have three cabinet members. The Freedom Front tallied 2,2%, the DP a disappointing 1,7%, the PAC and African Christian Democratic Party making up the rest with 1,2% and 0,5% respectively.

I had anticipated being a member of the new non-racial parliament and enjoying the fruits of more than thirty years of hard work to make such a parliament a reality. Uncomfortable doubts settled in as the results began coming through from the black townships and far-flung rural areas, and the percentage of DP votes started dropping towards the figure below which I would not be re-elected. At one stage I said to myself: 'How unfair it would be if I, who fought for 30 years against apartheid and for a non-racial democracy, was voted out of parliament and those bloody Nats, the architects of apartheid who brought South Africa close to the brink of disaster, would enjoy the pleasure and the honour of being members of South Africa's new democratic parliament – which they fought against for over forty years!'

When the final result was announced, I barely skimmed over the electoral hurdle and was number five in the DP team of seven. The election was less kind to Zach; indeed, it was cruel. In every election the party leader generally gets the credit for success and the blame for failure. This was even more so in the case of this election where voters chose a party, and in which the party leader, as its symbol, had a critically important role.

The dice were loaded against De Beer. He was up against De Klerk and Mandela, the most prominent leaders driving transformation and reconciliation. Millions had seen them debating on television – and rounding off by shaking hands as a symbol of mutual understanding and national unity. Zach, who remained a highly respected political leader, had not done particularly well. What people did not know was that he was under heavy medication for vascular and cardiac problems and contemplating retirement at an appropriate time after the election.

Senior members of the party called on Zach to advise him they thought the time had come for him to stand down. Zach asked me as a friend for my frank opinion. It was that if he was contemplating retirement, then it was in both his own interest and that of the party to do so at that time. Zach thanked me for helping him with his decision. Next morning he handed in his resignation as an MP to the secretary of parliament. Two weeks later, on Saturday 2 May, at a special DP meeting, Tony Leon was elected the new leader in preference to Ken Andrew, the only other candidate.

I had a high regard for Leon's capabilities. I thought at the time that his youthful drive and forceful style would be assets for the party. For all this, I felt that when it came to the judgement of people and issues, Andrew would be more reliable. Although I voted for Andrew, once Leon had been elected I had no difficulty in giving him my support and, at times, my advice. This is not to say that he always followed it.

On 7 April members of the newly-elected National Assembly met in the chamber that PW Botha had had built ten years before to house the Tricameral parliament. Their task that day was to elect South Africa's new president. I tried to imagine the feelings of the new members who had never before had either a vote or the opportunity to be elected to parliament. I considered the feelings and emotions of those who had spent years in exile, or who as MK members had fought a bush war, or been imprisoned on Robben Island, or been detained, or banned or silenced.

Amidst an outpouring of emotion, the Assembly unanimously elected Nelson Mandela, Prisoner No. 46664, as the first president of the new South Africa.

On 10 May Joyce accompanied me on a special flight to attend the swearing-in of President Mandela at the amphitheatre in front of the Union Buildings in Pretoria. Ill though Joyce was, nothing was going to prevent her from being present.

It was a very special occasion: powerful in its meaning and poignant in its symbolism. A peaceful, orderly transfer of power was effected: a triumph of good over evil, the dominance of reconciliation over revenge.

For me, among all the big moments, there were two very special ones. The first was when the bemedalled military and police generals saluted the former Robben Island prisoner as their president and commander-in-chief. The second was when military aircraft, followed by helicopters bearing the new South African flag, flew over in a low-altitude salute.

The following day Mandela announced his cabinet, and the Government of National Unity (GNU) got down to business. The Constituent Assembly consisting of the 400 members of the National Assembly, together with the 90 senators, met on 14 May and elected Ramaphosa and Leon Wessels as chairman and vice-chairman respectively.

The final phase of South Africa's constitutional transformation, that of drawing up the new constitution, commenced.

The new parliament in action

While the CA functioned from May 1994 to December 1996, the new Government of National Unity under Mandela's presidency found its feet and the members settled into their role as legislators and representatives of the people. I was amazed at how quickly people, with no prior experience of government or parliament, found their respective roles. This certainly dispelled the myth, believed by many white South Africans, that 'they' were not ready to assume public office.

During this period MPs, especially those in smaller parties such as the DP, carried a heavy workload. Generally, Mondays, Tuesdays and Wednesdays were devoted to normal parliamentary functions. On Thursdays and Fridays MPs became members of the CA and worked on the new constitution in various sub-committees – including what were termed theme committees.

The bills before parliament consisted largely of amendments to or the repeal of existing laws to bring them into line with the new constitution. But relatively soon bills started to reflect policy decisions of the GNU. The most important was that related to the Reconstruction and Development Programme (RDP), a socio-economic concept designed to address the inequalities and backlogs in housing, employment, and social and community services.

A blow to the government and a loss to parliament was Slovo's death on 6 January 1995. After only a few months in office, he had begun to make a real impact as Minister of Housing.

In addition to its changed racial composition the new parliament differed from the old in the system it adopted for carrying out its legislative and oversight functions. Instead of plenary sessions, there were 27 portfolio committees – one for each ministerial department. These meetings were open to the public and the media, and their procedures made provision for public participation in the form of submissions and relevant evidence.

While this method of functioning gave MPs more opportunity to influence the making of laws, and gave them greater access to the ministers and their departments, it increased the strain of work. Another new element was a sharp increase in the number of foreign visitors wanting to interact with parliament and its members, and in the number of overseas visits taken by MPs. This was understandable. For years the previous parliament had been cut off from Africa, shunned by most countries, and denied membership of international organisations such as the Commonwealth Parliamentary Association and the SADC Parliamentary Forum.

In addition, the budget of the new parliament made provision for portfolio committees to travel abroad to study and learn from the experience of other countries. I found that as the DP's chief constitutional negotiator and the party's representative on the portfolio committees of Foreign Affairs and Constitutional Development, my schedule of foreign visits, already substantial, increased enormously.

The DP's parliamentary team was led by Tony Leon, and consisted of the leader, Ken Andrew, Dene Smuts, Douglas Gibson, Mike Ellis, Kobus Jordaan and me in the National Assembly; and with three members in the Senate, we were developing into a small but effective opposition. By contrast the NP, led by Deputy-Executive President De Klerk, with 83 members in the Assembly, was struggling to establish its identity. Having been the majority party for so long, it had difficulty adjusting to the reality of being a minority party in an ANC-led government.

If the NP was struggling, its white supporters were totally confused. They had voted for the NP as an alternative, if not an opposition, to the ANC. Yet, having done so, they found that their MPs were in fact in a government with an ANC that called all the shots.

Their perception was that the NP was neither a government, nor an alternative, nor an opposition. This ambivalence marked the beginning of the decline of the NP, which led to its disintegration and, ultimately, its dissolution.

In September 1994 I decided to make another attempt to have the 'anti-defection' clause removed from the transitional constitution by introducing a private member's bill for its repeal. Procedure was that once a bill had been tabled it was referred to a portfolio committee on Private Member's Legislative Proposals and Petitions for analysis, debate and a decision on whether parliament should proceed further. My bill generated considerable debate, among not only politicians but members of the public and media.

By the time it came up for decision in the committee in February 1995, there were indications that support for the bill was growing. Ramaphosa, secretary-general of the ANC, in his end-of-year report had said the matter would have to be looked at again. The NP, which had previously adopted a reserved position on the issue, came out against the clause when De Klerk said, after an extended NP caucus meeting, that 'in principle we are not happy with this clause'. The NP 'believed that the right of elected members to re-group across party political lines be entrenched'.

Individual MPs from various parties objected to the regulation that anyone who resigned from his party would lose his seat, saying it restricted the constitutional right to freedom of speech and forced MPs to toe the party line. Dr Frene Ginwala, Speaker of the National Assembly, said in a public speech that the clause could indeed be considered a restriction on MPs' freedom of speech.

At the time there were calls for a free vote in parliament. However, when the bill finally came up for decision, the party whips swung into action. The ANC voted against the bill; the NP and the PAC abstained; and the IFP, FF and ACDP were not present. Only the DP voted for it. As far as parliament was concerned, my bill was dead. However, its impact had not faded. MPs as members of the CA resolved that there would be a provision in the final constitution to the effect that after a 'reasonable period of time' parliament could pass legislation that determined the circumstances in which MPs would not lose their seats if they ceased to be a member of the party that had nominated them.

It also provided for parties to merge or split. This meant that the 'anti-defection' clause did not need a vote of two-thirds of the members and a special constitutional procedure in order to amend or repeal it. It could be changed by a simple majority vote.

Early in 1995 I learned from friends in Italy that the various local communities were organising a series of functions to commemorate the 50th anniversary of the battle of Monte Solé and the liberation of the city of Bologna. Joyce and I decided to join a group of some twenty South African veterans planning to be in Italy for the anniversary. However, in view of the involvement of South African forces in this decisive battle, I felt that the South African government and the South African Defence Force should be represented as well.

Having received a negative response from the head of the SADF, I approached Ronnie Kasrils, deputy minister of Defence, who was in charge of matters relating to war veterans. He was sympathetic, and helped to get the wheels turning. The result was that the Speaker agreed to send three MPs representing parliament. A general would represent the SADF; Kasrils would represent the government; and a request would be made to Mandela to send a message.

In addition, Kasrils arranged for another group of veterans to be in Italy to take part in the commemorations during the period 18-21 April.

After my return I approached the Speaker to ask her to consider that parliament itself commemorate the 50th anniversary of VE Day on 9 May. She consulted the various parties, and it was decided that parliament would go ahead and simultaneously commemorate the first anniversary of our democratic parliament.

On 9 May MPs met in a solemn and reflective mood. I felt emotional as I spoke on behalf of the DP:

'We are gathered both to remember the sacrifices of our fellow citizens, and to celebrate the anniversaries of two profoundly significant events. The one the establishment, last year, of South Africa's first democratically elected parliament – a momentous event for the people of our country. The other the end, 50 years ago, of the war in Europe – a momentous event for all mankind.

'It is appropriate that the installation of our new democratic parliament and the end of the war in Europe should be celebrated on a shared occasion – for there is a vital linkage between these two events. Indeed, out of the agony of the last world war, was established the moral basis on which our democratic constitution is based. A war directed to the destruction of the system of Nazism and fascism based on the myth of racial superiority, had as a consequence the setting in motion of a process of the liberation of mankind from other prevailing systems based on racial discrimination, on colonialism and on domination.'

Members moved outside and gathered on the steps of parliament afterwards, around a flag-covered dais bearing the glass-covered caskets of the roll of honour of South Africans who had died in the two world wars. Representatives of the political parties laid wreaths in honour of the South Africans who had sacrificed their lives in all wars for freedom and democracy.

The final constitution, May 1994-December 1996

The deadline for the final constitution was 8 May 1996. Codesa and the MPNP had been very much part of a peace process between an oppressive government about to relinquish power and a liberation movement about to take over. The Constitutional Assembly did not reflect the struggle syndrome; it did not involve a massive transfer of power, but rather a means of devising a system in which that power could be exercised in an orderly way.

The CA was an agreed, structured process; the new constitution had to comply with 34 constitutional principles. If the negotiations had been characterised by a two-sided table, the CA process was represented, if not by a round, at least by an oval table. Decisions were to be taken not by the rule-of-thumb 'sufficient consensus' but by a vote of two-thirds of all the members of the CA. Nor would the CA sit in judgement of its own performance; once the constitution had been adopted by parliament it would still have to be certified by the Constitutional Court before it came into operation.

The CA was funded by the National Treasury from funds appropriated by parliament. It had an effective executive arm headed by an executive director, Hassan Ebrahim, and two deputy directors in a city office building near parliament. It decided to carry out its mandate through the following structures:

- The 490 members of the CA itself would meet periodically to receive interim reports and confirm progress made, and at the conclusion of its work would meet formally to adopt the final constitution.
- A constitutional committee of 44 members, drawn from all political parties, would be the 'engine of negotiation'.
- Six theme committees, assisted by committees of technical experts and legal draughtsmen, would deliberate on the various facets of the constitution and report regularly to the Constitutional Committee (CC) on progress. I was the DP's sole representative on the CC, with Andrew as my alternative. However, there was an agreement that smaller parties could bring other members of the CA to meetings of the CC when it dealt with reports from the various theme committees.
- A multi-party management committee, headed by chairman Ramaphosa and vice-chairman Wessels, met once a week to establish the programme of work, to decide on the process for resolving disputes, and to ensure that the process was kept moving forward. I was the DP's representative on the management committee. While this body did not have the benefit of the Van der Merwe-Maharaj secretariat, sensitive problems that arose between the ANC and the NP were often referred to an entity known as 'the channel' – Ramaphosa and Meyer.

From September 1994 the main burden fell on the six theme committees dealing with the nature of the democratic state, the structure of government, relationships between spheres of governance, fundamental rights, the judiciary, and public administration. A feature of the CA as a whole that pleased me tremendously – given the battle I had waged in the MPNP for the functions of government and constitution-making to be kept separate – was the independence adopted by its members. While the Constitutional Assembly occupied the same premises as parliament and comprised the same 490 members, it functioned entirely separately – and developed its own conventions and style of debate.

The CA did not take its cue from either parliament or the cabinet. My main objective was to ensure that the constitutional principles were fully complied with. Where there was room for differing interpretations, I consistently argued in favour of the most liberal, democratic interpretation. Among the chief of these was: 'There shall be a separation of powers between the legislature, executive and judiciary, with appropriate checks and balances to ensure accountability, responsiveness and openness.' Members of the CA with a special interest in constitutionalism supported the view that the provisions for accountability should be effective.

The final constitution mandated that members of the cabinet and 'State Institutions Supporting Democracy' – such as the Auditor General, the Public Protector, the Human Rights Commission and the Electoral Commission – would be accountable to parliament. It also directed that the National Assembly create mechanisms for holding them and other organs of state to account, and for oversight of their executive authority.

The distribution of powers and functions between national and provincial govern-ments was hotly contested. In general the NP, IFP and DP wanted greater authority for the provinces, and the ANC less. The political parties proposed more than three hundred amendments, of which 122 were from the DP.

Midway through the process, the IFP pulled out of the negotiations, partly on this issue but also because the government and the CA were not honouring the commit-ment made to the IFP for international mediation on outstanding matters relating to the Zulu king.

By early February 1996, with 65 contentious issues unresolved and only four months left, the pressure was on. Leapfrog procedures were adopted to speed up the process. During April, in a make-or-break move, the members of the Constitutional Committee met for a three-day *bosberaad* at a conference retreat on the Cape south coast. Driven by our determination to finish on time, and the whip being cracked by chairman Ramaphosa, we made up time in almost 72 hours of non-stop negotiation. When we returned to Cape Town, weary and exhausted, the number of contentious issues had been reduced to 20. But only 33 days remained.

The orderly and structured CA process was replaced by *ad hoc* bilaterals. Con-stand Viljoen, who was on the management committee, and I voiced our disapprov-al that a number of issues due for discussion had been agreed at bilaterals between the ANC and the NP. Dene Smuts, who had a torrid time fighting for improvements to certain clauses in the bill of rights, such as those dealing with hate speech, prop-erty rights, the right to independent schools, and the limitation of rights, noted: 'The country deserved better than to have the last few big issues outstanding settled be-tween the ANC and the NP.'

By the early hours of the morning of 19 May, when the last compromises had been made and amendments accepted, the drafting of the constitution was complete. Leon called an impromptu meeting of the DA members of the CA in the lobby adjoining the old Assembly chamber. He said the issue would be whether or not we cast our votes for the final draft. The way he put the issue made me realise that he had his doubts. I decided to have my say:

'For us to vote against a constitution that is the product of negotiation between the leaders of all sections of the South African people would be for us to turn our backs on the very thing that the DP and its predecessor parties fought for, for more than thirty years.

'Secondly, the adoption of the new constitution is going to be an historic occasion. To vote against it because of some matters of detail on which we could not get our own way would be to put us on the wrong side of history. Rather than concentrating on negative features we should see the bigger picture and claim to have been part-owners of the historic constitution-making process.

'Thirdly, to the extent that we are not satisfied that the draft complied with all the constitutional principles, it is implicit in our voting for the draft that it is still subject to the scrutiny of, and certification by, the Constitutional Court.'

The following day the full CA met to consider the recommendations. One by one the party leaders went to the podium to declare their party's attitude. Mbeki, who built his speech around the theme 'I am an African', gave the ANC's endorsement. De Klerk stated the NP's support. The IFP was still not present. Viljoen spoke positively about the draft but said that in view of the disagreement that the Freedom Front had over aspects of the constitution it would abstain from voting.

Leon, in what I considered one of his best speeches throughout the long negotiating process, stated that the DP would vote for it. He was followed by Clarence Makwetu of the PAC, who said his party would vote for it, and by Reverend Kenneth Meshoe who said the ACDP would vote against.

When the vote had been counted and Wessels announced that 421 votes had been cast in favour of the adoption of the new constitution, the CA broke out in spontaneous applause and cheering, with singing from the ranks of the ANC. The NP was markedly subdued.

In the latter stages of the negotiations, I had repeatedly stated that the DP believed the draft did not comply with a number of constitutional principles. The ANC argued that the DP and I were wrong. The DP notified the Constitutional Court that we intended to challenge certain sections of the constitution. We briefed senior counsel, and spent much time setting out and refining our case.

On 1 July I accompanied three of my DP colleagues to attend the proceedings of the Constitutional Court – and was able to appreciate the seriousness and sensitivity of the process, to give judgement on what was to become the supreme law of the land and knowing that in almost all the sections to be tested, politics and law were intertwined.

The Court had received written submissions from 147 objectors ranging from political parties such as the NP, IFP, DP, CP and the ACDP, to business, labour, legal and human rights organisations, professional associations, interest groups and individuals. During its sittings from 1-5 July and 8-11 July it was addressed by a number of the country's top advocates, some on behalf of the CA and others on behalf of the objectors.

On 6 September, in a 288-page judgement, the Constitutional Court ruled that 11 principles had not been complied with. Some were procedural; others dealt with the entrenchment of fundamental rights. Yet others went to the heart of the major debates involving the powers and functions of local government.

There was very little crowing by the DP and others whose objections were upheld by the Court; and equally no cries of disappointment from the ANC and its allies. It was generally accepted that the Constitutional Court's expression of its judicial independence had added to the legitimacy of the constitution itself.

The Constitutional Bill came back to the CA where appropriate amendments were made. On 11 October the amended draft constitution was approved by 369 votes with the various parties voting in the same manner as they had on the previous occasion. The final Draft Bill was certified on 4 December.

On 10 December, International Human Rights Day, we flew to Johannesburg and from there proceeded by coach to Sharpeville where President Mandela was to sign the Constitution Act into law. A moment or two before Mandela and his entourage arrived, Helen Suzman came bustling in to take her place next to us in a row of reserved seats. She had been about to leave home by car when Mandela phoned her and asked her to accompany him to Sharpeville by helicopter.

At Sharpeville before the signing Helen went with Mandela to the field outside the police station where the police had fired on the people in March 1961. Mandela unveiled a plaque recording the event and commemorating those who had died.

Mandela's action in inviting her to accompany him to this ceremony – with so much emotional content for those who had suffered under apartheid – was a demonstration of his respect for Helen and the role she had played in the fight against apartheid; a sensitive and powerful tribute of one great South African to another.

PART VIII

Mandela and after

27

South Africa under Mandela
1994-1997

One of the features of the Mandela presidency was his warm and inclusive style. While he recognised the dominant role of the ANC as the majority party, he tried to make all the parties feel they had a role to play in government. The NP and IFP, by virtue of the fact that each had polled more than 5% in 1994, were automatically included in the new Government of National Unity; the FF, DP and others, who had polled less, were not.

Mandela appeared to regret this and went out of his way to make us feel we belonged. On occasions when Leon, whose style was generally combative and blunt, expressed a view in parliament with which Mandela disagreed, he would phone Leon and suggest they meet and talk it over. On occasion he suggested that Leon bring me along.

The atmosphere was convivial: although Mandela and Leon often failed to reach agreement, their disagreement was always in the context of two men who understood and acknowledged the role each had to play.

Sometimes Mandela would tell Tony there was no need to go on the attack in parliament. Perhaps it would be better if, instead, the two of them just talked things over. This inclusiveness touched most of his dealings – when he was in the process of restoring relations with Buthelezi he asked Leon and me to lunch with him and 'Shenge' – as he called Buthelezi when they were together.

Again, a few months into his presidency, Mandela let it be known to Constand Viljoen and Leon that he would be pleased to consider appointing a member of each of their parties as a South African ambassador. Leon immediately put forward the name of Zach de Beer to Mandela, who in turn had no hesitation appointing him South African ambassador to the Netherlands.

Zach, however, was strangely ambivalent about his appointment. He tackled the task with typical thoroughness, and from all accounts did remarkably well. He appreciated Mandela's generosity and the confidence placed in him; yet he was not sure he really wanted to be an ambassador. Indeed, he was at a stage in his life when he was not sure that he wanted to do anything other than retire to his home in Clifton. After two years in The Hague, during which Zach and Mona became a much-liked and respected ambassadorial couple, Zach asked Mandela to relieve him of his position.

In 1997 Zach and Mona returned to their home in The Breakers, an apartment block across the road from mine and, like mine, overlooking Clifton First Beach.

In February 1997, in a move that surprised many, none more so than the ANC, Mandela invited Leon to join the cabinet of the GNU. Leon, as one would have expected, gave the matter much thought, and discussed it with his colleagues in the DP. We realised that the offer was in line with the mood of reconciliation that prevailed during the Mandela presidency. However, we felt that for Leon to become part of an ANC government would have emasculated the opposition. The key event that caused Tony to decide to thank Mandela, yet decline his offer, was when Mandela explained to him that the rule was that there could be robust debate on issues at cabinet meetings, but once a decision had been taken, all members were expected to support it.

I believed that Leon's decision was the correct one.

Mandela's actions early one morning on the Jewish holy day of Rosh Hashana illustrated his warmth and inclusiveness. As had been his habit since his Robben Island days, he rose early and, looking through his engagement book, noticed that it was Rosh Hashana. He decided it was a good occasion to phone his Jewish friends and wish them well. The first number he dialled was to the home of Chief Rabbi Harris – where the person who answered told him politely that the rabbi did not take telephone calls on that particular day. Mandela then decided to phone Tony Leon – and heard Tony's recorded voice saying that he was not available to take the call.

The scene shifted to my home in Clifton, where Joyce was fast asleep while I was somewhere over Africa winging my way back from Europe. The bedside phone rang and Joyce drowsily picked up and said, 'Hullo.'

The voice said: 'Good morning. It's Mandela here.'

Joyce was about to say, 'Don't try to pull my leg,' when she paused.

'Yes,' affirmed the voice. 'It's Mandela here. President Mandela.'

Joyce sat bolt upright and said as brightly as she could: 'Oh, good morning Mr President.' Whereupon the voice, now clearly that of Mandela, said, 'Can I speak to Colin, please?'

'I'm afraid not. He's only arriving back from Europe later this morning.'

'Oh,' said Mandela, and after a short pause: 'Would you please give him a message?'

'Certainly.'

'Please tell Colin that Mandela phoned to wish him well for Rosh Hashana.'

Joyce was completely flummoxed. She hesitated for a moment then replied: 'Certainly, Mr President, I'll pass on your message – but I must tell you that Colin is not Jewish. In fact, he is a member of the Methodist Church.'

After a longish pause Mandela said: 'Ah – I'm also a Methodist.'

Whereupon the two of them chatted for a minute or two with Joyce telling Mandela how the Methodist church in Pinelands was started in the home of Colin's father and mother.

'Strange,' said Mandela. 'I've always thought that Colin was Jewish.'

322

'Oh.'

Then Mandela said: 'When I was on Robben Island at a stage when we were allowed to get newspapers, I read in the *Cape Times* of a dispute over some Jewish issue in which Colin came out very strongly in support of the Jews!'

'Oh.'

Mandela wished Joyce a good day and rang off.

When I returned home and Joyce told me the story of Mandela's early morning call, I told her that she had missed making a good point. When Mandela said he thought I was Jewish, because I had come out in support of the Jews, she should have responded by saying: 'It was not because he was Jewish but because he was a very effective member of parliament for Sea Point!'

The new parliament and the new Constitution naturally triggered interesting changes in the ANC and NP. When the new basic law came into effect in December 1996 and the work of the CA had been completed, Ramaphosa resigned from parliament and as secretary-general of the ANC to start a new career in the business world. The following year – at the ANC congress in November-December 1997 – Mandela, who had announced earlier that he would not be seeking a second term as president, stood down as president of the ANC. Thabo Mbeki was elected ANC president; Jacob Zuma deputy president; and Mosiuoa 'Terror' Lekota its chairman.

The voters, accustomed to Mandela's style and comfortable with his message of unity and reconciliation, began asking what it would be like under a future President Mbeki, about whom they knew very little. I received many invitations from organisations, service clubs, and formations of the DP to speak on the subject of 'What happens when Mandela goes?' It was an uncontroversial way of asking me what I thought of Mbeki.

I predicted there would be a distinct difference in style; nevertheless I believed that the philosophical thrust Mandela had given to government and society around the concept of national unity and reconciliation would continue well into the life of the next presidency. I thought Mandela's judgement on the timing of his retirement was correct: he had laid the foundation, set the objectives, and perhaps South Africa now needed a managerial rather than a conceptual style of governance. Mbeki was an appropriate person to take the reins.

At the same time that the ANC was going through the process of leadership change, the NP was embarking on one of self-examination and fundamental restructuring. Having been active in politics in the years when the NP's mission was to protect and promote Afrikaner interests – later broadened to protect and promote those of white South Africans – I had no doubt that the NP had lost its fundamental reason for existence. If it was going to continue, it would have to fashion a new vision and look for a new constituency.

During January 1996 it undertook a reassessment of its political role. In February it issued a document stating the core values around which it proposed to mould the opposition to the ANC. De Klerk announced that Meyer would be resigning from the cabinet to become secretary-general of the NP with responsibility for negotiation with other parties and groups with a view to forming a new broad-based opposition. Four months later De Klerk announced that he and the other NP members would be resigning from the cabinet at the end of June and that the NP would become an opposition party.

I could understand the tactical reasoning. However, it was ironic that after De Klerk had fought tooth-and-nail during the negotiations for a power-sharing GNU written into the Constitution – and had gone to the white voters for a mandate to negotiate a power-sharing deal – his party turned out to be the first to withdraw from the unity government.

Meyer set about exploring the possibilities of forming a new value-based opposition. His team engaged in extensive discussions with opposition parties – including the DP – as well as with individual groups outside the formal party structures. In the DP we had to give serious consideration to the NP's proposals against the background of the changes taking place in the political environment. There was a case to be made both for and against the NP proposals, and this dichotomy of view was also prevalent within the DP.

I had never been opposed in principle to alliances, pacts or, on occasion, mergers. However, I believed that in considering any such action one had to be satisfied that its apparent short-term tactical advantages did not conflict with strategic objectives. On this occasion, while I recognised there was a case for an opposition regrouping around a set of core values (liberal-democratic, if one wanted to describe them by name), I was convinced that given the historical baggage the NP was carrying, and its identity crisis, any alliance, regrouping or merger with the Nationalists as the largest component was unwise.

Towards the latter part of 1996 the DP had started its own process of strategic review, and in the course of doing so had given attention to its relationship with the NP. This review culminated in a leadership *bosberaad* at Lourensford estate outside Somerset West in March 1997. The conference reached an unequivocal viewpoint on the issue of its relationship with the NP: 'The strategic objective of the DP is the development of a liberal democratic alternative to the ANC's policy and style of governance. The development of [this] would be impossible if it included the NP as it is currently constituted. Therefore it is necessary that the NP as an institution be destroyed.'

While this decision did not exclude pacts, agreements or alliances for short-term tactical goals, it confirmed my view that any short-term arrangements that the DP might enter into for tactical reasons had to be subject to overriding strategic objectives. The blunt message that the DP conveyed to Meyer's team was that the dissolution of the NP was a prerequisite for the emergence of a new opposition.

I assumed that other parties and individuals must have conveyed a similar message – since it emerged that Meyer came to the conclusion that this prerequisite was a reality the NP leadership had to face. Of course, they did not take kindly to Meyer's message, and on 7 May 1997 De Klerk announced that the task group had been dis-

banded. Ten days later Meyer resigned from the NP and went on to form the United Democratic Movement with Bantu Holomisa, the former military leader of the
Transkei, recently dismissed from his post as a deputy minister in the GNU and expelled from the ANC.

On 27 August De Klerk announced his retirement from politics. The disintegration of the NP was gathering speed. The leadership vacuum was filled by Marthinus
van Schalkwyk, a relative newcomer to parliament who, for all his tactical acumen,
lacked the personality and gravitas of De Klerk. He was not helped in his task of establishing himself as a leader of stature by acquiring the nickname of '*Kortbroek*'
('short pants') and having it used with great regularity in the media.

Just as the former Progressive Party, under my leadership in the 1970s, had gained
ground as a consequence of the disintegration of the UP, the DP under Leon's leadership gained from the collapse of the NP. Owing to the restrictive effect of the
'anti-defection' clause, the NP's representation in parliament remained intact: but
indications were that at grassroots level the slide from the NP to the DP was gaining momentum.

The DP embarked on two goal-orientated promotional campaigns. One – '1997:
The Year Of The Party' – was designed to strengthen the DP at grassroots level as a
viable and effective political party. The other – 'The Leader of the Opposition' – was
designed to establish Leon as a reliable, competent leader, who could stand up to the
ANC.

The DP under Leon became an acceptable political home for NP supporters disillusioned with their party and disenchanted with its leadership. This was the situation
prior to the scheduled 1999 parliamentary and provincial council elections.

The nature of my work in parliament changed. My task as the DP's chief constitutional negotiator was over, and I began to concentrate on my task as DP spokesperson on foreign affairs and its representative on the Portfolio Committee for Foreign
Affairs. South Africa had regained its membership of the Commonwealth. It was admitted to the OAU and the Non-Aligned Movement (NAM), and took up its seat in
the General Assembly of the UN once more. So my political remit was a fruitful and
expanding one.

Not least was the fact that the South African government started playing a meaningful role in the politics of Africa. Mandela became chairman of the Council of
SADC (the Southern African Development Community). The business community ventured into Africa and found trade opportunities that had been closed to them
for decades in countries around the world. Our sportsmen and sportswomen participated in international competition, and we acted as hosts to international sports
events.

In this new environment the responsibilities of the Department of Foreign Affairs
expanded exponentially as more and more South African embassies were opened
in other countries and, reciprocally, more foreign embassies were opened in South
Africa. Mandela was enthusiastically received on state visits abroad. Heads of state,

prime ministers and political leaders visited South Africa and addressed our parliament. Those who were grappling with their own constitutional dilemmas were keen to learn more about our constitutional transformation and the process by which it took place. Many saw our new Constitution as a model for multi-ethnic, multi-cultural, developing countries.

These factors all combined to keep me occupied in new fields of study – monitoring, making contacts, and keeping abreast of developments in foreign policy and international relations. They also increased my foreign commitments, the amount of international travel I had to do, and the number of international visitors with whom I had discussions. It was intense work, but a real pleasure to be involved at a time when South Africa was seen as an example of what was right, rather than shunned as an example of what was wrong.

'Talking to the enemy': The De Hoop Indaba

An example of what South Africa's experience had to offer the world came in early May 1997. In confidence, I was asked by Valli Moosa, Minister of Provincial Administration and Constitutional Development, whether I would hold myself in readiness to take part in discussions with a number of Northern Ireland political parties and some of the South Africans involved in the constitutional negotiating process.

On 12 May Moosa's ministry issued a statement that on the initiative of Padraig O'Malley, an Irish-American academic – and with the approval and co-operation of the Northern Ireland parties – the South African government would be hosting such discussions, tentatively scheduled for the last weekend of the month.

O'Malley's office gave further details of the background to the visit, and stated that 'all parties in Northern Ireland were satisfied that the South Africans neither sought, envisaged, nor wanted to play any mediating role in Northern Ireland, and that their sole interest was in sharing their experiences'.

The statement went on: 'While the parties in Northern Ireland will be in South Africa at the same time, the Unionist parties [are] insistent that there should be no meetings, seminars or workshops which would necessitate their being in the presence of members of Sinn Fein – or even for that matter in the same physical environment. The South Africans [have] agreed to honour this request.'

On Friday 29 May ten of us – all of whom had been involved in the negotiations – together with two generals from the SANDF met at Die Herberg, a conference complex a few kilometres from the coastal village of Arniston and adjoining the government-owned De Hoop nature reserve, to prepare for the weekend's discussions.

We were told of the conditions on which the Northern Ireland parties had insisted and which the South African government had agreed to honour. The visiting parties would be divided into two groups, one containing the Unionists and the other Sinn Fein; and these groups would be kept separate throughout the conference. They would arrive one after the other in separate aircraft at the nearby military airport and be brought to the conference complex in separate motor coaches – and housed separately.

There would be separate dining rooms, recreation rooms and bars. The groups would take part in discussions with the South Africans in two separate rooms, with the South Africans alternating between each of the groups. In this way, the programme had South Africans discussing a specific subject with one group for one-and-a-half hours; and then switching over to discuss the same subject with the other group for the same period. The subjects were:

- Commitment to finding a political solution.
- Creating the environment for talks and the politics of a ceasefire.
- Building trust.
- The peace process and the decommissioning of arms.
- Ownership of the negotiating process.
- Negotiated forums: structures and participants.

The process was cumbersome, but we accepted it as a condition for the discussions taking place at all.

On each day, and until 10.30 pm, extensive time was set aside for individual consultations on both a formal and an informal basis. Informal discussions took the form of a follow-up on the issues raised at formal discussion sessions. All went well until the second morning, when I was with the Unionist Working Group (which included Peter Robinson, deputy leader of Reverend Ian Paisley's Democratic Unionist Party, and David Trimble, leader of the Ulster Unionist Party) and we were dealing with building trust.

A message came through on the intercom for all South Africans to break away and assemble for a meeting in another room. Moosa, who was in charge of the whole operation, told us he had invited President Mandela to the indaba, if only for a short while. Only a few minutes before, he had received a message from Mandela's office saying that the president had already left Cape Town by air and would be landing at De Hoop within the next half-hour. Moosa explained that he had called the meeting to discuss the rearrangement of the schedule; and, more particularly, how we were going to deal with Mandela and the commitment to maintain separation of the two groups.

Would we have Mandela addressing the two groups simultaneously with each group sitting on one side of the room? Would we put a screen down the centre of the room? Would we have to arrange for Mandela to address each group separately, bearing in mind that he only had limited time?

When we reported back to our working groups, the Unionists were emphatic: the agreement was that the two groups would be kept separate at all times. This had to be carried out to the letter.

On arrival, Mandela, accompanied by Graça Machel, was taken to each group separately. I was with the Unionists when Mandela and Graça came to address its members. He was given a warm welcome; he walked slowly around the room shaking hands with each of the Northern Irish and saying a word or two to them.

Then he sat down at the table and spoke to them in a most conversational manner. Having welcomed them to South Africa, and adding how pleased he was to be with them, he explained that, based on his own experiences, there was something he would like to share with them:

'Firstly, the most difficult thing that you as a leader have to do is to talk to the enemy. Secondly, when you do so, you will find that he is not 100% wrong and you are not 100% right.'

After emphasising this simple message, he wished them well in the important task that lay ahead. He bid them farewell and left to talk to the other group.

When Mandela was preparing to leave, some of the Northern Ireland group asked if it was possible to have a photograph taken with him. So: was it to be a photograph of the group as a whole, or of two separate groups?

Mandela agreed to be photographed separately with each of the delegates of seven parties. Our Northern Irish guests were thrilled.

The South Africans were meticulous in sticking to the separation agreement. Even when there was to be an afternoon excursion to Cape Agulhas, the southernmost tip of Africa, the groups were taken in two separate coaches. Unfortunately for one of the groups, all the refreshments had been loaded on the other coach.

The only breach of the separation rule occurred one night when, led by a vocal Kader Asmal – who had spent some years as a professor at Trinity College, Dublin – the main bar echoed to the sound of Irish folk songs. Even on this occasion members from the two groups occupied opposite ends of the bar and tried to avoid making eye contact with one another.

On the final day there was a last round of personal discussions. From these I got the distinct impression that the exercise of telling our guests about our South African experiences had made an impression on them. I asked Martin McGuinness – who led the Sinn Fein group – what odds he would give on Sinn Fein being back soon, 'talking to the enemy'. He said he would give 80% odds that this would be so. There was 'no other place to be'. He did add, however, that it would require some persuasion.

In December the following year, representatives of the seven Northern Ireland parties returned to South Africa on a consultative visit around the theme: 'Political Parties and Governments in Power-sharing Arrangements'.

Joyce

While I was busy in the CA and parliament, as well as engaged in study tours and overseas visits, Joyce dealt in a very courageous and spirited way with the cancer diagnosed in March 1994. We spent as much time together as circumstances permitted, mainly at home overlooking Clifton or at our cottage in Berg 'n See, a retirement complex adjoining the golf course at Hermanus.

Unfortunately Joyce became unable to play the game she had enjoyed so much. On occasions we joined our daughter Susan (and her husband Peter and their sons Paul and Adam) at their holiday home on the Breede River at Malgas, near Swellendam. And there were times when, despite her deteriorating health, Joyce was able to join me on the overseas trips we both so much enjoyed. So when in July 1994 I received an invitation to take part in one of the Aspen Institute's executive seminars at Aspen, Colorado, it gave us a chance to travel together.

Joyce and I decided on a holiday linked to the Aspen event. We would go to London to see my daughter Caryl, husband Mark and two sons, with their third child due on 12 June that year. From there we would fly to Norway to embark on a cruise along the Norwegian coast, and then return to London. Joyce would stay with Caryl while I went to the Aspen seminar, after which we would each fly home.

On the 120-passenger *Charl Harald* we followed the rugged Norwegian coast of fjords and bays and stopped at small towns each day to allow passengers to embark and disembark and to offload sundry cargo. I was fascinated by the way North Sea oil had brought prosperity to Norway and changed the lives of remote fishing communities. A new freeway laced through the mountains across the fjords and bays and linked the fisher folk to the rest of the country.

Back in London, Joyce stayed on with the family at Chiswick and I went to Aspen. I learned that if you want to lead in an environment of cultural diversity you have to understand the others you want to relate to, and that the starting point of understanding is to understand yourself and who you are.

Before I returned to Cape Town, my daughter Linda came across from California and we looked around the picturesque town, went white-water rafting downriver, and went for an early-morning hot-air balloon flight down the valley and across the hills.

Back in South Africa I was in time for the next round of negotiations.

In July 1995 Joyce and I, with Susan and Peter and their sons Paul and Adam, joined friends and their children for a guletting holiday along the Azure Coast of Turkey. We chartered a fine-looking gulet with cabin accommodation for 12, and, complete with ship's captain, cook and a deck hand, sailed from Bodrum past Datça to Marmaris and back again to Bodrum.

We usually sailed in the morning and during the afternoon stopped in some small harbour or cove. While at anchor, we spent the afternoons swimming, snorkeling, canoeing or playing bridge or Scrabble; or if we were tied up in a harbour we explored the town and sampled the local wines. The scenery, the harbour towns, the villages and the sea itself all combined to make this one of the best family holidays we had all ever spent.

For Joyce's 70th birthday I asked whether she would like to fly to the US to see Linda and Caryl. The plan was for Linda to fly from San Francisco where she lived to meet Joyce in Miami. The two would then holiday in Florida before going on to Cancun in Mexico. After that Linda would fly back to San Francisco, and Joyce would go to Boston where she would meet Caryl who would fly in from London.

Joyce and Caryl would spend a few days in Boston with Edna Helfet, a Pinelands family friend who had emigrated to the US. They would fly to New York to meet Peter and Audrey Soal, since Peter was then serving as a counsellor in the South African mission to the UN.

Joyce, who was always ready for an adventure, jumped at the idea. She checked with her doctor who agreed she could go; worked out dates that would fall between her treatments; and took with her instructions of what to do in case of an emergency.

She returned three weeks later, exhausted but thrilled at the experience she had with her two daughters and friends in the US, and with the opportunity of seeing some of the treasures of the ancient Mayan civilisation in Mexico.

In September 1996 I was sent as a delegate from the South African parliament to a meeting of the Inter-Parliamentary Union in Beijing. Joyce was in two minds about coming with me; but she shed her hesitation when I suggested that after Beijing we could stay over for a few days at a seaside resort in Malaysia and that afterwards she could fly to Sydney to visit Doreen Sheares, her childhood friend and bridesmaid at our wedding.

In Beijing we stayed at the Continental Grand Hotel close to the stadium and sports centre that had been constructed for the recent Asian Games. While I was at my conference, Joyce joined the other wives on excursions around Beijing and environs. An old friend, Wang Zonghie, now worked in the burgeoning private sector. He explained that the style of employment had changed dramatically over the past few years. When we were last in Beijing in 1990 more than 90% of the people worked for the state or municipality and their associated enterprises; now more than 50% worked privately.

The benefit of working for state or municipality was that one had an assured job, and was provided with housing and medical benefits, schooling for children, and a degree of security on retirement. None of these was assured in the private sector. On the other hand, the wages were three times as high and if one succeeded as an entrepreneur the financial reward was even greater. According to Wang, younger people were taking the private-sector option. This was why it was possible for so many fashion-conscious young people to drive smart new cars to the sports centre and spa adjoining the hotel.

The city's physical appearance had changed: while the parks, public buildings, monuments and Tiananmen Square were still there, most of the hutangs in the city centre had been demolished and replaced by glass-fronted high-rise commercial buildings. A modern freeway ringed the city, and an underground linked one sector with another, while motor taxis and buses had replaced the cavalcades of cyclists.

Before the end of 1996 Joyce had another unexpected source of happiness when

Caryl and Mark, who had left Cape Town in 1984 to live abroad, returned with their three young sons to live in the Cape. After that happiness, 1997 was a traumatic year.

Joyce and I decided that, with her health deteriorating and with her requiring more medical care, we should move from our Clifton apartment with its many stairs to Woodside Village, a new retirement precinct in Rondebosch that had frail care as well as communal facilities. We bought life rights in an apartment still in the planning stage. I persuaded the parent company to adjust the plans to our requirements, and gave Joyce a free hand to handle the furnishing, equipping and interior decoration of our home-to-be. In April we moved from Clifton, where we had lived for 21 years, to Rondebosch.

Since it had been 40 years since I first entered politics, my friends and colleagues in the DP very kindly decided they would like to hold a gala banquet to honour Joyce and me. The banquet, which was held in the Rotunda at Camps Bay, turned out to be a splendid affair that reflected the inclusiveness and generosity of spirit that was the hallmark of the Mandela presidency. A formal dress occasion, it was attended not only by DP members and old Progressives from around the country but by Valli Moosa, Kader Asmal and Sue van der Merwe of the ANC; Ben Skosana of the IFP; Patricia de Lille of the PAC; Leon Wessels of the NP; as well as Constitutional Court judge Albie Sachs; Dr Mamphela Ramphele, vice-chancellor of UCT; and my sister Lorna, down from Kenya.

The cherry on top was the attendance for the first part of the evening of Nelson Mandela and his companion, as she was then, Graça Machel. After a greeting and photo session with members of our family and those who would participate in the proceedings, Mandela and Graça entered the banqueting hall to an enthusiastic standing ovation. Hennie Bester, leader of the DP in the Western Cape, was master of ceremonies. Zach de Beer welcomed Mandela and the guests in his customary elegant style. Members of an African band from the Camps Bay High School got going on their marimbas and drums.

Mandela turned to me and said: 'Colin, it's time to dance.' He took Graça and I took Joyce through the crowded hall to an open space in front of the stage. Mandela, in his own inimitable style and with a broad smile, led the dancing.

Mandela thanked the band for their music, and amid applause and handshakes made his way out to another engagement. Joyce, who had been in and out of hospital over the past few weeks and wore a metal brace to support her back, thoroughly enjoyed the occasion, if not the dancing itself.

Asmal read a special message from Mandela, and this was followed by speeches from Asmal, Skosana (on behalf of Buthelezi), Helen, Tony and me. Excellent catering, fine wine and good fellowship were rounded off by brief anecdotal comments from some of those present.

It was a great evening, with Joyce deserving the tributes more than anyone present realised.

In June UCT, my *alma mater* from the 1940s, did me the honour of conferring on me the degree of Doctor of Laws, *honoris causa*. I shared the occasion with Cyril Ramaphosa and Frene Ginwala – all recognised for our contribution towards the new South African Constitution. It was a moving and emotional experience as I stood on the platform as Prof. Annette Seegers, of the Department of Political Science, introduced me to the assembly and read out the citation: 'In awarding to Cyril Ramaphosa, Colin Eglin and Frene Ginwala each an Honorary Doctor of Laws, the University wishes to make public its own identification of the three persons who were at the heart of the democratic transition and who, honoured in a symbolic grouping, allow us to capture the inter-dependence of their unique and individual contributions.

'Colin Wells Eglin has been the archetypal "eighth man" of the democratic transition, a potent intellectual source of solutions and a pillar of integrity whenever expediency, self-interest or political inexperience threatened the negotiations that led to a new order and a new Constitution in South Africa. He is not an active politician, but rather a capable and principled person serving his country through political activity.

'In the severe apartheid years, when people of colour were systematically stripped of elementary political and economic rights, Eglin became one of the forward-looking United Party MPs who felt that policies of racial discrimination were at the heart of the country's ills. In 1959, this group broke away from the UP and founded the Progressive Party. When the era of negotiation eventually dawned, Eglin's negotiating skills were given due recognition and he became a key figure at the constitutional talks at Kempton Park.

'He was an omnipresent figure at the Codesa talks at the World Trade Centre, respected not only for his intellectual grasp and drafting skills, but because his integrity and overriding concern for the national interest were plain to all. After the initial Codesa debacle, Eglin formed part of the ten-person Planning Committee which resuscitated the multi-party negotiations with remarkable success.

'A democratic society is finally emerging from the turmoil of transition, and this University wishes to honour Colin Eglin as one of the core figures who helped to make this possible.'

I was capped by Vice-Chancellor Ramphele, on the same spot where I had been awarded my Bachelor of Science degree 51 years previously. I am sure that Joyce, sitting in the hall, shared my feelings and emotions.

The end was in sight. In the weeks that followed, Joyce's condition deteriorated. She was re-admitted to Groote Schuur hospital and taken from there to the intensive-care unit in City Park hospital in Cape Town. She lingered for ten days in a semi-delirious state. In a hushed voice she still inquired about the result of the examination she knew that Linda was due to write. She said she was worried that I would not be able to keep the books of household accounts she had managed so diligently over the years. She managed to smile slightly when one of the family was allowed to see her.

She died peacefully in her sleep on the morning of 27 August 1997.

Seeing her lying on her bed with no movement of her lips, or flicker of her eyes, I realised how irreversible death is. I was overwhelmed with messages of sympathy and support. I came to realise, perhaps more even than when Joyce was alive, how privileged I had been to be able to share 48 years with a great lady and wonderful wife.

Young Adam, Susan and Peter's son, without realising it, spoke for all of us close to Joyce when he said: 'Now that Grandma is gone, we won't really be a family, will we?'

The 1999 election: reshaping the opposition

Towards the end of 1998 I had to decide whether I would stand for re-election in May the following year. I was in two minds. The frustrations and irritations that go with being a public representative were building up: not least of these was that under the new electoral system, MPs were the agents of their political parties rather than representatives of the people.

My spell in public life and parliament had lasted for some thirty years. Perhaps at my age I deserved a break. On the other hand, I still enjoyed my work in parliament and the camaraderie among the members of the small DP caucus. I felt I had a role to play, both in helping to shape the conventions and thrust of the new parliament, and helping keep alive the liberal values for which so many of us had worked so long and hard.

I had no doubt that were Joyce still alive, I would have retired from parliament and we would have enjoyed life together.

However, I was on my own, and parliament was an important anchor. I put my name forward as a candidate for nomination. The DP had done extensive research and consultation in the preparation of a detailed policy manual. This set out both the shortcomings of government policy and performance, and the DP's alternatives for each ministerial portfolio and all major policy issues.

In addition, the DP had been working hard on the marketing side. As a consequence of the party list system, and the fact that the new parliament would elect the next president, election campaigns were more sophisticated and costly. Increasing use was being made of radio, TV and information technology to convey the message; and of market surveys, opinion polls, and focus group analyses to prepare it for consumption.

In addition to its own in-house experts, the DP engaged the services of Doug Schoen, a young American with experience of analysis and marketing in a number of US campaigns. A number of candidates, office-bearers and MPs were invited to Durban for a preview of the details.

A large banner in DP colours was unfurled, bearing in bold letters the words: 'FIGHT BACK'. There was a moment of silence, and then applause. When comments were invited, I said I had reservations.

'The slogan "Fight Back", standing on its own, could be the slogan of the New National Party (NNP), or even that of Eugene Terr'Blanche of the AWB. To be credible as the slogan for a party like the DP, it has to say what the party is fighting back about.'

The head table responded. The intention was that the slogan be used frequently in conjunction with phrases supporting human rights, the fight against crime, and for job-creation. The matter was left there.

'Fight Back' it was. The cover of each candidate's handbook carried a photo of a determined-looking Leon with the caption: 'The guts to fight back'. In due course the words became the symbol of the DP's political philosophy. The slogan aroused passions both for and against; and helped persuade hundreds of thousands of Nationalists and disillusioned right-wingers to vote for the DP for the first time. The DP's share of the vote increased.

The number of NNP seats fell from 83 to 27; the Freedom Front from ten to three; and the DP's rose from seven to 38. The party's tactical objective of becoming the second largest party and the official opposition was achieved. But for the vast majority of South Africans, who had been liberated from race discrimination and the oppression of apartheid, 'Fight Back' put the DP on the wrong side of history.

In May Zach de Beer died of a massive stroke. Three days later family members, friends, party colleagues, business associates, journalists and individuals whose lives had been enriched by their association with Zach gathered in the Bishops' Chapel at his old school in Cape Town to pay their last respects and remember his many-faceted life.

In the National Assembly the 38 DP members occupied the benches on the opposition side close to the Speaker; Leon had the seat of the leader of the opposition, with Joe Seremane, the party chairman, Ken Andrew and me joining him on the front benches. Spreading the work that had been handled by seven members to 38 certainly reduced the scope of the activity for which each of us was responsible. However, being the official opposition increased the intensity of our work and the demands of policy formulation.

As opposition spokesman on foreign affairs – and in particular on events in Africa and around the world that impinged on South Africa's interests – I had to keep abreast of developments and informed as best I could on all relevant foreign policy matters.

A few days after the election Leon came to speak to me in my new spacious, elegant office about my feelings as leader of the opposition in the 1970s and 1980s.

I told him I had found there were two differences between the leader of a small opposition party and the leader of the official opposition. A governing party could afford to be generous to the leader of a small party, since it posed no threat. The government's attitude to the official opposition was markedly different: 'The government party will not be generous. You will be its main target. If it can break you or damage you, it will be able to break or damage its main opposition.

'Secondly, as the leader of a small political party you could afford to be held to account for the small part of the nation that had voted for you, or to be seen to be promoting your party's interests ... You now hold the status of an alternative president, and will have to be seen speaking for the nation and putting the interests of the nation ahead of your party. You will have to give leadership and guidance not only to the members of your party but to opposition-minded people in general. Of course you are the leader of a political party, but as leader of the opposition you will have to rise above being merely the leader of your party.'

That night I must have been thinking of my conversation with Leon, for I dreamed about Sir de Villiers Graaff, leader of the opposition for 21 years, who had soldiered on with a great sense of duty but no breadth of vision until his party started disintegrating and finally disbanded. Next morning I told Leon of my dream. I said: 'Tony, make sure that you are not going to be another Graaff!'

The dramatic growth of the Democratic Party initiated a process of change in the character of the party. Before June 1999 the DP and its predecessors had been liberal-democratic formations committed to policies based on liberal values. After the election it acquired the character of a broad-based centre party focused on opposing the ANC. Perhaps this character change was inevitable; some would say it was desirable.

Inevitable, perhaps – because unlike during previous surges of rapid growth, the majority of more than a million citizens who had voted DP for the first time, and whom the DP now had to represent, were not liberals, nor on the way to becoming liberal democrats. The liberal core within the party was not large enough or strong enough to absorb the newcomers into the fold without diluting its liberal thrust. This character change was the direct consequence of the electoral success of the 'Fight Back' campaign.

On the desirability of the change I had reservations, for I believed that the liberal values written into the Constitution would only be secure when the public had come to embrace them, and the political parties to respect them. I believed that South Africans like me who believed in these values still had an important role to ensure that they were entrenched and not eroded.

Within the parliamentary caucus and around the country there were those who remained deeply committed to liberal values. Helen Suzman's influence remained a potent factor.

By this time I had decided that managing a political party was for younger people and not for septuagenarians. I no longer served on any executive committees or elected councils of the party. Despite this I was pleased to sense that my colleagues in caucus listened to my comments and suggestions with a degree of respect; and that at times individual members, including Leon, sought my opinion on matters of policy and tactics.

There was convergence among the opposition parties. In the Western Cape, where no party had achieved an overall majority at provincial level, the DP with five seats and the NNP with 17 formed a coalition to become the government of the province. At a meeting in Durban in June, the DP's federal council unanimously resolved 'to give a mandate to leadership to conclude agreements with opposition parties within the framework of the document presented to the council'.

The document, *inter alia*, considered that:

- The overriding consideration in South Africa today is the consolidation of our democracy.
- The greatest threat to the consolidation of democracy in our country is one-party dominance by the ANC.

Leon, in terms of this mandate, invited the NNP to fight the coming local government election under the DP banner. When I read of Leon's invitation and learned of the federal council's resolution, I was astonished at the speed with which the concept of opposition realignment was gaining ground. My view until then had been that, with the NNP clearly in deep trouble and the DP gaining strength, it would have been preferable for the DP to use the election to administer the *coup de grâce* to the NNP rather than provide it with a political lifebelt.

Van Schalkwyk, the NNP leader, did not accept Leon's invitation. However, he and Leon agreed to consider exploring co-operation between their parties.

Since I was not a member of Leon's inner circle on strategy, I was surprised when he asked me to take part in a meeting of representatives of the two parties. As the discussions progressed I realised that public opinion and electoral good sense pointed to the need for some form of unity between the DP and the NNP at the coming election. It would be better to achieve that by absorbing the NNP into a single opposition before the election rather than help keep it alive and have to deal with it afterwards. Although I had no specific mandate from the party leadership, I addressed the NNP members frankly about the DP's strategic objectives, the obstacles that stood in the way of achieving them, and the options open to the party.

I said there would be fundamental conditions for unification. These were that the visions and principles of the new party would be those of the DP; policies and programmes would be based on those of the DP; the organisational thrust would have to rely on the structures of the DP; the leadership would be that of the DP; and the name and logo of a coalition should bear no resemblance to that of the NNP.

I was given a mandate to ensure there was no misunderstanding of the conditions that the DP considered basic for achieving a single opposition party. On this basis, as the talks continued, I stated that there were only two realistic alternatives: a protracted war of attrition, or to use the local government election for moving ahead rapidly.

Representatives of the two parties worked hard at preparing the draft of an outline agreement. Essentially, the DP and NNP agreed to set in motion the process of establishing a new political entity, the values of which would be liberal-democratic (and would be spelled out). The party would be called the Democratic Alliance (DA).

I was pleased to know that Helen Zille, a principled liberal who as Minister of Education in the Western Cape had established herself as an up-and-coming political leader, was heading a small group from the two parties to draft the section of the agreement dealing with the values and principles of the new party.

In the week prior to the draft agreement being presented to the federal councils of the two parties, Leon told me that Van Schalkwyk wanted to do a deal, but needed the deputy leadership as a fig-leaf. I said that if this was to be the case, it should be made quite clear that the term 'deputy leader' did not mean a separate office or structure but referred to a person who would assist the leader as his deputy. I emphasised that if we were to form a new party with the NNP the various components and personalities should be integrated into a single structure as soon as possible.

A meeting of the federal council of the DP was held at Arthur's Seat Hotel in Sea Point on 24 June to discuss and decide on the draft agreement. When my turn came to speak, I explained my feelings and emphasised the conditions that the DP had laid down as a condition for forming a single opposition party:

'As someone who has fought the Nats for 40 years, it goes against the grain to form a single party with them; yet, if the DP is serious about building up an opposition party that could become a real alternative to the ANC, I realise one has to put one's personal feelings on one side.

'The existence of the NNP is a major obstacle to the DP achieving its objective. Unless we make use of the opportunity that the present situation presents, we will be stuck with the Nats for the next four years.'

In a remarkably swift but particularly top-down decision-making process, the parties adopted the agreement, and in June 2000 the DA was formed. Members of the parties would become members of the DA; the Alliance would be registered with the IEC as a political party for the local government poll. As a consequence, members of the DA elected to local government would serve as members of the DA.

However, DA members such as Leon, Van Schalkwyk and I, who had been elected to parliament or to the provincial legislatures as members of the DP or the NNP, would have to remain members of the DP or NNP since in terms of the anti-defection clause in the Constitution all would lose their seats if we ceased to be members of the party that had nominated us.

This requirement meant that although the DP and NNP had agreed to form the DA, its members, as representatives in parliament or the provincial legislatures, would continue to remain members of the old parties. The practical effect was that the core elements and structures of the NNP and the DP would remain intact until the 2004 election.

This unusual arrangement had a very negative and damaging effect on the new party. It was to be exploited by Van Schalkwyk, and in due course used by him as a mechanism to enable him and his supporters to defect from the DA without losing their seats in parliament. Meanwhile, the election campaign itself concentrated the minds of the candidates and party bosses on the task ahead, and had a cohesive and stimulating effect.

The DA's campaign went well. The NNP's 1999 election slogan of 'Hang murderers and rapists' and the DP's 'Fight Back' gave way to the new DA slogan of 'For all the people'. More than two million voters turned out for the DA; the percentage of the vote rose from the combined DP-NNP total of 16,3% in the 1999 election to 20,6%. More than twelve hundred DA municipal councillors were elected, and the Alliance held the majority of 24 municipalities in the Western Cape including the city of Cape Town. The DP component of the DA expanded; the NNP component was saved.

Raili, 2000

On 31 March 1999 I attended a late afternoon reception given by the Dutch ambassador at his home in Constantia in honour of the birthday of Queen Juliana of the Netherlands. I was enjoying moving around, talking to old friends and meeting other people for the first time, when I was introduced to an attractive and striking-looking silver-haired lady who, from her accent, I presumed to be from one of the Nordic countries.

We had both come to the reception on our own and started moving around together, nibbling at snacks, replenishing our champagne glasses, and generally enjoying one another's company. Later, when I felt it was time to leave, I explained that I had arranged to phone my daughter, who lived up the street, so that she could collect me by car. My companion felt that she too would like to leave, and said that as she lived close by, and had a car parked at the embassy, she would happily drive me to my daughter's house.

I phoned Caryl to tell her it would not be necessary for her to come and fetch me, but that instead she should put some champagne on ice; a lady I had met at the reception would bring me along instead.

Caryl invited us to come in. She produced the champagne, and after a few minutes explained that she would have to leave us since she was taking part in a half-marathon the following morning and needed to go to sleep early.

Mrs Raili de Keyser and I chatted for some time. When she left to get into her car, I thanked her, pecked her politely on her cheek, and said I hoped we would meet again. She drove to her home – which I discovered was only two doors away from Caryl – and I drove home in a thoughtful daze around the mountain to my apartment in Clifton.

Mrs de Keyser was 60. She had been born and grown up in Finland; married a prominent Belgian businessman; and she and her husband and two young daughters had come to settle in the Cape in 1983. Her husband had died in 1992, and for most of the time since then she had been living on her own in the family home, South Cross House in Constantia. Her daughters, Dominique and Stephanie, had gone to Herschel school in Cape Town. Both had married South Africans, and between them they had five children; and were all living in the Constantia area.

A couple of anxious days later I managed to get Mrs de Keyser's unlisted telephone number, and a phone call led to our first 'date': dinner at Mariner's Wharf at Hout Bay.

In the weeks that followed we saw as much of each other as we could, bearing in mind my political commitments, which included assisting in the campaign for the election due on 2 June. Over June, July and August, Raili went to Finland for six weeks to see her three brothers. I too was travelling at that time.

Our chance meeting blossomed into a romance. We started talking of sharing our lives together and of marriage. Both of us were wise enough and old-fashioned enough to discuss this with our daughters, with whom we had very strong bonds.

They approved, and we decided to get married at the start of the new year, 2000 – the beginning of the new millennium. On 8 January 2000, Raili Maria de Keyser (neé Sippo) (60) and Colin Wells Eglin (74) were married in the small village church of St Peter the Fisherman in Hout Bay. Raili's older daughter Dominique was her bridesmaid, and my eldest grandson Paul was my best man.

Donald Stewart, one of my quantity surveying partners, who was also an ordained Anglican priest, assisted at the service. At the reception for families and close friends Raili had some of the ladies close to tears with some lines of poetry she recited. I was more mundane. I referred to the fact that some people might have thought that our courtship was quite brief and our marriage hurried. I told them about Joyce's father, who some four months after his wife (Joyce's mother) had died following a long illness, came to Joyce to ask her if she had any problem with him marrying a near neighbour whom he had known for some time.

Joyce said: 'Dad, isn't it a bit soon?'

Joyce's father replied: 'I understand your feelings, but when you are close to 80 nothing is too soon.'

I also commented on the fact that so many of South Africa's former political leaders had married foreigners. PW Botha had married an '*Engelse dame*'; FW de Klerk a Greek; Van Zyl Slabbert a citizen of Swaziland; Mandela a Mozambican. And here was I marrying a Finn. I asked whether something was wrong with South African women – or whether political leadership does something strange to South African men.

Raili was a student of the history of Finland and knew a lot about that country's politics. She began to take a keen interest in what I was doing, and wanted to learn about our politics. I realised that a time was approaching when, before I became too stale and crusty, I would cut back on my public commitments – and I looked forward to the days when Raili and I would be free to do things and enjoy life together without being dominated by the priorities of politics.

The Nationalists swallow their tail

Not long after the 1999 election, the duality imposed on the DA by the provisions of the new Constitution – and the lack of personal trust – precipitated tensions in the new party.

Two issues in particular brought matters to a head. The one was the role of Van Schalkwyk as deputy leader, and the other was Peter Marais's performance as the mayor of Cape Town.

Although I did not serve on any DA committees, I stayed fairly well informed on what was going on behind the scenes. At times I was asked to take part in group discussions. Occasionally Douglas Gibson, the DA's chief whip, would invite me to attend a briefing because 'the leader would like to keep you in the loop'. On a more regular basis I was invited by Leon to join him at four-on-four meetings: himself plus three from the DP component, and Van Schalkwyk with three from the NNP.

At these four-on-four meetings I witnessed the concerns I had expressed to Leon about Van Schalkwyk as deputy leader becoming realities. Van Schalkwyk refused to integrate his deputy leader's office into that of the leader, or into the structure of the DA.

Physically, the NNP operated in separate offices from the DA, with separate personnel, separate budgets, and a separate programme of activities for Van Schalkwyk that projected him as an alternative leader rather than a deputy. I had the uncomfortable feeling that Van Schalkwyk was using his office to keep alive the concept of a distinct NNP component of the DA, and to ensure that it was available should the time come when he considered it necessary to use it as a fallback position.

For his part, Peter Marais had been brought across from being the NNP premier of the Western Cape to be the DA's candidate for mayor of Cape Town at the election, a position – following the DA's victory – he duly achieved.

Soon after taking office he started ruffling the feathers of the citizens of Cape Town with his flamboyant style and disregard for convention and sensitivities. These mayoral idiosyncrasies came to a head when, without consulting the citizens of Cape Town, he unilaterally announced that he intended renaming Adderley and Wale Streets – the two main thoroughfares in Cape Town – after Nelson Mandela and FW de Klerk respectively. This evoked an outcry from the citizens and was followed by a bizarre chain of events.

Leon and Van Schalkwyk instructed Marais to ascertain the views of the citizens by way of a referendum. A murky form of poll ensued – but along with its 'results' (in favour of Marais) there was evidence of fraud in the mayor's office. Leon and Van Schalkwyk then appointed a commission, headed by retired Judge Heath, to investigate the handling of the referendum, and the DA leader and his deputy persuaded Marais to 'take leave' while the commission was sitting.

The Heath Commission, while finding there had indeed been irregularities in the office of the mayor, cleared Marais of involvement, and a committee of the Cape

Town municipal council found that Marais had not transgressed any council rules or regulations. However, the storm over Marais's performance did not abate.

The tensions around Marais revealed and opened the divisions that were latent in the DA, and seriously affected the performance of the Alliance, which was in control of the Cape Town municipality. There were indications that public support for the DA was evaporating, and Leon decided the matter must be dealt with firmly.

Having obtained Van Schalkwyk's support for Marais to be redeployed as an MEC in the Western Cape provincial government, he wrote to Marais on 12 October informing him that 'he had lost confidence in his ability to continue as mayor of Cape Town'. He continued: 'I would earnestly request you to resign your post …'.

Leon added that should Marais decide not to resign he would put a motion that he should do so to a meeting of the federal council to be held on 19 October. Leon concluded: 'I continue to believe that you can make a valuable contribution to political life, but my judgement is that you cannot make this contribution as the mayor of Cape Town.'

Leon's letter immediately resulted in Van Schalkwyk making a public statement of support for Marais and launching an attack on Leon. This was followed by Van Schalkwyk convening a meeting of the federal council of the NNP, which in turn adopted a motion, stating:

'The NNP remains totally committed to the formation and success of the Democratic Alliance as a new political entity in terms of the vision, core values and principles contained in the Founding Agreement of the DA.

'The federal council endorses the viewpoints and conduct of Mr Marthinus van Schalkwyk in the current dispute on demands that Mr Peter Marais should resign as mayor of the Cape Town unicity.'

When Marais did not respond to Leon's letter, the National Management Committee (NMC) of the DA (on 19 October) adopted the following resolution, proposed by Leon. It stated that in 'the interests of the achievement of the objectives of the DA, and of the people it seeks to serve' the NMC:

- requires Peter Marais to relinquish his position as mayor of the unicity forthwith;
- in the event of him not complying with the decision of the NMC … terminates his membership of the Democratic Alliance with immediate effect.

Van Schalkwyk responded with a stinging attack on Leon .The NMC demanded that he issue a public apology. Van Schalkwyk's rebuttal was that the NNP component was withdrawing from the DA. He followed this up with a further announcement that the NNP was to open discussions on becoming part of the ANC government at every level.

This took me by surprise. I was aware of problems relating to personalities, style of management, membership lists and administrative arrangements within the party. I realised that tensions were building and that mistrust was a factor. But never at any stage, nor at any of the meetings that I attended, did Van Schalkwyk or any of his colleagues express criticisms or objections to the manner in which the DA was opposing the ANC; nor did they say anything to suggest they would renege on their commitment to a combined and united opposition and throw in their lot with the ANC.

Having endured some personal anguish at the time we entered into an agreement with the NNP to form the DA, my mood was not improved by long-time supporters of mine saying: 'You should have known you could never trust the Nats.'

I issued a statement: 'I derive no pleasure from the fact that the NNP national council has decided to withdraw from the DA. I am saddened personally, because an agreement which I helped to fashion and which I entered into in good faith in spite of my many years of opposition to the National Party has been shattered unilaterally by the people I had decided to trust: the leaders of the NNP.

'I am saddened politically by an attempt by the leadership of the NNP to destroy the DA. It is a setback for multi-party democracy in our country. Whatever the reasons now being advanced by the leaders of the NNP may be, their decision to break with the DA is a fundamental repudiation of the solemn agreement which we entered into to form the DA. It is a violation of the undertakings given to the voters of South Africa at the municipal elections.'

The DA continued to exist as a political party. However, as a consequence of the Constitution's anti-defection clause, a freak situation arose. MPs and Members of the Provincial Legislatures (MPLs) who had been elected to parliament or a provincial council in 1999 as members of the NNP all had to resign from the DA even if they had no wish to do so; for, if they did not, they would be expelled from the NNP and as a result lose their seats as MPs or MPLs.

Members of municipal councils who had been elected in the local poll of 2000 as members of the DA, and who wanted to resign to rejoin the NNP, could not do so – since if they did they would automatically lose their position as councillors.

The upshot was that sitting in the NNP caucuses in parliament and the provincial councils were some NNP members who wanted to be members of the DA; while sitting in municipal councils were DA members whose loyalty was with the NNP.

In the Western Cape Provincial Council the NNP called off the alliance it had with the DA and entered into an alliance with the ANC, effectively handing control of the Western Cape to the ANC.

In Cape Town and other municipalities where the DA had gained a majority in the election, the DA remained in office – for the time being.

Members of the public were bemused. Despite the withdrawal of Van Schalkwyk and his NNP MPs and MPLs, the DA remained a fact – and a functioning reality. There were resignations from some traditional NNP rank-and-file party loyalists, but opinion polls and municipal by-elections indicated that public support remained with the DA.

In July 2002 the ANC introduced a bill to permit public representatives to cross the floor in certain circumstances, and during certain prescribed window periods.

In October that year, when the window period in respect of municipalities occurred, DA councillors who had formerly been NNP members of the DA crossed the
floor to rejoin the NNP. In Cape Town the number who did so was enough to enable
the NNP to form an alliance with the ANC; to wrest control of Cape Town from the
DA; and effectively to hand it over to the ANC.

When a short while later a window period for floor-crossing for MPs and MPLs
opened, eight members of the NNP, who had formerly been members of the DA, resigned from the NNP to rejoin the DA. The number of DA members in the National
Assembly increased from 38 to 45.

All in all it was a depressing chapter in the history of South Africa's opposition
politics. It came to an end with the ANC – without a mandate from the electorate
– achieving its objective of gaining control of the governments of the Western Cape
and Cape Town. The NNP ceased to exist except as an appendage of the ANC. The
DA, battered and bruised, lived on to fight another day – the election of April 2004.

Mandela at 85

In July 2003, Raili and I flew to Johannesburg to attend Nelson Mandela's 85th birthday celebrations. The dinner and birthday party were to be held at the Sandton Convention Centre, and Raili and I checked in at the adjoining Sandton Sun hotel and
decided to make the most of our visit to 'Josi'.

On the Saturday morning 1 000 guests crowded the Johannesburg Civic Theatre for
a light breakfast and to listen to President Bill Clinton delivering the first of the annual
Nelson Mandela lectures. In the evening 1 500 guests were at the Convention Centre
to enjoy the birthday celebrations with their much-loved and respected Madiba.

The South Africans who were invited to the birthday party represented a cross-
section of movers and shakers in the country's broad society. Those from abroad
were among Mandela's special friends. They included Clinton, his wife Hillary and
daughter Chelsea; Queen Beatrix of the Netherlands and her son William and his
wife Maxima; the U2 singer Bono; Oprah Winfrey; and Richard Branson.

The musicians and artists were among the best from South Africa and abroad.
The screen presentation of Mandela's life and achievements, and the tributes paid to
him, were moving. In between speeches and stage and screen presentations, guests
enjoyed the opportunity of meeting and chatting with old friends.

Raili and I were seated at a table alongside Bantu Holomisa and his daughter. Opposite us were Pik Botha and his wife. Pik was his usual demonstrative and engaging self. At one stage he and Holomisa were engaged in earnest conversation ranging
over their experiences – which included the period when Holomisa was a military
general who seized power in a coup in the Transkei, and Pik, as Minister of Foreign
Affairs, was a chief protagonist of the 'independent homelands' with the responsibility of ensuring that the Transkei and others did not use that independence contrary
to South Africa's interests.

At one stage, Botha pointed to me and said earnestly to Holomisa: 'You see Colin Eglin sitting alongside you? In parliament he voted against independence for each of the four homelands.' He paused for a moment and continued: 'And he was right every time.'

Raili and I left the party at about midnight. The revelry continued until the small hours.

28

Mbeki, Leon, transformation

June 1999 to April 2004 defined the period of the Mbeki-Leon parliament, a period during which major developments occurred within and outside South Africa.

Consideration was being given to the reconfiguration of the economy at the same time as social relations. It was the time when black economic empowerment was being accelerated; and of socio-economic conditions in which tensions were building up because of rising crime, corruption and the inadequate delivery of services. At the same time, inter-personal and inter-group relations were changing as – even if in an uneven and patchy way – diverse people were becoming accustomed to living together in one country.

This mixed picture was reflected in Africa itself. There was the moral and economic deterioration of Zimbabwe; wars and civil strife in various parts of the continent; and the emergence of the African Union with its Nepad, Peace and Security Council, and Pan-African Parliament.

Further north the world was confronted by the escalating conflict between Palestine and Israel; tensions between the UN and Saddam Hussein over the issue of arms inspection and weapons of mass destruction; and the events of 9/11 followed by the 'war against terrorism' and the invasions of Afghanistan and Iraq.

Many of these issues were the subjects of statements, debates and questions in parliament – yet the character of parliament and the style of its proceedings were set by the interaction of the personalities of Mbeki, president of South Africa and leader of the ANC, and of Tony Leon, leader of the opposition and of the Democratic Alliance.

Both had deep commitments to their respective parties' causes; both had driving ambition and seemingly boundless energy. I was often with Leon both in South Africa and abroad and was amazed at his total dedication: he was a 24-hour politician. I often said to myself, thank heavens that when I was leader of the opposition there were no cellphones.

Judging from Mbeki's schedule as head of state, head of government and leader of the increasingly fractious Tripartite Alliance, he more than matched Leon for his involvement in work and the intensity of his activities.

The leaders both had gatekeepers protecting their interests. Mbeki had Essop

Pahad, Minister of State in the President's Office, who carried out his duties with aggressive bluntness. Leon had Gibson, the chief opposition whip, who carried out his mandates with oozing charm. Both leaders had a penchant for smart clothes, and were more at home in Western-style suits than T-shirts and jeans. Indeed, there were times when I looked at Mbeki with his neatly-trimmed beard, tailored suit, blue shirt with white collar and matching tie, and it seemed to me that he could have been a retired British naval officer.

Mbeki's dismissive style when dealing with Leon, and Leon's combative style when dealing with Mbeki, were the ingredients for an aggressive stand-off and fierce clashes across the floor of the House.

I was often disappointed by Mbeki's scorn towards the leader of the opposition; a person of his standing should have done better. I despaired at times when, instead of dealing with the substance of the arguments that Leon had put to him, he resorted to belittling jibes. What concerned me about Leon's input into debate was not the substance – for much of that was sound and needed to be said – but his excessively combative and hectoring style. I felt this often detracted from the force of his arguments, and that while it might have the effect of enthusing his supporters, it would have no persuasive impact at all on the ANC.

On a couple of occasions when I raised the issue of his style with Leon, his reaction was quite straightforward: 'Well, this is what I am.' Perhaps when I was leader of the opposition, I reacted in much the same way.

On occasion ANC MPs told me that while they had listened to what Leon had to say – and agreed with much of his substance – they always added: 'But I wish he would change his style and not be so aggressive and talk down to us.'

Many opposition supporters approved of Leon's style; but there were those who expressed their concern that this was the cause of the acrimonious relationship between him and Mbeki. My reaction was to tell them to bear in mind that 'it takes two to tango'. I reminded them that during Mandela's presidency Leon had a friendly and mutually interactive relationship with the president. Far from being dismissive or scornful towards Leon, Mandela on occasions would invite him privately to discuss matters on which they differed. At one stage Mandela had even invited Leon to become a member of his cabinet: 'If relations between Leon and President Mbeki are different from what they were when Mandela was president, it can't all be Leon's fault.'

To those ANC supporters who spoke to me, I argued that as far as the national interest was concerned, surely substance was more important than style? I put it to them that when it came to issues like HIV-AIDS; South Africa's attitude towards Mugabe's actions in Zimbabwe; the relaxing of the labour laws to enable small businesses to develop; and the emphasis on how a 6% economic growth rate could be achieved – who was right? Leon or Mbeki?

Taking all the factors into account, I believed that during Mbeki's first term of office and Leon's first five years as leader of the opposition, both, in spite of their differences of style and manner, had made valuable inputs on issues of substance. However, one of the consequences of the acrimonious relationship between Mbeki and Leon was that, although important policy statements were made, there was very little interactive or constructive debate in parliament on the dominant issue of the time: the transformation of the South African economy.

I believed that two inter-related components were essential to this pivotal change. The first involved not only freeing the economy from the restrictions imposed on it during the apartheid and sanctions era, but also making the reforms that would enable South Africa to participate successfully in the globalised economy of the modern world.

The second involved addressing the imbalances, inequalities and distortions that existed in the economic framework, in the fields of wealth ownership, power, knowledge, skills, opportunities and access. All were the legacy of the racially discriminatory policies of South Africa's colonial and apartheid past.

Apart from the imperatives of justice, economic development and social responsibility, I had no doubt that the demand for economic transformation would be the inevitable consequence of the transfer of political power.

During 1993 and 1994 while we were negotiating the Constitution and with it the political transformation of our nation, this was an issue to which I returned time and again. Addressing a gathering in Johannesburg organised by Davis Borkum Hare, a firm of stockbrokers, and shown on closed-circuit television around the country, I said:

'Allow me to identify four issues which decision-makers in both the public and the private sectors are not going to be able to avoid.

'The first is affirmative action, both to redress the injustices and inequities of the past, and to enable individuals from disadvantaged sections of our nation to develop to their full potential.

'The second is socio-economic reconstruction – the process of ensuring more equitable access to services, to housing, to education, to basic health care and to job opportunity.

'The third is economic empowerment, the process of making it possible for more and more people to have a share in the management, policy, decision-making and ownership within a market-orientated economy.

'The fourth is land ... Access to land, and more equitable distribution of land as well as ... the restitution and/or compensation for land dispossessed in terms of racial laws, are going to be potent political and economic issues in South Africa for decades to come.'

I saw essential changes in the socio-economic field as another phase in the wider process of transformation flowing from the talks at the World Trade Centre.

In 2000, in an interview with *Leadership* magazine, I was asked to deal with the DP's approach to economic transformation. I responded: 'The role of opposition is not just to talk to black South Africans about transformation but also to lead white

South Africa in transformation. The DP has got a leadership role to play in making transformation both rapid and successful.'

That Mbeki approached the issue of economic transformation in racial terms was reflected in his statement that there were two nations in South Africa: one white and rich, the other black and poor. His ANC-led government enacted laws and promulgated regulations that provided for compulsory racial quotas and for giving statutory recognition to the categorising of South Africans citizens as African, Coloured, Indian or white.

Leon approached the problem as primarily one of poverty, and the challenge as one of raising living standards. He relied on the redistribution that would be achieved by the overall growth of the economy and the opportunities this would create for individuals, rather than focusing on specific measures for redressing the imbalances and inequities caused by racial discrimination.

Given the importance of the issues, it was unfortunate that in parliament the proceedings were of such an adversarial nature that they never resulted in a meeting of minds.

Viewed from a marketing perspective, Mbeki succeeded in getting the public to see his policy on transformation as synonymous with the concept of transformation. As a consequence, when Leon attacked Mbeki on transformation he was seen to be attacking the concept itself. The reality was that Leon was in favour of it; however, he remained at a constant disadvantage, for unlike Mbeki, who had appropriated the word 'transformation' to encapsulate his policy, Leon did not have a marketable word or phrase for his alternatives.

I also had no doubt that the squalling relationship between Mbeki and Leon had an impact on the general quality of debates and on the behaviour of members of the House. MPs became more and more intolerant of one another. There was less desire to debate issues and more to score points off the other party. Penetrating interjections were giving way to unnecessary and unbecoming rowdiness.

All too often some of the ANC members, unlike in the days of the Mandela presidency, would resort to playing the race card instead of engaging in debate. Sadly, this reminded me of the old days in parliament when the Nationalists, not willing to deal with arguments put forward by the opposition, resorted to calling us *boerehater*s or *kaffirboeties*.

The question of human life

I had usually been in agreement with Leon on long-term strategic objectives of the DA. Areas on which, specifically, I did not see eye-to-eye with him arose when I felt that his short-term tactics were at variance with those long-term objectives. However, during the run-up to the April 2004 elections there was one issue on which I found myself in serious disagreement with him.

Five weeks before the election Leon announced a change of attitude on the issue of the death penalty. Previously, he had been an opponent of capital punishment. He had been committed to uphold the Constitution and to respect the values that it embraced, including the right to life. Now he stated that he was in favour of the re-instatement of the penalty for extremely violent crimes, such as murder with aggra-vating circumstances.

In view of the DA's policy of allowing its public representatives to have a free vote on matters such as the death penalty, Leon was entitled to a change of heart. How-ever, given the indications that there had been much activity on the issue of capital punishment in the strategic engine room of the DA, Leon's *volte-face* appeared rather more than a change of heart. I had no doubt it formed part of an electoral strategy to encourage the voters to believe the DA was in favour of the death penalty, without the Alliance leadership having to go to a congress for approval of a formal change of policy.

That it was indeed part of an electoral strategy was confirmed when – soon after Leon had made his statement – Douglas Gibson, Leon's closest confidant, issued the following in his capacity as the chief electoral spokesman for the DA:

'The DA views with amusement the NNP's anger and hysteria about the DA leader's support for the death penalty. No doubt it renders much of their election propaganda obsolete. Tony Leon has stated that he supports the death penalty for ag-gravated murders with no extenuating circumstances. The DA permits a free vote for this on matters of religion and conscience. Seventy-four per cent of DA MPs favour the death penalty while 26% do not. That is their right.

'The NNP is desperately clutching at straws. The ANC is resolutely opposed to the death penalty. And on this issue, as on so many others, the NNP's views have little or no influence whatsoever. Most South African voters will support Tony Leon's view no matter how cross the NNP might be about this issue.'

Apart from the fact that I believed the death penalty was barbaric and wrong on every rational count, I also believed that a *de facto* policy change of this nature on the eve of an election would undermine the credibility of the party and its leader without any additional votes being secured.

The constitutional factor also weighed heavily with me. I believed, as I still do, that nothing could be more dangerous than for a minority party to ask for a fundamental change to be made to the Bill of Rights in the South African Constitution. Doing this would be to invite the majority party to make the changes that it preferred.

The unravelling of the Bill of Rights – negotiated so carefully and such a key fea-ture of our Constitution – would be too high a price to pay for the pursuit of a few conservative votes at an election.

Helen Suzman issued a statement reiterating her rejection of capital punishment. I wrote a letter to Leon, the gist of which was this:

'While recognising the "free vote" policy of the party, I write to express my personal disappointment with you in coming out in support for the reinstatement of the death penalty. Taking into account the behind-the-scenes activities that have been taking place, I can't help coming to the conclusion that your statement is part of a strategy designed to avoid the requirements of the DA's constitution relating to the formulation of party policy, while at the same time have the voting public believe that in reality voting for the DA would be a vote for the reinstatement of the death penalty.

'Tony, whatever the impact on the election might be, I am concerned that by supporting the reinstatement of the death penalty, the DA will undermine its own credibility – and more than this it will do a disservice both domestically and internationally.'

The concept of a free vote on the death penalty had its origin in a policy decision taken by the PFP in the early 1980s, when capital punishment was constitutional and scores of executions were carried out each year. It was introduced to accommodate public representatives of the party who opposed the death penalty as a matter of conscience. Since then much had happened to the issue of the death penalty in South Africa and the DP's attitude to it.

President FW de Klerk effectively ended judicial capital punishment in South Africa in October 1989 when he placed a moratorium on executions, which at that stage averaged approximately a hundred each year.

During the constitutional negotiations when dealing with the Bill of Rights the political parties, including the DP, overwhelmingly rejected a proposal by the NP that, in respect of certain serious crimes, parliament could legislate that the death penalty could apply. A year later, on 5 June 1995, the Constitutional Court, in a unanimous judgement, found the death penalty to be unconstitutional. From that time on the DP gave no indication that it would favour the reintroduction of capital punishment. On the contrary, its policy position was that it 'supports the Constitution and abides by the decision of the Constitutional Court. Individual members of the DP are, however, given a free vote on this issue.'

When, at that time, the NP proposed a motion in parliament calling for a referendum to test public opinion on the issue, Leon rounded on the Nationalists for wanting to overturn the judgement of the Constitutional Court. He reminded the House of a speech that a National Party member, NJJ van R Koornhof, described by Leon as a wise and balanced politician, had made in parliament two years earlier. Quoting Koornhof Leon said:

'Many people, especially the public, argue that the death penalty should be retained simply because public opinion wants it. Nowhere in the world have governments permitted themselves to be prescribed by public opinion on such a moral case. If this were so, what would we do in this parliament if public opinion chose torture? Would we introduce it?

'Public opinion in South Africa is emotionally loaded in favour of the death penalty at present. The public must not turn the death penalty into a magic formula which will restore law and order. This will not happen.

'The real issue at stake here is getting tough on crime and coming to grips with the causes of crime.'

Leon's attack on the hypocrisy of the NP for wanting to overturn a carefully reasoned and unanimous judgement of the 11 judges of the Constitutional Count left
no room for doubt that, as the leader of the DP, he was committed to upholding
that judgement. During the 1999 election, when the NP campaigned under the slogan 'Hang murderers and rapists', the DP had its counter-slogan, 'Nail them and jail
them'.

However, after the formation of the DA and with the approach of the 2004 election, I sensed a restiveness developing in the Alliance on the issue. Some DA MPs,
when making statements in favour of the death penalty, emphasised that they were
doing so in their personal capacities. But others spoke on behalf of the party. Thus
Tertius Delport, the DA's spokesperson on justice, said: 'Crime has reached a point
where extreme measures are necessary. These include the death penalty – even if this
necessitates an amendment to the Constitution.'

Andries Botha, the leader of the DA in the Free State, was reported as saying:
'Most DA parliamentarians are in favour of the reinstatement of the death penalty.
The DA agrees with Judge Arrie Hattingh who called for the reinstatement earlier
this week, saying that the state was failing in its duty to protect its citizens.'

Theuns Botha, Western Cape leader of the DA and the DA's candidate for premier
of the province, taking part in an election debate against his ANC and NNP counter-
parts, said: 'I am a champion of the death penalty. I shall do my best to promote it.'

Leon's statement so soon before the 2004 election, followed by Gibson's reinforce-
ment, attracted sufficient media attention to persuade members of the public who
cared about such matters that the DA had changed its policy and was now in favour
of the reinstatement of the death penalty.

The election took place on 14 April. Whether the DA's shift of policy resulted in it
gaining any votes from conservative members of minority groups is a matter for conjecture. I believe it did not. But what was beyond conjecture was that this tactical shift
brought the DA no additional votes from members of the black majority. As with the
'Fight Back' slogan in 1999, the DA's short-term tactical decision in the 2004 election
was not in harmony with its long-term strategic objectives. Was it worth it?

A time to bow out

On 7 October 2003 I issued the following statement: 'I have decided not to make
myself available as a candidate in next year's general election. I have had a long and
eventful innings as a public representative. Since 1958 I have stood as a candidate in
11 successive elections, during which process I have experienced both victories and at
times defeats. I have also had the privilege of having played a part in the negotiations
which led to the adoption of South Africa's democratic Constitution.

'At times my heart tempts me to stay on. However, my head tells me that the next
election will be the time to go. After all, 79 years will hardly be an appropriate age
at which to start another five-year stint as a public representative. When the 2004

election takes place it will be time for me to make way for someone of the younger generation.

'I have discussed the matter with Tony Leon who understands the reasons for my decision. My task in the months ahead will be to do what I can to ensure that the Democratic Alliance does well in the election.'

My announcement was received in a very generous spirit by friends and political foes alike. Letters, statements and articles in the media were kind and complimentary, and generally commented on the role I had played in keeping liberal values alive during the dark days of apartheid, and the contribution I had made to the success of the negotiations on the new South African Constitution.

As an old hand at politics, I realised there would be those who would be pleased to see the last of me. However, on this occasion they had the good grace not to go public on their views. Having read the kind articles and statements, I quipped to my friends: 'It is comforting to be alive and to read one's own obituary.'

I was especially touched by Boy Geldenhuys, one of the senior members of the NNP with whom I had many battles across the floor of the Assembly, who said most generously: 'The Hon. Colin Eglin was named by *Leadership* magazine as the parliamentarian of the century. In my view it is a well-deserved nomination. Allow me to salute a parliamentarian *par excellence* who has served his country well over many years.'

To my surprise, *Die Burger*, one of my political foes from the apartheid era, and its sister newspaper *Die Beeld* carried a warm and incisive centre-page article complete with a colour photo of an ageing Eglin seated in his parliamentary office. During the interview with Johan van Zyl, who wrote the article, he asked me if I had any specific adjective in mind that would be appropriate in describing me. I thought for a few moments, and then said that I did not want to be too brash, but neither too reticent, so perhaps the most appropriate adjective would be 'durable' (*duursaam*).

Van Zyl must have liked the description duursaam, for in the headline of his article I became '*Meneer Duursaam*' ('Mr Durable'). There was a comment that said I had seen what Nazism stood for – and was firm that it should never happen in South Africa.

I rather enjoyed being called *Meneer Duursaam*, and the vision it conjured of a life stretching out into the years ahead. On 7 January 2004 I was brought back to reality as I lay in a semi-sedated state on a movable hospital bed being wheeled into theatre for an emergency operation to deal with a perforated ulcer. It was as if a voice said softly to me: 'Colin, you may be durable, but remember no-one is indestructible!'

While convalescing I was delighted to receive a letter from Olusegun Obasanjo in Nigeria. After wishing me a recovery to good health, he wrote: 'No doubt, you have found your [service to] active politics not only bruising in its excitement but equally rewarding in its service to humanity. I have very fond memories of our relationship, which incidentally was brought about by the nature and terrain of the apartheid system in South Africa.

'I will always recall with nostalgia your untiring and positive contributions to the eradication of apartheid, and warmly congratulate you on your well-deserved bed to retire from active politics.

'I hope you will continue to lend your experience and wisdom to the more immediate and urgent task of transformation, and to continue to serve your country in a new capacity.'

I recovered from the surgery and was back in time for a short pre-election session of parliament – my last.

As for my travels, they continued apace. In the month that I announced my retirement, I returned to Dakar to attend a congress of Liberal International (LI). It was a pleasure to be back and to meet my Senegalese friends. There was a familiarity about the place – Gorée Island, Independence Square, the corniche drive, the fishermen's cove, the arts and crafts market, the university, and the restaurants where Helen Suzman and I had dined in 1971.

There was the luxury of enjoying the hospitality of the redoubtable Maitre Abdoulaye Wade, once a political prisoner and now president of his country.

The congress focused on the theme: 'Islam and the West, the Liberal View'. This was most appropriate: Senegal, where 94% of the people were Islamic, was an example of tolerance and respect for the rights of minorities. The congress also marked the end of my period in office as vice-president of LI. With my retirement from parliament only a few months away, I decided to stand down and proposed Tony Leon as the DA's nominee for the position.

My involvement with Liberal International had deepened over time. One crowning moment came in the early years of the new millennium when I flew to the Iberian peninsula, to Barcelona, the capital city of the Catalan region of Spain. My reason for going there was not to attend a meeting or to act as a resource person, but to receive the Ramon Trias Fargas Memorial Award (2002) from the Funducio Llibertat I Democracia, a Catalan liberal foundation. Fargas was the founder of modern liberalism in Catalonia, and an outspoken critic of General Franco's fascist regime; the award is conferred annually on someone deemed to have defended liberal values and promoted liberalism internationally.

There was continuing interest in our new Constitution, its functioning, its content, and the process by which it had been drawn up. Delegations of parliamentarians and political leaders from developing countries came to South Africa for discussions on these matters. I received invitations to go abroad to take part in workshops and symposiums in which I pointed out the lessons to be learned from the South African experience.

I went to Tanzania and the Ivory Coast to address members of parliament and senior government members on the role of parliament, and in particular on that of the government party and the opposition within the parliamentary system. In Nairobi, Kenya, I was a resource person at a conference attended by delegates from 18 African countries on the role of parliament in the budgetary process.

I went further afield: on two occasions to Fiji and on another two to East Timor to assist MPs, members of the relevant constitutional assemblies, and political leaders on the process of drawing up their countries' constitutions and ensuring that their new parliaments and executives functioned effectively.

While there was no exact parallel between the constitution-making process in these countries and that of South Africa, the foreign participants appeared to appreciate a first-hand account of the South African experience. I was also requested to submit a written assessment of the proposals to be put to Afghanistan's constitutional assembly when it met in Kabul to draw up a new constitution for the nation.

In November 2003 I was one of three MPs who flew to Khartoum to attend the 25th conference of the African Parliamentary Union (APU). I had not been in Khartoum since 1944, when as a young soldier I had stopped *en route* to joining the African forces in North Africa. Sudan had been in the news recently over the long-drawn-out civil war between the North and the South; the problems along its borders with Chad; the allegations of human rights violations; and the discovery of oil.

There were lively workshops on Nepad and the Pan-African Parliament – which revealed conflicting views and sharp disagreements on interpretation and implementation. Inevitably, these were set to continue as the Darfur crisis escalated. My exposure to such crises in the nascent structure of African co-operation have, at least, given me a broader perspective than I would have had from the tip of Africa.

Back home again in November, the Green and Sea Point Hebrew congregation invited me to be the guest of honour at the Friday evening service in the shul and after that at a dinner in the shul hall. I had been to the shul on occasions as member of parliament for Sea Point. Indeed, I had made a habit of keeping a yarmulke in the cubbyhole of my car for use on Jewish occasions. However, this was to be a very special one for me as I had been told that I was the only South African politician, other than Nelson Mandela, who had been honoured in this way.

Rabbi Jack Steinhorn thanked me on behalf of the congregation for my years of service and for the contribution I had made in helping to change the attitudes of the people of Sea Point. In turn I thanked the members of the congregation for the support and encouragement they had given me over the years.

The dinner that followed was a very friendly affair. I returned home that night in a relaxed frame of mind.

Thinking about the evening's proceedings and looking back to 1974, when I was first elected in Sea Point, I couldn't help recalling the contrast between my first and last public address as the parliamentary representative for the area.

My last was from the pulpit of the Marais Road synagogue when I said farewell and thank you to the well-clad and largely elderly members of the congregation. The first was standing on a box on the nudist beach of Sandy Bay where I was taking part in a protest against the commercial development of that pristine piece of mountain and seascape – and speaking to a youthful group of protestors, a few of whom were modestly wearing bathing costumes!

In December I took my grandson Paul on a visit to the US as a present for his 21st birthday. Thanks to the assistance and hospitality of friends in Washington, Philadelphia and New York, we were able to do and experience far more than the casual visitor. I tried to steer clear of politics; however, my American friends did not. For a change the discussions were not about South Africa, but the war in Iraq and where the US was heading under President George W Bush.

I sensed I was tiptoeing through a deeply divided American society. Sadly, I felt that the US was no longer the place to which I should come to recharge my liberal batteries.

I departed from my no-politics rule on my last day in New York when Paul and I visited Maurice Templesman in his apartment and then went on to lunch in a nearby restaurant. Templesman and I engaged in a far-ranging discussion on the politics and the personalities of the US. The issues involved the presidential election due the following year, the war in Iraq, and the problems facing the world in the wake of the terrorist attacks of 9/11.

I imagined Paul being bored to tears listening to his grandfather talking politics yet again. To my surprise and my delight, when we were back in South Africa a few weeks later, Paul told his parents that listening to Templesman and me talking had been one of the highlights of his visit.

On 21 January 2004 the Cape Town Press Club held a luncheon in my honour. When the organisers of the lunch heard I had been rushed into hospital they must have wondered whether they should postpone – or perhaps even cancel it. It turned out to be a good occasion enhanced by the attendance of a number of old-time Progressives who did not normally attend press club functions, and by the fact that Helen Suzman flew down especially from Johannesburg to be the guest speaker.

Parliament opened two weeks later for what was going to be the last session for my benchmate Ken Andrew and me. As one expected, with the election round the corner, MPs used the debate on the president's State of the Nation speech and the Minister of Finance's budgetary proposals, as well as parliament's question time, to indulge in some early electioneering.

I had known from my own experience how much importance MPs attached to this pre-election parliamentary politicking – although there were moments when I wondered if the general public paid any attention to it.

The last piece of legislation I had to attend to before I retired was the second reading of the Powers, Privileges and Immunities of Parliament Bill and the Provincial Legislatures Bill. There was a long and interesting background to this legislation, starting in July 1997 when a sub-committee of the National Assembly had been established to review the 1963 Powers and Privileges of Parliament Act and related issues. Soon after the sub-committee was established I expressed my opinion that the 1963 Act would have to be scrapped, since it was enacted at a time when parliament was sovereign – and this was now in conflict with the concept of the South African Constitution as the supreme law of the nation.

Previously parliament could confer on itself any powers and privileges it wished. Under the new Constitution parliament only had such powers and privileges as were conferred on it by the Constitution. This limitation of parliament's powers was brought sharply to the attention of members when, in May 1998, a judgement of the Cape High Court set aside a resolution of the National Assembly. The essence was that 'the Constitution permits the Assembly to determine and control its internal arrangements, proceedings and procedures. It does not, however, follow that the Assembly can do so in a manner that is inconsistent with the Constitution.

'The exercise of the power conferred on the Assembly remains subject to the Constitution and subject to constitutional review by the courts ... To the extent that the Powers and Privileges of Parliament Act purports to place issues of parliamentary privilege beyond judicial scrutiny and thus beyond the supremacy of the Constitution on the mere ipse dixit of the Speaker, it is undoubtedly unconstitutional.'

Despite the Speaker informing the members of the National Assembly that the matters identified in the court judgement required urgent attention, the sub-committee, reconstituted again after the 1999 election, only brought the bill to parliament six years later, in 2004. In the end the bill was relatively brief – for as I pointed out in my speech in the House, the core powers and privileges were to be found in the Constitution.

Although the process of producing the bill was protracted, I enjoyed taking part in it for it led one to consider the nature and importance of parliament as an institution in shaping democracy, and of the relationship of parliament with the executive, the judiciary, the citizens, and the Constitution itself.

I was pleased that in a small way I had had an opportunity of helping to shape the character and the conventions of the new democratic parliament.

The last sitting days of parliament before the election were 26 and 27 March – and the occasion for members to make farewell speeches. Andrew and I each made short ones; we both received standing ovations from our DA colleagues and polite, yet nevertheless friendly, applause, from the ranks of the ANC.

I said: 'Forty-six years have elapsed since, as a nervous backbencher, I made my first speech in parliament. I've been around a long time. I was elected in 1958. In 1961, with 11 of my colleagues of the Progressive Party, I was voted out of parliament by the white voters. They resented us saying that racism was wrong and that apartheid must go, and that sooner rather than later the representatives of all the people of South Africa must negotiate a new non-racial and democratic constitution.

'I was re-elected in 1974 and have been here ever since. I have fought in 11 successive elections. I have served during the term of the last seven presidents and prime ministers, Strijdom, Verwoerd, Vorster, Botha, De Klerk, Mandela and Mbeki. And, believe it or not, I have served in parliament under five different constitutions: the Union, Republican, Tricameral, interim and the final Constitution of 1996.

'I've taken part in many bruising political battles. I've shared the joy of victory. I've experienced the disappointment of defeat. I shall leave parliament with a kaleidoscope of memories. But I shall leave with no regrets.

'You might ask, what was your most satisfying moment? Undoubtedly when on 9 May 1996 parliament endorsed our new democratic Constitution. To have had the privilege of taking part in the constitution-making process was satisfying in itself. But to realise when the Constitution was adopted, that close on forty years of opposition to the National Party's apartheid and authoritarianism had not been in vain, was the cherry on the top.

'Like many of you I have enjoyed my ten years in South Africa's democratic parliament. It is very different from the old parliament. Different fundamentally in its composition of both race and gender. Different in its procedures through the development of the committee system. Different in that it is less concerned with ideology and more concerned with people. [But similar] in sensing the increasing dominance of the executive over parliament and its members. I believe that good governance requires that MPs, irrespective of party affiliation, unite in ensuring that the rights of parliament are protected both in letter and in spirit.

'If I am disappointed it is because, although in this House there are many well-prepared speeches, often they are read with much speed but little passion. There have been very few real debates. There has been very little constructive interaction across the floor of the House on matters which are of vital concern to our people. On occasions when debates look like getting underway, speakers at the podium are greeted by a barrage of noisy and intolerant interjections. Parliament would do better, and enjoy more esteem by members of the public, if in future there were fewer speeches and more debates, less noise and more tolerance.

'I would like to thank all who have enriched my experience as an MP, to members of parliament and members of the staff in general for their courtesy and to many of them my thanks for friendship. I wish you all a peaceful election, and of course to all the members of my own party I trust that you will return to the House in greater numbers to play a constructive role in strengthening multi-party democracy and to ensure that good governance prevails in South Africa.

'Finally I trust, too, that in the next parliament there will be a common recognition of the fact that the underlying threat to our democratic order lies not so much in personalities or parties or party politics, but in the existence in our country of pervasive poverty, of rising unemployment and the widening gap between the rich and the poor.

'This is the greatest challenge facing politicians of all parties, and the one that will be facing those of you who will be coming back to parliament next session.

'I thank you once again. I wish you well. I say, *sterkte*. I say, *hamba kahle*.'

A few days before the end of the parliamentary session, Speaker Frene Ginwala– at that time chairperson of the steering committee for the inauguration of the Pan-African Parliament (PAP) – told me it had been decided that each country's delegation to the inauguration, in addition to its five PAP members, could be accompanied by three official observers. It had been the decision of the whips of the party that I would be one of these observers. I decided to go to Addis Ababa.

The ceremony was held in the OAU conference hall, preceded by some pomp and ceremony. I foresaw great difficulties in moulding the PAP into an effective instrument that would stand up for the people and hold the executive of the African Union – which consisted of the heads of states of the African countries – to account.

Among these difficulties were finance; communications; the availability of members of the PAP who were also MPs in their own countries; and differing political cultures ranging from genuine parliamentary democracies to 'deliberative organs' operating within the framework of a dictatorship. Nevertheless, I believed that provided the PAP was able to develop momentum as a people's parliament speaking in its own right, it could create the balance of power lacking in the former OAU.

I was fortunate that the Deputy Speaker Baleka Mbete – who was noted for her keen dress sense and excellent taste for attractive African clothes – was one of the five members from South Africa. She asked me to join her shopping at a couple of fashionable boutiques 'so that I could buy something for my wife'. I enjoyed my outing; my purchases were modest, but were appreciated when I got back home.

So my last parliamentary visit would be to Addis Ababa. Who could have foretold it in 1958?

As 14 April, the date for the election drew near, I became attuned to the reality that my parliamentary career was drawing to a close. Strangely enough I was helped in adjusting to this pending lifestyle change by the fact that for the first time since 1958 I was not a candidate. I had a foretaste of the pleasure of being able to take an interest in politics, its events and personalities, without being involved personally in the hurly-burly.

On 13 April Raili and I went to the apartment of Barry Streek and Donwald Pressly, his journalist colleague, where they hosted us together with Bennie and Shirley Rabinowitz, Ken and Adrienne Andrew, my daughters Susan and Caryl and their husbands Peter and Mark, for a relaxed dinner and a social get-together. At midnight Ken and I ceased to be MPs and I entered my 80th year. We drank a toast to the days gone by and to the new life ahead.

As polling went smoothly around the country, there were no reports of significant problems. The DA did well, although perhaps not as well as it had hoped. It won 50 seats, up from 38 in the 1999 election, and up from the 45 it held after the recent crossover. The Inkatha Freedom Party slipped back to 28 seats, and the NNP ended up with a meagre eight. The ANC increased its hold on parliament by winning 279 seats.

My farewell to politics was not as abrupt as the termination of my membership of parliament. Since 24 April was exactly 30 years after the PP's breakthrough and my election victory in Sea Point in 1974, I decided it would be appropriate to have a 'get-together evening' for individuals who had been active workers in the old campaign. With the help of Marlene Silbert and Bennie Rabinowitz – both of whom had been keen supporters – we managed to organise a function attended by about seventy people.

The get-together took place in the home of Dr Silbert and his wife Marlene, ven-ue for many meetings and get-togethers in the early days of the PP. Key people in the campaign – including Herbert Hirsch, my provincial council running mate, and his wife Shirley – were there. Posters, newspaper articles and photographs from the campaign were on display. Individuals recounted anecdotes from the past. Others just wanted to express their feelings. It was a nostalgic and heartwarming occasion that brought together people who worked and made personal sacrifices for a cause in which they believed and to which they were committed.

The following week the Cape Town Club, of which I have the honour to be the president, held a formal dinner at which a portrait of me was to be unveiled. I was pleased when I learned that Pravin Gordhan, the effective and hard-working direc-tor-general of the South African Revenue Services, had agreed to fly down from Pre-toria to address the dinner and unveil the portrait.

Gordhan had been my opposite number in many negotiation tussles at Codesa, the MPNP, the Constitutional Assembly, and later in parliament; and he had been my colleague and co-chairman in the Transitional Executive Council. I appreciated his kindness in participating in a function in my honour.

Gordhan's presence added lustre to the occasion. He spoke with warmth and gen-erosity. The fact that he and I – with our very different personal backgrounds and political ideologies – could share this Club function as friends reflected not only the respect each had for the other, but said something about the magic of the change that had taken place in South Africa.

A few days later I e-mailed a photograph of the portrait to a few friends overseas. One of them, Stanley Uys, at one time one of South Africa's most senior journalists and political commentators, sent me the following response from London:

'Splendid portrait. Usually portraits make one look like Dracula – Thatcher's was like Boudicea and a recent one of Prince Philip was straight from a Rocky Horror show. You look very dignified and benign. No-one would suspect you were as tough as an old boot.

'Regards, Stan.'

Afterword

I have continued to take a keen interest in political developments. Not surprisingly, I have assessed their significance against the background of the constitutional and democratic processes set in motion a decade ago.

Given the seismic nature of the transfer of political power, I am of the opinion that constitutional democracy in South Africa is in reasonably good shape. The constitutional structures and organs of state have functioned in an orderly – if not always effective – manner.

There has been a decade of political stability during which elections took place at national, provincial and local level. There is a growing understanding of the central role the Constitution is intended to play in shaping society, creating the framework for governance, and protecting the rights of individuals.

But while they are pluses, there are also minuses.

There is growing scepticism about the constitutional structures owing to the failure of those operating within their framework to deliver services required by the people. There is mounting cynicism as it is noted how often individuals with political connections are being enriched, while the poor are being left behind.

The shockingly high level of violent crime – robbery, assault, murder, rape and child abuse – has revealed the extent to which the entrenched values of respect for property, life and human dignity are being ignored. And the dominance of a single political party, the ANC, whose leader is head of party, head of government and head of state, has resulted in an increasing centralisation of power and a growing intolerance of the political interaction between government and opposition essential to multi-party democracy.

On one issue the intention of the Constitution has not been fulfilled. This is the current party list system through which political parties nominate members of parliament. As parliament is at present composed, the manner in which members are appointed is not promoting representative democracy to the extent that it should. MPs are not elected by the people; they are appointed by the political parties. They are accountable not to the voters but to the party authorities. They are not public representatives, but party agents.

In addition, because citizens are not allowed to elect those who are to represent them and who they can call to account between elections, they are prevented from participating in the critically important process of representative democracy. The system is retarding the development of a democratic culture, and there are signs of growing resentment. This is having a negative impact on the political parties themselves: ordinary citizens play less of a role in their activities, and the parties are the poorer for being deprived of the people's input. Decision-making is becoming ever more top-down.

A constituency-linked MP elected directly by voters provides an essential link between parliament and the public – and conversely between the public and parliament. This principle lies at the heart of representative and participatory democracy.

The Constitution, in stating that the electoral system should, in general, result in proportional representation, does not entrench the party list system. What it does say is that the National Assembly consists of persons 'elected as members', and that the Assembly is 'elected to represent the people and to ensure government by the people'.

The present party list system was included in the Constitution as an interim measure for the 1994 and 1999 elections. It was used again in 2004. Two-and-a-half years have passed since then. I believe that government and parliament should take steps in time to introduce a system that makes provision for directly-elected constituency MPs in the next election in 2009.

Two developments in 2005-2006 should have alerted South Africans to the fact that our new democracy was not safely entrenched.

One was the series of somewhat bizarre events in the months following the statement by High Court judge Hilary Squires, in finding Schabir Shaik guilty on a charge of corruption, that 'mutually beneficial symbiosis' existed between Shaik and Deputy President Jacob Zuma, and President Mbeki's dismissal of Zuma as Deputy President.

There were emotional protests and demonstrations of support for Zuma, while Mbeki and his government were attacked by prominent members of Cosatu and the South African Communist Party, both of which, together with the ANC, were members of the ruling Tripartite Alliance.

The fault lines in the body politic were exposed – along with the potential for an emotionally driven division in the wider society along the lines of ethnicity, culture, personalities, policies and political power.

Democracy can not be taken for granted.

The second event was a brazen attempt by the ANC majority in the Cape provincial government to try to seize power in the Cape Town city council after the ANC had actually been voted out of office. In a recent local government election, Helen Zille of the opposition Democratic Alliance had been elected Executive Mayor. Here was the spectacle of a political party that held power at national level, in all nine provinces, in most of the municipalities, and in five of the six metropolitan councils, refusing to abide by the result of the election in the one metropolitan council where it had been voted out. Faced by Mayor Zille's resolute defence of the constitutional *status quo*, and the prospect of losing at the Constitutional Court at the end of a protracted and divisive constitutional dispute, the ANC abandoned its attempted power grab. The immediate danger was over; but the forebodings for the future remained.

In my final speech to parliament in March 2004 I said that the greatest threat to our new democracy was widespread unemployment, pervasive poverty, and the widening gap between the rich and the poor. The situation has since worsened: despite the economy growing at a faster rate, unemployment has increased, widespread poverty has persisted, and the gap between rich and poor has widened. Ironically the government's Black Economic Empowerment policy has contributed to the widening of the gap, by creating a new rich elite, often of persons with strong political connections, and by leaving the millions of impoverished out of the employment process.

These factors are having an impact, turning people away from the values that underpin our constitutional system, and eroding confidence in our democratic institutions. They are driving people towards populism as a cure for their problems. In short, they are undermining our new democracy.

The warning and its challenges are there. Much will depend on the quality of our leadership over the next few years.

Tony Leon, party leader and the leader of the opposition, has announced that he will retire from office in May 2007 at a DA federal congress where a new leader will be elected.

Thabo Mbeki will continue as president until his ten-year term in office expires at the national election in 2009. In the meanwhile, in December 2007, the delegates to the ANC national congress will elect the ANC's leadership cadre for the next three years. This will include the person destined to be Mbeki's successor as president of South Africa.

In the field of leadership 2007 could be a watershed year.

While I have learned to take nothing for granted, I believe we South Africans have the ability to overcome our problems. I remain quietly confident that the democracy for which so many have worked and fought is going to prevail.

Acknowledgements

Two years elapsed from the time I commenced working on *Crossing the Borders of Power* to 5 May 2006, when I handed my manuscript to Jonathan Ball. Perhaps I could have produced the manuscript in a shorter time had I not decided to adopt a do-it-yourself approach.

On the administrative side, I had no secretarial assistance: save for a few short chapters that I dictated directly into my computer using a voice recognition programme, I wrote the first draft by hand. Then I took charge of subsequent phases of the development and production of the final manuscript.

I was most fortunate. Bernard James and Partners kindly made an office and its facilities available to me. I received assistance from the Ernest Oppenheimer Memorial Trust. I was encouraged and assisted by many individuals whom I approached for information or advice.

In the evenings and over weekends – when the computer desk and dining-room table of our home was my workplace – I had the benefit of Raili, my understanding wife. For the willing assistance of the friends, acquaintances and members of the public whom Peter Soal and I contacted during the course of our work, I have the utmost gratitude. They included:

Wendy Masters, my secretary at the time when I embarked on the initial stages of the project;
Ester van der Bergh of the South African Media Department, University of the Free State;
Carol Archibald of the Cullen Library, University of the Witwatersrand;
Sunet Swanepoel and Juanita van Zyl of the Parliamentary Library in Cape Town;
Peter Fabricius, foreign editor of the Independent Newspapers; and
James Selfe of the Democratic Alliance.

In addition there were Lesley Hart and her assistants Isaac Ntabankulu and Yasmin Mahomed of the Manuscripts and Archives Department, UCT, where in 1994 I lodged my papers and documents. These included 38 volumes containing newspaper reports on my activities from 1971 to 1988 that Joan Fowle, my thoughtful and enterprising secretary, had cut and filed.

Three people in particular played an especially important role in the production of the manuscript. Barry Streek, at that time the senior editor at Jonathan Ball Publishers, read my draft manuscript in two-monthly tranches, made pertinent comments and suggestions, and gave guidance, advice and encouragement from the publisher's perspective.

Sadly, in March 2005, Barry took ill. His health deteriorated to the point that he could no longer carry out his publishing duties. He died in September 2006, loved and respected by his many friends, colleagues and associates.

Peter Soal, a long-time Progressive and parliamentary colleague during the 1980s and 1990s, assisted me with research, checking facts, figures and dates, and the production of the manuscript. With his strong liberal commitment, his knowledge of politics and political personalities, and his bubbling enthusiasm, he was a great member of my team.

Fiona Chisholm, a freelance journalist, who typed almost all of the manuscript, was a tower of strength. Her comments and suggestions, both as a journalist and as an interested member of the public, were most helpful. In spite of the stress of our intense interaction over many months, Fiona and I remain good friends!

At an early stage I wondered whether I would have the staying power to complete the task. However, later, when on rare occasions I was not working on my manuscript, I developed a guilty feeling that I was playing truant.

I enjoyed reliving experiences of my past, meeting and talking with people many of whom I had not been in contact with for years, filling the gaps in my memory, and on occasions discovering that it was not as accurate as I had imagined it to be.

I became so engrossed in writing, and Barry so involved in reading, that the draft manuscript grew to a length that far exceeded the number of words required for publication.

Eva Hunter, a research fellow at the University of the Western Cape, was given the task of recommending how the manuscript could be reduced in length, and the final task of editing the manuscript was assigned to Peter Wilhelm, journalist and author in his own right.

Peter and I consulted regularly during the course of his work. I appreciated his sensitivity and concern and the respect that he had for the integrity of the manuscript he had been given. I am most grateful to him for the significant contribution he made to *Crossing the Borders of Power*.

Index